Date Due

Bitter Harvest identifies the principles governing Franklin Roosevelt's development and use of a presidential staff system and offers a theory explaining why those principles proved so effective. Matthew Dickinson argues that presidents institutionalize staff to acquire the information and expertise necessary to better predict the likely impact their specific bargaining choices will have on the end results they desire.

Once institutionalized, however, presidential staff must be managed. Roosevelt's use of competitive administrative techniques minimized his staff management costs, while his institutionalization of nonpartisan staff agencies provided him with needed information. Matthew Dickinson's research suggests that FDR's administrative approach could be used today as an alternative to the White House staff-dominated institutional presidency upon which most of his presidential successors have relied.

Bitter Harvest

Bitter Harvest
FDR, Presidential Power and the Growth of the Presidential Branch

MATTHEW J. DICKINSON
Harvard University

CAMBRIDGE
UNIVERSITY PRESS

Published by the Press Syndicate of the University of Cambridge
The Pitt Building, Trumpington Street, Cambridge CB2 1RP
40 West 20th Street, New York, NY 10011-4211, USA
10 Stamford Road, Oakleigh, Melbourne 3166, Australia

First published 1997

Printed in the United States of America

Library of Congress Cataloging-in-Publication Data
Dickinson, Matthew J.
    Bitter harvest : FDR, presidential power and the growth of the
    presidential branch / Matthew J. Dickinson.
        p.   cm.
    Includes bibliographical references and index.
    ISBN 0-521-48193-7 (hc)
        1. Presidents – United States – Staff.   2. United States – Politics
    and government – 1933–1945.   3. Roosevelt, Franklin D.
    (Franklin Delano), 1882 – 1945.   I. Title.
    JK518.D54   1996
    353.03 – dc20   95–48903
                                                                       CIP

A catalog record for this book is available from the British Library.

ISBN 0-521-48193-7 Hardback

Contents

Preface and acknowledgments

It was as Richard Neustadt's graduate student, and later as his teaching assistant, that I first began to think about the presidential "branch," the White House-centered advisory system that is an increasingly influential actor in presidential politics. Neustadt, of course, as a former Bureau of the Budget official, a White House aide to Harry Truman, and informal adviser to almost every one of Truman's presidential successors, knows perhaps as much as anyone about this topic. But *Presidential Power*, his seminal book on the American presidency, touches only tangentially on presidential advising, and then only to warn presidents not to expect aides to provide the support and advice presidents need, when they need it.

The rapid growth of the presidential branch since *Presidential Power* was first written, however, and its evident role in a series of disastrous presidential decisions – escalating the American presence in Vietnam, the Watergate cover-up, and the Iran-contra affair are perhaps the most prominent – convinced me that the subject deserved more study. What explains the rate and locus of presidential branch growth? How to understand its internal configuration, including levels of hierarchy and role specialization? Most important, what overall impact does it have on a president's effective influence on governmental outcomes?

Previous scholarship evinces no consensus on these questions. In part, this reflects the diversity of research methods that have been utilized. Presidential advisory systems have been viewed through the analytic lens of historical methods and case studies; as a function of presidents' personal characteristics, e.g., temperament, background, and operating style; using organization theories, particularly decision-making schemas; and, most recently, through formal models deduced from simplifying assumptions and ideas familiar to economists – optimizing behavior, equilibrium outcomes, and social choice axioms.

Each approach has it merits, and collectively they help illuminate important aspects of the presidential branch. As yet, however, these findings are not well integrated with what scholars have learned about presidents, and their place in the American political system. In particular, we still do not understand the link between presidential staff and presidential power.

This book is a first step in explicating that linkage. So that the work might be cumulative, I have consciously sought to build on Neustadt's bargaining paradigm, as introduced in *Presidential Power* and subsequently refined and elaborated through two generations of research. The argument that follows is anchored in a simple supposition: if bargaining is the primary basis of presidential power, then ideally presidents will try to organize staffs to facilitate effective bargaining. But what does that entail? To find out I decided to compare how presidents actually organized their advisory systems, and with what effect on bargaining outcomes.

My research began with Franklin Roosevelt. Most scholars, Neustadt included, believe FDR to be the most effective modern president. And he is typically credited with formally planting the presidential branch, as it were; Roosevelt established, with congressional acquiescence, the Executive Office of the President, including the White House Office. The Roosevelt presidency, then, seemed a logical place to begin the study of branch origins.

After several months immersing myself in archives and secondary sources, however, I was forced to conclude that Roosevelt could take little credit for creating the White House-centered advisory system in use today. Indeed, Roosevelt rejected the approach adopted by most of his successors. Rather than centralize advisory support within the White House, he opted for a significantly different staff system, one that proved remarkably effective despite the leadership burdens imposed by the Great Depression and World War II. This finding led me to refocus my research more narrowly on FDR. In particular, I sought answers to three questions: what were the details of his advisory system? Why did it work (if, indeed, it did)? What lessons can be gleaned from his experiences?

This book contains my answers, however tentative, to those questions. Although the substantive focus on FDR is much narrower than I originally intended when I first began this project, the larger issue to which the argument is addressed remains pertinent today: how best to organize the presidency? If Alexander Hamilton was right when arguing that in our constitutional system an energetic president is a prerequisite for effective government, then it behooves us to know what contribution, if any, presidential advisers should make towards this end. By extending Neustadt's bargaining framework to include the role of advisers, my hope is that this book makes a modest step in that direction.

To be sure, I have likely raised more questions than I have answered. But generating a testable theory is a first step on the research road, however long. My hope is that I will be joined on that journey by others who share my interests. Presidents (and their advisers) need all the help they can get.

So do scholars. I have been fortunate in this regard. As the reader will discover, in researching this book I have borrowed from a variety of research approaches and findings, ranging from archival-based case studies to deductive formal models. Roosevelt, too, sought advice from a range of substantively and ideologically diverse advisers. But he was beholden to none of them. I cannot say the same; my indebtedness to my "advisers" is great.

Of course, everything begins with my parents, Henry and Carol, whom I owe more than I can ever repay.

My advisers at Harvard, some of whom are now colleagues, deserve special thanks. Mark Peterson epitomizes the ideal Harvard professor: intellectually curious, a dedicated teacher, and committed to using research to advance the public interest. He also has a sense of humor, to my good fortune. Paul Peterson's enthusiasm and guidance were, and continue to be, tremendously helpful. In addition to constantly urging me forward, he was also responsible for giving me one wonderful year at the Brookings Institution and a helluva lot of frequent flier miles. Having sent me out into the professional world, Morris Fiorina has had to cope with my return to Harvard as one of his junior colleagues. He continues to put up with more abuse from me than any individual deserves – and continues to dish out twice as much in return. I have learned more from him than I care to admit.

Other professors who provided invaluable feedback include Gary King, Steve Macedo, H. W Perry, and Margaret Weir. I've greatly benefitted from co-teaching the American presidency course at Harvard with Roger Porter. I also thank the undergraduates at Dartmouth, Harvard, and Middlebury colleges who served as guinea pigs when I tried out my ideas there in classes and seminars.

Of course, Harvard is run not by faculty, but by the secretarial staff. Two in particular helped me immeasurably while I was a graduate student: Sally Mackacynas and Steve Baker. During my time here as a professor, Mary Jane Brown, Ben Kawachugi, Judy Rapping, and Ann Wigglesworth have continued that tradition.

Financially, this research benefitted from a variety of sources. Harvey Mansfield, Jr., provided summer grants through the auspices of the American Center for Constitutional Studies. Archival research was made possible by scholarships from the Roosevelt, Truman, Eisenhower, Kennedy, Johnson, and Ford libraries. The Eisenhower World Affairs Institute gave me a fellowship for which I am very grateful. I spent a year at the Brookings Institution, and I thank Tom Mann and the other members of the

Governmental Studies program there. While I was in Washington, D.C., my Uncle Gene and Aunt June Trone put me up, to my good fortune.

Special thanks are extended to Mr. Benjamin Ulin, without whose assistance this project – and the next to come! – would not be completed. He has demonstrated extraordinary patience while waiting for this book to reach the bookstore shelves. Andy Rudalevige, Adele Grignon, Amanda Spector, and Ilya Somin provided much needed editorial and research assistance. Andy's help proved particularly invaluable.

I also owe a debt of gratitude to the editorial staff at Cambridge University Press, especially Herbert Gilbert and Alex Holzman. Herb in particular has proved a sharp-eyed but congenial critic.

Finally, two people deserve special mention for seeing this project through. Richard Neustadt taught my first class at Harvard, gave me my first teaching job, chaired my dissertation committee for six long years, and was lured out of retirement to co-teach a graduate seminar on the presidency with me. Despite his extensive knowledge of this topic, he has demonstrated remarkable patience with my rather slow-witted attempts to assimilate even the most elementary history. Professor Neustadt's counsel has been invaluable, especially his constant admonishment to get the story straight before I gallop off into the never-never land of social science theory. He also taught me that because politics *matters*, our research should be directed toward some greater good.

My wife Alison deserves the most credit for reminding me of what is important in life. While in graduate school she gave me excuses to travel to England, Scotland, Japan, and France, not to mention California. She has also read countless versions of this argument, from dissertation to book manuscript, through the years. All this she did while carrying on her own duties, whether it was showing state officials in Massachusetts how to weather a fiscal crisis without breaking the backs of the underclass, or the eminently more important task of giving birth to and raising our sons. While I traveled the country on various research junkets, or commuted from Vermont to Cambridge, Alison has borne the brunt of responsibility for feeding, clothing, and nurturing Seth and Ethan. More than anyone she knows the time and effort I've invested in this project. And yet I'd gladly start the damn thing from scratch again if it gave me a few more years with her. Thanks, Alison.

Introduction: The fruits of his labor? FDR and the growth of the presidential branch

In the United States we like to "rate" a president. We measure him as weak or strong and call what we are measuring leadership. . . . We are quite right to do so.

Richard Neustadt[1]

Only three American presidents – George Washington, Abraham Lincoln, and Franklin Delano Roosevelt – are consistently rated "strong" leaders.[2] Among the post-1933 presidents, FDR stands alone in this regard.[3] Indeed, he largely defined the standards by which his "modern" presidential cohort is judged.[4] Roosevelt's groundbreaking innovations – the use of radio, rhetoric, and the media; the development of legislative programs; the wielding of prerogative powers; and the creation and utilization of a presidential staff system – carved new leadership pathways in the presidential landscape. His successors were, in historian William Leuchtenberg's words, expected to "tread in the rows that he had furrowed."[5]

1 Richard E. Neustadt, *Presidential Power and the Modern Presidents: The Politics of Leadership From Roosevelt to Reagan* (New York: Free Press, 1990), p. 1.
2 Of six polls conducted from 1948 through 1982 asking political scientists, historians, and other presidency scholars to rate the presidents, FDR was judged either the second or third "greatest" president, just below Lincoln and, in four cases, Washington. For a summary, see James Pfiffner, *The Modern Presidency* (New York: St. Martin's Press, 1994), pp. 222–3. Because the most recent poll took place in 1982, neither Ronald Reagan, George Bush nor William Clinton are rated, but it is doubtful any of these three will be ranked above FDR.
3 Among FDR's successors only Truman consistently breaks the top ten, and he is never ranked higher than eighth (although the 1970 Maranell – Dodder poll of historians rates the Truman administration sixth best in terms of "accomplishments" [cited in Pfiffner, *The Modern Presidency*, pp. 222–3]).
4 On the concept of a "modern" presidency, see Fred Greenstein, "Changes and Continuities in the Modern Presidency," in Anthony King (ed.), *The New American Political System* (Washington, D.C.: AEI, 1978). For a differing, although not incompatible, perspective regarding whether there is a distinct modern presidency, see Stephen Skowronek, *The Politics Presidents Make* (Cambridge, Mass.: Harvard University Press, 1993).
5 William Leuchtenberg, *In the Shadow of FDR: From Harry Truman to Ronald Reagan* rev. ed. (Ithaca, N.Y.: Cornell University Press, 1983), p. xi.

In the field of presidential staffing, however, Roosevelt's precedents have been ignored.[6] Here, rather than tread the staffing furrows FDR first marked out, the modern presidents have largely plowed them under. And they have resodded the presidency with soil conducive to the growing of a "presidential branch": a large, White House–centered presidential staff bureaucracy, its members functionally specialized and hierarchically arranged.[7]

The fruits of that branch have often been bitter. Vietnam, Watergate, and the Iran-contra scandal revealed the dangers of staff misjudgment and outright malfeasance. These incidents, however, are indicative of more deep-rooted problems; as Chapter 1 argues, there is systematic evidence suggesting that, on balance, the political harvest from increasing White House staff size, hierarchy, and functional specialization has proved harmful to presidents and the body politic.[8]

To be sure, scholars differ regarding the extent to which the presidential branch is flawed, and whether presidents possess the will or the power to enact solutions. But the ongoing debate regarding how best to organize the presidency typically ignores the administrative lessons of Franklin Delano Roosevelt. This book attempts to redress that oversight. It argues that FDR's staff practices pose an effective staffing alternative to a large, functionally specialized White House advisory system.

Admittedly, this is an unconventional proposition. Prevailing scholarly sentiment is that FDR himself planted and nurtured the seed from whence the presidential branch grew.[9] His presidential successors merely emu-

---

6 The centerpiece of that legacy is, of course, FDR's 1939 creation of the Executive Office of the President (EOP), including the White House Office (WHO). (See E.O. 8248 [Sept. 8, 1939], issued under Reorganization Plan I, pursuant to authority granted Roosevelt by the 1939 Reorganization Act.) Although the relevant statutes remain on the books, subsequent presidents have for the most part paid little attention to FDR's underlying motives.

7 First coined by Nelson Polsby, the term "presidential branch" has been popularized by John Hart's indispensable book of the same title. See Nelson Polsby, "Some Landmarks in Modern Presidential-Congressional Relations" from Anthony King (ed.), *Both Ends of the Avenue* (Washington, D.C.: AEI, 1983), p. 20; and John Hart, *The Presidential Branch: From Washington to Clinton*, 2nd ed. (Chatham, N.J.: Chatham House Publishers, 1995).

   Note, however, that the term is somewhat misleading; the locus of staff growth and functional specialization is centered within the White House Office, not the outlying executive branch departments and staff agencies. That is, the topic is really a "White House," as opposed to a "presidential," branch. Nevertheless, in deference to popular usage, the latter term is used throughout this book, although both Hart and Polsby are absolved from any responsibility for my treatment of the subject.

8 For arguments along these lines, see Hart, *The Presidential Branch*; and Stephen Hess, *Organizing the Presidency*, 2nd ed. (Washington, D.C.: The Brookings Institution, 1988).

9 See, for example, Terry Moe's argument that:
    Today's presidency is vastly different from what it was in Franklin Roosevelt's time . . . but the real transformation was initiated by . . . Roosevelt

lated FDR's attempt to "manage" the executive branch through "the basic structure of a large-scale, multifunctional White House staff."[10] From the conventional perspective, then, FDR's use of staff is unlikely to provide clues for remedying presidential branch flaws. John Burke, a leading presidency scholar, makes this point well:

> FDR's highly personalized style could perhaps work at the onset of the institutional presidency, but it placed great demands on the president's time and failed to create coherently organized and lasting procedures. Roosevelt thus left his successors with the emerging structure of a White House staff but little they could emulate by way of managing it and making it effectively serve their ends.[11]

Conventional portraits of presidential staff institutionalization, however, tend to be painted with an exceedingly broad historical brush. These typically gloss over significant details distinguishing FDR's administrative practices from his successors'. To fully appreciate Roosevelt's distinctive approach, one needs a more finely pointed impression. That is the research strategy adopted here. Drawing from archives and secondary material related to Roosevelt's staff choices, I conclude that although Roosevelt did seek to bolster presidential staff support, he did not nurture the growth of the presidential branch.[12] Indeed, rather than increase

himself, who, in fashioning his New Deal and leading the nation in war, revolutionized public expectations about the office. . . . While these expectations far outstripped the president's means of meeting them, presidents responded as best they could by incrementally developing their institutional capacity for governance. The result has been a trajectory of change in which, over the decades, policy making has become more centralized in the White House organization and the bureaucracy has become more politicized (or, more accurately, presidentialized) through appointments and top-down control. Terry Moe, "Presidents, Institutions and Theory," in George C. Edwards III, John H. Kessel, and Bert A. Rockman, eds., *Researching the Presidency: Vital Questions, New Approaches* (Pittsburgh, Pa.: Pittsburgh University Press, 1993), p. 341.

See also Hess, *Organizing the Presidency*, p. 6; and Terry Moe "The Politicized Presidency" in John E. Chubb and Paul E. Peterson, eds., *The New Direction in American Politics* (Washington, D.C.: The Brookings Institution, 1985), Chapter 9, 235–71.

10 John Burke, *The Institutional Presidency*, (Baltimore, Md.: Johns Hopkins University Press, 1992), p. 12.

11 Burke, *The Institutional Presidency*, p. 3. See also Terry Moe, "Presidents, Institutions and Theory," p. 341.

12 For useful overviews regarding FDR's contribution to the evolution of the institutional presidency, see Herbert Emmerich, *Federal Organization and Administrative Management* (Birmingham: University of Alabama Press, 1971), p. 86; A. J. Wann, *The President as Chief Administrator: A Study of Franklin D. Roosevelt* (Washington, D.C.: Public Affairs Press, 1968), p. 109; Hart, *The Presidential Branch*, p. 1; Clinton Rossiter, "The Constitutional Significance of the Executive Office of the President," *American Political Science Review* 43 no. 6 (December 1949); Alfred Dick Sanders, *A Staff for the President: The Executive Office 1921–1952* (New York: Greenwood Press, 1989), p. 2; George Graham, "The Presidency and the Executive Office of the President," *Journal of*

White House staff size and hierarchy, he limited his personal staff to a handful of general-purpose aides. And instead of regularized staffing procedures, FDR violated traditional administrative canons by assigning overlapping staff duties, utilizing duplicate communications channels, and mixing the lines of authority connecting him with his advisers.

Nor did he "politicize" the non–White House executive office staff agencies in the manner pursued by his successors. Although the size and influence of these staff agencies increased during FDR's presidency, the bulk of the growth was centered within the career civil service, and not in Roosevelt's political staff.

To be sure, these distinguishing aspects of FDR's staff practices are not entirely unfamiliar to all scholars.[13] But few take pains to distinguish FDR's methods from those utilized by his presidential successors. Fewer still assert their relevance today, a half-century after his death. Instead, most argue that Roosevelt's administrative strategy is outmoded due to the growth in demands for presidential leadership since 1945. Scholars point to a new presidential selection process and decline in party influence, the increase in policy complexity and interrelatedness, a larger and more active public sector, especially at the state and local level, the atomization of Congress, the fragmentation of the executive branch, a more assertive role for courts, the growing influence of interest groups and the electronic media, and the increased vulnerability of the United States to both economic and military threats from abroad, as changes that have collectively rendered FDR's administrative practices irrelevant, or worse.[14]

In short, the dominant impression among scholars is that FDR governed in a simpler time. In fact, however, he presided during perhaps the two greatest crises facing the American political system in the twentieth century: the Great Depression and World War II. As I try to demonstrate

Politics 12, no. 4 (1950), pp. 599–621; Robert Sherwood, *Roosevelt and Hopkins*, rev. paperback ed. (New York: Universal Library, 1950), p. 210; John Burke, *The Institutional Presidency*, pp. 1–3; and Greenstein, "Changes and Continuities in the Modern Presidency," p. 45.

13 See, for instance, Richard E. Neustadt, "Approaches to Staffing the Presidency: Notes on FDR and JFK," *American Political Science Review* 57, no. 4 (December 1963), pp. 855–64; Arthur Schlesinger, Jr., *The Coming of the New Deal*, vol. II of his *The Age of Roosevelt* (Boston: Houghton-Mifflin, 1959), pp. 511–73; John Hart, "No Passion for Brownlow: Models of Staffing the Presidency," *Politics* 17, no. 2 (November 1982), pp. 89–95; and Wann, *The President as Chief Administrator*.

14 For details and documentation, see the several articles in three useful anthologies: King, *The New American Political System*, and the two Brookings' publications edited by Chubb and Peterson, *The New Direction in American Politics*, and Chubb and Peterson, *Can the Government Govern?*

in later chapters, these two events posed administrative complexities that arguably have not been matched since. Yet Roosevelt's administrative system proved equal to the task. This suggests that his staff practices, suitably modified to take into account the contextual changes listed above, are relevant today.

One reason for scholars' tendency to overlook the continuing relevance of FDR's staff choices is the lack of an analytic framework for explaining why presidential staffs exist, and what they are supposed to do. Instead of explicit theorizing regarding the causes and consequences of presidential branch growth, most studies of presidential staffing have utilized descriptive means for prescriptive ends. During the 1940s and 1950s, scholars argued that staff growth and specialization was a necessary response by presidents to increasing demands for presidential leadership.[15] By the 1960s, however, in reaction to the role of presidential aides in the decision making processes leading to the United States' involvement in Vietnam, and the Watergate scandal, scholars began to have doubts about these staffing trends. The "aggrandizement" of the White House staff and the use of "administrative" strategies by presidents were now seen as contributing to an "imperial presidency."[16]

Whether viewed positively or negatively, then, the growth of the presidential branch was judged largely in normative terms. Those scholars who did try to conceptualize the causes and consequences of staff growth typically focused on individual presidential management or operating styles.[17] Critics pointed out, however, that the emphasis on presidential

---

15 See "The Executive Office of the President," a symposium by Louis Brownlow, Harold D. Smith, Charles E. Merriam, William H. McReynolds, Lowell Mellett, and Luther Gulick, *Public Administration Review* 1, no. 2 (Winter 1941), pp. 101–89; Rossiter, "The Constitutional Significance of the Executive Office of the President"; and Lester G. Seligman, "Presidential Leadership: The Inner Circle and Institutionalization," *The Journal of Politics* 18 (1956), pp. 410–26. For an early exception to these favorable reactions, however, see Stephen Bailey, "The President and His Political Executives," *Annals of the American Academy of Political and Social Sciences* 307 (1956), pp. 24–36.

16 George E. Reedy, *The Twilight of the Presidency*, paperback ed. (New York: New American Library, 1971); Hess, *Organizing the Presidency* esp. pp. 171–3, 218–33; Thomas Cronin, "The Swelling of the Presidency: Can Anyone Stop the Tide?" in Peter Woll (ed.), *American Government: Readings and Cases*, 8th ed. (Boston: Little, Brown & Co., 1984).

17 See Richard Tanner Johnson, *Managing the White House* (New York: Harper & Row, 1974); Alexander George, *Presidential Decision-making in Foreign Policy: The Effective Use of Information and Advice* (Boulder, Colo.: Westview Press, 1980); and Roger B. Porter *Presidential Decision Making: The Economic Policy Board* (New York: Cambridge University Press, 1980).

styles could not explain why some staff structures seemed to outlast the presidential administrations in which they were constructed.[18]

Not until the last fifteen years have scholars begun explicitly theorizing about the presidency's institutional staff dynamics. Two overlapping research strands dominate this literature. The first blends organization theory and microeconomics; here scholars deduce general theories of staff development from core assumptions about individual behavior within specified political contexts.[19] The second is descriptive, inductive, and macro-oriented; its practitioners derive theory from detailed historical surveys of the major institutional innovations affecting the presidency.[20]

Both research programs are beginning to enlarge our understanding of the institutional presidency. Interestingly, however, neither make much use of the dominant paradigm in presidential studies: Richard Neustadt's conception of the bargaining president, first articulated more than three decades ago in his classic *Presidential Power*. Indeed, new institutionalists express skepticism that Neustadt's bargaining paradigm will help scholars understand the growth and behavior of presidential staff.[21]

That skepticsm is derived from the scholarly findings inspired by *Presidential Power* to date, none of which focus on the institutional presidency. Neustadt's insights have spawned at least three research programs: Efforts to measure the sources of presidential legislative "success" in Congress, attempts to isolate the origins and impact of public opinion on presidential power, and assessments of the types and relative influence of different presidents' bargaining skills. Although the findings are by no means definitive, there seems to be a growing consensus that scholars have delimited the boundaries of the answers to each question.

18 Hugh Heclo, "The Changing Presidential Office" in Arnold J. Meltsner (ed.), *Politics and the Oval Office* (San Francisco: Institute for Contemporary Studies, 1981), pp. 161–83; Moe, "Presidents, Institutions and Theory."

19 Terry Moe, "The Politicized Presidency,"; Gary Miller, "Formal Theory and the Presidency," in George C. Edwards III, John H. Kessel, and Bert A. Rockman, *Researching the Presidency: Vital Questions, New Approaches,* (Pittsburgh, Pa.: Pittsburgh University Press, 1993); Thomas Weko, *The Politicizing Presidency: The White House Personnel Office, 1948–1994* (Lawrence: University Press of Kansas, 1995); and Charles Walcott and Karen M. Hult, *Governing the White House: From Hoover Through LBJ* (Lawrence: University Press of Kansas, 1995).

20 Burke, *The Institutional Presidency*; Hart, *The Presidential Branch*; Sidney Milkis, *The President and the Parties: The Transformation of the American Party System Since the New Deal* (New York: Oxford University Press, 1993); and Skowronek, *The Politics Presidents Make.*

21 In this regard, see Stephen Skowronek, *The Review of Politics* 49, no. 3 (Summer 1987); and Moe, "Presidents, Institutions and Theory."

Thus, presidency researchers are now relatively confident that presidential influence within Congress is in fact primarily shaped by contextual factors, especially the legislature's partisan and ideological composition[22]; that a president's public prestige is largely, but not entirely, determined by forces outside his control[23]; and that prestige exercises at most a marginal impact on legislative outcomes[24]; and, finally, that individual presidential bargaining skills are, in select cases, probably quite critical but that they are difficult to measure in any systematic fashion and are usually swamped by other factors.[25]

Presidential Power has clearly helped illuminate scholars' understanding of the presidency, then, but not in ways that new institutionalists

22 Two methodological approaches characterize these efforts: single case studies utilizing "thick description" of presidential attempts to influence congressional processes, and multivariate aggregate data analysis in which scholars measure the relationship between several variables, e.g., the partisan and ideological composition of Congress, a president's public popularity, the state of the economy, and legislative outputs. See Barbara Kellerman, *The Political Presidency* (New York: Oxford University Press, 1986); George C. Edwards, *Presidential Influence in Congress* (San Francisco: W. H. Freeman, 1980), and George C. Edwards, *At the Margins; Presidential Leadership of Congress* (New Haven, Ct.: Yale University Press, 1989); Jon Bond and Richard Fleisher, *The President in the Legislative Arena* (Chicago: University of Chicago Press, 1990); Mark A. Peterson, *Legislating Together: The White House and Capitol Hill from Eisenhower to Reagan* (Cambridge, Ma.: Harvard University Press, 1990), and Charles O. Jones, *The Presidency in a Separated System* (Washington, D.C.: The Brookings Institution, 1994).

23 See John Muellar, "Presidential Popularity from Truman to Johnson," *American Political Science Review* 64 (March 1970), pp. 18–34; Samuel Kernell, "Explaining Presidential Popularity," *American Political Science Review* 72 (1978), pp. 506–22; Charles W. Ostrom and Dennis M. Simon, "Promise and Performance: A Dynamic Model of Presidential Popularity," *American Political Science Review* 79 (1985), pp. 334–58; Richard Brody, *Assessing the President: The Media, Elite Opinion, and Public Support* (Stanford, Calif.: Stanford University Press, 1991); and Paul Brace and Barbara Hinckley, *Follow the Leader: Opinion Polls and the Modern Presidency* (New York: Basic Books, 1992).

24 Douglas Rivers and Nancy Rose, "Passing a President's Program: Public Opinion and Presidential Influence in Congress," *American Journal of Political Science* 29 (1985), pp. 183–96; Edwards, *At the Margins: Presidential Leadership of Congress*; Bond and Fleisher, *The President in the Legislative Arena*; Jones, *The Presidency in a Separated System*.

25 Kellerman, The Political Presidency; Charles O. Jones, *The Trusteeship Presidency: Jimmy Carter and the United States Congress* (Baton Rouge, La.: Louisiana State University Press, 1988); Erwin Hargrove, "Presidential Personality and Leadership Style" in George C. Edwards III, John H. Kessel, and Bert A. Rockman, *Researching the Presidency: Vital Questions, New Approaches* (Pittsburgh, Pa.: Pittsburgh University Press, 1993), pp. 69–109; Bond and Fleisher, *The President in the Legislative Arena*; Peterson, *Legislating Together*; Barbara Sinclair, "Studying Presidential Leadership," in George C. Edwards III, John H. Kessel, and Bert A. Rockman, *Researching the Presidency: Vital Questions, New Approaches* (Pittsburg, Pa.: Pittsburg University Press, 1993), pp. 203–32; Terry Moe, "Presidents, Institutions and Theory"; and Terry Sullivan, "Bargaining with the President: A Simple Game and New Evidence," *American Political Science Review* 84, no. 4 (December 1990), pp. 1167–95.

necessarily find helpful. Accordingly, rather than utilize Neustadt's paradigm, they have sought alternative analytic frameworks for understanding the presidency's institutional dynamics.[26] Methodological pluralism is undoubtedly healthy for presidential studies, and should be encouraged. But, for several reasons, I believe that scholars interested in the institutional presidency should think twice before relegating *Presidential Power* to the shelf of classic period pieces. First, unlike organizational or economic-based approaches, *Presidential Power* is specifically formulated to explain presidential behavior within the dictates of the American political system. Hence it "fits" empirical observation in this area rather well. Second, because Neustadt's insights have been extensively tested and have generally held up well, research based on his premises is potentially cumulative. By using alternative research paradigms to understand the American presidency, in contrast, scholars are essentially starting from scratch. Third, the logic contained in *Presidential Power* is widely disseminated among scholars; most have some knowledge of Neustadt's terms and assumptions.

Most importantly, however, the Neustadt paradigm *is* adaptable for institutional analysis.[27] Admittedly, this fact is easy to miss because, as Moe points out, although *Presidential Power* is institutionally based, the narrative focuses predominantly on individual presidential behavior.[28] If Neustadt's paradigm is to help scholars uncover the link between

26 Moe, for instance, draws on the "new economics of organizations" literature, with its emphasis on principal-agent models and transaction-cost theories, to explain why presidents should centralize staff support within the White House and infiltrate the surrounding staff agencies with partisan appointments. He claims that the American political system distributes incentives and resources in a manner that encourages presidents to adopt these tactics. Moreover, as unitary actors, presidents have advantages over Congress and other political actors when it comes to influencing the process of executive branch growth. This produces, in the long run, a presidential tilt to the administrative playing field.

   However, Roosevelt's experiences suggest that this viewpoint understates the management costs associated with strategies of White House staff centralization and politicization. See Moe, "The Politicized Presidency"; and Terry Moe and Scott A. Wilson, "Presidents and the Politics of Structure," *Law and Contemporary Problems* 57, no. 2 (Spring 1994), pp. 1–44. For an introduction to the ideas on which Moe's argument is based, see Terry Moe, "The New Economics of Organizations," *American Journal of Political Science* 28 (November 1984), pp. 739–77; Gary J. Miller, *Managerial Dilemmas: The Political Economy of Hierarchy* (New York: Cambridge University Press, 1992); and Terry M. Moe and Gary J. Miller "The Positive Theory of Hierarchies" in Herbert F. Weisberg, (ed.) *Political Science: The Science of Politics* (New York: Agathon Press, 1986), pp. 167–98.

27 For more on this point, see Matthew J. Dickinson, "Neustadt and New Institutionalism: New Insights on Presidential Power?" (paper delivered at the Annual Meeting of the American Political Science Association, Chicago, Sept. 1–4, 1995).

28 Moe, "Presidents, Institutions and Theory."

presidential staff and presidential power, then, it needs to be extended and elaborated.

I begin to address that task in the remainder of this introductory chapter. My fundamental claim is that presidents institutionalize advising structures to reduce bargaining uncertainty within recurring bargaining arenas. This basic postulate, as elaborated below, serves as a starting point for understanding FDR's staff choices throughout his presidency. The details of his choices, from the onset of the New Deal through the end of World War II, are recounted in Chapters 2–7. Chapters 2–3 describe the collapse of "cabinet" government under the administrative weight of the New Deal and FDR's search via the Brownlow Committee for an administrative alternative. Chapters 4–5 examine how FDR modified that alternative to cope with the demands of economic mobilization during World War II. Chapters 6–7 scrutinize his staff choices in military and foreign affairs during the war. Chapter 8 then reformulates the underlying instincts on which FDR's staff system was based into "principles," and tries to explain their effectiveness in terms of Neustadt's bargaining paradigm. Roosevelt's methods, I conclude, proved particularly effective at balancing his need for expertise and information against the costs of managing an advisory system. In contrast, the presidential branch has frequently posed insuperable management costs on FDR's successors. The final chapter explores in preliminary fashion why FDR's practices have not been emulated, and what might be done to encourage their use today.

Presidential staff and presidential power: A conceptual starting point

Following Neustadt, I begin by assuming that all presidents, including Roosevelt, seek power. By *power*, I mean they want to maximize their effective influence on governmental outcomes, whether policies, elections, or some other objective. *Ceteris paribus*, presidents want more power, not less. (I am not concerned here with whether presidents should seek power, nor how much.)

By extension, then, an effective presidential staff is one that helps presidents increase their power. By *staff* I refer primarily to those individuals and agencies within the Executive Office of the President (EOP), formally established in 1939, including the White House Office (WHO) and the other primary staff agencies; and the political secretaries heading the major executive branch departments and agencies that collectively constitute the traditional presidential "cabinet." More formally, staff is

any individual tied to the president through hierarchical authority relationships. *Hierarchical authority relationships* are those in which a president possesses formal control over the individual's work-related
incentives: *pay, tenure, jurisdiction, and prestige.*

In practice, a president's influence over staff incentives varies; typically
it is shared with other actors, especially members of Congress. I assume
the greater a president's control of an aide's work-related incentives, the
more responsive that aide is to presidential directive. Aides whose work-
related incentives are almost entirely subject to presidential influence are
labeled *personal* advisers. *Institutional* advisers, in contrast, are career
civil servants whose job tenure and pay are less amenable to presidential
influence. (As envisioned by FDR, the EOP was to be divided accordingly;
personal advisers were housed in the WHO, and institutional aides in
the rest of the EOP staff agencies. His successors, however, have blurred
this distinction.[29])

Note that both institutional and personal staff roles can be *institutionalized.* By that I mean the positions and related incentives are
grounded in statute, executive order, or some other formal foundation.[30]
However, although E.O. 8248 institutionalized the WHO in 1939, members of the White House staff remain personal, as opposed to *institutional*
staff. This holds true for members of the presidential cabinet as well: Departmental secretaries' positions are institutionalized by statute, but they
are not institutional staff since their work-related incentives are largely
subject to presidential influence. The Bureau of the Budget (BoB, now the
Office of Management and the Budget), however, was both institutionalized (through the 1921 Budget and Accounting Act) and provided FDR
institutional advice because it was predominantly staffed by career civil
servants.[31]

Presidents also utilize *non-institutionalized* advisers. As defined in this
book, political consultants, party leaders, members of Congress, family
and friends (e.g., FDR's wife Eleanor), government officials borrowed

---

29 This is discussed more fully in Chapter 1.
30 This is not how other scholars define "institutionalized"; compare to John Burke, "The
    Institutional Presidency" in Michael Nelson, (ed.) *The Presidency and the Political
    System,* 4th ed. (Washington, D.C.: Congressional Quarterly Press, 1995), pp. 385–9;
    Nelson W. Polsby, "The Institutionalization of the U.S. House of Representatives,"
    American Political Science Review 52 (1968) pp. 144–68; Robert S. Gilmour, "The In-
    stitutionalized Presidency: A Conceptual Clarification," in Norman Thomas (ed.), *The
    Presidency in the Contemporary Context* (New York: Dodd, Mead, 1976), pp. 147–59;
    and John Kessel, "The Structures of the Carter White House," *American Journal of
    Political Science* 27 (August 1983), pp. 431–63.
31 To be sure, the BoB was led for much of FDR's presidency by a politically-appointed
    director and assistant director. But they were not partisan appointments in the conven-
    tional sense. See Chapters 2,3, and 5 for details.

from other departments and agencies, and others all functioned as presidential advisers whenever their work-related incentives came under FDR's purview. But these advising roles are not considered institutionalized because their duties were not formally subject to presidential control.[32]

Presidents are presumed to exercise influence primarily through bargaining.[33] A *bargain* is a transaction among two or more political actors in which goods, services, or other political resources are exchanged on terms negotiated by all involved.[34] It is defined, from the president's perspective, by its *objective*, its *participants*, its *frequency*, and its *cost*.

By objective, I simply mean the president's bargaining goal. What does he (someday she) hope to accomplish? Bargaining participants are chosen

32 It is worth noting that these distinctions between personal, institutional, and institutionalized staff are important to FDR's conception of an effective staff system, a point that will become more apparent in the next several chapters.

33 Scholars have raised at least three objections to the bargaining model. Peter Sperlich, in his perceptive analysis of *Presidential Power*, argues that a president who perpetually bargains creates unnecessary work. He notes that presidents possess alternative means for inducing cooperation; they can appeal to others' loyalty or shared ideology. See Peter Sperlich, "Bargaining and Overload: An Essay on Presidential Power," from Aaron Wildavsky (ed.) *Perspectives on the Presidency* (Boston: Little, Brown & Co., 1975).

   Sperlich's point is useful, but in my view successful presidential appeals for cooperation based on loyalty or shared values are exceptions to the rule; the evidence at least during FDR's presidency is that bargaining was the primary method by which he achieved objectives in a political system that distributed power across several institutions and numerous actors, including presidential aides.

   More recently scholars have argued that presidents can utilize rhetoric and public appeals for support from voters as an alternative to bargaining. For variations on this theme, see Samuel Kernell *Going Public: New Strategies of Presidential Leadership* 2nd ed. (Washington, D.C.: Congressional Quarterly Press, 1993); Jeffrey K. Tulis *The Rhetorical Presidency* (Princeton, N.J.: Princeton University Press, 1987) and Theodore Lowi *The Personal President* (Ithaca, N.Y.: Cornell University Press, 1985). A full rebuttal to this argument is impossible here, but other scholars have pointed out that the evidence in support of a decline in the importance of bargaining is open to a different interpretation. They argue that "going public" serves at best to supplement bargaining; it cannot replace it in a system in which political power is shared across governing institutions. See, for instance, Marc Bodnick "Going Public Reconsidered: Reagan's 1981 Tax and Budget Cuts, and Revisionist Theories of Presidential Power" *Congress and the Presidency* 17 (Spring 1990), pp. 13–28.

   Finally, some scholars argue that Neustadt slights the importance of a president's formal powers in achieving political and policy objectives. See, for instance, Terry Eastland *Energy in the Executive: The Case for a Strong Presidency* (New York: Free Press, 1992), pp. 7–10. In fact, however, Neustadt's bargaining paradigm is derived from the president's formal powers; he argues that constitutional and statutory powers provide presidents with "vantage points" from which to bargain effectively. By themselves, however, formal powers do not guarantee the president a successful bargaining outcome since other actors share in the exercise of those powers.

34 I use the term inclusively to encompass the process of establishing bargaining objectives, determining alternatives, conducting negotiations, implementing decisions, and monitoring and evaluating outcomes. In practice, of course, bargains frequently consist of more numerous "smaller" bargains, each a step toward the ultimate bargaining outcome.

from among those whose help the president needs to achieve an objective, and who need the president's services in return. Typically participants include some subset of the following: congressional legislators and staff; executive officialdom at the national, state and local levels; organized interests; the media; party leaders and party rank and file; the general public; and the international community.³⁵

Frequency is the number of times a particular type of bargain takes place in a specified time period. Roosevelt distinguished between bargaining exchanges that took place daily, those that recurred at longer intervals, and others whose frequency could not be predicted. White House aides handled daily appointments, paperwork, and media contacts; institutional staff took primary responsibility for more long-term bargaining processes, such as budgeting and legislative clearance; and assistance with other bargains was farmed out to staff sources on an *ad hoc* basis.³⁶

Cost refers to the resources, or capital, presidents expend to achieve a desired bargaining outcome.³⁷ It includes any tangible resource under a president's control or influence that is valued (either positively or negatively) by others engaged in the bargaining process.³⁸ Capital is primarily derived from a president's formal powers (or vantage points) which ensure that others must look to the president for help to achieve their own objectives.³⁹ But these bargaining resources are made more or less fungible, in Neustadt's schema, according to a president's professional reputation and public prestige. By professional reputation, Neustadt means a bargainer's assessment of the president's skill in utilizing those formal powers. By prestige, he means the likely support among the bargainer's constituents for the president's bargaining objectives.

Neustadt's objective in *Presidential Power* is to shed light on a fundamental issue: Given an array of bargaining options and preferences, how does a president choose the bargaining terms most likely to produce the

---

3 5 See Neustadt, *Presidential Power*, p. 8; and Lester G. Seligman and Cary R. Covington, *The Coalitional Presidency* (Chicago: Dorsey Press, 1989), p. 9. Neustadt identifies the "Washington community" as those bargaining participants with an immediate stake in what the president does (defined, then, by interest rather than locale). Neustadt, *Presidential Power*, p. 50. Because bargaining is a multistep process presidents often negotiate with different audiences during a single bargaining transaction.

3 6 In reality, staff functions were not so neatly compartmentalized. Frequently there was a good deal of overlap; his White House staff worked with the BoB in putting together the annual State of the Union address, for instance.

3 7 Note that Neustadt does not use the term "capital"; I have superimposed it on his framework.

3 8 Its intrinsic value is determined by the importance attached by bargaining participants to the good or service in question.

3 9 The best overview of the president's formal powers remains Edward S. Corwin, updated by Randall W. Bland, Theodore T. Hindons, and Jack W. Peltason, *The President: Office and Powers* 5th rev. ed. (New York: New York University Press, 1984).

desired outcome? For Neustadt, the answer is rooted in a president's individual characteristics: experiences, temperament, and sense of power. Presidents who, like FDR, possess the proper mix of individual characteristics are more likely to make the correct choices.[40]

Contrary to some scholars' perceptions, however, Neustadt's analysis does not preclude a role for presidential staff. By expanding his analytic focus to include presidential advisers, Neustadt's basic question can be reformulated as follows: How do advisers help presidents make the proper bargaining choices? The answer, I argue, is by providing resources that enable presidents to better predict the likely impact of their bargaining choices on their preferred outcomes.[41] In short, advisers can help reduce bargaining uncertainty.

Uncertainty exists for two fundamental reasons: presidents bargain instrumentally, but under conditions of bounded rationality. Because presidents and their bargaining partners occupy different roles and institutional vantage points, they usually have competing bargaining objectives.[42] And because they are "intendedly rational," but "limitedly so," they do not know what their optimal bargaining strategy should be.[43] Hence bargaining takes place under uncertainty; terms must be negotiated.

What types of resources do presidents require to reduce uncertainty? This depends on the bargaining objective and participants. To simplify matters, in what follows bargaining resources are classified as one of three types: political, policy, or administrative.[44] Political resources help illuminate a bargain's likely impact on a president's standing with his bargaining audiences; policy is applied knowledge pertaining to the nonpolitical substance of a bargaining exchange; and administrative resources refer to the gathering, processing and dissemination of these other

40 Neustadt, *Presidential Power*, pp. 128–51.
41 Note that I distinguish these staff-based resources from the bargaining "capital" cited above as crucial to presidential bargaining success. Capital is largely derived from a president's formal powers and is expended in the exchange between presidents and their bargaining audiences. Staff resources, on the other hand, are used by presidents to decide what bargaining terms to accept. (Economists sometimes label the costs associated with establishing bargaining terms "transactions costs".) The distinction I am drawing parallels, I think, Paul Light's discussion of internal and external presidential resources. Light writes: "Capital reflects the president's political strength, while the internal resources help to absorb decisionmaking costs." See Paul Light, *The President's Agenda*, (Baltimore, Md.: Johns Hopkins University Press, 1983), pp. 14–25.
42 Note, then, that one need not posit selfish, opportunistic behavior on the part of bargaining participants to understand why they must negotiate bargaining terms; in most cases, those who pursue competing bargaining objectives are simply fulfilling the dictates of their professional roles.
43 Compare to Herbert Simon, *Administrative Behavior* (New York: The Free Press, 1976), and Oliver Williamson, *Markets and Hierarchies: Analysis and Anti-trust Implications* (New York: The Free Press, 1975).
44 Compare to Light, *The President's Agenda*, pp. 14–25.

bargaining resources. These collectively constitute the staff resources which presidents need to bargain effectively.

How much of each is required depends in part on the nature of the bargain. But it is also a function of how important the bargain is to the president, and his uncertainty regarding the likely impact of his bargaining choices on his preferred outcomes.[45] *Ceteris paribus*, the more important the bargain, and the less certain the outcome, the more resources the president wants to clarify his bargaining stakes.

Conclusion

I have proposed a simple framework for understanding the role of presidential advisers. Beginning with Neustadt's *Presidential Power*, I argue that presidential bargaining effectiveness depends on the skill with which a president acquires and utilizes the resources necessary to determine the most favorable bargaining terms.[46] This is partly a function of how well advisers are selected and utilized.

Comparatively speaking, history indicates that FDR's advisory system served him well in this regard. Evidently he acquired the resources necessary to bargain effectively with the actors whose cooperation was essential for achieving presidential objectives.

But this begs the question: Why? What made his methods effective? This book is an attempt to provide an answer and, in the process, correct misperceptions regarding FDR's administrative approach. Although he carved the contours of an institutionalized presidency into the political landscape, he did not sow the seeds of the presidential branch. It was his presidential successors who did that.[47]

Why did Roosevelt avoid planting the branch of White House staff growth and specialization? I argue it is because he did not think it enhanced his bargaining influence, and hence his power, in a constitutionally mandated system of shared powers. To the extent that system remains in place today, and bargaining continues to be central to presidential leadership effectiveness, FDR's administrative lessons remain relevant.

45 By importance, I mean the relative placement of the bargaining objective in a president's hierarchy of goals.

46 This means that presidential power as discussed in this book is situational; it cannot be measured without first defining bargaining parameters: objective, resources, participants, and frequency.

47 Which of FDR's successors are to blame is a controversial question. John Hart suggests Eisenhower begins the buildup of a presidential branch. See John Hart, "Eisenhower and the Swelling of the Presidency," *Polity* 24, no. 4 (Summer 1992), pp. 673–91.

This does not mean presidents should replicate the specifics of FDR's advisory organization. The changes in the last half century in both politics and presidents make this unfeasible. Instead, I urge presidents and their advisers to understand why Roosevelt organized his staff as he did, and why it worked under circumstances as demanding as any faced by his successors. The staffing "principles" enunciated in Chapter 8 are meant to help presidents adapt FDR's system to the political context in which they operate, in light of their own personality, style, and bargaining objectives. Suitably modified and properly implemented, I argue, that system will help a president govern more effectively, and with more accountability, than by relying on a White House–centered presidential branch.[48]

Of course, the argument I present can be at best only suggestive; space constraints prevent a full-fledged comparison of the two staffing approaches. Nevertheless, although my primary goal in writing this book is to revise conventional portraits of FDR's staffing practices, a brief discussion of the strengths and weaknesses of the presidential branch is useful for placing Roosevelt's approach in context. Before documenting Roosevelt's staff practices, then, Chapter 1 examines the presidential branch. What are its flaws? How bitter the harvest?

---

48 Note that this is a *ceteris paribus* argument; all other factors being equal, I claim, a president who relies on a staff organized according to FDR's principles is likely to be more effective than one who utilizes a White House–centered staff branch. In making this assertion, I am *not* suggesting that presidential branch growth is the cause of every disease afflicting the modern presidency, nor that FDR's approach will cure them. Instead, my sentiments echo Eisenhower's as revealed in his frequently quoted comment regarding the virtues of sound organization; although "organization cannot make a genius out of an incompetent . . . disorganization can scarcely fail to result in inefficiency and can easily lead to disaster." Dwight D. Eisenhower *The White House Years: Mandate for Change, 1953–56*, (Garden City, N.Y.: Doubleday, 1963), p. 87. Similarly, I argue, although FDR's approach may not guarantee a successful presidency, relying on the presidential branch is more likely to prevent one.

PART I

Concepts and controversies

1

Bitter harvest: The presidential branch and the Iran-contra affair

There is an emerging consensus among scholars that the presidential branch is flawed, perhaps fatally so.[1] However, the scholarly criticism, while trenchant, is not typically theoretically explicit. Critics generally do not concern themselves with conceptualizing the causes and consequences of White House staff growth, hierarchy, and functional differentiation. This chapter does address those issues, however, using the conceptual framework presented in the introductory chapter. The Iran-contra affair – in many respects the paradigmatic example of the flaws inherent in the presidential branch – provides the empirical grist for the conceptual mill.

Although details of the Iran-contra affair remain shrouded in controversy, on balance it is one of the best researched and most accessible cases of presidential decision making. Four official investigations,[2] several

---

1 Thomas Cronin, "The Swelling of the Presidency: Can Anyone Stop the Tide?" in Peter Woll (ed.) *American Government: Readings and Cases*, 8th ed. (Boston: Little, Brown & Co., 1984) pp. 345–59; John Hart, *The Presidential Branch: From Washington to Clinton* 2nd ed. (Chatham, N.J.: Chatham House Publishers, 1995); Stephen Hess, *Organizing the Presidency*, 2nd ed. (Washington, D.C.: The Brookings Institution, 1988); and Samuel Kernell "The Evolution of the White House Staff" in John E. Chubb and Paul E. Peterson (eds.), *Can the Government Govern?* (Washington, D.C.: The Brookings Institution, 1989).

2 Immediately after the disclosure of the diversion of funds to the contras, Reagan appointed the three-person President's Special Review Board, commonly called the Tower Commission, which issued its report in February 1987. See *The Tower Commission Report: The Full Text of the President's Special Review Board* (New York: jointly published by Bantam Books, Inc. and Times Books, 1987) (paperback version) (hereafter *Tower Commission Report*).

In early January 1987, the House and Senate each set up select committees to investigate the Iran-contra affair. Later, they merged into a twenty-six member joint Congressional Committee that held televised hearings on the Iran-contra affair from May 5 through Aug. 3, 1987. Its findings, issued on Nov. 17, 1987, consist of a majority report signed by every Democratic Committee member, as well as several Republicans, and a minority report signed by the remaining Republicans. See U.S. Congress, Select Committee of the House and Senate, *Report of the Congressional Committees Investigating the Iran-Contra Affair* (Washington, D.C.: Government Printing Office, 1987) (hereafter *Joint Report*).

insider accounts,[3] and numerous books and newspaper and journal articles have been devoted to explaining what happened, and why.[4] Because
of the extensive documentation, the case is a useful illustration of the
more general criticisms scholars make regarding the White House-
centered presidential staff.[5]

The Iran-contra events are by now familiar: In 1985, the Reagan administration, disregarding its own stated policy, undertook a covert operation to sell American arms to Iran. It did so in part to influence Iranian
"moderates" to pressure Mideast terrorist factions to release the Ameri-

The reports of these two committees are the primary sources for my account. Two very
useful indexes to them are provided by James Joseph Sanchez. See James Joseph Sanchez,
Index to the Tower Commission Report (Jefferson, NC: McFarland & Co., Inc., 1987)
and James Joseph Sanchez *Index to the Iran-Contra Hearings Summary Report* (Jefferson, NC: McFarland & Co., Inc., 1987).

In addition to the Tower Commission and the joint Congressional Committee, there
were at least two other official investigations into the Iran-contra affair. Attorney General
Meese, when disclosing the diversion of funds to the contras, asked that an independent
counsel investigate whether criminal charges should be brought against any of the participants. That led to the lengthy investigation by Special Prosecutor Lawrence Walsh.

The Senate Select Committee on Intelligence also held closed-door hearings on the un-
folding scandal in December 1986, although their efforts were handicapped by the refusal
of key Reagan aides to testify unless granted immunity from prosecution for anything
they said during the hearings. In addition, CIA Director William Casey, fatally stricken
with a brain tumor, was rushed to the hospital on the day before he was scheduled to testify to the committee. As perhaps the critical player in the entire Iran-contra affair, his
death effectively buried an important source of knowledge.

3 Among the "insider" accounts consulted for this chapter are: Ronald Reagan, *An Ameri-
can Life* (New York: Simon & Schuster, 1990); Oliver North, *Under Fire: An American
Story* (New York: Harper Collins, 1992); Edwin Meese, *With Reagan: The Inside Story*
(Washington, D.C.: Regnery Gateway, 1992); Donald T. Regan, *For the Record: From
Wall Street to Washington* (New York: Harcourt, Brace, Jovanovich, 1988); Michael A.
Ledeen, *Perilous Statecraft: An Insider's Account of the Iran-Contra Affair* (New York:
Charles Scribner's Sons, 1988); and Constantine C. Menges, *Inside the National Security
Council: The True Story of the Making and Unmaking of Reagan's Foreign Policy* (New
York: Simon & Schuster, 1988). Ledeen was a consultant to the National Security Coun-
cil (NSC) who served as an intermediary with Israeli officials in the early stages of the
Iran-contra affair. Menges served on Reagan's national security staff for three years, leav-
ing in the summer of 1986, before the Iran-contra story broke.

As this chapter was edited the first excerpts from Robert McFarlane's memoirs were
being published. They are most noteworthy for apparently claiming that Vice-President
George Bush knew much more about the planning and implementation of the operation
than he ever acknowledged while president.

4 The most detailed accounts by journalists are Bob Woodward, *Veil: The Secret Wars of
the CIA 1981–1987* (New York: Pocket Books, 1987) (paperback ed.); and Jane Mayer
and Doyle McManus, *Landslide: The Unmaking of the President, 1984–1988* (Boston:
Houghton-Miflin, 1988). The best analysis I have seen by a political scientist, especially
regarding Reagan's motives, can be found in Richard E. Neustadt, *Presidential Power and
the Modern Presidents: The Politics of Leadership from Roosevelt to Reagan,* (New York:
Free Press, 1990), pp. 279–94.

5 Note that it is meant to be illustrative only; there are obvious hazards to generalizing from
a single case. More detailed evidence in support of the conclusions I draw from the Iran-
contra affair are presented below.

cans they held hostage. Despite Reagan's subsequent assertions to the contrary, however, in retrospect the Iran initiative was perceived by many observers as little more than a plan to pay ransom to kidnappers.[6]

To make matters worse, members of Reagan's national security staff, apparently without Reagan's knowledge, diverted "residual" profits from the arms sales to the United States-backed resistance fighters in Nicaragua.[7] This occurred despite existing legislation that prohibited U.S. aid to the "contras."[8]

When the details of the Iran-contra affair began leaking during the fall of 1986, politicians, pundits and other presidency watchers immediately characterized the undertaking as another instance of major presidential miscalculation, deception, and, perhaps, malfeasance.[9] And all for no measurable gain; when finally exposed, the covert operation appeared to have achieved none of its implied objectives. The Iranian government was still controlled by extremists hostile to the United States; American

6 To this day, Reagan steadfastly resists such a characterization. His logic is as follows: The arms initially shipped to Iran were not U.S. weapons, but Israeli. Moreover, U.S. representatives never negotiated directly with groups holding American hostages – only with members of the Iranian government. See Reagan, *An American Life*, pp. 523, 528–9.

7 As revealed at the Nov. 25, 1986, national televised news conference. After Reagan opened the conference with a brief statement, Attorney General Edwin Meese then took the podium and shocked his audience by announcing that Reagan's NSC adviser John Poindexter and Poindexter's assistant Lieutenant Colonel Oliver North had been fired for diverting funds received from the Iranian arms sales to the Nicaraguan resistance fighters.

8 This was the so-called Boland Amendment, sponsored by Representative Edward P. Boland, Democrat from Massachusetts. In fact, the term refers to two pieces of legislation, dubbed Boland I and Boland II.
   Boland I was an amendment to the Defense Appropriations bill for fiscal year 1983. It prohibited the use of CIA funds for the purpose of overthrowing the Sandinista government in Nicaragua, but allowed the United States to continue to fund the contras.
   Boland II was attached to an omnibus appropriations bill and signed into law on Oct. 12, 1984. It restricted the CIA, the Defense Department, "or any other agency or entity involved in intelligence activities" from spending appropriations in support of the contras. However, it included a proviso that the administration could seek a $14 million appropriation for aid to the contras on an expedited fashion after Feb. 28, 1985.
   The practical implication of Boland II was to drive North's efforts to support the contras underground, away from scrutiny by the public, Congress, or other executive branch officials. Whether in fact the Boland Amendment applied to the national security staff was to be a matter of continuing controversy. See *Joint Report*, pp. 32–3, 41–2.

9 The first official acknowledgment was Reagan's Nov. 13, 1986, televised address, which confirmed the rumors then circulating through Washington regarding an effort to open a dialogue with the Iranian government. Those rumors had begun Nov. 4 (the day of the U.S. congressional elections), when wire services first reported that *Al Shiraa*, an Arabic-language magazine published in Lebanon, ran a story claiming that the United States supplied Iran with spare military parts and that Reagan's former national security adviser Robert McFarlane visited Teheran in September to negotiate the release of American hostages.

hostages remained captive in the Middle East[10]; the Nicaraguan conflict seemed no closer to resolution; and Congress was as unwilling as ever to support Reagan's efforts to aid the contras.[11]

Reagan, of course, bore the brunt of the criticism regarding the failed operation. Despite damage control efforts by his top aides, he suffered the greatest one-month drop in job performance public approval ratings ever recorded.[12] His public standing did not rebound until late in his second term, when he was effectively a lame-duck president.[13] This loss of public credibility compounded his already weakened status as a second-term president prohibited from running for reelection. The 1987 reports of the two major investigations into the Iran-contra affair, one by the Tower Commission and the other by a joint Congressional Committee, further damaged Reagan's credibility.

But Reagan's presidential aides did not escape unscathed. Key White House assistants, including NSC staff members John Poindexter and Lieutenant Colonel Oliver North, and Reagan's chief of staff Donald Regan were forced from office.[14] Robert McFarlane, another Reagan national security adviser, attempted suicide, apparently overwhelmed by his culpability in the scandal. Officials in the Central Intelligence Agency,

---

10 Whether the arms deal would in fact have led to freedom for all the American hostages held in the Mideast remains a subject of controversy. It was not until 1991 that the last American hostage finally came home.

11 Eventually, the Nicaraguan conflict came to an uneasy end when the Sandinista-backed government agreed to hold elections, only to see itself voted out of office. The contras have since disbanded. Nicaragua remains in a state of political unrest, but military violence has, for now, ceased.

12 Through 1985 and most of 1986, Reagan's job performance public approval rating hovered in the low 60 percent range, with a high of 65 percent reported in November 1985, one year after his reelection. After the revelations regarding the Iran-contra affair, Reagan's job performance approval rating plummeted from 63 percent in late October 1986 to 47 percent in a poll conducted Dec. 4 and 5, 1986.

His approval rating remained stable throughout 1987, at just below the 50 percent level. The sharpest drop occurred in late February, just after the release of the Tower Commission report, when approval fell from 48 percent to 40 percent. It climbed back to 46 percent after Reagan's televised address on the Iran-contra affair in early March 1987.

All data is from the Gallup Polls, based on responses to the question, "Do you approve or disapprove of the way Ronald Reagan is handling his job as president?" See George Gallup, Jr., *The Gallup Poll* (Wilmington, Dela.: Scholarly Resources, Inc., 1986–9).

13 Beginning in 1988, his approval ratings finally began inching up. In January, he was at 49 percent; in mid-July, he reached 54 percent; and by December 1988, when he was a lame-duck president, Reagan's job approval rating was 63 percent, the highest of any president leaving office since Franklin Roosevelt. Gallup, *The Gallup Poll*.

14 Officially, of course, North was not a member of the White House Office.

which provided logistical support for the initiative, were indicted and placed on trial for lying to Congress.

Ironically, until the story first broke, both Reagan's critics and supporters generally agreed that he had snapped the string of "failed" presidencies stretching back to the Johnson administration.[15] Iran-contra, however, changed that perception. Nor was the damaged limited to the Reagan presidency; the arms-for-hostage deal tarnished his successor's term in office as well. During the 1988 and the 1992 presidential campaigns, George Bush was pressed by the media and by rival candidates to provide a more complete account of his involvement, while Reagan's vice-president, in the Iran affair.[16] Indeed, revelations regarding Bush's alleged role in the Iran decision-making process, released only days before voters went to the polls in 1992, may have cost Bush a chance at reelection.[17] Bush himself added additional fuel to the flames of controversy by pardoning, as one of his last presidential acts, several members of Reagan's presidential staff for any legal improprieties they may have committed during the Iran initiative. Critics viewed Bush's pardon as a self-serving attempt to prevent Iran-contra investigators from incriminating him.

The disastrous consequences of the Iran initiative begs the inevitable question: Why? What prompted Reagan to pursue such an inherently contradictory policy? As the Tower Commission noted,

> The Iran initiative ran directly counter to the administration's own policy on terrorism, the Iran/Iraq war, and military support to Iran. This inconsistency was never resolved, nor were the consequences of this inconsistency fully considered and provided for. The result taken as a whole was a U.S. policy that worked against itself.[18]

How did such a flawed policy reach fruition? What went wrong?

---

15 Recall that Johnson's presidency was doomed by Vietnam; Nixon's destroyed by Watergate; and Ford's essentially still-born, due in part to his early decision to pardon Nixon. Although Carter avoided major scandals, he was not reelected.

16 Critics essentially suggested that Bush choose among one of the following two scenarios: Either he was a key player during Iran-contra, and thus culpable for a faulty and possibly illegal decision, or he was cut out of the decision process, and therefore served merely as a figurehead vice-president. Understandably, Bush refused to accept either premise.

17 Only days before the election, Special Prosecutor Lawrence Walsh released documents that suggested Bush knew more about the decision-making process during the Iranian covert operation than he had so far acknowledged. Prior to this, of course, Bush had also been haunted by the so-called October surprise scenario – the claim, never proved, that officials close to Reagan delayed the release of Iranian-held hostages until after the 1980 presidential election so as not to boost then president Jimmy Carter's reelection chances. A congressional investigation failed to substantiate the charges.

18 *Tower Commission Report*, p. 62. See also the *Joint Report*, pp. 11–12.

The flaws in the branch: Why the Iran initiative failed

The Iran-contra affair, I argue, stems in large part from basic flaws inherent in the presidential branch.[19] Specifically, in this case White House staff growth and specialization made it difficult for Reagan to judge whether his advisers were providing him the information and expertise necessary to predict the most likely consequences of the Iran initiative.

By indicting the presidential branch during the Iran affair, of course, I do not mean to exonerate Reagan himself; his congenial nature made him susceptible to advisers' pleas to help the hostages, and his passive management style and intellectual flaccidness allowed those aides to extend the operation beyond the limits Reagan initially set.[20] Nor do I argue that Reagan's White House aides were somehow pawns in a malevolent staff system. Their combination of excessive zeal, questionable ethics, and inexperience surely contributed to the botched outcome.

Nevertheless, the impact of Reagan and his aides' personal characteristics during the Iran affair were exacerbated, I argue, by the large, functionally specialized White House-dominated advising system in which they operated. This is evident in a review of the decision-making process.

First, the decision-making process violated standard administrative procedures for formulating national security policy. Due to security concerns, the initiative was never fully vetted at the subcabinet level; record-keeping was faulty; intelligence expertise was ignored; and the operation unfolded with limited political and legal oversight.[21]

These administrative shortcomings were compounded by the lack of political acumen exhibited by key presidential aides, especially Casey, McFarlane, Poindexter, and the redoubtable North.[22] All felt they were

---

19 As evidence, see Tower Commission member Edmund Muskie's summary of sixteen different factors that together contributed to the failure of the Iran-contra plan. All sixteen relate to performances by Reagan's subordinates, including his national security assistant and staff, the CIA, key cabinet heads, and his chief of staff. *Tower Commission Report*, pp. xvii–xix. Similarly, the *Joint Report* is rife with comments critical of the role of Reagan's advisers, esp. pp. 13–19.

   To be sure, neither investigation indicts the White House staff system more generally, nor do they advocate the reforms suggested here; the Tower Commission recommendations (pp. 87–99) are largely designed to make the presidential branch more effective, not to dismantle it. Similarly, the *Joint Report* is primarily concerned to ensure that, in the future, Congress is not cut out of the foreign policy decision-making process.

20 The *Tower Commission Report*, pp. 79–80.

21 As the Tower Commission concluded, "In the case of the Iran initiative, the NSC process did not fail, it was simply ignored." See the *Tower Commission Report*, p. 80. Similarly, the joint Committee report states, "The record of the Iran-contra Affair also shows a seriously flawed policymaking process," p. 12.

22 Some argue that McFarlane at this time was already burdened by the emotional troubles that would lead him to attempt suicide a short time after the joint congres-

helping Reagan achieve desired objectives, but their actions, when uncovered, in fact decreased the likelihood those objectives – and others Reagan wanted – would be obtained.[23] None seemed to fully anticipate the impact of public revelations that senior White House officials were pursuing a covert operation running counter to expressed administration policy. Nor, apparently, did they foresee the backlash from disclosures that proceeds from the arms sales were being diverted to the contras at a time when such aid was banned by Congress.

Those who might have anticipated these consequences were not fully engaged in the decision-making process.[24] Secretary of State George Shultz and Secretary of Defense Caspar Weinberger voiced opposition to the Iran initiative on at least two occasions, but evidently their warnings were not transmitted at a time or in terms that might have encouraged Reagan to reconsider his decision.[25] And offsetting their warnings were the assurances of McFarlane and Poindexter, and probably Casey, that the plan could work. Moreover, both secretaries later admitted they were largely uninformed as to the full extent of the operation until the public disclosures in November 1986.

The failure to warn Reagan, in terms he understood, of the Iran initiative's potentially disastrous domestic consequences demonstrates the difficulty presidents have relying on a staff whose functional or institutional roles may blind them to the president's bargaining interests. Although there is some controversy on this point, the bulk of the evidence suggests Reagan was ignorant of North's decision, with Poindexter's concurrence, to transfer arms profits to the contras. Reagan's ignorance, combined with his strong political convictions, created the wrong operating climate for his national security advisers; in order to give Reagan "plausible deniability," his aides used his publicly stated bargaining objectives as policy-making cues, rather than clear their actions directly with him. In their preoccupation with secrecy, however, Reagan's national security staff underestimated the legal and political ramifications of their actions.

---

sional hearings on the Iran-contra affair. On this point, see Ledeen, *Perilous Statecraft*, pp. 145–51. As for North, Ledeen describes him as "a great talent and a great risk" who required "good management and careful supervision." Evidently he received neither. *Perilous Statecraft*, pp. 292–3.

23 See the *Tower Commission Report*, pp. 79–83.

24 Michael Deaver, who had demonstrated excellent political judgment in Reagan's first term, had by this time left the White House, and Nancy Reagan, who also was adept at protecting her husband, was evidently not kept informed.

25 Shultz and Weinberger aired their opposition to the plan in a meeting with Reagan at the White House on Dec. 7, 1985, and at a full NSC meeting on Jan. 7, 1986. See the *Joint Report*, pp. 193, 197–8. This was several months after McFarlane had already broached the issue with Reagan, and the initial phase of the operation was already under way.

Moreover, CIA Director Casey was apparently intent on augmenting the nation's intelligence capabilities by using the "residuals" from the Iranian arms sales to develop a free-standing "company" capable of conducting covert operations.[26] Again, his institutional bias may have blinded him to Reagan's perspective.

Reagan, of course, expected Chief of Staff Don Regan to manage the White House on his behalf. But despite the public perception cultivated by Regan that the White House office was under his close supervision, Regan apparently had no jurisdiction over McFarlane's or Poindexter's activities, and evidently did not know the details of what they were doing.[27]

Departmental parochialism may also have colored Shultz's and Weinberger's input; some argue that both were more concerned with protecting their departments from involvement in the Iran initiative than in warning Reagan of its likely consequences.[28]

Advised by a staff that in retrospect appears insufficiently sensitive to the potential dangers, then, Reagan pursued an undertaking that failed to achieve his preferred objectives: an opening to Iranian moderates and the release of American hostages. Instead, the Iran initiative jeopardized his sources of bargaining power, reduced his ability to effect political outcomes, and destabilized the American political system as a whole.

To be sure, it is worth repeating that primary blame for the Iran-contra affair must rest with Reagan himself. But, as the several investigations into the affair conclude, a series of factors related to the advising process certainly contributed to Reagan's decision to undertake the Iran initiative.

Of course, had Reagan been able to fully disassociate himself from those parts of the initiative of which he claimed to be ignorant, the repercussions of its failure might have been minimized. But members of the "Washington community," and the general public inevitably held Reagan

---

26 On this issue, see the *Joint Report*, p. 413. Meese, however, argues that Casey was unaware of the diversion, although North disagrees. See Meese *With Reagan*, pp. 289–90.

27 See Regan, *For the Record*, pp. 1–54, 375–9.

28 That is, having protected the interests of their respective departments by going on record as opposed to the Iran initiative, Weinberger and Shultz then relaxed their guard, allowing the covert operation to continue when more dogged opposition might have stopped it. Concerning Shultz on this point, see especially Menges, *Inside the National Security Council*, pp. 371–8; and Ledeen, *Perilous Statecraft*, pp. 73–4, 143–4, 241–2, 277. See also the *Tower Commission Report*, pp. xvii–xix; the *Joint Report*, pp. 178, 197–9, 203, 263; Woodward, *Veil*, pp. 473–5, 492, 498–9, 562, 566–70, 583–4.

On Weinberger and the vigor of his opposition, see Ledeen, *Perilous Statecraft*, pp. 143, 256, 277–8. See also the *Tower Commission Report*, pp. xvii–xix; Menges, *Inside the National Security Council*, esp. 378–9; the *Joint Report*, pp. 198–9; and Woodward, *Veil*, pp. 473–5, 498–501, 562.

accountable for the entire affair.[29] Despite North's willingness to "fall on the sword," or Poindexter's assertion that the "buck stops here," Reagan ultimately shouldered responsibility for everything his advisers did in his name – whether he knew of it or not.[30]

This is the fundamental lesson of the Iran-contra affair: Because the president is invariably held accountable for almost every White House staff action, he must actively manage staff operations to ensure his aides will provide the bargaining resources he needs.

The flaws in the branch: Conceptualizing the argument

Unfortunately, Iran-contra is not an isolated event; in fact, many critics believe that presidential branch growth during the last half century has made it more difficult for presidents to extract the political, policy and administrative resources necessary to reduce bargaining uncertainty. Presidents are thus less able to gauge the likely impact of their bargaining choices on preferred outcomes.

By "presidential branch," of course, I mean to suggest that the weaknesses of the presidential advisory system are primarily centered in the White House Office (WHO), rather than the rest of the EOP. Since its inception in 1939, the WHO has become progressively larger, more functionally specialized, and internally differentiated.

There are now White House advisers for national security, domestic, and economic policymaking; media and communications; liaison to Congress, interest groups, and other government actors and institutions; and internal staff coordination and administration.[31]

In theory, this growth in staff size and specialization expands the bargaining resources available to presidents. In fact, however, it has frequently made it less likely these resources will be accessible to presidents in a manner most useful to them. This is because presidents must integrate the separate streams of resources that different administrative, political, and policy staffs provide to fully understand the consequences of particular bargaining choices. But staff specialization and differentiation make the job of integrating these separate streams of advice more difficult.[32]

---

29 Recall that by Washington community, Neustadt means those who have a direct stake in what the president chooses to do; the term is defined by interest, not locale.

30 As the joint Committee report states, "[T]he ultimate responsibility for the events in the Iran-Contra Affair must rest with the President. If the President did not know what his National Security Advisers were doing, he should have." *Joint Report*, pp. 21–2.

31 For documentation, see the relevant sublistings in the U.S. Government Manual during the last half century.

32 On this point, see particularly Bruce Buchanan, "Constrained Diversity: The Organizational Demands of the Presidency," in James P. Pfiffner, *The Managerial Presidency*

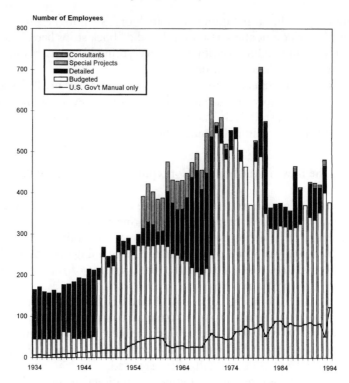

Number of Employees

Figure 1.1. Size of the White House staff, 1934–94. *Source:* 1934–76 from James Connor File, Ford Library (from OMB); 1979–93 from Hart 1995; 1977–8, 1989, 1994 from *United States Statistical Abstract.*

The activities of Reagan's White House foreign policy advisers during the Iran-contra affair offer a case in point. Neither McFarlane nor Poindexter, Reagan's two assistants for national security affairs, nor their assistant North, nor CIA director Casey ever seemed to grasp the likely

(Pacific Grove, Calif.: Brooks-Cole, 1991); Hugh Heclo, "The Executive Office of the President" Occasional Paper no. 83–4 (Cambridge: Harvard University Center for American Political Studies, 1983); Roger Porter, "Advising the President," *PS* Vol.19 (Fall 1986), pp. 867–9; and Richard Rose, "Organizing Issues in and Organizing Problems Out" in Pfiffner, *Managing the Presidency*, pp. 105–19.

   An oft-stated corollary of this point is that staff specialists, by virtue of professional training and background, are less likely to possess a "generalist" outlook. Staff recruitment patterns thus reinforce role specialization, to the detriment of presidential bargaining. To my knowledge, however, no one has systematically tested this point. For some evidence regarding staff backgrounds, see, generally, Patricia Florestano, "The Characteristics of White House Staff Appointees from Truman to Nixon," *Presidential Studies Quarterly* 7, no. 4 (Fall 1977), pp. 184–91; Alex Lacey, "The White House Staff Bureaucracy," *Trans-Action* 6, no. 3 (July 1969), pp. 50–6; and James W. Riddlesperger, Jr. and James D. King, "Presidential Appointments to the Cabinet, Executive Office, and White House Staff," *Presidential Studies Quarterly* 16, no. 4 (Fall 1986), pp. 691–9.

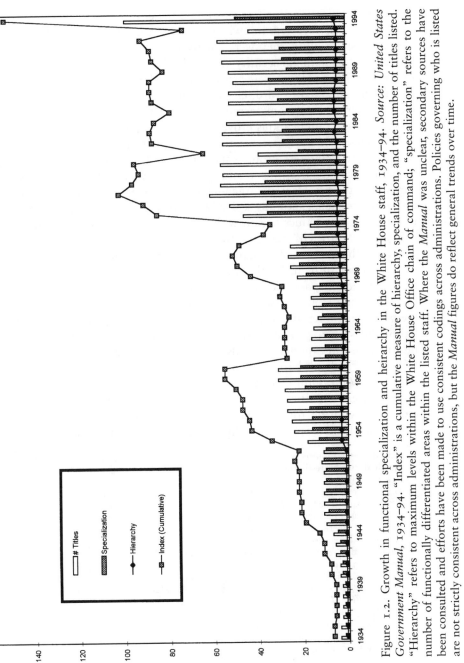

Figure 1.2. Growth in functional specialization and heirarchy in the White House staff, 1934–94. *Source: United States Government Manual, 1934–94.* "Index" is a cumulative measure of hierarchy, specialization, and the number of titles listed. "Hierarchy" refers to maximum levels within the White House Office chain of command; "specialization" refers to the number of functionally differentiated areas within the listed staff. Where the *Manual* was unclear, secondary sources have been consulted and efforts have been made to use consistent codings across administrations. Policies governing who is listed are not strictly consistent across administrations, but the *Manual* figures do reflect general trends over time.

domestic ramifications for Reagan should the covert Iran-contra operations be publicly revealed. But why should they have? By virtue of training and responsibility, they were chiefly responsible for evaluating the
Iran initiative's national security and intelligence-gathering implications.
In contrast, none of them were officially charged with, nor were their specific talents oriented toward, clarifying the full gamut of the likely domestic repercussions from secretly dealing with Iran.[33] Unfortunately,
those domestic ramifications proved most damaging to Reagan.

The dangers of staff specialization also apply to presidential relations
with Congress, interest groups, state and local governments, agencies
within the federal government, and to the non – Washington, D.C., press
corps.[34] As the presidential bargaining universe expands in both size and
diversity, presidents naturally seek additional aides with the expertise and
information to conduct liaison with these specialized audiences. But in
delegating "outreach" activities to specialized staff, a president's direct
contact with members of his bargaining audience inevitably lessens. This
makes it more difficult for the president to accurately assess their needs
and likely actions, and vice versa. The result, as Stephen Hess warns, is
that the White House liaison staff may become special pleaders, serving
the bargaining interests of the targeted audiences, not the president.[35] If
liaison aides, then, provide a president with more specialized bargaining
information and expertise, they also do so from a vantage point less helpful to the president's bargaining needs.

As the White House staff becomes internally differentiated, it also
grows bigger.[36] But this spawns an additional problem. Because there are
more staff with narrower concerns, managing their activities becomes
more crucial and more difficult. In response, every president since Nixon

33 Indeed, Casey reportedly viewed the diversion of residual payments as "a neat idea."
   North, during his testimony on Capitol Hill, repeatedly chastised Congress for meddling
   in foreign affairs.
34 For a survey of some of these staff liaison developments, see Eric L. Davis, "Congres-
   sional Liaison: The People and the Institutions" in Anthony King (ed.), *Both Ends of the
   Avenue: The Presidency, the Executive Branch, and Congress in the 1980's* (Washing-
   ton D.C.: American Enterprise Institute, 1983), pp. 59–95; Joseph Pika, "Interest
   Groups and the Executive: Presidential Intervention," in Allen J. Cigler and Burdett A.
   Loomis (eds.), *Interest Group Politics* (*Washington D.C.: Congressional Quarterly
   Press*, 1983), pp. 298–323; Mark A. Peterson, "The Presidency and Organized Interests:
   White House Patterns of Interest Group Liaison," *American Political Science Review*
   86, no. 3 (September 1992), pp. 612–25; and John Maltese, *Spin Control: The White
   House Office of Communications and the Management of Presidential News* (Chapel
   Hill: North Carolina University Press, 1992).
35 Hess, *Organizing the Presidency*, pp. 172–3.
36 Interest in specifying the size of the presidential staff has become something of a cottage
   industry, to some extent obscuring the more relevant issues. For an overview see generally Cronin, "The Swelling of the Presidency", pp. 345–59; Hart, *The Presidential
   Branch*, pp. 97–109; and Hess, *Organizing the Presidency*, pp. 225–6.

has routinely delegated internal management functions to senior aides, thus creating additional hierarchy within the White House.[37] But this layering of positions removes the president from direct oversight of staff activities. Consequently, he is less able to ensure that they are working in his interest.

Equally important, as staffs grow larger, members are less able to gauge the probable impact of their actions on a president's bargaining preferences.[38] This means the information and expertise they transmit to the president may be less relevant to his needs. He, in turn, must then expend more time and energy to extract the necessary bargaining resources, or risk the consequences.

Again, Iran-contra is illustrative. Most of the initial decisions regarding Iran-contra were made without Chief of Staff Don Regan's knowledge. Reagan, of course, assumed Regan was protecting his interests, but his chief of staff was not positioned to do so.[39]

Furthermore, effective staff management and the provision of bargaining resources are jeopardized not only by increasing staff specialization and size, but also by the locus of branch growth. Specifically, by centering staff development during the last half-century within the White House Office, presidents have merged two types of aides – personal and institutional – within one advising organization.

As noted in the introduction, Roosevelt's E.O. 8248 essentially divided the presidential staff into a White House Office and the rest of the EOP staff agencies.[40] White House aides included Roosevelt's personal and political assistants who largely concerned themselves with his day-to-day bargaining needs. In contrast, the EOP housed the institutional staff agencies that played a relatively greater role in recurring but longer-term

---

37 Eisenhower was the first to appoint a chief of staff, of course, but neither Kennedy or Johnson followed suit. Thereafter, however, every president has delegated staff management to an aide or aides. The rationale for appointing a "chief-of-staff" is explored in Buchanan, "Constrained Diversity," pp. 96–104; Richard E. Neustadt, "Does the White House Need a Strong Chief of Staff?" in Pfiffner, *Managing the Presidency*, pp. 29–32; and Samuel Kernell and Samuel Popkin, *Chief of Staff: Twenty-Five Years of Managing the Presidency* (Berkeley and Los Angeles: University of California Press, 1986).

38 As Francis Rourke argues, "One serious problem . . . is the extent to which . . . the White House staff, can itself, with or without the president's knowledge, become an irrational force in executive policymaking, capable of inflicting far more damage on the president's and the nation's welfare than any of the executive agencies whose errors it has been charged with preventing." Francis Rourke "Presidentializing the Bureaucracy: From Kennedy to Reagan," in Pfiffner, *Managing the Presidency*, p. 134.

39 On this point, see Reagan's comments in Reagan, *An American Life*, pp. 536–9.

40 On this distinction, see generally *The President's Committee on Administrative Management: Report with Special Studies* (Washington, D.C.: Government Printing Office, 1937) (hereafter the *Brownlow Committee Report*). It is discussed more fully in Chapter 3.

bargaining processes, such as the annual budgeting process. Moreover, they did so with an eye toward protecting the interests of the presidency, not just the president.

As I document in later chapters, this division of institutional and personal staff was an important bargaining safeguard for Roosevelt. By incorporating institution-based staff resources into the bargaining process, Roosevelt created an administrative warning device that helped avert decisions that might otherwise erode long-term presidential bargaining leverage for short-term personal political gains. Of course, the two perspectives frequently overlapped – what benefitted the presidency usually helped the incumbent president – but the obverse was not always true.[41]

The distinction between personal and institutional staff survived at least through the Truman years, but has since gradually eroded.[42] Today both institutional and personally oriented bargaining support sources are merged within one White House-dominated staff branch. Short-term personal bargaining considerations are thus more likely to drive out long-term institutional concerns.[43] By losing the means to evaluate the likely impact of today's decisions on presidential bargaining effectiveness tomorrow, presidents ultimately jeopardize their sources of power.

The loss of institutional perspective manifests itself in other ways as well. By merging institutional advice with political service, and politicizing institutional staff agencies, presidential staffs are less likely to anticipate the probable policy consequences of particular presidential bargains.[44] This is

---

41 This is not to suggest that institutional advising sources are not politically involved. To the contrary, institutional agencies do take political stances, but from a perspective looking beyond the president's immediate horizon. [For a slightly different view equating institutional perspectives with "neutral competence," see Hugh Heclo, "The OMB and the Presidency – the Problem of 'Neutral Competence,'" *Public Interest*, [no. 38, (Winter 1975), pp. 80–98.]
    For more on institutional outlooks, see also Buchanan, "Constrained Diversity,"; Colin Campbell, *Managing the Presidency: Carter, Reagan and the Search for Executive Harmony* (Pittsburgh, Pa.: University of Pittsburgh Press, 1986); Hugh Heclo, "The Executive Office of the President"; Neustadt, "Does the White House Need a Strong Chief of Staff?" p. 30; Porter, "Advising the President," and Roger Porter, *Presidential Decision Making: The Economic Policy Board* (New York: Cambridge University Press, 1980), pp. 221–52; and Walter Williams, *Mismanaging America: The Rise of the Anti-Analytic-Presidency* (Lawrence: University Press of Kansas, 1991).
42 On this point, see Patrick Wolf, "Reorganization, Competition, and Crises: Fundamental Explanations for the Bureau of the Budget's 'Golden Era,'" Occasional Paper 93–114 (Cambridge: Harvard University Center for American Political Studies, 1993). The observation is also partly derived from correspondence with Richard Neustadt, who worked in both the BoB and the White House during Truman's presidency.
43 See specifically Heclo, "The Executive Office of the President," pp. 33–4, and Rourke, "Presidentializing the Bureaucracy," p. 134. But this is a point made by nearly every critic of White House staff bureaucratization.
44 Williams, *Mismanaging America*; Heclo, "Neutral Competence"; Lester G. Seligman and Cary R. Covington, *The Coalitional Presidency* (Chicago: Dorsey Press, 1989). For

partly due to the loss of staff institutional memory; politicization means there are fewer aides with knowledge of basic governmental administrative processes or the past details of policy proposals. The result are policies that do not achieve stated objectives or that produce unintended consequences. Again, Iran-contra is telling in this regard.[45]

Parallelling the decline in institutional expertise is a fourth adverse consequence of presidential branch growth: the loss of political sensitivity. Staff enlargement and differentiation pull functions once performed by other political actors into the domain of the White House-centered bureaucracy.[46] Consequently, presidents find themselves relying primarily on the White House staff to gauge the likely impact of presidential bargains on a president's sources of influence. But aides clustered within a White House-centered orbit simply do not possess the knowledge to adequately advise presidents in this regard.

This is partly due to the gradual divorce between a president's political interests and those of his party. Formerly, in the party-dominated era of presidential politics, presidents relied on party leaders, especially at the local and state levels, to gauge the likely impact of specific bargains on the president's party support.

But beginning in the mid-1960s the ties that bound presidents to parties dissolved, victimized by electoral and other political reforms. The White House staff gradually absorbed the functions, but not necessarily the expertise, once possessed by the party hierarchy.[47] Recall that neither

---

an early indictment of presidential policy capabilities, but with recommendations somewhat in variance with mine, see William Carey, "Presidential Staffing in the Sixties and Seventies," *Public Administration Review* 29 (September/October 1969), pp. 450–8.

45 For another recent example, consider the unpredicted long-term effects, especially the massive budget deficits, resulting from Reagan's 1981 economic program as enacted by Congress, encompassing both tax cuts and a reduction in some federal expenditures. An overview is provided by Donald Kettl, *Deficit Politics: Public Budgeting in its Institutional and Historical Context* (New York: MacMillan, 1992); for inside accounts, see David Stockman, *The Triumph of Politics: Why the Reagan Revolution Failed* (New York: Harper & Row, 1986); and Paul Craig Roberts, *The Supply-side Revolution: An Insider's Account of Policymaking in Washington* (Cambridge: Harvard University Press, 1984).

46 See generally Seligman and Covington, *The Coalitional Presidency*, pp. 150–8.

47 For details, see Roger G. Brown, "Party and Bureaucracy: from Kennedy to Reagan," *Political Science Quarterly* 97, no. 2 (Summer 1982), pp. 279–294; Godfrey Hodgson, *All Things to All Men: The False Promise of the Modern American Presidency from Franklin D. Roosevelt to Ronald Reagan*, (New York: Simon & Schuster, 1980), pp. 161–82; Theodore Lowi, *The Personal Presidency: Power Invested, Promise Unfulfilled*, (Ithaca, N.Y.: Cornell University Press, 1985), pp. 67–96; Austin Ranney, "The Political Parties: Reform and Decline" in King, *The New American Political System*, pp. 213–48; Sidney M. Milkis, *The President and the Parties: The Transformation of the American Party System Since the New Deal* (New York: Oxford University Press, 1993); and Matthew J. Dickinson and Katie Dunn Tenpas, "Governing,Campaigning, and Organizing the Presidency: An Electoral Connection?" (Paper delivered at the annual meeting of the Midwest Political Science Association, Chicago, 1994.)

North or Casey evidently concerned themselves with the possible danger to the Republican party should their Iran-contra activities be disclosed. This despite the fact that Casey, prior to becoming CIA director, served previously as Reagan's campaign manager, and North, while a member of Reagan's NSC staff, actively solicited contributions from party donors to support the contra movement.

Their ignorance of partisan concerns is understandable; the White House-centered staff branch is beholden primarily to the president – not his party.[48] As the White House staff absorbs political functions, then, a president's contact with other political actors who have independent political bases lessens. So, too, does the likelihood he will be warned of politically foolish bargains.[49]

At the same time, a larger White House staff attracts more business less directly related to the president's bargaining priorities. As bargaining resources are stretched thin and management costs grow, the president is held accountable for more decisions of which he has less knowledge. This fuels unrealistic expectations among Washingtonians and the public regarding what a president might feasibly accomplish.[50]

Moreover, the centralization of authority within the White House staff branch has adverse system-wide repercussions. As Joel Aberbach and Bert Rockman observe, it tends "to induce retaliatory behavior" among other governing institutions.[51] Emulating executive branch staff growth, Congress has expanded its own staff capacities. And, as James Pfiffner argues, attempts by the White House staff to politicize the federal bureaucracy may decrease presidential bargaining effectiveness: "The more political appointees there are and the more layers which separate the agency head and career executives, the longer it will take to establish effective control."[52] The end result is political and policy stalemate – not expanded presidential power.

48 On this point see Nicole Woolsey Biggart, "A Sociological Analysis of the Presidential Staff," *The Sociological Quarterly* 25 (Winter 1984), pp. 27–43; and Matthew Holden, "Why Entourage Politics Is Volatile," in Pfiffner, *Managing the Presidency*.

49 Independent actors include cabinet heads, party officials, congressional leaders and influential state and local politicians. See also Richard E. Neustadt "The Constraining of the President: The Presidency After Watergate," *British Journal of Political Science* 4, no. 4 (1974), pp. 383–97.

50 These issues are addressed in Hess, *Organizing the Presidency*, p. 172; Samuel Kernell *Going Public: New Strategies of Presidential Leadership* 2nd ed. (Washington, D.C.: Congressional Quarterly Press, 1993); and Jeffrey K. Tulis *The Rhetorical Presidency* (Princeton, N.J.: Princeton University Press, 1987).

51 Joel D. Aberbach and Bert Rockman, "Mandarins or Mandates?: Control and Discretion in the Modern Administrative State," in Pfiffner, *The Managerial Presidency*, p. 165.

52 James P. Pfiffner, "Political Appointees and Career Executives", in Pfiffner, *Managing the Presidency*, p. 179. See also Aberbach and Rockman, "Mandarins or Mandates?"

Perhaps most importantly, critics argue that the presidential branch undercuts presidential accountability, resulting in decisions – escalating the U.S. presence in Vietnam, covering up the Watergate break-in, selling arms to the Iranians and funneling the proceeds to the Nicaraguan contras – which show little sensitivity to democratic principles.[53]

Branch flaws: Empirical indicators?

The logic of this argument suggests, then, that a larger, White House-dominated presidential staff, internally differentiated and functionally specialized, may in fact decrease a president's bargaining effectiveness, by diffusing bargaining resources and increasing management costs. This lessens a president's bargaining success and his effective influence on outcomes. But although the logic may seem persuasive, it begs the question: Are there other empirical measures beyond the Iran-contra case that support the claim?

Unfortunately there has yet to my knowledge been any systematic attempt to test this assertion, in part because scholars asserting branch weakness typically do not do so in a way that is easily amenable to empirical study. Nevertheless, there are indicators that the argument has some validity, although the measures are admittedly imprecise. Typically, scholars cite three: other presidential bargains that also do not achieve desired outcomes; more general indicators of declining presidential influence, such as opinion polls, reelection rates, and historical reputations; and the administrative actions of recent presidents who, since 1972, seem intent on finding alternatives to the White House-centered staff system.

The Iran-contra affair is but the latest of several well-publicized presidential bargains that did not achieve stated objectives, in part due to ill-advised staff actions. Two others stand out. During the period 1964–5, of course, Lyndon Johnson committed more than half a million American soldiers to Vietnam, effectively mortgaging his presidency to a war that had no immediate prospects of resolution. Three years later, with

An interesting case study is provided by the Reagan administration's attempts to relax environmental regulation by the EPA. For an inside account of the political backlash, see Anne M. Burford and John Greenya, *Are You Tough Enough? An Insider's View of Washington Power Politics* (New York: McGraw-Hill, 1986).

53 The problem here has more to do with evading bargaining than in constructing bargains that do not serve a president's interest. In the long run, however, attempting to circumvent bargaining constraints does not seem to serve presidential interests.

    The issues are explored more systematically in John Burke, "Responsibilities of Presidents and Advisers: A Theory and Case Study of Vietnam Decision Making," *Journal of Politics* 46, no. 3 (August 1984), pp. 818–45.

the U.S. still mired in the war, and facing a bitterly divided country, Johnson declined to run for reelection. In retrospect, scholars have questioned whether Johnson was well-served by the advising process which helped produce the decision to escalate the American presence in Vietnam.[54]

The Watergate scandal, which unfolded during the period 1972–4, is a second major staff-related debacle. Again a president was forced from office, victimized not just by his own mistakes but by those of his assistants. In this case, members of Richard Nixon's campaign organization, pressured by Nixon's senior White House advisers to ensure the president's reelection, engaged in a series of "dirty tricks," including the bungled attempt to bug the headquarters of the Democratic National Committee in the Watergate hotel. Nixon's subsequent efforts, with the complicity of his senior staff, to control the repercussions from the break-in destroyed his presidency.

Together with the Iran-contra affair, Vietnam and Watergate illustrate the hazards of presidents relying on a large, layered, functionally specialized White House staff for administrative assistance. And yet these high-visibility cases, no matter how significant, also represent a selective use of evidence; skeptics can argue that they were chosen to prove the point. Rather than any systemic flaws in the presidential branch itself, then, they may simply reflect the isolated failings of particular staff members and presidents.

However, the highly publicized staff travails of the Johnson, Nixon, and Reagan entourages are not the only evidence of branch weakness. Consider also the staff-related mishaps of Gerald Ford, Jimmy Carter, George Bush, and, most recently, Bill Clinton. These additional cases demonstrate a perhaps less noticeable but no less worrisome aspect of presidential branch weakness: that it manifests itself not only in spectacular instances of staff misjudgment and scandal, but also in an almost imperceptible erosion of presidential power through time.

Recall that Ford, Carter, and Bush were all one-term presidents generally characterized as politically ineffective, an ineffectiveness traced in part to poor judgment pressed upon the president or exercised by staff. And Clinton, three years into his presidency, appears in danger of

---

54 For arguments along these lines, see Alexander George, "The Case for Multiple Advocacy Making in Foreign Policy," *American Political Science Review* 66 (September 1972), and Fred Greenstein and John Burke (with Larry Berman and Richard Immerman), *How Presidents Test Reality: Decisions on Vietnam, 1954 and 1965* (New York: Russell Sage Foundation, 1989).

For a contrary argument that LBJ had all the information he needed to make the "right" decision regarding Vietnam, see Hess, *Organizing the Presidency*, pp. 101-2.

sharing their fate, again due in part to the mistakes and misperceptions of his aides.[55]

Look first at recent presidents' inability to get reelected. Since the full maturation of the presidential branch during the mid-1960s, only Reagan succeeded in serving two full terms in office, and his second term was clouded by the Iran-contra scandal. Ford, Carter and Bush were defeated in bids for reelection, Johnson declined to run due to adverse political conditions, and Nixon was forced from office because of a staff-related scandal. In contrast, in the period 1940–64, no president lost a bid for re-election and all but two – JFK and Truman – served out at least two full terms.[56]

Critics also cite the increasing volatility of presidential approval polls as evidence of presidential weakness.[57] This instability in mass sentiment was most recently illustrated by George Bush's free-fall in public opinion, from a high near 90 percent in the aftermath of the Persian Gulf War, to one below 35 percent during his reelection campaign less than two years later. More generally, goes the argument, as presidents institutionalize staff to help cultivate a favorable public image, they foster unrealistic public expectations and become more susceptible to sudden shifts in mass opinion.

A third measure of declining political effectiveness is presidents' inability to translate backing in one issue area to more general support across the range of presidential policies. Support for presidential programs, some argue, is increasingly fragmented, idiosyncratic, and of short

55 From the start of his presidency, when campaign manager Mickey Kantor was blocked from becoming White House chief of staff, Clinton's advising arrangements have been the subject of controversy. The biggest concern, of course, centers on allegations that senior Clinton aides improperly interfered with investigations into his and his wife's pre-presidential Arkansas land deals. Congress and an independent prosecutor are currently investigating these charges.

But Clinton's staff were also embroiled in controversies regarding the budget and health-care policy, as well as lesser issues that, although not as significant, nevertheless point to disarray within the White House. Among the more damaging incidents traced in part to advice from Clinton's staff were the decision to raise taxes substantially on the middle class, in part through a broad-based energy tax, despite campaign promises to the contrary; the public commitment to developing a health-care reform package within the first one hundred days of Clinton's administration, although most observers thought this unfeasible; the decision to immediately push the military to accept acknowledged homosexuals into their ranks; and the failure to consult Republican members of Congress before submitting a jobs stimulus package that subsequently died in the Senate, victimized by a Republican filibuster. Other miscues include firing and then rehiring members of the White House travel office, and allowing the President to receive a $200 haircut in Air Force One, creating the perception that he blocked air traffic at the Los Angeles airport in the process.

56 The EOP was established in 1939, hence the use of 1940 as my starting date. Note that there is some doubt whether Truman could have been reelected in 1952.

57 Cited in Seligman and Covington, *The Coalitional Presidency*, p. 33.

duration. For instance, George Bush's favorable foreign policy ratings apparently did not help him in the domestic realm. Nor did Ronald Reagan's personal popularity translate into support for much of his policy agenda. And Clinton is finding that he must create new coalitions of support for almost all his major legislative initiatives. Gone are the days when presidential programs attracted broad-based partisan backing.

Of course, these barometers of declining presidential bargaining effectiveness surely are driven by more than excessive White House staff growth and specialization. Changing issues pools and reconfigured voting coalitions are coterminous with branch growth. At the same time, key political institutions – the press, party, and Congress – have been drastically transformed.[58] But it is equally plausible that some of these trends are, at least in part, the result of presidential branch growth. The adversarial media coverage of the presidency, for instance, reflects presidents' efforts to conceal decisions during Vietnam and Watergate. And Congress has sought to match presidential staff institutionalization by acquiring its own independent staff support.

Moreover, judging by their search for administrative alternatives, presidents evidently believe their White House-dominated presidential staffs must share some of the blame for recent cases of presidential ineffectiveness.[59] Clinton, for instance, stung by charges that his staff were inexperienced, arrogant[60] and exercised poor judgment, and with several aides under investigation by both branches of Congress, undertook three major administrative overhauls in his first two years in office.[61]

58 For details, see generally the articles in King, *The New American Political System*; John E. Chubb and Paul E. Peterson, *The New Direction in American Politics* (Washington, D.C.; The Brookings Institution, 1985), and John E. Chubb and Paul E. Peterson, *Can the Government Govern?* (Washington, D.C.; The Brookings Institution, 1989).

59 For instance, early in his first term Clinton admitted that his performance to date "lacked focus," a failing he attributed in part to his staff. See his remarks in "Clinton Weighs a Shuffle in Top White House Staff," *Boston Globe*, May 5, 1992, pp. 1, 24.
Reflecting that lack of focus, Clinton's standing in the polls was the lowest ever recorded for a president at that time in office.

60 Regarding staff arrogance, see Burt Solomon, "Even Clintonites Worry About Arrogance," *National Journal*, Apr. 10, 1993, p. 888; see also Richard L. Berke, *The New York Times*, Feb. 22, 1994, p. 1A.

61 The first major staff shake-up occurred in May 1993, when key campaign operative George Stephanopoulos was removed from his high-visibility post as White House communications director and replaced by David Gergen, previously a White House aide under three Republican presidents.
Three weeks before hiring Gergen, Clinton had brought in a deputy chief of staff, Roy Neel, to assist the president's longtime confidant and chief of staff, Thomas F. McLarty. Neel, a member of Vice-President Al Gore's staff, was widely viewed as more experienced in government than McLarty. (See "Clinton Sees Need to Focus His Goals and Sharpen Staff," *New York Times*, May 5, 1993, pp. 1A, 9B; and "Clinton Weighs a Shuffle in Top White House staff" *Boston Globe*, May 5, 1992, pp. 1, 24.

Nor are Clinton's actions unprecedented. Since at least Nixon's reelection, every president has sought to significantly reform the presidential branch, usually by reducing White House staff size.[62] In 1972 Nixon, concerned that his staff had grown too unwieldy, resolved to reduce staff size by reallocating administrative power to a few senior aides and cabinet officials.[63] Although his efforts were scuttled by the Watergate revelations, they set a precedent that most of his successors have emulated.

In Watergate's wake, Gerald Ford also embraced staff reductions, in part to end repeated clashes between Nixon holdovers and Ford appointees.[64] Although he trimmed almost one hundred people from the

A second organizational restructuring took place a little more than a year later, in June 1994, when McLarty was replaced by Office of Management and Budget Director Leon Panetta. McLarty was retained as a senior adviser with unspecified functions, and Panetta's assistant Alice Rivlin became the new head of the OMB. At the same time, amid criticism of Clinton's handling of foreign policy, Gergen was moved to the State Department to advise Secretary of State Warren Christopher.

For additional details regarding the first staff shuffle, see Ruth Marcus, "GOP Insider to Be Clinton Counselor," *The Washington Post*, May 30, 1993, p. 1A; John M. Broder, "Gergen Reveals He Has Sweeping Power," *Los Angeles Times*, June 8, 1993, p. 16A; Michael Kranish, "Clinton to Reduce White House Staff," *The Boston Globe*, Feb. 10, 1993, p. 3; and Carl P. Leubsdorf, "It Can Be Too Much Fun," *The Dallas Morning News*, Dec. 23, 1993, p. 17A.

On the second staff shakeup, see Douglas Jehl "Clinton Shuffles His Aides, Selecting Budget Director as White House Staff Chief," *The New York Times*, June 28, 1994, p. A1; Michael Kranish "McLarty out, Panetta in as Clinton Shakes Staff," *Boston Globe*, June 28, 1994, p. 1; Marshall Ingwerson, "Deficit Hawks Rise to the Top in White House," *The Christian Science Monitor*, June 29, 1994, p. 1; and Suzanne Garment, "Starting Over: Is Lack of Focus the Problem?," *Los Angeles Times*, July 3, 1994, Part M, p. 1.

In September 1994, the Clinton White House underwent still another staff shake-up. This primarily involved clarifying the functions of various staff members. (See the White House press release, dated Sept. 23, 1994 for details).

62 For an overview of some of these attempts, see Hart, *The Presidential Branch*; Hess, *Organizing the Presidency*; Peri Arnold, *Making the Managerial Presidency: Comprehensive Reorganization Planning, 1905–1980* (Princeton, N.J.: Princeton University Press, 1986); and Harold Seidman and Robert Gilmour, *Politics, Position, and Power*, 4th ed. (New York: Oxford University Press, 1986).

63 The growth had in part been spurred by Nixon's efforts to implement the recommendations of the Ash Council, appointed by him in 1969 as one in a succession of presidential commissions with a mandate to reorganize the presidency. Its recommendations led to the establishment of a Domestic Council and staff, and the conversion of the Bureau of the Budget into the Office of Management and Budget. Both were implemented by Reorganization Plan no. 2, submitted to Congress in March 1970. An assessment of their effectiveness is given in Arnold, *Making the Managerial Presidency*, ch. 9; and Seidman and Gilmour, *Politics, Position, and Power*. For Nixon's later efforts to reduce the White House staff, see Seidman and Gilmour, *Politics, Position, and Power*; and Richard P. Nathan, *The Plot That Failed: Nixon and the Administrative Presidency* (New York: John Wiley, 1975). Inside accounts include John Ehrlichman, *Witness to Power: The Nixon Years*, (New York: Simon & Schuster, 1982), and Richard Nixon, *In the Arena: a Memoir of Victory, Defeat and Renewal* (Norwalk, Conn.: Easton Press, 1990).

64 See Robert Hartmann, *Palace Politics: An Inside Account of the Ford Years* (New York: McGraw-Hill Book Co., 1980), pp. 34–6, 272–302; and Gerald Ford, *A Time to Heal:*

White House Office, these peripheral cuts did not touch the staff branch's core. His successor, Jimmy Carter, campaigned in 1977 on a promise to reduce White House staff size. But Carter's efforts proved largely symbolic; rather than eliminate personnel, he shifted them from the White House to other executive staff agency payrolls.[65]

Reagan broke the run of presidents pressing for smaller staffs and his apparent first-term administrative success temporarily quelled talk of White House staff reform. But Iran-contra resurrected the issue. Ultimately, rather than reduce the White House staff size, Reagan opted for more staff hierarchy and a reversion to regularized staffing procedures. However, his successor, former Vice-President George Bush, evidently found these reforms inadequate, at least in domestic affairs. After a term in office plagued by the failings of key aides, most notably Chief of Staff John Sununu who eventually resigned under fire, Bush promised a major overhaul of the White House Office, only to see himself voted out of office.[66]

Most recently, of course, Clinton campaigned on a promise to cut his White House staff size by some 25 percent – a pledge he has since tried to fulfill.[67] To date, however, the reductions seem not to have helped his bargaining power, although it remains to be seen whether they will prove beneficial in the long run.

The historical record, then, while not conclusive, certainly lends credence to claims that presidential branch growth has not increased presidential power. Indeed, it may have produced the opposite effect. Since at least the mid-1960s and the escalation of the American presence in Vietnam, successive presidents seem prone to making poor bargaining choices, based in part on the advice of their White House staff-dominated advisory organizations. Nor are staff sins restricted to the substance of policy and political judgments; White House aides have also been guilty of ethical and legal improprieties in this period.

Conclusion

If the preceding argument is correct, then, the presidential branch is flawed in two respects: It does not provide presidents with the resources

the *Autobiography of Gerald Ford* (Norwalk, Conn.: Easton Press, 1987; originally published New York: Harper & Row, 1979).

65 See Dom Bonafede, "White House Reorganization: Separating Smoke from Substance," *The National Journal*, 10, no. 46 (1977), pp. 1307–11, and Jimmy Carter *Keeping Faith: Memoirs of a President*, Paperback ed. (New York: Bantam, 1982), pp. 115–17.

66 Sununu's replacement as chief of staff, Sam Skinner, fared no better and was himself eased out by Jim Baker during the presidential campaign.

67 "Clinton Trimming Lower-Level Aides," *The New York Times*, Feb. 10, 1993, pp. 1A, 20A. Clinton aides acknowledged that the initial cuts did not constitute 25 percent of staff, but they promised additional reductions.

necessary to assess the political and policy implications of presidential bargains, and it makes presidential management of staff activities much more difficult.[68] The growth in White House staff size, increased specialization, merging of institutional and personal advice, and gradual decline in input from independent political players collectively work to erode presidential bargaining effectiveness. In extreme cases, this contributes to the political and policy disasters typified by Vietnam, Watergate, and the Iran-contra affair. More frequently, however, its erodes a president's effective influence on outcomes in more insidious fashion.[69]

Ironically, the negative effects of branch growth are multiplied as presidential aides assume more responsibility for exercising the means of influence FDR pioneered: rhetoric, radio and media relations,[70] the development of legislative programs,[71] and the use of presidential prerogatives.[72] In short, as the presidential branch has grown, the bargaining tools bequeathed by Roosevelt to his successors have become less effective from a presidential perspective.

The real concern for many observers is that a branch-induced decline in presidential bargaining effectiveness will have repercussions beyond its impact on the fortunes of an incumbent president. Lacking an effective

---

68 Compare to Rourke, "Presidentializing the Bureaucracy," pp. 133–4.

69 For one of the few attempts to measure the relationship between presidential staff organization and presidential power, see Matthew Kerbel, *Beyond Persuasion: Organizational Efficiency and Presidential Power* (Albany: State University of New York, 1991). Kerbel, while not arguing against White House staff bureaucratization per se, does present evidence that how presidential staff are organized and employed measurably impacts a president's effective influence on outcomes.

70 On Roosevelt's use of rhetoric, see Samuel I. Rosenman, *Working with Roosevelt* (New York: Harper & Row, 1952); Robert Sherwood, *Roosevelt and Hopkins*, rev. paperback ed. (New York: The Universal Library, 1950), pp. 212–19; and Graham J. White, *FDR and the Press* (Chicago: The University of Chicago Press, 1979). For developments in this sphere since FDR, see Roderick Hart, *The Sound of Leadership: Presidential Communication in the Modern Age* (Chicago: The University of Chicago Press, 1987); Lowi, *The Personal President*; Kernell, *Going Public*; and Tulis, *The Rhetorical Presidency*.

71 See Richard E. Neustadt, "Presidency and Legislation: The Growth of Central Clearance," *American Political Science Review* 48 no. 3 (1954), pp. 641–71. For developments since FDR, see generally John Kessel, "The Structures of the Carter White House," *American Journal of Political Science* 27, no. 3 (August 1983), pp. 431–63; Stephen J. Wayne, *The Legislative Presidency* (New York: Harper & Row, 1978); Paul Light, *The President's Agenda: Domestic Policy Choice from Kennedy to Carter* (Baltimore: Johns Hopkins University Press, 1982); and Mark A. Peterson, *Legislating Together: The White House and Capitol Hill from Eisenhower to Reagan* (Cambridge: Harvard University Press, 1990).

72 By prerogatives I refer to the unilateral exercise of powers by the president as a means for achieving political objectives. These include the use of executive orders, reorganization authority, appointments, administrative rule making and budget impoundments. Scholars occasionally group these activities under the rubric "administrative presidency." See Richard P. Nathan, *The Administrative Presidency* (New York: John Wiley & Sons, 1983), and Richard Waterman, *Presidential Influence and the Administrative State* (Knoxville: The University of Tennessee Press, 1989.)

presidency to serve as an energizing force, the remaining American political institutions will themselves weaken. Neustadt, echoing Alexander Hamilton in Federalist paper #70, argues:

> [The] pursuit of presidential power, rightly understood, constitutionally conditioned, looking ahead, serves purposes far broader than a President's satisfaction. It is good for the country as well as for him. The President who maximizes his prospective influence within the system helps to energize it in the process.[73]

If Neustadt is correct, then presidential branch development erodes not just the foundation of presidential power. More ominously, it also threatens to sap the vitality of the American political system.

And yet, even if one accepts this evidence as damning, it cannot by itself justify uprooting the presidential branch. As Terry Moe cautions in his seminal defense of White House staff centralization and executive branch politicization:

> This cannot tell us whether politicization and centralization are good or bad. It does tell us something about our criteria of evaluation: that it must take account of the systemic forces on presidential choice. . . . However we appraise [presidential administrative choices] in absolute terms, the practical issue is inevitably one of feasible alternatives.[74]

Documenting the flaws within the presidential branch, then, should not blindly drive us to chop it down. Presidents, as Moe argues, must determine whether there is a viable administrative alternative. Given the current level of bargaining demands, can presidents realistically expect to construct another type of advisory system that provides more bargaining resources, but at equal or less management cost?

As the next several chapters demonstrate, Roosevelt's experiences as president, particularly during World War II, suggest the answer is yes. There is a viable administrative alternative to the White House-centered staff branch. To understand his methods, and why they worked, however, we must document how FDR constructed and utilized a staff system under bargaining circumstances as demanding as any his successors confront. The story begins in 1933, with FDR's ill-fated experiment with cabinet government in the depths of the Depression. Here lie the origins of the modern presidency – and of FDR's means for managing it.

---

73 Neustadt, *Presidential Power*, p. xix. See also Alexander Hamilton *Federalists Paper* #70.
74 Moe, *"The Politicized Presidenecy,"*, pp. 269–70.

PART II

From cabinet to presidential

government, 1933–9

2

Creating the resource gap: Bargaining costs and the First New Deal, 1933–5

Roosevelt's First New Deal was, in essence, a single, gigantic preservation operation, designed to restore confidence in the free enterprise system at home and abroad.[1] His primary objectives were to end the crippling deflation, lighten the debt carried by lower-income groups, put the unemployed to work, and offer structural relief to the nation's most important economic actors, particularly banks, railroads, insurance companies, real estate and mortgage firms, homeowners, and farmers.

In responding to the economic demands from these sectors FDR permanently broadened the scope, frequency, and importance of presidential bargaining, and thus its cost. This exposed a bargaining resource gap within the presidential advisory system. Essentially, Roosevelt had inherited a cabinet-centered advising system that was severely limited in its ability to collectively provide the resources required to accurately predict the likely consequences of his New Deal bargaining choices.

Because he primarily focused during the first term on resuscitating the nation's economy, however, FDR temporarily bridged this gap by utilizing a jerry-rigged administrative system. It was composed primarily of four staff components: an expanded cabinet and staff secretariat; institutional staff agencies, particularly the Bureau of the Budget; a corps of White House aides, supplemented by other government officials detailed to the White House; and an assortment of friends, politicos, and other advisers drawn from the public and private sectors.

Of these, the cabinet was historically the most important source of advice and the one FDR initially turned to most frequently.[2] From July 1933,

---

1 Albert U. Romasco, *The Politics of Recovery (Roosevelt's New Deal)* (New York: Oxford University Press, 1983), p. 29.
2 For revealing glimpses of the Roosevelt cabinet from an inside perspective, see Interior Secretary Harold L. Ickes, *The Secret Diary of Harold L. Ickes: The First Thousand Days*, vol. 1 (New York: Simon & Schuster, 1953) (hereafter Ickes, *Secret Diaries*); Frances Perkins, *The Roosevelt I Knew* (New York: Harper & Row, 1964); and Grace Tully, *F.D.R. My Boss* (New York: Charles Scribner & Sons, 1949), pp. 170–97. An overview can be found in Frank Friedel, *FDR Launching the New Deal*, (Boston: Little, Brown & Co., 1973), pp. 137–60. Richard F. Fenno *The President's Cabinet; An Analysis in the Period from Wilson to Eisenhower*, (New York: Vintage Books, 1959, paperback ed. [original edition from Cambridge:

through September 1935, he experimented with at least five different cabinet-level coordinating councils. But, despite his repeated attempts to make their deliberations more effective, these coordinating councils proved unable to meet his bargaining needs. By the end of 1935 he was genuinely worried that his administrative shortcomings might jeopardize his reelection chances. Consequently, with the economy stabilizing, Roosevelt turned his efforts toward rationalizing his institutional house and putting it on a more permanent footing. His choices in this regard, beginning with his decision to appoint the Brownlow Committee in March 1936, ultimately spelled the death of cabinet government as it had been practiced in the United States for a century and a half.

Roosevelt's first term helps illuminate the weaknesses in the proposals for "cabinet government" frequently espoused by presidents and others seeking alternatives to the White House staff-centered president branch. As he discovered, presidential objectives in the modern era typically require the coordinated action of several departments and agencies. But cabinet secretaries have little incentive to subjugate their departmental needs to the president's broader bargaining interests. As Hugh Heclo explains: "First the Constitution binds executive bureaucracies to a powerful legislature independent of the president. And, second, our constitutional system vests executive branch leadership in a president and department heads whose personal and political fates are not closely tied together."[3]

Presidents have few means to counter these centrifugal forces. Roosevelt's experiences suggest that no staff coordinating instrument, no matter how powerful, can be expected to overcome such divergent incentives. But if the presidential cabinet is simply not well suited to perform collectively as an instrument of advice and consultation, what to plant in its stead? As we shall see, it was Roosevelt's first-term experiences that primed the soil for his administrative seed.

Implementing the New Deal

The "nationalization" of politics begun by FDR's New Deal can be measured in at least three ways: through legislation Congress passed to expand the general authority of the federal government, by the specific

Harvard University Press, 1959]), surveys the presidential cabinet during the twentieth century through the end of the Eisenhower administration. Stephen Hess, *Organizing the Presidency*, 2nd ed., (Washington, D.C.: The Brookings Institution, 1988), takes the reader through Reagan's cabinet.

3 Hugh Heclo "One Executive Branch or Many?" in Anthony King, ed. *Both Ends of the Avenue*. Washington, D.C.: American Enterprise Institute, 1983, p. 27.

powers it granted directly and indirectly to the president, and by the growth in governmental institutions necessary to implement that expanded authority, presidential or otherwise.[4]

Legislatively, the New Deal expanded the government's role across a range of policy arenas, including industrial production and regulation, agriculture, banking, monetary policy, housing, taxation, natural resources, employment and relief activities, securities, and foreign trade.[5] Much of this legislation was passed by the special session of the 73rd Congress Roosevelt called to order soon after taking office. When this Congress finally adjourned on June 16, 1933, it had:

> [C]ommitted the country to an unprecedented program of government-industry co-operation; promised to distribute stupendous sums to millions of staple farmers; accepted responsibility for the welfare of millions of unemployed; agreed to engage in far-reaching experimentation in regional planning; pledged billions of dollars to save homes and farms from foreclosure; undertaken huge public works spending; guaranteed the small banks deposits of the country; and had, for the first time, established federal regulation of Wall Street.[6]

The significance of much of this legislation is that it invested formal powers and political expectations in the presidency, by directly granting powers to FDR or to those working for him.[7] Consider the National Industrial Recovery Act (NIRA), the centerpiece of the First New Deal.[8] It

---

4 The phrase "nationalization" is E. E. Schattschneider's. See E. E. Schattschneider, *The Semi-Sovereign People* (Hinsdale, Il: Dryden Press, 1975), pp. 3–18.

5 Thus, the Home Owners' Loan Act, passed June 13, 1933, created the Home Owner's Loan Corporation and provided that mortgage holders could turn in defaulted mortgages for government bonds; the Securities Act of 1933 and the Securities and Exchange Act of 1934 created a regulatory body (the Security and Exchange Commission) to oversee the stock market; and the Revenue Act of 1934 (approved May 10, 1934), among other provisions, shifted some of the tax burden from low-income taxpayers toward those whose incomes came generally from "unearned sources." For further details, see Arthur Schlesinger, Jr., *The Coming of the New Deal* vol. 2, *The Age of Roosevelt* (Boston: Houghton-Mifflin, 1973) and below.

6 William Leuchtenberg, *Franklin D. Roosevelt and the New Deal*, paperback ed. (New York: Harper Torchbooks, 1963), p. 61.

7 An overview of the expansion of presidential powers in the first months of the New Deal is provided in a document contained in Louis Howe's files. See "memorandum of enumerated powers given to FDR" (May 25, 1933), "Part I" and "Part II," Louis Howe Papers, Howe A3 Folder, FDRL.

8 An omnibus bill, the National Industrial Recovery Act was intended to stimulate economic recovery by relaxing antitrust statutes so that businesses might draft cooperative code agreements regulating their activities. It also funded a massive public works program. Signed into law by FDR on June 16, 1933 (48 *Stat.* 195), the NIRA actually consisted of two sections. Title I, in addition to supporting codes of competition, also guaranteed the right of unions to use collective bargaining (Section 7a) and stipulated that provisions for minimum wages and maximum hours be incorporated into the codes. Title II called for the creation of a Public Works Administration, funded by a $3.3 billion appropriation.

was "a piece of enabling legislation, a law that gave the president un-precedented peacetime powers to reorganize and regulate an obviously ailing and defective business system."⁹ Roosevelt essentially determined the impact of that legislation through his administrative decisions.¹⁰

The story is much the same for the other important New Deal legisla-tion. The Emergency Banking Act authorized FDR to regulate the bank-ing system¹¹; the Agricultural Adjustment Act gave him control of agricultural commodity production,¹² whereas amendments tacked on to it empowered the president to fix the weight of gold and silver dollars, to

The Act was to be in effect for two years. By early 1934, however, dissatisfaction with the NRA was evident. Critics charged that the codes merely encouraged price fixing by major industries, while hampering small businesses through needless regulation. To make matters worse, Hugh Johnson, in charge of administering Title I of the NRA, was a political loose cannon, whose broadsides were fueled by excessive use of alcohol and exacerbated by overwork. He eventually became a political liability to Roosevelt and was eased out of government. See Leuchtenberg, *Franklin D. Roosevelt and the New Deal*, pp. 63–71, and Schlesinger, Jr., *The Coming of the New Deal*, pp. 87–176.

The NIRA was already a political liability by the time the Supreme Court invalidated it in 1935. In its lifetime, however, the NRA enacted 546 codes of fair competition, for-mulated some 11,000 orders through which the codes were interpreted, issued another 139 administrative orders regarding NRA administrative procedures, and promulgated 70 presidential executive orders to deal with rights, procedures and privileges. See Lev-erett Lyon et. al., *The National Recovery Administration* (Washington, D.C.: The Brookings Institution, 1935), p. 30. Ellis W. Hawley provides an excellent overview of the NIRA. See Ellis W. Hawley, *The New Deal and the Problem of Monopoly* (Prince-ton, N.J.: Princeton University Press, 1966), pp. 3–146.

9   Hawley, *The New Deal*, pp. 19–20.
10 Among its provisions, the act authorized the president to designate or create appropri-ate administering agencies; to approve codes or to impose his own codes when none were devised; to control imports that might have an adverse affect on codes; to issue li-censes to industry to prevent destructive wage and price cutting; to prescribe the neces-sary rules, regulations, and fees for administering the act; to enter into voluntary agreements with business firms; to approve and give the force of law to collective bar-gaining agreements between business and labor; and to regulate pipeline companies, preventing interstate shipment of oil produced in excess of the limit prescribed by state law. See Hawley, *The New Deal*, pp. 32–3.
11 Roosevelt's first presidential act closed the nation's banks by presidential proclamation (Proclamation no. 2039 [Mar. 6, 1933], reprinted in *The Public Papers of Franklin De-lano Roosevelt* [New York: Random House, 1938–50], vol. 2, pp. 24–6). (hereafter *FDR's Public Papers*). He did so by invoking the "Trading with the Enemy Act," passed and amended during World War I, which gave the president power to control transac-tions in foreign exchange and to prohibit hoarding of currency. This action was con-firmed by passage of the Emergency Banking Act (Mar. 9, 1933), which empowered the president to regulate banking transactions, including foreign exchanges, and gold and currency movements. Subsequently, the Glass-Steagall Banking Act, approved June 16, 1933, separated commercial from investment banking, created the Federal Deposit In-surance Corporation to insure deposits, and provided for additional Federal Reserve open market activities.
12 The Agricultural Adjustment Act, passed on May 12, 1933, was in essence another om-nibus bill. It sought to aid farmers through a combination of three approaches: direct attempts to raise commodity prices through crop production restrictions, expanding the role of federal farm credit agencies and creating new ones to protect farmers against fore-

revalue the dollar, and to issue three billion dollars of greenbacks.[13] The Reciprocal Trade Agreements Act authorized the president, for a period of three years, to unilaterally enter into commercial trade agreements with foreign nations and to raise and lower tariffs.[14] The 1933 Economy Act handed the president broad powers to reduce veterans' pensions and the salaries of government employees.[15] The 1935 emergency relief appropriation gave FDR discretionary power to spend $5 billion in relief and recovery efforts.

True, not all of this authority was permanent. But even temporary grants of power tended to expand the size of Roosevelt's bargaining audience, and to make it more likely to look to him for solutions to its bargaining needs. Moreover, those New Deal measures, such as federal relief payments to the unemployed, that did not add to the president's statutory powers nevertheless extended the range of influence wielded by the federal government, thus indirectly centering attention on the president as well.[16]

Such broad-based grants of authority did more than raise expectations for presidential leadership, they compelled FDR to devise means to implement them. The New Deal saw the rapid institutionalization of new government organizations and the overhaul of existing ones. Between Mar. 4, 1933 and July 1, 1934, Roosevelt and those under his authority, working with Congress, created more than sixty agencies,

---

closure, and a variety of monetary powers to raise farm produce prices and lower farm debt by cheapening the dollar. See Romasco, *The Politics of Recovery*, pp. 157–64.

13 In fact, a series of actions strengthened the president's monetary powers. On June 5, 1933, a joint congressional resolution cancelled the gold clause in all federal and private obligations; the Gold Reserve Act of 1934 (approved Jan. 30, 1934) authorized FDR to revalue the dollar at fifty to sixty cents in terms of its gold content, and set up a $2 billion stabilization fund; and the Silver Purchase Act (approved June 19, 1934) authorized the president to monetarize silver.

14 Signed into law by FDR on June 12, 1934, the Reciprocal Trade Agreements Act authorized the president, for a period of three years, to enter into commercial trade agreements with foreign nations without the need for Senate consent, and to raise and lower tariffs by not more than 50 percent. The goal was to reduce tariffs worldwide.

15 See the "Act to Maintain the Credit of the United States Government" (Mar. 20, 1933), in *FDR's Public Papers* vol. 1., pp. 52–4.

16 The Federal Emergency Relief Act, approved May 12, 1933, created a Federal Emergency Relief Administration charged with doling out $500 million in direct relief payments to states to support the unemployed. Half the $500 million was assigned on a matching basis, one dollar of federal money for three dollars of state funding. The remaining half was spent according to need, with no requirement for matching funds.

In addition, the Civil Works-Emergency Relief Act (approved Feb. 15, 1934) appropriated an additional $950 million to continue civil works projects and direct relief. And the Civilian Conservation Corps Reforestation Relief Act (approved Mar. 31, 1933) authorized the president to provide employment through conservation-related jobs. Under the CCC, more than 1,000 camps were established to recruit young adults to help with reforestation and other natural resource – related tasks, as a form of national service.

almost all independent and reporting directly to him.[17] Some of these, like the Tennessee Valley Authority, originated through congressional legislation.[18] Others, like the National Recovery Administration, were established by executive order, pursuant to statutory authority contained in New Deal legislation.[19] Still others were created by department heads in the process of carrying out their statutory functions on Roosevelt's behalf.[20] And existing institutions, such as the Reconstruction Finance Corporation (RFC), created under Hoover, and the Federal Reserve Board, vastly expanded the scope of their authority during Roosevelt's presidency.[21]

Never before, except for the war years 1917–18, had a national government spent more, employed more workers, or wielded more authority.[22] From fiscal years 1933 to 1936, the number of federal employees grew from 572,091 to 824,259, a good deal of it attributable to FDR's patronage. Total federal expenditures during this same period, meanwhile, almost doubled from $4,622,865,000 to $8,493,486,000.[23] Much

17 Cited in Harold H. Roth, *The Executive Office of the President: A Study of Its Development with Emphasis on the Period 1939–1953*, doctoral dissertation, The American University, Washington, D.C. (1958), p. 111. Original source is Laurence F. Schmeckbier, *New Federal Organizations: An Outline of Their Structure and Functions* (Washington, D.C.: The Brookings Institution, 1934).

18 Signed on May 18, 1933, the Tennessee Valley Act created the Tennessee Valley Authority (TVA) to oversee the development of the Tennessee Valley water resources through projects for flood control and for the generation of hydroelectric power.

19 Pursuant to the NIRA, FDR issued E.O. 6340 (Oct. 16, 1933), creating the Commodity Credit Corporation (chartered under Delaware state laws). By issuing loans to farmers, the Commodity Credit Corporation attempted to maintain a floor under farm prices by encouraging farmers not to dump produce on the market when demand was low, thereby further depressing commodity prices. The NIRA also gave FDR the legal means to create the Resettlement Administration, the Works Progress Administration, and the National Youth Administration. See *FDR's Public Papers* vol. 2, pp. 404–7.

20 For instance, the National Planning Board was established on July 30, 1933, by Secretary of the Interior Harold Ickes in his capacity as head of the Federal Emergency Administration of Public Works.

21 The RFC, under the leadership of Texas banker Jesse Jones, operated during the New Deal essentially as the world's largest bank. During the years prior to World War II, the RFC loaned $10.5 billion, including more than $1 billion to 89 railroad agencies; $90 million in loans to 133 insurance companies; and another $1.5 billion to farmers. It also aided cities, cooperatives and individuals through the creation of new lending agencies, including the Export-Import Bank, the Rural Electrification Administration, and the Disaster Loan Corporation. See Romasco, *The Politics of Recovery*, pp. 64, 54–5; John Blum, *Roosevelt and Morgenthau: A Revision and Condensation of the "From the Morgenthau Diaries"* (Boston: Houghton-Mifflin Co., 1970), pp. 45–67.

22 It is not insignificant, I think, that Roosevelt served as Wilson's Assistant Secretary of the Navy, and thus was acquainted with the administrative difficulties posed by "big government." He would draw on this experience again during World War II.

23 Budget figures taken from James D. Savage, *Balanced Budgets and American Politics* (Ithaca, N.Y.: Cornell University Press, 1988), Appendix 3. Personnel figures cited in A. J. Wann, *The President as Chief Administrator: A Study of Franklin D. Roosevelt* (Washington, D.C.: Public Affairs Press, 1968).

of that was attributable to the massive relief and recovery programs sponsored by Roosevelt, including the $4.88 billion appropriated for relief and recovery efforts in 1935.[24]

This growth in government's formal powers and expectations multiplied Roosevelt's bargaining costs. And it exposed a serious weakness in the presidency: the lack of bargaining resources under direct presidential control. To compensate for his resource deficiencies, Roosevelt pursued three strategies. First, he increased membership in the presidential cabinet and sought institutional mechanisms to better coordinate its activities. Toward this end he established a small cabinet staff secretariat under an Executive Secretary. Its goal was to bring administrative coherence to cabinet meetings. In addition, Roosevelt devised a number of low-profile interdepartmental coordinating agencies to provide services and advice in specific policy areas. Typical were committees dealing with foreign trade,[25] land reform,[26] federal power use,[27] civil international aviation,[28] and health and welfare activities.[29]

Second, he began strengthening his institutional staff support, primarily by overhauling the Bureau of the Budget (BoB). This meant giving the BoB formal authority to "clear" governmental bargains on FDR's behalf. It also meant increasing the BoB's payroll and personnel, although these changes came slowly.

Third, he developed an extensive network of policy and political aides who, while on the payroll of other executive branch departments,

24 On the 1935 relief appropriation, see Romasco, *The Politics of Recovery*, pp. 64–5.
25 The Executive Committee on Commercial Policy, composed of representatives of government agencies dealing with foreign trade under the recovery programs, was charged with coordinating the commercial policy of the government regarding all activity affecting export – import trade. See FDR's letter to the Secretary of State (Nov. 11, 1933); and E.O. 6656 (Mar. 27, 1934) and E.O. 7260 (Dec. 31, 1935), both of which extended the life of this committee.
      The Committee for Reciprocity Information, created by E.O. 6750 (June 27, 1934), was directed by the Executive Committee on Commercial Policy. It was composed of representatives from various government agencies and received the views of any person affected by proposed trade agreements.
26 E.O. 6693 (Apr. 28, 1934), charged with conducting surveys and a general study for the purpose of developing a national land program. It was later abolished and its function taken over by the National Resources Board.
27 As directed by FDR in a letter to Ickes (dated July 9, 1934), a committee was formed from members of several government agencies and charged with developing a national power policy.
28 The Interdepartmental Committee on Civil International Aviation was created by presidential letter (June 20, 1935) to conduct a study of activities pertaining to this subject. It was abolished after the organization of the Civil Aeronautics Agency.
29 The Interdepartmental Committee to coordinate Health and Welfare Activities, first appointed by FDR on Aug. 15, 1935, was directed to increase cooperation among government agencies dealing with this area. It was reestablished by E.O. 7481 (Oct. 27, 1936).

circulated through the White House providing information and expertise on an ad hoc basis. (These were supplemented by numerous ad hoc bodies, usually created by FDR to deal with bargains of limited duration and impact, e.g., industrial dispute resolution,[30] industrial analysis,[31] and inquests and investigations.[32])

Of these, FDR initially invested the most time in an attempt to integrate the newly established emergency agencies into the traditional cabinet, and to make this larger entity a more effective coordinator of New Deal policy. It was to prove a losing effort.

The search for bargaining support: Government by cabinet committee

Approximately four months into his first term, on July 11, 1933, FDR issued an executive order creating a temporary Executive Council (EC) consisting of twenty-four people: himself, the ten heads of the regular cabinet departments, the director of the BoB, the heads of the nine emergency organizations, and three others.[33]

The EC, which met a handful of times through 1933 and into the following summer, was in effect an enlarged cabinet.[34] Frank Walker, supported by a small staff, served as Executive Secretary responsible for

30 See, for example, the Board of Inquiry for the Cotton Textile Industry, created by E.O. 6840 (Sept. 5, 1934).
31 The Committee of Industrial Analysis was created by E.O. 7323 (Mar. 21, 1936) to report on the NRA.
32 For instance, the National Recovery Board (the Darrow Commission, named after its head, Clarence Darrow), created by E.O. 6632 (Mar. 7, 1934) to investigate charges that the NRA encouraged industrial monopoly at the expense of small businesses.
33 E.O. 6202A (July 11, 1933), pursuant to power granted FDR under the Federal Emergency Relief and National Recovery acts. The twenty-four members included FDR's entire cabinet, as well as the Director of the Budget, the Assistant Secretary of the Treasury, the Administrator of National Industrial Recovery, the Administrator of Agricultural Adjustment, the Administrator of Federal Emergency Relief, the Federal Coordinator of Transportation, the Governor of the Farm Credit Administration, the Chairman of the Board of the Reconstruction Finance Corporation, the Chairman of the Board of the Home Owners Loan Corporation, the Chairman of the Board of the Tennessee Valley Authority, the Director of the Emergency Conservation Work, the Secretary to the President, and an Executive Secretary.
   The Emergency Council was "to provide for the orderly presentation of business to the President, and to coordinate the inter-agency problems of organization and the work of the new governmental agencies established pursuant to the emergency legislation" (*FDR's Public Papers*, vol. 2, p. 281).
34 Meeting notification memorandum to Howe, who was officially a member of the EC, suggests that it met at least on the following dates in 1933: Aug. 1, and Sept. 5; and in 1934: January 4, 16, 20 and 30, March 13, April 25, and June 19 (Louis Howe Files; Executive Council Folder; FDRL).

administering the EC meetings.³⁵ Despite Walker's best efforts, however, Roosevelt's administrative style undercut the Council's coordinating effectiveness. The president ran EC meetings without a formal agenda, and with little advance planning, much as he did the Friday meetings of the traditional cabinet.

Compounding the problem, the Council lacked the formal power to direct the work of departments or agencies, and Walker did not have enough staff to enforce EC decisions even had it possessed such authority. Moreover, it was poorly funded and too unwieldy, especially as it began breeding subcommittees.³⁶ A. J. Wann, in his perceptive review of FDR's administrative practices, assesses EC effectiveness as follows: "In itself [the exchange of ideas and information] was undoubtedly of considerable value in the early days of the New Deal, but neither the council nor the Executive Secretary served in an important way to make decisions of a coordinative nature for the President."³⁷

To compensate for the EC's unwieldiness, FDR established the ten-member National Emergency Council (NEC) in November 1933.³⁸ Also under Walker's aegis, the NEC ostensibly functioned as the Executive Council's working secretariat, leaving the larger EC to operate more as a debating forum.³⁹ One month after its inception, the NEC absorbed the

35 A Montana lawyer and businessman, Walker was a close political friend of FDR's and Treasurer of the Democratic National Committee. As Executive Secretary he was expected to coordinate the activities of the entire apparatus and to report directly to FDR, thus becoming the first of a long line of what observers dubbed "Assistant Presidents." The notoriety achieved by these presidential assistants, especially Walker's successor Donald Richberg, was one factor that soured Roosevelt on the idea of appointing a chief of staff.

After leaving the EC Walker remained a close although relatively unpublicized confidant of FDR's, serving as Postmaster General during the period 1940–5.

36 See Louis Brownlow, *A Passion for Anonymity* (Chicago: University of Chicago Press, 1955–8), pp. 319–20; Wann *The President as Chief Administrator*, pp. 50–2.

37 Wann, *The President as Chief Administrator*, p. 51. The intelligence functions of the EC were supplemented by the creation, at Howe's request, of a "Clipping Bureau" placed under Hugh Johnson's control and responsible for clipping newspapers circulating in every major city with a population 50,000 or more. More sophisticated variations on this procedure have continued within the White House to this day. See Louis Howe to Frank Walker (July 25, 1933), Louis Howe Papers, Executive Council Folder, FDRL.

38 The NEC was established by E.O. 6433A (Nov. 17, 1933), pursuant to authority granted FDR under the NIRA, the AAA, and the Federal Emergency Relief Act. Membership included the secretaries of the Interior, Commerce, Agriculture, and Labor departments, the Administrator of Agricultural Adjustment, the Administrator of FERA, the Administrator for Industrial Recovery, the Chairman of the Home Owners Loan Corporation, the Governor of the Farm Credit Administration, and a representative of the Consumers' Council.

39 Walker was authorized "to execute the functions and to perform the duties vested in the Council by the President." A $10,000 appropriation, drawn from the NRA budget, was included to cover NEC administrative expenses.

Special Industrial Recovery Board, originally created by FDR to supervise Hugh Johnson and the National Recovery Administration.[40] Three purposes motivated FDR to create the NEC. First, he was concerned the New Deal economic recovery efforts were beginning to lose steam after seven months of initial success.[41] He hoped the NEC would reverse this trend by clarifying the program objectives and eliminating the functional overlap, especially at the state level, of his three major New Deal programs – the NIRA, the AAA, and the FERA.[42]

Second, he wanted the NEC to give him the administrative means to screen legislation submitted to Congress by the various executive branch departments and agencies. Toward this end Roosevelt issued a directive ordering agencies and departments to submit legislative proposals to the NEC before transmitting them to Capitol Hill. However, compliance with

40 E.O. 6513, issued Dec. 18, 1933, incorporated the Attorney General, the BoB director, and the chairman of the FTC into the NEC. The Special Industrial Recovery Board had been the first of several top-level watchdog committees Roosevelt formulated in an attempt to control the NRA. For more on it, see below.

41 As FDR told Council members during their first meeting: "The general thought . . . in organizing this Emergency Council is to centralize the work of putting the country back on its feet, especially in the relationship of that work to the general public" ("Proceedings of the National Emergency Council" meeting no. 1, Dec. 19, 1933, in Lester G. Seligman and Elmer E. Cornwell, Jr. [eds.], *New Deal Mosaic: Roosevelt Confers with his National Emergency Council, 1933–1936* [Eugene: University of Oregon Books, 1965], p. 2.) The transcripts of the thirty-one meetings of the NEC, partially reproduced in Seligman and Cornwell's book, provide probably the most revealing portrait of FDR available in any historical record. These verbatim transcripts indicate that he was a president constantly in search of information. He also possessed a tremendous grasp of the complexities involved in administering the New Deal program, as well as a detailed working knowledge of the federal government.

42 Partly in reaction to Harry Hopkins' pleas, Roosevelt at this time was moving from a policy of providing direct economic relief, administered by the Federal Emergency Relief Act (FERA, created in May 1933), to one of work relief through the provision of federally funded jobs. For this purpose he created the Public Works Administration (PWA) under Title II of the National Industrial Recovery Act as the major agency to stimulate economic revival and employment through large-scale public works projects. But under Ickes' direction, the PWA got off to a slow start, in part because Ickes carefully scrutinized the feasibility of each project before spending taxpayers' money.

Consequently in the fall of 1933, FDR created the Civil Works Administration (CWA), directed by Hopkins, to help the unemployed survive the coming winter while the PWA gathered steam. The CWA provided more than four million people with short-term jobs on a variety of federally funded projects before the program was largely terminated early the next year.

Despite the different objectives, however, the line of demarcation between the two programs was not very distinct, leading to repeated clashes between Ickes and Hopkins regarding which federal agency retained control of what relief projects. See Perkins, *The Roosevelt I Knew*, pp. 183–6 and Schlesinger, Jr., *The Coming of the New Deal*, pp. 268–81.

this directive was never strong to begin with, and it progressively lessened, especially with regard to major legislative initiatives.[43]

Rather than submit their proposals to review by the NEC, and risk rejection, agency and department heads preferred to negotiate directly with the relevant congressional committees and interest groups.

Third, Roosevelt wanted the NEC to serve an information-gathering and -disseminating purpose; as he told its members in their initial meeting: "[I]t is tremendously important for every one of us to get a cross-section from every one of the forty-eight states, as to how the whole recovery program is working out."[44]

Roosevelt, however, was wary of investing too much authority in the NEC. Although it would function as "a sort of alter ego . . . going around and acting as my legs and ears and eyes and making certain – what might be called suggestions," it would not have the power to decide policy; "I would not call them decisions, because we don't do things that way."[45] Presumably decision making remained solely FDR's prerogative.

By June 1934, still another cabinet-level coordinating committee – the Industrial Emergency Committee (IEC) – was established, this time to

43 In a study conducted for the Brownlow Committee, E. E. Witte examined the effectiveness of legislative clearance under the NEC and found that the total number of bills passing through the NEC's executive director's office in 1936 was less than in the previous year, primarily because the heads of departments failed to comply with the president's directive that the NEC provide such clearance. See E. E. Witte, "The Preparation of Proposed Legislative Measures," *President's Committee on Administrative Management, the Report with Special Studies*, (Washington, D.C.: Government Printing Office, 1937).

44 Roosevelt's remarks, Dec. 19, 1933, NEC meeting, reproduced in Seligman and Cornwell, Jr., *New Deal Mosaic*, pp. 13–25. In fact, the NEC proved most useful as an intelligence source. Members decided during the first meeting to appoint a regional NEC director in each state with the responsibility to supervise and coordinate the field representation of the emergency agencies. This led to the creation of a Division of Field Operations. Roosevelt evidently hoped these local branches would disseminate information to people regarding relief programs, and gather feedback on how these programs were being received. See also his Dec. 6, 1933, statement clarifying the NEC's role.

Other subordinate divisions spawned by the NEC, including the United States Information Service (USIS), a Consumer's Bureau, and a Better Housing Division, served similar intelligence-related purposes. For more on the NEC, see Brownlow, *A Passion for Anonymity*, pp. 320–1, and Wann, *The President as Chief Administrator*, pp. 54–5.

45 Seligman and Cornwell, Jr., *New Deal Mosaic*, p. 3. That the Council was expected to make "suggestions," and not decisions, reveals Roosevelt's resistance to delegating presidential authority to subordinates. See also the unsigned and undated memorandum listing the objectives of the proposed NEC (Louis Howe Papers, National Emergency Council, 1933, February 1935 Folder, FDRL) and the White House statement clarifying the council's organization and objectives (reprinted in *FDR's Public Papers*, vol. 2, pp. 514–15).

supervise the National Recovery Administration. This was one of several attempts by FDR to oversee the implementation of the NIRA.[46]

By that fall, however, the system of cabinet coordinating councils was in danger of collapsing from its own administrative weight. To eliminate overlapping membership and blurred jurisdictions Roosevelt moved in October 1934, to consolidate the NEC, EC, and the IEC into one super-coordinating entity, which retained the label of National Emergency Council.[47] He evidently hoped that integrating his three top-level administrative bodies into one thirty-four member "super" cabinet committee would reduce bargaining uncertainty through more effective interagency coordination of New Deal programs.[48] The NEC's centralized reporting

46 The Industrial Emergency Committee, established by E.O. 6770 (June 30, 1934), pursuant to authority granted the president under the NIRA, functioned largely as a clearinghouse for NIRA policy proposals. Membership in the IEC included the Secretary of Interior, the Secretary of Labor, the Administrator of Federal Relief, the Administrator for Industrial Recovery, and Donald Richberg, appointed as Director. Later that summer Roosevelt added the Administrator of Agricultural Adjustment. Brownlow, *A Passion for Anonymity*, pp. 320–1; Wann, *The President as Chief Administrator*, p. 55.

47 The actual sequence of events was slightly more complex. When Hugh Johnson resigned as head of the NRA, FDR, through E.O. 6859 (Sept. 27, 1934) created the National Industrial Recovery Board (NIRB) to administer NRA affairs, subject to the oversight of the Industrial Emergency Committee (IEC). At the same time, E.O. 6860 (Sept. 27, 1934) placed the NIRB chair on the IEC, and the IEC was transformed into an advisory committee to FDR in the area of relief, public works, industrial recovery, agriculture and labor. The IEC also became the policy-making council for the NRA, determining, under FDR's direction, the general policies to administer the National Industrial Recovery Act. (See the agenda of IEC meetings scheduled for Nov. 8 and 20, and Dec. 18, 1934. The primary topics concerned the NIRA and related recovery measures. [Louis Howe papers, Industrial Emergency Committee Folder, FDRL].)

Through this chain of events the membership and functions of the IEC came generally to overlap those of the NEC, and the EC duplicated both. In fact, combined meetings of the EC and the NEC were held seven times between June 26 and Oct. 30, 1934 (Louis Howe Files, National Emergency Council Folder, FDRL). Consequently, the three were combined under E.O. 6889A, issued Oct. 31, 1934. Under this order all the members of the EC were appointed to the NEC, and the EC was terminated, with all its functions and duties transferred to the NEC. The IEC became a subcommittee of the newly formed NEC.

Donald Richberg, the former counsel to the NRA, was appointed director of the IEC at the same time as he replaced Walker to become Executive Director of the NEC.

48 The NEC functioned: "(a) To provide for the orderly presentation of business to the President; (b) to coordinate interagency problems of organization and activity of Federal agencies; (c) to coordinate and make more efficient and productive the work of the field agencies of the Federal Government; (d) to cooperate with any Federal agency in performing such activities as the President may direct; and (e) to serve in advisory capacity to the President and Executive Director of the National Emergency Council." Its thirty-four members included: the president, the heads of the ten cabinet departments, the director of the BoB, the Secretary to the President, the Assistant Secretary of the Treasury, the Administrator of Agricultural Adjustment, the Administrator of Federal Emergency Relief, the Chairman of the Board of Reconstruction Finance Corporation, the Chairman of the Board of the Tennessee Valley Authority, the Chairman of the Federal Home Loan Bank Board, the Chairman of the Federal Trade Commission, the Director

functions would also help publicize New Deal accomplishments while soliciting public feedback. And to improve New Deal relief and recovery efforts, the NEC devoted considerable time managing federal – state relations in the field.[49]

To administer the NEC, Roosevelt at this time replaced Walker as Executive Secretary with Donald Richberg, former counsel to the NRA. On paper, at least, Richberg was invested with significant coordinating authority; Roosevelt essentially authorized him to make any rules and regulations necessary to achieve the president's objectives as determined through the NEC.

Many observers viewed Richberg as the de facto "Assistant President," – a phrase bandied about in press accounts detailing Richberg's appointment, much to Roosevelt's chagrin (not to mention that of his cabinet members).[50] Richberg evidently shared this perception, at least initially: "In one of our discussions he [FDR] told me he was considering creating a special office of Assistant to the President. He would appoint

of Emergency Conservation Work, the Federal Coordinator of Transportation, the Governor of the Farm Credit Administration, the Adviser on Consumer Problems, the Chairman of the National Industrial Recovery Board, the Chairman of the Federal Alcohol Control Administration, the Adviser on Consumer Problems, the Federal Housing Administrator, the President of the Export-Import Bank, the Chairman of the Federal Deposit Insurance Corporation, the Chairman of the Federal Power Commission, the Chairman of the Federal Communications Commission, the Chairman of the Securities and Exchange Commission, the Governor of the Federal Reserve Board, and the Executive Director.

49 The NEC's state directors were responsible for gathering and consolidating reports from field agencies operating within their jurisdictions and reporting periodically to the Washington, D.C., office. The NEC also disseminated information to the general public regarding the various functions of the government agencies, especially those involved in relief and recovery programs. In part this was accomplished by the creation of the *United States Government Manual*, a book describing the creation, authority, and functions of all the executive units of the federal government. See the letter from Richberg to Howe (Dec. 29, 1934); Louis Howe Files, National Emergency Council Folder, FDRL. The *Manual* is still published.

On the NEC field reporting requirements, see the unsigned and undated four-page memorandum beginning, "It is proposed that there be established the National Emergency Council." (Louis Howe Files, National Emergency Council folder, FDRL). See also Wann, *The President as Chief Administrator*, pp. 54–6.

50 *The New York Times* opined that Richberg's powers "are too great for any one man, or any one governmental machine, no matter how large or smooth running" *(The New York Times*, Nov. 2, 1934 [cited in Seligman and Cornwell, Jr., *New Deal Mosaic*, p. xix]). Roosevelt reacted angrily to these accounts: "[t]his kind of thing is not only a lie . . . it is a deception and a fraud on the public. It is merely a continuation of previous lies such as the headlines that [Raymond] Moley was running the government; next that [Bernard] Baruch was Acting President; next that Johnson was the man in power; next that [Felix] Frankfurter had been put over the Cabinet and now that Richberg has been put over the Cabinet . . . "(Schlesinger, Jr., *The Coming of the New Deal*, pp. 546–7). See also Ickes' comments regarding Richberg's role in Ickes, *Secret Diaries*, pp. 242–3.

me to this post so that I could work under his direction and take some of the load off him. I had an immediate premonition of trouble."[51]

Richberg's premonition proved accurate. Within six months he had resigned, effective May 1935, a victim of sniping from cabinet members, and FDR's lukewarm administrative backing. Roosevelt evidently could not bring himself to give Richberg the authority necessary to coordinate cabinet activities, despite the wording of the executive order authorizing Richberg's appointment. In the frequent disputes between Richberg and the NEC's members, FDR frequently sided with the latter, thus undercutting Richberg's influence. Frank Walker, temperamentally closer to FDR's notion of the ideal Executive Secretary, replaced Richberg.[52]

But Richberg's demise foreshadowed Roosevelt's decreasing confidence that the cabinet could serve as his primary source of bargaining support. By December 1935, with Walker's resignation, Roosevelt's experiment with cabinet coordinating committees had effectively ended.[53] Meetings of the NEC dwindled in frequency, and even these were increasingly attended by second-echelon staff. Its thirty-first, and last, meeting took place on Apr. 28, 1936.[54]

Looking behind the cabinet

The failure of Roosevelt's initial efforts to utilize cabinet coordinating committees merely underscored the paucity of his other staff resources.

---

51 Donald Richberg, *My Hero: The Indiscreet Memoirs of an Eventful But Unheroic Life* (New York: Putnam, 1954), p. 178.
52 Richberg's resignation occurred about a week after the Supreme Court handed down its ruling in the Schechter case, which effectively invalidated the NRA. In his memoirs, Richberg argues that he resigned in order to carry on the government's appeal against the Schechter decision.
53 Walker was replaced by his assistant, Lyle T. Alverson.
54 However, its administrative staff and field offices continued with information gathering and reporting activities, serving as a valuable staff arm to the president by providing regular updates on the status of government agencies. These embodied several functions. The NEC's Central Information Bureau, in addition to publishing the *United States Government Manual*, handled over 100,000 information requests a year by 1938. The NEC's state and local offices, meanwhile, continued to coordinate and transmit information for the various government agencies. Finally, the press clipping service continued to function.
   Roosevelt intended to officially abolish the NEC by the end of 1937, based on the recommendations of the Brownlow Committee. But FDR continued to use its information services through June 30, 1938, under the direction of Lowell Mellet who was appointed the NEC's Executive Director. Apparently Roosevelt was also prepared to again utilize the council in a coordinating capacity should worsening economic conditions once again require large-scale emergency programs. Roosevelt's E.O. 7906 (issued June 6, 1938), extended the NEC for another year, but prior to then it was finally effectively dissolved, and its functions transferred to the newly created Executive Office of the President. There its information functions were carried on through the new Office of Government Reports, under Mellet's direction. See Wann, *The President as Chief Adminstrator*, pp. 63–5.

These included a handful of White House aides, backstopped by the Executive Clerk's office; the Bureau of the Budget, an agency historically focused almost exclusively on budget cutting; and whomever he could borrow from executive branch departments and agencies.[55] During his first term this patchwork advisory system provided much of his bargaining support. Eventually, it formed the nucleus for his staff reforms as institutionalized in 1939.

The BoB and other institutional staff agencies

In 1921, the BoB became essentially the first noncabinet, institutionalized source of presidential bargaining resources.[56] It primarily assisted the president in reviewing and consolidating all departmental and agency requests to Congress for funding.[57] By locating the BoB within the Treasury Department, however, rather than directly under the president, Congress compromised the agency's usefulness as a source of presidential bargaining support.[58]

This proved less problematic to FDR's three Republican predecessors, who had largely utilized the BoB as a fiscal watchdog guarding against excessive spending by executive branch departments and agencies.[59]

---

55 For background on some of these individuals and institutions, see Schlesinger, Jr., *The Coming of the New Deal*, pp. 17–20; James M. Burns, *The Lion and the Fox*, (New York: Harcourt, Brace, Jovanovich, 1956), pp. 172–3; and Leuchtenberg, *Franklin D. Roosevelt and the New Deal*, pp. 63–4.

56 As established by the Budget and Accounting Act, passed June 10, 1921, after a decade of congressional debate. The Executive Clerk's Office, discussed more fully below, provided primarily clerical, as opposed to policy, assistance.

57 The 1921 act replaced the traditional budgeting method, in which departments and agencies submitted individual requests to different congressional committees, with a single presidential budget. The BoB Division of Estimates was responsible for putting this document together based on budget requests from agencies and departments. The Division was divided into groups of investigators. Each group was headed by an assistant director, and took responsibility for reviewing particular government agency budgets. The assignments were made on a functional basis. See Alfred Dick Sander, *A Staff for the President: The Executive Office, 1921–52*, (New York: Greenwood Press, 1989), p. 16.

58 Although officially located within the Treasury Department, the BoB was in fact supposed to be a "presidential" agency, reporting directly to the president. Roosevelt himself had testified before Congress in 1919 on the president's need for help coordinating the work of the executive branch agencies and departments. He had recommended creating a special agency to inspect government activities, to coordinate fiscal estimates, and to generally control expenditures. See Roosevelt's testimony before the U.S. House of Representatives, Select Committee on Budget, *Hearings* (Washington, D.C., 1919), 66th Cong, 1st sess., pp. 649–77.

59 In fact, under Budget Circular 49 (issued Dec. 19, 1921), the BoB initially possessed formal authority to review, on the president's behalf, all legislative proposals and views emanating from executive branch agencies and departments, not just budget requests.

Although Roosevelt, too, was initially wedded to budget cutting, his bargaining priorities changed soon after taking office. Unfortunately, the BoB did not, at least not quickly enough to suit Roosevelt's new bargaining purposes.[60]

The difficulty, however, was not simply the BoB's location within the Treasury Department. Roosevelt's choice of Lewis Douglas as his first BoB director complicated any attempt to change the BoB's priorities.[61] Douglas was a proponent of balanced budgets and limited government expenditures. He (erroneously as it turned out) thought FDR was, too.[62] At first, Roosevelt fulfilled Douglas' expectations; on Mar. 20, 1933, he signed the Economy Act that the Budget Director had largely drafted. It cut government salaries by 25 percent (saving $100 million) and gave FDR the power to slash another $400 million in veterans' payments.[63]

But when FDR later downplayed efforts to cut costs and balance the budget, Douglas' leading role began to diminish.[64] A month after signing the Economy Act, FDR restricted gold imports, signaling his turn toward

But Charles Dawes, the first BoB director (appointed June 28, 1921), saw his role primarily as the business manager of the executive branch, and he helped mold the BoB toward that end by emphasizing the agency's cost-cutting functions. Following Dawes' precedent, a succession of BoB directors pulled back from this sweeping interpretation, refusing to interpose the BoB as an organ of legislative clearance between the president and the various departments and agencies. In this they were supported by presidents Harding, Coolidge, and Hoover. For details, see Richard Neustadt, "Presidential Clearance of Legislation: Legislative Development, Review and Coordination in the Executive Office of the President," Ph.D. dissertation, Harvard University (1950), pp. 27–43.

60 Dawes' imprint on the agency had, Roosevelt complained to Louis Brownlow, left it ill-prepared to fulfill its other statutory duties: "[T]he Bureau of the Budget had never exercised its functions with respect to continuing examination of the organization because it had been led astray by General Dawes' decision that the budget bureau should keep a small staff and thereby be an example of economy to other bureaus; . . . [t]his precept . . . had been followed by other budget directors" (Brownlow memorandum for the record, Document A-II-7 [Mar. 4, 1936]; President's Committee on Administrative Management (hereafter PCAM), FDRL, p. 4.

61 Actually, Roosevelt's first choice for Budget Director was former House Appropriations Committee chairman Swager Sherley, who declined the post. See Roosevelt's letter to Sherley, dated Jan. 17, 1933, reprinted in Elliot Roosevelt (ed.), *F.D.R. His Personal Letters, 1928–1945* (New York: Duell, Sloan & Pearce, 1950), p. 321 (hereafter *FDR's Personal Letters*).

62 Roosevelt, much to his later regret, had promised during a 1932 presidential campaign speech in Pittsburgh to cut federal expenditures and balance the budget. Douglas took him at his word.

63 Leuchtenberg, *Franklin Roosevelt and the New Deal*, p. 45; Schlesinger, Jr., *The Coming of the New Deal*, pp. 9–11.

64 Douglas was, Roosevelt wrote Colonel House on Apr. 5, 1933, "in many ways the greatest 'find' of the administration . . ." (reprinted in *FDR's Personal Letters*, p. 342). Moley recounts that he and Douglas had standing 9:00 a.m. appointments with FDR in the first heady days of the New Deal. See Moley's listing of the daily schedule in Raymond Moley, *After Seven Years* (New York: Harper & Brothers, 1939), p. 166. See also Perkins, *The Roosevelt I Knew*, pp. 268–74.

inflationary measures.[65] A distraught Douglas reportedly proclaimed, "Well, this is the end of Western civilization."[66] Instead, it proved to be the end of Douglas; his influence waning, and opposed to Roosevelt's inflationary monetary policies, he chose to resign.[67]

Douglas' departure magnified the increasing divergence between FDR's bargaining needs and the Bureau's dominant area of expertise.[68] Before

Douglas' early influence is also reflected in two executive orders FDR issued, both designed to give Douglas control over emergency expenditures. E.O. 6166 (issued June 10, 1933) transferred from department heads to Douglas the power of making, waving, and modifying apportionments of appropriations, in order to ensure against deficiencies. However, this still left Douglas little control over the lump-sum emergency appropriations granted FDR by Congress to finance the emergency recovery and relief programs. Consequently, FDR issued E.O. 6548 (Jan. 3, 1934), extending the BoB director's budgetary control over emergency expenditures by prohibiting further obligations prior to approval of estimates by Douglas. Predictably, Roosevelt's cabinet heads protested that this gave Douglas de facto veto power over the new emergency programs. Accordingly, FDR issued E.O. 6550 three days later revoking the budget-control order, replacing it with the milder requirement that Douglas receive weekly reports of obligations of emergency relief funds (see also Schlesinger, Jr., *The Coming of the New Deal*, p. 291).

65 Roosevelt's changing objectives are spelled out in a letter to long-time presidential advisor Colonel House, dated Apr. 5, 1933: "While things look superficially rosy, I realize well that thus far we have given more of deflation than of inflation – the closed banks locked up four billions or more and the economy legislation will take nearly another billion out of Veterans' pay, departmental salaries, etc. It is simply inevitable that we must inflate and though my banker friends may be horrified, I am still seeking inflation which will not wholly be based on additional government debt" (reproduced in *FDR's Personal Letters*, p. 342).

66 Moley, *After Seven Years*, p. 160. Douglas' agony at Roosevelt's policy reversal is captured in a letter he sent the president, pleading with apocalyptic fervor that FDR return to the fold of fiscal austerity. "Permit me," Douglas' memorandum began, "with all the sincerity at my command and with great earnestness, to make this last plea against further large undertakings involving huge governmental expenditures." After presenting a point-by-point rebuttal of FDR's New Deal profligacy, the ten-page memo concluded with a stark warning: "The issue . . . is clearly drawn, either we will change our social order and deliberately abolish all private enterprise . . . or we must maintain the credit of the Government. If you choose the former course, I prophesize many years of intense suffering on the part of millions" (Lewis Douglas to FDR [Dec. 30, 1933], President's Secretary's File [hereafter *PSF*] – Subject, Lewis Douglas Folder, FDRL). Evidently FDR was unmoved.

67 Douglas left in mid-1934. Roosevelt, much to Treasury Secretary Henry Morgenthau's chagrin, considered replacing him with Thomas Corcoran who, while working for the RFC, had helped draft New Deal legislation. Morgenthau thought Corcoran too political and suggested Daniel Bell, a career Treasury man, instead. Bell was initially hired as acting Director for a sixty- day period, but continued to serve in an "interim" role for four years and seven months. He refused, however, to become the permanent BoB director for fear of losing his civil service status. On Bell's appointment, see Schlesinger, Jr., *The Coming of the New Deal*, p. 292.

68 The divergence was partly FDR's fault. Upon taking office he made a clean sweep of the upper layer of BoB employees, thus losing what institutional memory the agency possessed. Moreover, acting Director Bell, unlike Douglas, was not invited to sit in cabinet meetings although he was serving simultaneously as assistant secretary of the treasury. The lack of intimacy between FDR and Bell together with the BoB's traditional emphasis on cost-cutting helps explain the agency's mixed influence during FDR's first six years

resigning, Douglas had lopped thirty-one employees from the BoB payroll to comply with FDR's emphasis on economizing,[69] and had entirely eliminated the Federal Coordinating Service.[70] Roosevelt, however, was soon asking the BoB to expand its functions to include legislative clearance and other duties.[71] In late 1934 he ordered all executive orders prepared for his signature by departments and agencies subjected first to BoB review, which would circulate them to the relevant departments for comments, and then to the Attorney General for a legal ruling.

He also began gradually expanding the bureau's authority to clear legislative proposals.[72] Beginning in 1934, enrolled bills – those that Congress had already passed – were submitted to the BoB before presidential review.[73] At first this directive applied only to relief bills involving expenditures of funds, but during the next several years, as the NEC de-

(see Larry Berman's overview of the BoB during this period in Larry Berman, *The Office of Management Budget and the Presidency, 1929–1979* [Princeton, N.J.: Princeton University Press, 1979], pp. 3–16).

69 See Roth, *The Executive Office of the President*, pp. 120–1. During the Republican period under Harding, Coolidge, and Hoover, yearly BoB personnel had never exceeded forty-eight people. After Douglas' cuts and subsequent departure, it never went higher than forty-five until its incorporation into the EOP by Roosevelt in 1939. This total included about ten clerical staff.

Of course, additional personnel were employed under both Republicans and Democrats through the practice of detailing employees from other agencies. The primary sources included the War and Navy Departments, and the Federal Coordinating Service. See also Sander, *A Staff for the President*, pp. 16–18.

70 The Federal Coordinating Service was an organization separate from, but under the direction of, the BoB, charged with monitoring the routine business transactions of the government. Created by Dawes, it consisted of a chief coordinator, General Supplies, and a number of interagency boards and committees dealing with government procurement, disposal of surplus property, real estate, transportation, forms, and hospital construction. In addition to its Washington, D.C., office, the coordinating service operated a number of field services. It fell into disuse under Hoover, but it was left to FDR to abolish it entirely. Some services were absorbed by the BoB. See Sander, *A Staff for the President*, p. 18; and Neustadt, "Presidential Clearance of Legislation," p. 19, n. 5.

71 Some of the growth in responsibilities reflects staff functions the BoB absorbed from other agencies abolished during FDR's first term. The Bureau of Efficiency was eliminated by Congress, effective June 3, 1933, on the grounds that it duplicated functions vested by law in the BoB. All of its records and duties were transferred to the BoB. The Business Organization of the Federal Government was formally abolished by E.O. 6166 (June 10, 1933). A committee consisting of the President, BoB director, and the heads of all executive branch departments, independent agencies, and bureaus, it had met twice a year during 1921–9, pledging adherence to economizing and good management, in meetings that Neustadt describes as strictly "devotional" (see Neustadt, "Presidential Clearance of Legislation", p. 19, n. 5). The BoB took over some of these functions, while others went to different agencies.

72 A decision prompted in part by FDR's displeasure that department proposals were being leaked to newspapers before he knew of them.

73 Simultaneously he directed that the National Emergency Council clear proposed legislation. See the "Proceedings of the National Emergency Council," meeting no. 19, Dec. 11, 1934, reprinted in Seligman and Cornwell Jr., *New Deal Mosaic*, pp. 374–5.

clined in influence, the BoB's clearance functions were extended to other bills.[74] By 1938, with the demise of National Emergency Council, the BoB was reviewing practically all congressional legislation on FDR's behalf.[75] Thereafter it was incorporated into the EOP, becoming FDR's primary institutional staff workhorse.[76]

Detailees, politicos, and informal advisers

Institutional staff agencies like the BoB helped FDR protect the bargaining interests of the presidential office.[77] For resources to clarify his personal bargaining interests, however, FDR cultivated a loose assortment of detailees, politicians, and other advisers. Some, such as James Farley, the Democratic National Chairman appointed Postmaster-General by FDR, and Edward J. Flynn, a long-time associate of FDR's in New York state

74 Initially other legislation was cleared through Donald Richberg, the Executive Director of the National Emergency Council. This practice was discontinued in 1937. See the "National Emergency Council memorandum" (Dec. 13, 1934), from Richberg to BoB director Daniel Bell, reprinted in Neustadt, "Presidential Clearance of Legislation," Appendix A, p. 5.

75 The evolution of central clearance is highlighted by the memoranda contained in Neustadt, "Presidential Clearance of Legislation," Appendix A, pp. 6–11.

76 Its wartime duties are detailed in chapter six; see also Berman, *The Office of Management Budget and the Presidency*; and Wolf, "Reorganization, Competition and Crises."

77 Several other institutionally oriented staff agencies provided bargaining resources during this period:

   (1) The Central Statistical Board, created in August 1933. It served as a central clearinghouse for governmental reports, thus providing FDR with reliable statistical data. Composed of members designated by the heads of various departments and agencies, the board formulated standards for, and effectuated the coordination of, the statistical activities of government related to recovery efforts. It largely took over the functions of the Federal Statistical Board (see E.O. 6225 [July 27, 1933]).

   E.O. 6240 (Aug. 3, 1933) made Winfield W. Riefler, a member of the statistical board, the Executive Council's economic adviser (see Roth, *The Executive Office of the President*, pp. 123, 126). Riefler's appointment was meant to prevent the problems that had plagued FDR's predecessor, Herbert Hoover, who had caused political controversy when he inadvertently stated publicly that unemployment figures were dropping in 1930, when in fact they were increasing. Roosevelt's Industrial Commissioner in New York, Frances Perkins, challenged Hoover's claim, using figures she had drawn from the Bureau of Labor, thus pointing out the president's need for a source of reliable statistical data. (See the "Memorandum Concerning Industrial Emergency Committee Meeting" Nov. 8, 1934, *PSF* – Subject, Louis Howe File, FDRL, p. 2, in which FDR stresses the importance of accurate statistical information; see also "Proceedings of the National Emergency Council," meeting no. 19, Dec. 11, 1934, reprinted in Seligman and Cornwell, Jr., *New Deal Mosaic*, pp. 377–8.)

   (2) The Science Advisory Board, created in 1933. Working under the authority of the National Academy of Sciences, it appointed committees to deal with special problems regarding scientific activities of the government. These oversaw government agencies such as the Weather Bureau, the Bureau of Mines, the Bureau of Standards, and the Geological Survey (E.O. 6238 [July 31, 1933]).

politics, served in purely political capacities, overseeing patronage and other party-oriented and election-related functions.[78]

Others were borrowed from departments and agencies for extended stays at the White House working under Roosevelt's direction. These "detailees" were the prototype for the administrative assistants later specified in the Brownlow Committee Report. They, and not FDR's permanent White House staff or his cabinet, were most often the catalysts for major New Deal policies. For instance, Thomas Corcoran, a Hoover appointee working in the Reconstruction Finance Corporation, and Ben Cohen, first with the Public Works Administration and later with the National Power Policy Committee within the Interior Department, drafted significant chunks of New Deal legislation on FDR's behalf and helped sell it on Capitol Hill.[79]

In addition to generating policy, Roosevelt used detailees to gather information, track down rumors, mediate disputes, write speeches, and serve as all-purpose troubleshooters, providing bargaining support as he needed. Although they were White House aides in all but name, detailees were not paid from FDR's White House budget. Instead, Roosevelt used them on a per-bargain basis; someone was borrowed to handle a specific assignment and then returned from whence they came when the bargain was consummated.

(3) The Office of Special Adviser to the President on Foreign Trade. Its roots were George N. Peek's activities as Special Assistant to the President on American Trade Policy. Beginning in December 1933, Peek headed a committee charged with devising permanent machinery for coordinating all government activities relating to foreign trade. The Special Adviser was directed to keep the president informed on trade matters and to direct others seeking assistance on trade to the appropriate government agency (E.O. 6651 [Mar. 23, 1934]). Peek had been appointed Dec. 11, 1933. The office ceased to exist on expiration of the National Recovery Administration.

78 See James Farley, *Jim Farley's Story: The Roosevelt Years* (New York: Whittlesey House – McGraw-Hill Book Company, Inc., 1948); and Edward J. Flynn, *You're the Boss* (New York: Viking Press, 1947).

79 Correspondence by FDR's appointments secretary Marvin McIntyre indicates that Corcoran and Cohen were being asked to perform special tasks for the president at least as early as September 1934 (see McIntyre's letter to Rudolph Forster, reproduced in *FDR's Personal Letters*, p. 420; FDR's letter to Corcoran [Nov. 8, 1935], p. 518, and to Cohen [May 14, 1936] pp. 590–1.)

Together or separately, the two were responsible for drafting much of the Securities Act of 1933, the Securities and Exchange bill of 1934, the Public Utility Holding Company Act of 1935, the Fair Labor Standards Act of 1938, the National Housing Act and legislation creating the Tennessee Valley Authority. Several fascinating oral histories regarding how they worked and the young lawyers who supported them are provided in Frank Watson, Joseph L. Rauh, Jr., and Kenneth Crawford, "The Draftsmen," in Katie Louchheim (ed.), *The Making of the New Deal: The Insiders Speak* (Cambridge, Mass.: Harvard University Press, 1983), pp. 105–18. See also Tully, *F.D.R. My Boss*, pp. 141–2; the Samuel Rosenman Oral History, FDRL; Schlesinger, Jr., *The Coming of the New Deal*, pp. 440–1; 456–67; and, regarding Corcoran, Louis Koenig, *The Invisible Presidency* (New York: Rinehart & Co., 1960), pp. 249–98.

One benefit of this approach was that it disguised the "true" size of Roosevelt's White House, thus minimizing friction with Congress during the yearly appropriations process. Recall that Roosevelt's predecessor Herbert Hoover had created a "national sensation" when trying (successfully as it turned out) to get Congress to appropriate money so to allow him to expand his White House staff from one to three permanent secretaries of equal rank.[80] Roosevelt evidently learned from Hoover's experience. Having campaigned in 1932 on a platform of fiscal austerity, FDR would grant only Louis Howe the title "Secretary to the President"; Roosevelt's other two senior White House aides, Steve Early and Marvin McIntyre, were made assistant secretaries, at a lower salary.[81] This remained the authorized size of the White House staff, as spelled out in the yearly appropriations bill, until the 1939 Reorganization Act, when FDR was appropriated money to pay for up to six administrative assistants.[82] In the meantime, he borrowed aides from other departments as needed.

80 Sander, *A Staff for the President*, p. 52–3. Although Roosevelt is typically credited with having the first true "White House staff," Charles Walcott and Karen Hult argue that "Herbert Hoover first introduced a prototype of the modern staff," because he was the first president with multiple White House aides performing more than clerical duties (see Walcott and Hult, "Management Science and the Great Engineer: Governing the White House During the Hoover Administration," paper delivered at the annual meeting of the Midwest Political Science Association, Apr. 9, 1987, p. 1).

Hoover's three White House secretaries were George Akerson, in charge of appointments; Lawrence Richey, who handled personal affairs; and Walter H. Newton, who oversaw legislative affairs. Akerson was replace by Theodore Joslin on Mar. 16, 1931. French Strother served as the administrative assistant (although George Hastings served during Strother's approximately year-long absence during 1931–2). In addition, Hoover's White House included two military aides, and about forty clerks, typists and messengers (see also Herbert Hoover, *The Memoirs of Herbert Hoover: 1920–1933*, the Cabinet and the Presidency [New York: The MacMillan Company, 1952], pp. 218–19.)

81 Howe was paid $10,000 annually, the other two $9,500. Hoover's three secretaries had been paid $10,000 annually. This compares to $15,000 for cabinet secretaries, the highest paid members of the executive branch next to the president and vice- president. The president was paid $75,000, and the vice- president, $15,000 (see Document E-VIII-2 "List of Positions with Salaries $9,000 and Over," Brownlow Papers, JFKL).

Raymond Moley recalls that Roosevelt did not bother to tell either Marvin McIntyre or Stephen Early until after they were appointed that their titles were, in effect, being downgraded from those of their predecessors. His decision partly reflects Howe's pre-eminence as FDR's chief adviser, a position Howe jealously guarded. But it also indicates that Roosevelt was acutely sensitive to congressional prerogatives, even when it came to his own personal staff. That sensitivity was well founded, as he discovered when attempting to implement the Brownlow Committee report. Not until 1937, after Howe's death, did Roosevelt acquiesce to formally having three secretaries of equal rank. See Moley, *After Seven Years*, p. 80, n. 65; and Raymond Moley and Elliot A. Rosen, *The First New Deal* (New York: Harcourt, Brace & World, 1966).

82 Sander, *A Staff for the President*, p. 53. The yearly appropriation act covering the White House office usually included variations closely approximating the following language: "Salaries: For personal services in the office of the President, including the Secretary to the President, and two additional secretaries to the president at $10,000 each:[total

But FDR's use of detailees did more than stretch his wallet. It provided him with specific bargaining resources at less strain to his management capabilities. Roosevelt evidently believed that aides who did not provide resources that he needed on a daily basis had no business getting paid from his permanent White House budget. Hence everyone with positions in the White House were there for a specific bargaining purpose known to both FDR and them. Accountability to FDR was thus enforced. At the same time, this provided him some political insulation, because he was less likely to be held responsible for the actions of detailees working unofficially on his behalf.[83]

Unfortunately, Roosevelt's tendency to borrow aides has misled scholars into thinking his staff support, and thus his bargaining costs, were less than was actually the case. Officially, his White House staff numbered between thirty-five and forty individuals, most of them clerical aides (a total largely unchanged from Hoover's last three years, which remained the same through fiscal year 1939).[84] But these totals, as Figure 2.1 demonstrates, overlooks FDR's use of detailees.

In fact, a BoB statement covering fiscal year 1942 lists 189 aides working for Roosevelt while on other payrolls, in addition to the 40–50 authorized White House aides. Almost half – 94 – of those on detail worked under FDR for the entire year, performing in effect as full-time White House aides. Another thirty-eight detailees worked six months or more for FDR while on other payrolls.[85]

appropriation listed here]; provided, that employees of the executive departments and other establishments of the executive branch of Government may be detailed from time to time to the office of the President of the United States for such temporary assistance as may be deemed necessary."

83 For instance, Corcoran played an unofficial role in FDR's unsuccessful attempt to purge the Democratic party of conservatives in the 1938 election. Thereafter Roosevelt refused to lend his name to Corcoran's efforts to secure a more prestigious government post. Had Corcoran been an official member of the White House staff, of course, it may have been more difficult for FDR to disown his activities. See Koenig, *The Invisible Presidency*, pp. 294–8.

84 During fiscal years 1931–3, the official "average" yearly number of White House staff was 37, 36, and 36, respectively. These totals do not include building maintenance and ground crews, which numbered about 60 individuals in this period.

 By 1940, with the addition of some administrative assistants, FDR's White House staff climbed to about 50 aides. In 1942, official figures placed the total at "40.5 man-years." By this time, however, FDR was drawing on two other appropriations – one for emergencies related to national defense and the other administrative expenses associated with Defense Aid (Lend-Lease), to pay some White House employees. Neither are included in the official figures (see the Records of the White House Office of Budget and Accounting; W. H. Budget and Accounting, Budget Reports, Estimate File, FDRL, for the appropriate years, and the Budget Bureau Circular dated Aug. 26, 1942, in these same files, FDRL).

85 White House Budget and Accounting, Budget Reports and Estimates, 1944 File, FDRL.

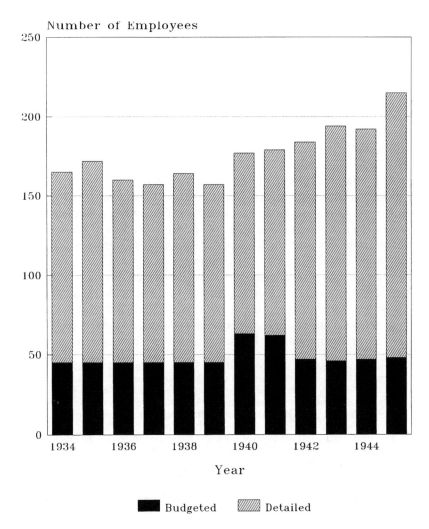

Number of Employees

Figure 2.1. Size of the Roosevelt White House staff. Source: James Connor File, Ford Library (from OMB records).

These aides were drawn from a variety of departments and agencies and paid from several different appropriations.[86] Judging by their salaries, which were low in comparison to what FDR's White House senior aides were paid, many detailees undoubtedly performed clerical functions. But

---

86 For instance, in 1942 detailees were drawn from the Farm Credit Administration, the Commodity Credit Corporation, the Civil Aeronautics Authority, the National Defense

others, such as Corcoran and Cohen, were clearly involved in substantive political and policy issues.

Another favorite tactic FDR used was to place key advisers in senior positions within executive branch departments from where they continued to work closely with FDR. This was the fate of several members of the so-called brains trust, a group of academics who assisted FDR with policy issues during the 1932 campaign. Two of them, Raymond Moley and Rexford Tugwell, were appointed assistant secretaries in cabinet departments.[87] Both were particularly influential in the initial stages of the New Deal, helping draft and implement significant components of emergency legislation. Tugwell played a key role hatching the National Industrial Recovery Act and advising FDR on agricultural issues.[88] Moley was a major player in the efforts to get a banking holiday and subsequent overhaul of the nation's banking system.[89] Adolf Berle, a third brain truster, worked primarily with the Reconstruction Finance Corporation, helping compose railroad and banking legislation.[90]

Other long-time confidants and associates served informally, drafting speeches, doing ad hoc research, giving advice, and performing other duties without holding any official position in FDR's administration. Of these, the most important were Samuel Rosenman, a valued speech writer who had been appointed by Roosevelt as a New York state judge[91]; Basil

Housing Administration, the National Park Service, the Fish and Wildlife Service, the Bureau of Mines, the Department of Justice, the Labor Department, the Bureau of Ships, the U.S. Coast Guard, the Office of Emergency Management, the Office of Government Reports, the Railroad Retirement Board, the Department of State, the Internal Revenue Service, the Emergency Relocation Bureau, the Foreign Exchange Control, the Securities and Exchange Commission, and the Signal Corps (*ibid.*).

87 The brains trust consisted of three Columbia University professors, Raymond Moley, Rexford Tugwell, and Adolf Berle, recruited by Samuel Rosenman to provide FDR with ideas as well as "words with which to express them" during the 1932 presidential campaign (Schlesinger, Jr., *The Coming of the New Deal*, pp. 270–1.) Upon FDR's election Moley became Assistant Secretary of State, and Tugwell was appointed Assistant Secretary of Agriculture. Their influence, however, began declining almost from the day FDR was inaugurated. Roosevelt's use of both is partly chronicled in their books. See Moley, *After Seven Years*; Moley and Rosen, *The First New Deal*; and Rexford G. Tugwell, *The Democratic Roosevelt* (N.Y.: Doubleday, 1957).

Berle initially refused an official government position, but nevertheless continued to regularly advise Roosevelt. He later entered the State Department (see FDR's letter to Berle, dated June 27, 1932, thanking him for his campaign assistance [reproduced in *FDR's Personal Letters*, p. 286]).

88 On the origins of the NIRA, see Perkins, *The Roosevelt I Knew*, pp. 197–208. On Tugwell, see Schlesinger, Jr., *The Coming of the New Deal*.

89 Raymond Moley gives a detailed account of the events leading to the banking holiday; see Moley and Rosen, *The First New Deal*; see also his account in Moley, *After Seven Years*.

90 Schlesinger, Jr., *The Coming of the New Deal*, pp. 182–3.

91 His influence became particularly acute beginning in FDR's second term. Some of the flavor of their relationship is captured in their correspondence; see, for example, the fol-

O'Connor, FDR's former law partner; Bernard Baruch, a long-time presidential confidant dating back to the Wilson administration[92]; and Felix Frankfurter, eventually appointed to the Supreme Court by FDR.[93] Generally speaking, these individuals were valued by Roosevelt because they provided bargain-specific support without FDR's having to permanently expand his management duties.

His comparatively smaller White House staff, then, does not mean Roosevelt governed when bargaining costs were lower. Instead, it reflects his tendency to forgo White House staff institutionalization in favor of "spot contracting," whereby aides were enlisted for the duration of a particular bargain. During "down time," they returned to the department or agency paying their salary. In this way he received adequate bargaining support while minimizing his supervisory costs.

However, certain recurring bargaining activities could not be delegated on an ad hoc basis. These required a more dependable source of resources. Such functions were entrusted to FDR's permanent White House staff.

The White House staff

Roosevelt's permanent White House staff provided resources he needed to carry out his day-to-day presidential activities: correspondence, speechwriting, appointments, press relations, and other official duties. These were recurring activities thrust on FDR by the nature of his job. The core of FDR's first-term White House staff was his three senior political secretaries: Howe, Early, and McIntyre. Howe served in effect as FDR's minister without portfolio, acting as a political troubleshooter and policy adviser.[94] Early was in charge of press

---

lowing FDR letters to Rosenman (all reproduced in *FDR's Personal Letters*): Mar. 3, 1933 (p. 336); Mar. 3, 1936 (p. 567); and Aug. 4, 1937 (p. 705).

   Rosenman eventually became a full-time member of Roosevelt's White House staff as Special Counsel in 1943. For details, see Samuel Rosenman, *Working with Roosevelt* (New York: Harper & Row, 1952); his oral history at the FDR Library; and Tully, *F.D.R. My Boss*, pp. 137–9.

92 See Tully, *F.D.R. My Boss*, p. 163.

93 See *ibid.*, pp. 139–41. The relationship between Frankfurter and Roosevelt is chronicled in their correspondence, reprinted in *Roosevelt and Frankfurter Their Correspondence 1928–1945*, annotated by Max Freedman (Boston: Little, Brown & Co., 1967). Frankfurter brought a number of his proteges, including Corcoran, Cohen, and James Landis, into the New Deal.

94 A Progressive, Howe was more conservative than many of FDR's New Dealers. His strength was an ability to sense FDR's moods and restrain his rasher impulses. From his West Wing office, Howe served as a buffer, shielding FDR from outsiders, shunting supplicants to the proper authorities, and often taking on the undesirable tasks of firing

relations.⁹⁵ McIntyre handled appointments.⁹⁶ Together, they rendered political advice, put out fires, and generally insured that fundamental administrative tasks were discharged.⁹⁷ Most importantly, they did so from a perspective more nearly matching FDR's.

These senior aides worked alongside a corps of private secretaries and stenographers; the Executive Clerk's staff; and additional clerical aides. The private secretaries were brought by FDR from his governor's office in New York. Marguerite "Missy LeHand", who lived on the third floor of the White House, was the most important. She was assisted by Grace Tully. Both LeHand and later Tully, by virtue of their close daily proximity to FDR, were more than stenographers; they also served as political sounding boards, occasionally proffered advice and took charge of personal chores Roosevelt felt comfortable delegating.⁹⁸

subordinates and delivering bad news. During his time on FDR's staff Howe lived in the White House. Because he was a sick man, however, his influence was already waning when Roosevelt was elected president. He continued as FDR's chief political aide until his death on Apr. 18, 1936. See Alfred Rollins, Jr., *Roosevelt and Howe* (New York: Alfred A. Knopf, 1962).

95 Early, a Virginian, had served many years with the Associated Press before joining Roosevelt. (Both he and McIntyre had worked for Roosevelt in his 1920 vice-presidential campaign.) Early assisted with FDR's first press conference announcing the Bank Holiday in 1933, and he was still serving as press secretary when FDR died in April 1945.

Early thus continued the succession of presidential aides whose primary function was to administer a president's press relations. Nathaniel Hawthorne had informally performed this function for President Franklin Pierce in the 1850s. Archie Butt, under Teddy Roosevelt, and Joseph Tumulty, Wilson's principal aide, performed similar functions. But it was Early's predecessor George Akerson who, under Hoover, was first designated "Press Secretary." See William C. Spragens, *From Spokesman to Press Secretary: White House Media Operations* (Lanham, Md.: University Press of America, 1980).

96 Like Howe and Early, McIntyre too was a former newspaperman. He subsequently worked for FDR while the latter was Assistant Secretary of the Navy. When McIntyre fell ill during the second term, he was replaced at Early's suggestion by Edwin "Pa" Watson, one of FDR's military aides. See Early's memo to FDR (Feb. 23, 1939), PSF – Subject, Stephen T. Early Folder, FDRL. On McIntyre's background, see (no author listed) *The New Dealers*, (New York: The Literary Guild, 1934), pp. 225–30.

97 For a capsule summary of their duties from an inside perspective, see Tully, *F.D.R. My Boss*, pp. 135–7, 150–4.

98 Schlesinger, Jr., writes: "Of all the staff, Marguerite LeHand, the President's personal secretary, was undoubtedly closest to him and had most influence upon him." Roosevelt let LeHand reply to the many letters that he felt did not warrant personally dictated responses. She was also one of the few individuals who could tell Roosevelt he was making a mistake.

There is some question whether Roosevelt's relationship with Lehand was more than professional. Roosevelt's son James makes a strong argument that this was probably not the case. See James Roosevelt, *My Parents: A Differing View* (Chicago: Playboy Press, 1976).

Tully assumed most of LeHand's duties when the latter became ill during Roosevelt's second term and eventually became FDR's private secretary, serving from 1941 until his death. See Schlesinger, Jr., *The Coming of the New Deal*, pp. 516–17; and Tully, *F.D.R. My Boss*, pp. 39–40.

The permanent institutional staff within the White House, numbering approximately forty individuals, with another twenty or so on detail, provided a third source of support. They were headed by the Executive Clerk, Rudolph Forster, and his assistant, Maurice Latta, both of whom had served under seven presidents beginning with McKinley at the turn of the century.[99] The Executive Clerk's office supervised clerical services, including the mail room, oversaw White House building and grounds crews, handled all official papers, and generally provided the "institutional memory" for incoming White House administrations.[100]

The bargaining gap, 1933–5

In the initial bargaining flux that was the New Deal, Roosevelt attempted to govern through an enlarged cabinet, backstopped by a loose assortment of advisers and agencies. Despite the formal creation of cabinet coordinating agencies, however, he tended to utilize this system in an ad hoc contingent fashion, haphazardly drawing bargaining resources from it as needed. This bargaining approach, compounded by his management style, however, demonstrated the weakness of the presidential advising system at this time.

In retrospect, it appears the attempt to govern through cabinet-based committees failed for several reasons. To begin, the cabinet committees were generally too big to be effectively administered. At thirty-four

99 On the Executive Clerk's duties, see Roth, *The Executive Office of the President*, pp. 114–15; Tully, *F.D.R. My Boss*, pp. 348–50; Robert Sherwood, *Roosevelt and Hopkins*, rev. paperback ed. (New York: The Universal Library, 1950), pp. 208–9; and William Hopkins' oral history at the Truman Library. (Hopkins served as Executive Clerk for a number of years.)

In addition to Forster and Latta, the permanent White House staff included an extensive mail room force and a large pool of stenographers to prepare the letters that went out daily under Roosevelt's name. There was also a household staff of messengers, filing clerks, telephone operators, and other aides.

See the thirteen-page memorandum (unsigned, no date but presumably written in 1933) listing the background, pay and duties of the White House executive office staff (Louis Howe Papers, Report on the White House Executive Office Folder, FDRL.) This lists forty-one employees working for the executive staff, with another twenty-seven on detail. In addition, six more were temporarily detailed to the executive office for the "social season." Based on the background details as listed in the memorandum, one can deduce the following rough distribution of functions: two clerks responsible for official documents, including tracking executive orders and enrolled bills; one head usher and one head doorkeeper; five working in the White House garage on transportation; two "washers" and "two laborers" handling building and grounds; a social secretary to the First Lady; four stenographers; three telephone/telegraph operators; six "messengers"; and the rest working on correspondence and in the mail room. The detailees were spread approximately evenly among all these functions.

100 They also supervised building upkeep and maintained the grounds.

members, the NEC was more akin to a "town meeting" than a coordinating agency; while it provided an opportunity for debate and the exchange of ideas and views, it rarely achieved consensus.

Roosevelt, of course, might have lowered his management costs by delegating real authority to a staff subordinate, like Richberg. But he was unwilling to do so. With his penchant for making decisions outside established channels, and his proclivity for listening to appeals from those nominally under the Executive Secretary's authority, FDR effectively undercut any chance Richberg or anyone else might have had to manage the cabinet on his behalf. Others realized that Richberg's authority could be circumvented by direct appeals to the president. With no one short of FDR to enforce a unified perspective, then, the NEC's chance to act collectively was doomed.

In the final analysis, Roosevelt seemed reluctant to delegate coordinating authority to any individual or committee short of himself. Perhaps he recognized that the only way a subordinate could truly coordinate the cabinet on his behalf was if FDR delegated inherently presidential powers to that person. But that FDR refused to do so.

At a more fundamental level the cabinet committees were stymied by their pursuit of an inherently impossible task: coordinating a program whose parts were mutually incompatible. Roosevelt's bargaining agenda evinced no specific ideological or policy cohesion. Indeed, he had been elected on a platform most noteworthy for its attacks on his opponent's record.

He thus took office with tremendous bargaining flexibility when it came to choosing objectives. The result, as Leuchtenberg observes, is that "Roosevelt welcomed all the advice he could get, but he had no intention of being confined by rigid adherence to any particular doctrine." Frances Perkins, his Secretary of Labor, concurs, noting that Roosevelt "was a great believer in alternatives. He rarely got himself sewed tight to a program from which there was no turning back."

To maintain bargaining flexibility, Roosevelt frequently embraced contradictory bargaining objectives. For instance, when challenged by Raymond Moley to choose among two campaign statements, one advocating protectionist tariffs, the other proposing lower tariffs to encourage trade, Roosevelt replied "weave them together." Indeed, his major New Deal initiatives, the NIRA and the AAA, are really pieces of omnibus legislation whose separate components are in ideological tension. As James MacGregor Burns points out more generally:

> There was nothing but contradiction between the spending for public works and the economy act, between the humanitarianism of direct relief and the miserliness of veteran's cuts, between the tariff-raising provisions of the AAA [Agricultural Adjustment Act] and the

new internationalism of the State Department, between Roosevelt's emphasis on the strengthening of government as a tool for social betterment and his reducing the cost of government, including salaries of government workers.[101]

With a program this controversial and contradictory, agreement among warring cabinet secretaries and emergency heads, barring a unilateral decision by FDR, was unlikely. Thus bargaining consensus among his advisers was possible on only the most minor issues.[102]

For this reason the cabinet could not be a decision-making body. Indeed FDR rarely relied on it for collective support. As Roosevelt's Secretary of the Interior Harold Ickes complained:

> The cold fact is that on important matters we are seldom called upon for advice. We never discuss exhaustively any policy of Government or question of political strategy. The President makes all of his own decisions and, so far at least as the Cabinet is concerned, without taking counsel with a group of advisers. On particular questions he will call into his office persons directly interested, but it is fair to say that the Cabinet is not a general council upon whose advice the president relies or the opinions of which, on important matters, he calls for.[103]

Of course, the bargaining interests of presidents and their cabinet members have never been identical. But until the New Deal these differences did not usually prove fatal because most presidential bargains fell substantially within the purview of one or, at most, two executive branch departments. Beginning in 1933, however, the expanding presidential bargaining agenda made cabinet disputes more likely.[104] For this reason FDR frequently bypassed cabinet meetings completely, preferring to deal directly with the relevant cabinet and agency heads.

Wann summarizes Roosevelt's first-term administrative strategy this way:

> [I]t can be said that Roosevelt went to considerable lengths . . . to try and devise new coordinative machinery, such as the Executive Council, the Industrial Emergency Committee, and the National Emergency Council, to aid him in meeting the need for Presidential coordination. These agencies . . . were unquestionably of value in helping him perform his coordinative functions. The evidence is abundantly clear, however, that he used them only as means to help him coordinate, and not as effective coordinating devices in themselves. He delegated authority and controlled his subordinates in such

---

101 Burns, *The Lion and the Fox*, p. 179. See also Friedel, *FDR Launching the New Deal*, pp. 60–82.
102 On this point, see Seligman and Cornwell, Jr., *New Deal Mosaic*, p. xxii.
103 Ickes *Secret Diaries*, vol. 1, p. 308.
104 See Fenno, *The President's Cabinet: An Analysis in the Period from Wilson to Eisenhower*, pp. 219–49; Perkins, *The Roosevelt I Knew*, pp. 134–5; and Tully, *F.D.R. My Boss*, p. 170.

a way that the power to make final coordinative decisions almost always remained in his own tight grip.[105]

Roosevelt's first-term experience presents an underappreciated primer on the virtues and vices of cabinet government. But scholars studying the evolution of the presidential office usually gloss over this period. This is ironic, for cabinet government has been the administrative reform movement's clarion call since before Roosevelt's time. Woodrow Wilson, among others, was an early advocate. More recently, Nixon, Ford, Carter, and Reagan all took office extolling the virtues of a "collegial cabinet." And today, when it comes to rescuing the presidency from the dangers of White House staff bureaucratization, many reformers still keep time to this familiar tune.

Given FDR's experiences – not to mention those of his successors – the persistence with which presidents and reformers trumpet the virtues of cabinet government is puzzling. For the plain truth is that FDR's attempt to govern through his agency and department heads did not succeed.[106] To be sure, the cabinet councils were not totally unproductive. They served effectively as an information exchange and policy debate forum, and helped alert FDR to bargaining problems. They also helped keep key agency and department heads on board the New Deal ship. When it suited his purposes, then, as when using the NEC to provide oversight of the NIRA, cabinet committees could prove useful. But generally speaking, these committees were not very effective.

Their failure was exacerbated by FDR's tendency to split responsibility for implementing New Deal programs among more than one subordinate, and his habit of handing out identical assignments to two or more staff members. For instance, Hugh Johnson, charged with drawing up and enforcing codes, and Harold Ickes, responsible for public works, jointly administered the NIRA.[107] Similarly, to disburse the 1935 Emergency Relief appropriation Roosevelt pitted Ickes, in charge of large-scale capital ex-

---

105 Wann, *The President as Chief Administrator*, p. 71.

106 Brownlow, in his memoirs, argues that FDR's failure to exercise administrative control through cabinet councils was predictable. The problem, he wrote, is that multiple-member coordinating committees tend to "institutionalize," thus creating new operating divisions and entering into activities that compete with those they are trying coordinate. This presents the president with a new problem: "how to co-ordinate the co-ordinator with those who were to have been coordinated. In plain words, the multiple-member co-ordinating body nearly always transfers its identification of interests from that of the general manager who appointed it to its own interest as a separate and distinct institution" (Brownlow, *A Passion for Anonymity*, pp. 321–2).

107 For Johnson's reaction to this unexpected blow to his prestige, see Perkins, *The Roosevelt I Knew*, pp. 200–4.

penditures, against Harry Hopkins, head of the WPA and responsible for individually oriented unemployment relief programs.[108]

Although maddening to his subordinates, however, these administrative practices served FDR's purposes. As Donald Richberg notes, they helped him retain administrative control, thus lowering his management costs:

> It was . . . quite characteristic of President Roosevelt that, through caution or desire to keep all the reins of government either in his hands or within close reach, he repeatedly divided authority in such a manner that he could always balance the recommendations of one administrator against the opinions of perhaps a subordinate or some-one of equal and confusing co-authority.[109]

Administrative overlap and staff competition meant in practice that FDR's advisers monitored one another on his behalf. He thus gained information, advice, and options, all of which reduced his bargaining

---

108 This was part of the celebrated "five-ring circus" FDR devised to dole out emergency relief money. It included:

1. A Division of Application and Information, placed within the National Emergency Council and administered by Frank Walker. It served as a central clearinghouse, reviewing all proposals to spend money for relief and recovery projects.
2 The Advisory Committee on Allotments chaired by Interior Secretary Ickes. This twenty-three-person committee (including FDR) processed the projects sent up by Walker, making recommendations on the merits and comparing priorities.
3. The Works Project Administration (WPA) under Harry Hopkins, formerly Roosevelt's federal emergency relief administrator. His job was to get people off the relief rolls in the shortest time possible, and to oversee the development of small work relief projects to ensure maximum employment. (To get WPA approval, projects had to have local sponsors, be "useful," conclude in one year or less, take place on public property, and not compete with private employment.)
4. The Treasury Department, under Secretary of the Treasury Henry Morgenthau, controlled – under FDR's direction – the disbursement of funds.
5. The Bureau of the Budget, under acting Director Daniel Bell, tracked the administrative expenses associated with the activities of the relief agencies.

The process of administering the funding worked as follows: Applications for projects were sent to Walker for initial approval. In turn, Walker directed them to the huge committee nominally presided over by Ickes, although in fact FDR held the final veto. If the project cleared this hurdle, it went to Hopkins for implementation, with Morgenthau keeping financial account of the cost of relief activities, and Bell doling out funds for administrative overhead expenses.

Despite the complex setup, the five-ring circus succeeded in effectively administering the 1935 appropriation, primarily because FDR undertook "the tremendous burden of the actual task of co-ordination" (Brownlow, *A Passion for Anonymity*, p. 325).

109 Richberg, *My Hero*, p. 166. Richberg, of course, found himself undercut by these tactics while serving as Roosevelt's Executive Secretary to the National Emergency Council. As he recalled, "I found it frequently difficult to determine whether the president was relying on one of two or three persons of overlapping or interlocking authority, or whether he really was not relying on anyone's judgement except his own."

uncertainty.[110] Of course, these practices frustrated subordinates who took government posts in the naive belief that Roosevelt would allow them unfettered responsibility for particular tasks.[111] Not surprisingly, Roosevelt spent a large portion of his waking hours soothing ruffled feathers and resolving administrative disputes.[112] "The maintenance of peace in his official family took up hours and days of Roosevelt's time that could have been used on other matters," Tully recalled.[113] Burns notes, "He was forever acting as umpire between warring administrators or congressmen."[114]

Roosevelt exacerbated these disputes by his penchant for entrusting new government programs to new agencies, rather than vesting them in

110 Indeed, Roosevelt's methods turned public administration theory on its head; rather than separating line and staff support, clarifying staff jurisdictions, and establishing hierarchical channels of authority, Roosevelt took the opposite tack. The heads of line agencies also served as staff; jurisdictions were purposely mixed; and key subordinates reported directly to him, with little regard for proper administrative channels. In this, he violated many of the tenets espoused by public administration experts; see particularly Luther Gulick and Lyndall Urwick (eds.), *Papers on the Science of Administration* (New York: Institute of Public Administration, Columbia University, 1937), pp. 1–45, 191–7.

111 Frustration among staff caused by Roosevelt's unorthodox administrative habits were compounded by his personal characteristics. Many who worked for him later testified to his habit of nodding his head in apparent agreement with whomever he was conversing. On more than one occasion a visitor left Roosevelt's office convinced the President had adopted his or her views, when in fact no such agreement had occurred. See Moley and Rosen, *The First New Deal.*

112 There is no doubt FDR's administrative tactics contributed to the departure of several presidential aides, including Lewis Douglas, Hugh Johnson, Ray Moley, and Donald Richberg. Others, such as Harold Ickes and Cordell Hull, periodically threatened to quit, although Ickes never did during his presidency. Roosevelt was aware his administrative tactics took a toll on aides' morale; his papers contain several letters intended to mollify disenchanted subordinates. See, for instance, the exchange between FDR and Johnson prior to the latter's resignation as head of the NRA (reprinted in *FDR's Personal Letters*, pp. 412–15).

When Roosevelt decided an aide had reached a limit in usefulness, he felt no aversion to letting them resign. However, he generally refused to fire them himself. Instead, he preferred either to ignore them until they simply quit or to transfer them out of harm's way. For instance, see James Rowe's account regarding FDR's efforts to remove Leon Henderson from the Securities Exchange Commission, in Loucheim, *The Making of the New Deal*, pp. 286–7. Similarly, Hugh Johnson was offered an overseas position when FDR relieved him from the NRA. Ditto for Donald Nelson after his demise as head of the War Production Board.

113 Tully, *F.D.R. My Boss*, p. 170.

114 Burns, *The Lion and the Fox*, p. 183. The conflict between Johnson and Richberg is an early example of this. See Richberg's threat to resign as General Counsel to the NRA due to his deteriorating relationship with Johnson (June 26, 1934, letter to FDR, attached to a cover letter to Marvin McIntyre and a draft of a resignation letter to Johnson): "There are some conditions to which no self-respecting man expects any other self-respecting man to submit," Richberg wrote (*PSF*, Richberg folder, FDRL).

See also Roosevelt's response (Dec. 12, 1934), encouraging Richberg to continue as NRA counsel, after the latter complained that ill health and financial problems were making continuance in government difficult (reprinted in *FDR's Personal Letters*, p. 442.)

existing departments. At least five reasons, all related to his bargaining needs, help explain his approach.

First, Roosevelt evidently believed existing departments and agencies had enough problems coping with the economic emergency without entrusting new functions to them. Second, Roosevelt felt more confident a new agency would devote all its energies to the specific task at hand. Third, when and if the Depression ended, he thought it would be easier to terminate an emergency agency than to wrest a supposedly temporary function from a permanent department. Fourth, talented individuals seemed more willing to come to Washington to work for a new agency devoted to an issue of interest to them, than to work within an existing department pursuing several competing objectives. Finally, emergency agencies addressed Roosevelt's political needs. After twelve years out of power, Democrats were pushing FDR to make good on patronage opportunities. He did so by establishing new agencies outside of the civil service regulations, and then filling them with Democrats. This bypassed the existing civil service lists, most of which were outdated and filled with Republicans.[115] Thereafter he was able to lock these Democrats into permanent government service by bringing them within the fold of civil service.

The cumulative impact of FDR's organization strategy, however, was administrative disarray. "Administratively, the structure of the Executive Branch grew without plan or symmetry, neatness, or order."[116] As more bargains transcended departmental jurisdictions, FDR found it increasingly difficult to coordinate programs, despite a proliferation of coordinating committees.[117] By 1934, Richberg, working at FDR's behest, had catalogued at least 124 interdepartmental committees, boards, and commissions, served by 224 interdepartmental subcommittees, for a total of 348 interdepartmental committees operating at various levels.[118]

Roosevelt might have tackled the problem through executive branch reorganization intended to align departmental jurisdictions more closely

---

115 Congress in the several emergency relief appropriations acts of the New Deal exempted from civil service requirements all positions drawing salaries of $5,000 or more a year. Instead of drawing from civil service lists, appointees needed Senate confirmation. This allowed Roosevelt to appoint some 300,000 people in the newly created emergency agencies in his first two years as president. Wann, *The President as Chief Administrator*, pp. 26–7.

116 Roth, *The Executive Office of the President*, p. 112.

117 For instance, foreign trade was carried on by 27 bureaus spread across 20 departments and independent agencies, encompassing 22 related tasks. To synchronize their activities, some 44 interdepartmental committees related to foreign trade were established.

118 When asked by FDR how to remedy this administrative behemoth, Richberg, in the ultimate irony, suggested forming a committee to study the problem (see Proceedings of NEC, meeting no. 19, Dec. 11, 1934, reprinted in Seligman and Cornwell, Jr., *New Deal Mosaic*, pp. 355–7).

to recurring bargaining arenas. In fact, Roosevelt inherited extraordinary reorganization power in 1933.[119] Under existing law Congress could block presidential reorganization plans only through the normal legislative process, not by legislative veto as was later the case.[120] As Wann notes: "All in all, the wide authority given to Roosevelt under the above legislation constitutes the most extensive grant of power to effect administrative reorganization ever entrusted to a President by Congress in peace-time."[121]

Roosevelt, during the 1932 campaign, promised to use this power as a budget-deficit reducing tool.[122] As one of his first presidential acts he asked each cabinet head to submit reorganization proposals, and he appointed a special committee to study those plans.[123] But then Roosevelt allowed his reorganization authority to lapse without making more than a number of minor administrative changes.[124] As Interior Secretary

119 The reorganization authority had actually been granted to Hoover. Part II of the Legislative Appropriations Act, approved June 30, 1932, gave the President wide powers to make transfers or other changes in government organizations by executive orders. Initially, there was no time limit on this power. However, any executive order for governmental reorganization could be vetoed by either House through a resolution of disapproval adopted within sixty days of the executive order.
       By the time Hoover made use of this power and issued sweeping governmental reorganization orders in December 1932, however, he had already lost the election to Roosevelt and faced a hostile Congress. In January 1933, the House voted to reject all of Hoover's reorganization plans.

120 On Mar. 3, 1933, Congress amended the Legislative Appropriations Act by expanding the President's power to abolish the whole, or any part, of an agency or its functions. Abolition of entire departments was prohibited, however. This amendment also stipulated that Congress could reject reorganization orders only by enacting legislation, which was subject to a Presidential veto. It also put a two-year limit on the president's reorganization authority. (On Mar. 10, 1933, the act was amended once more to state that any reorganization plan would go into effect in sixty days even if Congress was not in session.)

121 There were two other instances in which presidents had the authority to veto congressional attempts to block presidential reorganization plans. The first occurred under the 1918 Overman Act, and the second under the First War Powers Act of 1941. Both of these acts were passed in times of war. See Wann, *The President as Chief Administrator*, p. 24.

122 Ibid., p. 20–1.

123 As early as Dec. 21, 1932, Roosevelt gave Moley a memorandum from Owen Young advocating reorganization as a tool to combat the Depression (see the letter to Moley from FDR, reprinted in *FDR's Personal Letters*, pp. 311–2). Subsequently he met with Congressman Swagar Sherley to set up an informal committee to examine reorganization proposals (letter from FDR to John N. Garner, Jan. 26, 1933, reprinted in *FDR's Personal Letters*, pp. 322–3).

124 Before his reorganization authority lapsed on Mar. 3, 1935. FDR created an Office of National Park Buildings and Reservations within the Department of the Interior; created a Division of Disbursements and Procurement in the Treasury Department; abolished the U.S. Shipping Board and transferred its functions and those of the Fleet Corporation to the Department of Commerce; consolidated the separate bureaus of Immigration and of Naturalization Services into a new Immigration and Naturaliza-

Harold Ickes observed, Roosevelt sought only "to sign executive orders bringing about departmental changes about which there is no dispute, leaving debatable matters to be considered more carefully later."[125] Apparently FDR feared politically controversial reorganization plans would jeopardize congressional support for his economic recovery plan.

Roosevelt's reluctance to fully utilize his reorganization powers suggests the more general political constraints he faced in attempting to rework the traditional presidential advisory system. The constitutionally mandated system of separate institutions sharing power gave Congress, the Supreme Court, and other government institutions incentives to thwart Roosevelt's attempts to modernize his bargaining support system.

As Hoover discovered, Congress' willingness to exercise administrative oversight extended even to the president's personal White House staff. It would not, therefore, submit passively to presidential efforts to restructure the executive branch. Indeed, Congress was soon actively considering its own plans for reorganizing the executive branch. In 1936, led by Senator Harry F. Byrd (Democrat, Va), the Senate created the Select Committee to Investigate the Executive Agencies of the Government.[126] The House soon followed suit.

At the same time, the Supreme Court was also moving to constrain Roosevelt's administrative efforts. In its Schechter and Butler rulings, it essentially declared unconstitutional the two major cornerstones of FDR's New Deal program.[127] In *Humphrey's Executor v. United States,* issued

tion Service within the Department of Labor; transferred the functions of the Federal Board for Vocational Education to the Interior Department, where it was assigned to the Office of Education; consolidated all government agricultural credit agencies into a new Farm Credit Administration; transferred the Office of Alien Property Custodian and its functions to the Department of Justice; abolished the Board of Indian Commissioners, transferring its functions to the Department of Interior; and created a Division of Territories and Insular Possessions in the Department of Interior to consolidate all government functions pertaining to territories.

See Roosevelt's message accompanying E.O. 61660 (June 10, 1933), *FDR's Public Papers,* vol. 2, pp. 222–8, and Wann, *The President as Chief Administrator,* p. 25.

125 Ickes, *The Secret Diaries* vol. 1, p. 47; and Roth, *The Executive Office of the President,* pp. 130–1.

126 See Senate Resolution 217, 74th Cong., Feb. 24, 1936, 80 Congressional Record, 2674, 2802. Byrd had achieved nationwide recognition some years before as governor of Virginia when he had reorganized that state government to save money.

John Millett, a Committee staff member, recalls, "My recollection of the chronology is that the [Brownlow Committee] was set up in part as a presidential response to the leadership of Byrd" (Frederick C. Mosher, *The President Needs Help* [Lanham, Md.: University Press of America, 1988], p. 27).

127 In *Schechter Poultry Co. v. the United States* (1935), the Court ruled that Congress did not delegate to Roosevelt the authority to regulate hours, wages, trade practices, and other business practices. It thus effectively nullified the National Industrial Recovery Act and all agencies created pursuant to that act. Similarly, in *United States v. Butler* (1936), the Court invalidated the Agricultural Adjustment Act of 1933.

the same day (May 27, 1935) as the Schechter decision, meanwhile, the Court decreed Roosevelt could not legally remove a member of the Federal Trade Commission nor anyone serving on any independent regulatory commission.[128] This dealt a severe blow to Roosevelt's efforts to control administrative personnel. Moreover, the Court's conservative bent had a chilling effect on Roosevelt's attempts to construct other New Deal measures, such as wage and hours legislation.[129]

Still another obstacle to FDR's administrative authority existed in the person of John J. McCarl, appointed Comptroller-General by Republican President Warren G. Harding, and a former secretary of the Republican Congressional Committee. By utilizing his "pre-audit" authority, McCarl could void appropriations for New Deal programs, including those intended for WPA and PWA projects.[130]

But it wasn't simply institutional constraints that stymied FDR in his search for bargaining support. His own personal style played a role as well. He was unfailingly accessible to almost all subordinates, regardless of official hierarchy. "Almost a hundred people could get through to him by telephone without stating their business to a secretary," Schlesinger notes; Brownlow put FDR's estimate of regular telephone contacts at about 125

Roosevelt's concern with Schechter is reflected in a memo he sent to the Justice Department, asking it to assess the impact of the Schechter ruling on the legal status of the emergency agencies (OF 285, Government Departments File [May 29, 1935], FDRL). See also the reply of Assistant Solicitor General Angus D. Maclean (June 1, 1935), OF 285, Government Departments File, FDRL.

128 See *Humphrey's Executor v. United States*, 295 U.S. 602 (1935). Humphrey had been appointed by Hoover in 1931 to a seven-year term on the FTC, but FDR felt that Humphrey was opposed to the New Deal political philosophy. On the basis of an earlier court ruling in *Myers v. United States* 272 U.S. 52 (1926), in which the Court upheld President Wilson's removal of a postmaster, Roosevelt and his advisers felt that they had authority to request Humphrey's resignation. The Court ruled otherwise.

129 On this issue, see Perkins, *The Roosevelt I Knew*, pp. 246–56.

130 Herbert Emmerich, a New Deal official, later complained: "To recall the abundant examples of both flagrant and petty interference by the Comptroller-General in executive management is to review a 'parade of horribles'" (Herbert Emmerich, *Federal Organization and Administrative Management* [Birmingham: The University of Alabama Press, 1971], p. 54).

See the legal opinion on the role of the Comptroller-General in disbursing NRA funds, submitted to Howe by the Assistant Secretary of the Treasury (Aug. 28, 1933), with attached letters from Daniel Bell (Aug. 25, 1933) and Comptroller-General McCarl (Aug. 11, 1933). See also Howe's letter to McCarl, asking for clarification (Aug. 29, 1933) of McCarl's ruling. (Louis Howe Papers, National Industrial Recovery Act Folder, FDRL). McCarl had vetoed an effort to raise the price paid by the U.S. government for services rendered by a private firm under the terms of the NIRA. The ruling raised the more general issue of presidential discretion to allocate funds appropriated by Congress.

FDR's frustration with McCarl is revealed in a letter sent from the President to Harry Hopkins (Oct. 31, 1935), inquiring about McCarl's disapproval of certain WPA expenditures (reprinted in *FDR's Personal Letters*, p. 515). Ultimately, FDR's dissatisfaction with the powers of the Comptroller-General's Office would lead the Brownlow

people.[131] This meant he spent almost a quarter of his fourteen-hour working day on the phone. He also averaged, prior to World War II, four to six hours of daily appointments spread among ten to fifteen people.[132] This included almost daily three- to four-hour meetings with Congressional leaders during the legislative session.[133]

He also dealt with a staggering amount of paperwork. Despite admonishing his subordinates to keep memoranda to one page, Roosevelt found himself flooded with approximately one hundred times the amount of official papers faced by his predecessors.[134] This included the numerous official daily cables and periodic sampling of public mail.

A lack of administrative knowledge compounded the problem. Simply put, there were few precedents for what Roosevelt was trying to accomplish; except perhaps for Wilson and the National Industrial Advisory Council during World War I, no president had attempted to coordinate such a complex administrative program. Roosevelt had neither institutional machinery nor experienced personnel on which to draw for support. That left him only his political instincts as a guide to constructing a first-term administrative structure.

To further complicate matters, his bargaining needs slowly evolved during the course of the first term. Initially, he valued speed and flexibility; stop-gap institutions were created as needed to implement his New Deal economic recovery program, but with little thought to permanently integrating them into the established institutional framework.[135] But as the economy stabilized the political climate began to change. Both Congress and the Supreme Court began to reassert their institutional prerogatives, and Roosevelt's ad hoc administrative approach threatened to become a 1936 campaign liability. Alf Landon, the Republican candidate for president, charged: "This administration has gone hog-wild in adding new agencies and accumulating new powers. It has created 75 new alphabetical what-nots. Many of these are little more than duplications of agencies already in existence. . . . This is not good government."[136]

Committee to advocate a restructuring of the government's accounting procedures. See chapter 3.
    For a detailed examination of the issues, see Harvey C. Mansfield, *The Comptroller-General* (New Haven, Conn.: Yale University Press, 1939); see also Barry Karl, *Executive Reorganization and Reform in the New Deal* (Chicago: University of Chicago Press), pp. 195–9.
131 Schlesinger, Jr., *The Coming of the New Deal*, p. 523; and Wann, *The President as Chief Administrator*, p. 196, n. 7.
132 Wann, *The President as Chief Administrator*, p. 34.
133 Schlesinger, Jr., *The Coming of the New Deal*, pp. 545–6.
134 Ibid., p. 523.
135 Karl, *Executive Reorganization and Reform in the New Deal*, pp. 196–8.
136 Speech at Pittsburgh, Oct. 27, 1936. Quoted in Roth, *The Executive Office of the President*, p. 131. Rosenman later recalled that Roosevelt spelled out a strategy by

By mid-1935, then, FDR realized the administrative chaos engendered by the New Deal program threatened his political support.[137] By spot contracting on an ad hoc basis for bargaining resources, he had survived the onslaught of demands produced by the New Deal, but just barely. The New Deal measures had helped stabilize the economy, but at the cost of creating a large budget deficit. To reduce the deficit Roosevelt wanted the emergency agencies brought into the budgeting and accounting procedures governing established departments. This would also address alienation felt by those cabinet secretaries excluded from administering a large portion of the New Deal emergency recovery program. It would also counter Comptroller-General McCarl's continued efforts to periodically invalidate New Deal emergency financing.

His primary need, however, was for a more reliable source of staff resources oriented toward his bargaining objectives. That realization prompted continuing discussions between FDR and several public administration experts who comprised the advisory board to the National Resources Committee (NRC). This committee was the administrative descendant of the National Planning Board (NPB), a three-member board created by Interior Secretary Ickes in 1933 to assist him in developing a "comprehensive program of public works."[138] Among

which Landon might have won the 1936 presidential election: "I would say: 'I am for social security, work relief, etc., etc., but the Democrats cannot be entrusted with the administration of these fine ideals.' I would cite chapter and verse on WPA inefficiency – there's plenty of it – as there is bound to be in such a vast emergency program. "You know,' he added reflectively, almost longingly, 'the more I think about it, the more I think I could lick myself'" Rosenman, *Working With Roosevelt*, pp. 131–2.

137 "The joints of the federal machinery began to creak; sheer weight of numbers of units responsible to the President made the job of Chief Executive almost unbearable. It seemed evident that I had to be provided with expanded staff facilities to assist in the job of administrative management" *FDR's Public Papers*, 1938, pp. 498–9.

138 Established by order of Ickes on July 20, 1933, under authority granted him in his role as administrator of public works. Ickes was a Bull Moose Progressive with an abiding interest in governmental planning. Planning, of course, had ambivalent connotations in the United States, but it was implicit in the Progressive movement. It was Roosevelt's predecessor, Hoover, who had appointed the President's Committee on Recent Social Trends, a first step toward using social scientists to aide governmental planning for policymaking. Subsequently, in 1931, the Federal Employment Stabilization Board (later disbanded by FDR) was established to advise the president regarding employment trends and business activities. See Sander, *A Staff for the President*, pp. 19–23.

The NPB was chaired by Roosevelt's uncle Frederic A. Delano, assisted by Charles Merriam and the economist Wesley C. Mitchell. All served on a part-time basis. Mitchell and Merriam had been members of Hoover's Research Committee on Recent Social Trends, and were veterans of the city planning movement. The board was supported by a small staff working under the auspices of Charles W. Eliot II. Although its name changed three different times, this organization served continuously until 1943 as Roosevelt's chief source of national planning advice. For an overview of New Deal planning activities, see especially Marion Clawson, *New Deal Planning: the National*

the discussants were Louis Brownlow, Charles Merriam, and Luther Gulick.[139]

Roosevelt, like Ickes, had a long-standing interest in instituting governmental planning at the national level.[140] In fact, FDR unsuccessfully attempted on several occasions to get Congress to create a permanent planning agency attached directly to his office.[141] The NPB thus appealed to him as a mechanism by which he might yet achieve that goal. In this he was supported by the NPB itself, which issued a report in 1934 advocating the creation of a permanent planning agency directly responsible to the president.

Resources Planning Board (Baltimore, Md.: Johns Hopkins University Press, 1981), and Otis L. Graham, Jr., *Toward A Planned Society: From Roosevelt to Nixon* (New York: Oxford University Press, 1976), pp. 49–90. See also Sander, *A Staff for the President*, p. 20–3.

139 Brownlow chaired the Social Science Research Council's (SSRC) Committee on Public Administration, was a member of the Public Administration Clearinghouse (PACH), and served as a consultant to Roosevelt's National Planning Board, making him perhaps the nation's foremost expert in the field of public administration. He had contacts with many officials in the Roosevelt government, including Charles Merriam, which enabled him to get a firsthand glimpse of the administrative problems FDR faced. (Indeed, Brownlow had offered the services of PACH to Roosevelt in the early days of the New Deal to help with reorganization issues. See the memorandum [dated Apr. 7, 1933] from Frank O. Lowden to FDR "covering the subject of reorganization of federal agencies"; also the memorandum [June 16, 1933] of Brownlow to Roosevelt reaffirming the offer [OF 3795, Brownlow folder, FDRL].)
        Merriam was a member of the advisory board to the National Planning Board. He had created the SSRC to bring together research of scholars working in different fields. Brownlow, *A Passion for Anonymity*, p. 297.
        Gulick was formerly director of the Bureau of Municipal Research in New York, and later director, president, and then chairman of the Institute of Public Administration in New York.
        A fascinating examination of their backgrounds and views toward the presidency and administrative management is found in Karl, *Executive Reorganization and Reform in the New Deal*, pp. 37–165.

140 Sander believes the NRC gave Roosevelt a source of planning and advice at the presidential level similar to that provided by the brains trust during the early New Deal days. Sander, *A Staff for the President*, p. 22–3.

141 See his memorandum to Senator Joseph T. Robinson (Apr. 20, 1936), urging enactment of legislation creating a National Resources Board in order to rationalize the nation's planning for public works: "I think it is very important, in order to stop wild raids for Public Works at the next session," FDR wrote (reprinted in *FDR's Personal Letters*, p. 582). However, during the next decade, attempts to legislate the existence of a national planning office were all thwarted. See Graham, Jr., *Toward a Planned Society*, pp. 54–9.
        Much of the congressional opposition to FDR's efforts was motivated by the Army Corps of Engineers, which did not want to relinquish control of natural resource development. See, for example, the confidential memorandum from Lauchlin Currie to FDR (Jan. 22, 1940). That memo relayed a message from Corcoran, who was told by Representative Sam Rayburn that "the real opposition to the Planning Bd is the Army Engineers who have been actively lobbying against the Bd" (*PSF*, Lauchlin Currie Folder, FDRL).

Acting on these sentiments, and prompted in part by a congressional resolution asking the president for a comprehensive plan to utilize the nation's rivers, FDR tried first to incorporate the NPB within his own appointed office. But Ickes, supported by several cabinet members, resisted, arguing that in effect FDR was delegating oversight of the nation's natural resources to three appointed officials with little accountability.[142] To mollify Ickes, Roosevelt created the National Resource Board (NRB), a six-member cabinet committee chaired by Ickes, with the three-member NPB reconstituted as an advisory board. Later in 1935, when it became clear the legal basis for the NRB would be invalidated by the Supreme Court's Schechter decision, FDR transformed it by executive order into the National Resources Committee (NRC).[143]

It was an NRC report, issued Dec. 1, 1935, that provided the catalyst for FDR to sponsor a study of his own management needs.[144] That report, which advocated the creation of a permanent national planning body, came at an auspicious time. Across the globe, people mired in a worldwide economic depression were beginning to wonder if fascism and communism were superior to liberal democracies as forms of government.[145] Brownlow and his colleagues disagreed, of course. But they believed that for the American system of separated powers to effectively address the economic emergency, there had to be an energetic executive whose powers matched expectations for leadership.[146] And to sustain that energy in

142 Ickes complained, "The plan as outlined would have made this Planning Board . . . supreme in its field, without any Cabinet responsibility . . . I hit the ceiling when I learned of this plan" (Ickes, *Secret Diaries*, vol. 1, p. 171). Ickes was supported by Secretary of Labor Perkins, Secretary of Agriculture Wallace, and relief administrator Harry Hopkins.

143 The change was largely cosmetic. Because the NRB had been created by authorization of the NIRA, Roosevelt needed an alternative means to maintain a planning staff. He found it in the provisions of the 1935 $4.88 billion Emergency Relief Appropriation Act. With that legislation FDR created the NRC, which was essentially an expanded version of the NRB. See E.O. 7065 (June 7, 1935), pursuant to the Emergency Relief Appropriations Act of 1935 (49 *Stat.* 115).

144 "We recommend the establishment of a permanent advisory National Planning Board responsible directly to the President and charged with the duty of preparing plans and general policies . . . and advising the President on progress and development of planned proposals" (Charles Merriam with input from Louis Brownlow who at this time was serving as a consultant to the NRB, "A Plan for Planning" National Resources Committee, *Regional Factors in National Planning and Development* [Washington D.C.: Government Printing Office, 1935], p. xi). The rest of the report was largely devoted to analyzing land and water use in the United States.

145 Brownlow was particularly struck by the prevalence of this sentiment during a trans-Atlantic tour at the height of the Depression. He noted the increasing pessimism of Europeans regarding the ability of democracies to act decisively and effectively in the teeth of the prevailing political and economic calamities.

146 "It was our belief that the Presidency of the United States was the institution . . . behind which democrats might rally to repel the enemy. And, to that end, it was not only desirable but absolutely necessary that the President be better equipped for his

the face of rising demands for executive leadership, the presidency must have adequate staff support. Their call for a national planning agency, then, was but one element in a larger plan to reinvigorate the presidency, and by extension the American political system.

Roosevelt's own political predicament thus converged with his planners' desire to resuscitate the American presidency as a bulwark against totalitarianism both home and abroad. The upshot was Brownlow's, Gulick's, and Merriam's appointment in March 1936 as the President's Committee on Administrative Management – more commonly known as the Brownlow Committee. That landmark in presidential staffing embodied FDR's first-term lessons and begins the second phase in FDR's presidential staff development. To understand its recommendations, however, one must look closely at its origins and approach. That is the task of the next chapter.

tremendous task" (Brownlow, *A Passion for Anonymity*, pp. 335–6). Gulick, in a 1941 symposium reviewing the EOP's creation, concurred: "But you will find in that action [the creation of the EOP] one part of America's answer to the taunt of the dictators that democracies cannot meet the demands of the modern world and still remain democratic" (Gulick, "Conclusion", in the "Symposium on the Creation of the Executive Office of the President," p. 139).

3

The president needs help: The Brownlow Committee frames the Roosevelt response

As John Hart notes, "The Brownlow Report, the Reorganization Act, Reorganization Plan No. 1, and E.O. 8248 together were a watershed in the history of presidential staffing."[1] They mark the first significant institutionalization of presidentially controlled sources of bargaining support.[2] Roosevelt's belief that, in the oft-quoted phrase from his introduction to the Brownlow Report, "the president needs help" provided the impetus for staff reform.[3] But the details of reform, as first laid out in that Report, were dictated by his specific bargaining needs, particularly information and expertise regarding policy planning, budgeting and fiscal affairs, personnel selection, administrative management, and economic regulation.[4]

---

1 John Hart *The Presidential Branch: From Washington to Clinton*, 2nd ed. (Chatham, N.J.: Chatham House Publishers, 1995), p. 36. The 1939 Reorganization Act, passed by Congress on Apr. 3 of that year, authorized the President to prepare reorganization plans which, unless disapproved by Congress, became law. Under this authority, FDR sent Plan I to Congress on Apr. 25, 1939, followed by Plan II on May 9, 1939. A resolution stating "that Congress does not favor the Reorganization Plan I" was defeated in the House. A similar resolution regarding Plan II was defeated in the Senate. Ordinarily, that meant Plan I would have gone into effect sixty days later, on June 25, whereas Plan II would have become law on July 9. Since, however, the fiscal year ended on June 30, Congress by joint resolution made both plans effective July 1, 1939.

   Under the authority of Plan I FDR then issued E.O. 8248, (Sept. 8, 1939) formally establishing the Executive Office of the President (EOP) and transferring into it the BoB, a National Resources Planning Board, the Office of Government Reports, the White House Office, and an Office of Emergency Management. Reorganization Plan II was concerned mainly with intradepartmental transfers and consolidations. See Louis Brownlow "The Executive Office of the President," *Public Administration Review* 1, no. 2 (Winter 1941), pp. 101–2.

2 Recall from Chapter 2 that, although the Bureau of the Budget was established in 1921 as a presidential agency, its location within the Treasury Department had compromised its utility for presidents.

3 Gulick actually wrote the introduction to the Committee Report that Roosevelt signed. Thus the phrase may be his. See *The President's Committee on Administrative Management: Report with Special Studies* (Washington, D.C.: Government Printing Office, 1937), p. 5 (hereafter *Brownlow Committee Report*).

4 The Brownlow Report's major recommendations, which largely dictated the subsequent agenda for administrative reform, include: (1) appoint up to six more White House assistants; (2) strengthen the management agencies of government, especially those deal-

In modernizing the presidential office, however, Roosevelt conspicuously avoided planting the seed of the presidential branch; the acquisition of additional White House staff was but a small part in his otherwise ambitious plan to reorganize the presidency.[5] As he explained to Senator James Byrnes, who led the floor fight for legislation to implement the Brownlow Report on FDR's behalf: "[A]s a matter of fact, I would hardly know what to do with six Executive [White House] Assistants if I do not have any authority to put the government as a whole on a businesslike basis. It is a little like giving the President the envelope of the letter without any letter in it!"[6]

As the blueprint for FDR's staff reforms, the Brownlow Report is in many respects the most thoroughly articulated synopsis of his response to escalating demands for presidential leadership.[7] Congress, however, viewed the recommendations with suspicion, particularly the sections dealing with civil service reform, executive branch reorganization, and the duties of the Comptroller-General's Office.[8] Indeed, many critics viewed

ing with planning, budgeting, personnel, and administrative reorganization; (3) streamline the executive branch by bringing almost one hundred agencies, including the independent regulator commissions, under departmental auspices (and providing the president with permanent reorganization authority); (4) extend the merit system upward, outward, and downward to cover all nonpolicy-making positions as part of a general reorganizatin of the civil service system; and (5) revise the federal government's fiscal system, especially the role of the Comptroller-General's Office. See the *Brownlow Committee Report*, esp. the conclusion, pp. 51–3; and Harold H. Roth, *The Executive Office of the President: A Study of Its Development with Emphasis on the Period 1939–1953*, Ph.D. dissertation (Washington, D.C.: The American University, 1953), p. 142.

5 Note that the Report's section on the White House staff takes up but two of its fifty-three pages. (The bound volume of the Report, including "special" studies, totals 382 pages.) Moreover, its recommendation that FDR be authorized to hire not more than six additional White House administrative assistants really set no precedent; as documented in Chapter 2, he was already using at least this many detailees from other agencies in much the same capacity as Committee members envisioned.

6 Letter from FDR to James F. Byrnes, July 26, 1937, (reprinted in Elliot Roosevelt (ed.) *F.D.R. His Personal Letters, 1928–1945* (New York: Duell, Sloan & Pearce, 1950), p. 696 (hereafter *FDR's Personal Letters*). Byrnes was serving as FDR's floor leader in the Senate fight to ratify the Brownlow legislation.

7 Brownlow told Neustadt in 1963 that Roosevelt approved the final draft of the Report without making any significant changes. He could do so in part because he had reviewed earlier drafts to ensure it fulfilled his needs, and because committee members largely shared FDR's vision regarding the role of staff.

8 The political firestorm ignited by the Brownlow Report is well documented in Richard Polenberg, *Reorganizing Roosevelt's Government 1936–1939: The Controversy over Executive Reorganization* (Cambridge, Mass.: Harvard University Press, 1966), pp. 28–191. Note, however, that there was little opposition to the recommendations to increase the White House staff by up to six administrative assistants; in fact, this section was adopted almost without discussion by the Senate and the House in 1937. See the transcripts of the 75th Congress, 1st session, U.S. Congress, Joint Committee on Government Organization, *Hearings on Reorganization of the Executive Departments* (1937). See also Don K. Price, *America's Unwritten Constitution Science, Religion, and Political Responsibility*

the Report as a stalking horse in FDR's bid to acquire more power, perhaps even establish a dictatorship.[9] His Committee members, in contrast, believed that without real reform, the presidential office would prove incapable of meeting the leadership demands thrust on FDR by the Great Depression. As Brownlow recalled:

> The committee was unanimous in the opinion that what was needed was an exploration of the ways and means to equip the President . . . to carry out the task of executive top management of the government and . . . if possible, of practical ways in which the president's authority might be made more nearly commensurate with his responsibility.[10]

A diminished presidency, they argued, threatened the very fabric of the American constitutional system itself – a fabric already strained by economic crisis and the challenge of dictators. With these clashing perspectives as backdrop, Roosevelt undertook the delicate task of administrative reform.

The decision to appoint the Brownlow Committee

Two memoranda, one written by Lewis Meriam, the other by Charles Merriam, helped define the Brownlow Committee's intellectual boundaries.[11] Meriam's, submitted to Merriam in October 1935, argued that

(Cambridge, Mass.: Harvard University Press, 1985), pp. 99–128; Roth, *The Executive Office of the President*, pp. 146–56; and Alfred Dick Sander, *A Staff for the President: The Executive Office of the President, 1921–52* (New York: Greenwood Press, 1989), p. 26.

9 Ironically, Roosevelt expanded the Committee's research purview largely against the advice of Louis Brownlow, Charles Merriam, Luther Gulick, and Lewis Meriam. They sought a narrower, less politically controversial examination of what Gulick characterized as FDR's "top-level management" needs. In practice, this meant focusing primarily on Roosevelt's staff support. But Roosevelt encouraged the Committee to broaden its agenda because he felt it served his larger bargaining interests. Once having steered the Committee into politically dangerous waters, however, Roosevelt then almost scuttled its efforts by unwisely choosing to unveil his Court-packing plan just as Congress was on the brink of passing many of the Committee's recommendations. That led to the two-year fight to get congressional approval of the Committee's plan, as documented by Polenberg in his *Reorganizing Roosevelt's Government 1936–1939*.

10 Louis Brownlow, *A Passion for Anonymity* (Chicago: University of Chicago Press, 1955) p. 349.

11 See "An Executive Staff Agency" prepared by Lewis Meriam for Charles Merriam, (Oct. 10, 1935), President's Committee on Administrative Management Papers (hereafter PCAM), Franklin Delano Roosevelt Library (hereafter FDRL); and Charles Merriam, "Proposed Study of Management in the Federal Government," National Resources Committee File, PCAM, FDRL. Lewis Meriam, although not formally a Committee member, was influential in developing the conceptual foundation for the Brownlow Report. Ironically, he eventually played a significant role in producing the Brookings Institution study of the executive branch sponsored by Byrd's Senate Committee. That report, issued in serial form in 1937, differed in several significant respects from the Brownlow Committee's recommendations. Those differences were magnified by Roosevelt's opponents and helped fuel the controversy regarding the Brownlow Report. See

industrialization and the impact of modern technology had utterly transformed the character of modern democracies by shifting power from elected representative assemblies to appointed government officials: "[R]ealists know today that legislatures must delegate to the administrative agencies a host of questions involving policy."¹² However, the proliferation of appointed agencies in the United States taxed the president's management capacities: "This inescapable change is throwing an ever increasing burden on the President of the United States, who as chief executive, is held responsible for the efficient operation of the great and growing administrative machine."¹³

And, because bargaining demands frequently pitted cabinet advisers against one another, the president could no longer rely on "cabinet government" for support:

> When two of them [cabinet secretaries], representing different agencies with different clienteles, with different economic and social objectives get at loggerheads, they bring the scrap to the President to settle, and the President is extremely fortunate if each of them has not previously turned loose at a press conference so that public attention is focused on the row.¹⁴

Nor could presidents expect to solve their administrative problems through "bureau shuffling."¹⁵ Reorganization was a one-shot deal, and

the *Investigations of Executive Agencies of the Government* August 16, 1937 (Senate Report 1275, 75th Congress, 1st session).

For a bound version of the Senate-sponsored Brookings Report, see the Preliminary Report of the Senate Select Committee to Investigate the Executive Agencies of the Goverment, *Investigation of Executive Agencies of the Government* (Washington, D.C.: Government Printing Office, 1937) (hereafter the *Brookings Report*).

12 Meriam "An Executive Staff Agency".

13 Ibid. p. 3. Or, as Barry Karl put it in his overview of presidential staff development in this period: "The growth in executive responsibility since the end of the Civil War had not been accompanied by a corresponding development in the instruments of executive power" (Barry Karl *Executive Reorganization and Reform in the New Deal* [Chicago: University of Chicago Press, 1963] p. 239). Karl noted that without administrative reform presidents were faced with unenviable alternatives: They could either refuse to take on the additional responsibilities, or risk delegating inherently presidential authority to subordinates to see that they were carried out – but in essence this meant abdicating executive responsibility. Conversely, they could accept the additional responsibilities and try to govern without the means to fulfill these demands.

14 Meriam, "An Executive Staff Agency," p. 4.

15 As Meriam noted, "Whenever the Federal debt rises and further taxation seems imminent the representatives of large private interests and the press demand a reorganization of the executive branch of the United States Government." But, he argued, "Actual savings through reorganization of the executive branch cannot possible amount to much, . . ." and he doubted "the anatomical rearrangement of bureaus and independent establishments . . . [would] result in elimination of overlapping or prevent offices at times from working at cross purposes" (Meriam, "An Executive Staff Agency," p. 4.)

Brownlow concurred: "It may also be assumed in this study that a probable cause of the relative failure of previous efforts effectively to reorganize the Federal Government its traditional emphasis on economy and efficiency was not, in Meriam's view, particularly useful.[16]

Instead, Meriam advocated bolstering the president's "executive top management" resources, focusing specifically on the organization of and services provided by the president's staff. The president, he observed, "has at his disposal an exceedingly small staff to aid him."[17] He noted in particular the president's lack of staff-based sources of institutional memory.

> Curiously the White House Office has no large accumulated files. . . .
> When a new President wants the papers in a given case he must ordinarily get them from the department, dealing through a new Secretary who is not himself familiar with the situation.[18]

Hence,

> The question which should be studied carefully is whether the President should not have a considerable office of his own, made up in part of new people of his own selection and in part of persons who serve through administration after administration; whether such an office would help him in coordination and controlling the growing administrative machine, whether it could be made to furnish him at once with all information needed for day to day control . . . that could study problems that cut across departmental lines and involve interdepartmental conflicts.[19]

At about this same time Charles Merriam drafted a memorandum, at FDR's behest, echoing many of Meriam's recommendations.[20] This three-

---

is that, in large part, they have proceeded on the theory that consolidation, the elimination of overlappings and conflicts, the shifting of bureaus and divisions hither and yon, and the like, and not enough attention has been given to the central problem of over-all management and the arming of the President with effective means of making his direction and control commensurate with his responsibility" (Louis Brownlow *Management Study* [Mar. 14, 1936], document A-II-11, PCAM, FDRL). See also Brownlow, *A Passion for Anonymity*, p. 370; and Sander, *A Staff for the President*, p. 26.

Historically, of course, executive branch reorganizations in the name of economy and efficiency were the favored tools of presidents seeking enhanced administrative control. See Peri Arnold, *Making the Managerial Presidency: Comprehensive Reorganization Planning: 1905–1980*, (Princeton, N.J.: Princeton University Press, 1986)), for an excellent review of the history of executive branch reorganization.

16 As Meriam put it, "[R]eorganization is static whereas Presidential control of the administrative departments must be dynamic" (Meriam, "An Executive Staff Agency," p. 5).

17 Ibid.   18 Ibid.

19 Such a project, he concluded, "seems infinitely more promising than any new study of the reorganization of the administrative departments. . . ." (ibid., p. 5).

20 Merriam, "Proposed Study of Management in the Federal Government." See also Marion Clawson, *New Deal Planning: The National Resources Planning Board* (Baltimore, Md.: Johns Hopkins University Press, 1981), p. 47; Edward H. Hobbs, *Behind the President: A Study of Executive Office Agencies* (Washington, D.C.: Public Affairs Press, 1954), p. 79; and Charles E. Merriam, "The National Resources Planning Board: A Chapter in American Planning Experience," *The American Political Science Review* 38, no. 6 (December 1944).

page outline proposed analyzing "the institutional arrangements, general understandings and practices which would most effectively aid the Executive in the double task of management plus political leadership and direction." The focus would be the President's "over-all administration supervision or management of technical problems"[21]:

> The study would deal primarily with the staff which the Executive should have to exercise over-all management, how this staff should be organized, what its functions should be, and its relations to the operating agencies.[22]

These two memoranda accurately capture the intellectual genesis underlying many of the Brownlow Report's recommendations. Simply put, each argues that the proliferation of demands for government services had exposed the presidency's institutional shortcomings and that the remedy lay in expanding FDR's sources of staff support.

It was several months, however, before FDR took action on the proposals. In the interim, he made sure nothing could be done without his consent.[23] Finally, on Feb. 20, 1936, he met with the principals to discuss whether and how the study might be done.[24] The tenor of the hour-long meeting is captured in Merriam's note to Brownlow: "I had quite a discussion but believe it will come out alright."[25]

Evidently Roosevelt agreed with the basic diagnosis as outlined in the two memoranda. But he wanted to control all attempts to develop and implement a cure. His caution during this election year was politically

21 Merriam, "Proposed Study of Management in the Federal Government," p. 1; see also Brownlow, *A Passion for Anonymity*, pp. 327–30.
22 Merriam, "Proposed Study of Management in the Federal Government."
23 "The President asked me to telephone the Secretary of the Interior [Ickes] and tell him that before he does anything he would like a specific proposal that will limit the whole affair and the President suggests that nothing be done until he has had a chance to talk it over with the Secretary" (Grace Tully to Rudolph Forster [Dec. 12, 1935], PCAM, FDRL.
   Merriam's memo was forwarded by Ickes to FDR on Dec. 20, 1935. Ickes added a cover letter expressing his support, and suggesting financing the project through private funding, perhaps from the Social Science Research Council's (SSRC) Committee of Public Administration (memorandum from Ickes to FDR [Dec. 20, 1935], PCAM, FDRL). Frederick Delano, chairman of the National Resource Committee advisory board, also expressed his support, but only if the study's recommendations were released after the 1936 presidential election.
   Ickes wrote to FDR again on Feb. 8, asking whether he had permission to authorize the study. Apparently, Delano also met with FDR on this day to discuss the proposal. See Official Files, Brownlow Folder 3795, memorandum titled "National Resources Committee, Chairman of" (Feb. 8, 1936), FDRL.
24 The meeting included Merriam, National Resources Committee advisory board chair Frederic Delano, and secretary Charles Eliot II, and Secretary of the Interior Harold Ickes. Brownlow was in Florida at the time, and Ickes stayed for only a portion of the meeting.
25 Merriam to Brownlow (Feb. 20, 1936), PCAM, FDRL.

motivated, in part because, as noted in Chapter 2, Congress was beginning to launch its own study of the executive branch.[26] Also, Roosevelt
did not want a presidentially-appointed committee to bring forth recommendations with which he did not agree: "The President seemed appre-
hensive that recommendations might be brought in of a kind which might
embarrass him in the development of some alternative plan of his own.
What he had in mind apparently was, for example, a recommendation for
three or four Assistant Presidents or a recommendation for an Executive
Committee of the Cabinet."[27]

In fact, FDR wanted a broader study that examined the Comptroller-
General's functions, the organization of the Civil Service Commission, the
handling of executive orders, the delegation of powers to administrative

26 On Feb. 29, 1936, the Senate appointed the five-member Byrd Committee to examine
the executive branch organization "with special reference to overlapping and conflicting functions and simplification of the governmental structure." The Committee chair,
Harry Byrd, met with Brownlow on Mar. 4 to ask that Brownlow, Harold W. Dodd,
and Gulick advise the Senate Committee. Byrd told Brownlow that the Senate had authorized $20,000 for the study, and that it planned to ask the Brookings Institution to
undertake the actual research. The Senate Committee, Byrd assured Brownlow, was not
motivated by any desire to politically embarrass FDR.
    The Byrd Committee posed something of a dilemma to FDR. As Brownlow recorded
FDR's thinking: "if he took no action until the Senate committee came to see him that
two things would happen, that it might appear the Senate committee had forced his
hand, although as a matter of fact, he had been considering this problem for months,
and that it would leave the House of Representatives out." (Brownlow, *A Passion for
Anonymity*, p. 349). Roosevelt decided to have Brownlow draft letters to the Senate and
House leadership, suggesting that the House create a counterpart to the Byrd Committee. Brownlow wrote the letters, but he pointed out to FDR the long-run problems likely
to accrue if Roosevelt linked himself to the two congressional studies in addition to
sponsoring his own. In this, Brownlow was remarkably prescient. (See Brownlow's account of his meeting with FDR, summarized in memorandum A-II-7 [Mar. 4, 1936],
PCAM, FDRL, p. 6. See also Brownlow's memorandum to Delano [Mar. 5, 1936] expressing his reservations about three simultaneous studies [document A-II-10, PCAM,
FDRL].)
    To limit research overlap, Brownlow agreed to advise the Senate project, along with
Dodd and Gulick (who had also been suggested for the president's committee). But he
suggested dividing the labor, with the Byrd Committee examining broader questions of
department reorganization, and the President's committee focusing more narrowly on
issues of presidential management. Eventually the Byrd Committee and its companion
in the House, established on Apr. 29, 1936, jointly contracted with the Brookings Institution to conduct a survey of government organizations. Their report was submitted in
a series of installments to the Senate Committee, with the last segment transmitted June
19, 1937. See the *Brookings Report*.
27 Recall that FDR had tried both during his first term, with unenviable results. Memorandum, Merriam to Brownlow (Feb. 20, 1936), PCAM, FDRL.
    Roosevelt also worried about the politics of financing the study. For this reason, he
refused to accept Social Science Research Council funding because the SSRC received
money from the conservative Rockefeller Foundation. See Gulick's recollection in Frederick Mosher *The President Needs Help* (Lanham, Md.: University Press of America,
1988), pp. 25–6.

agencies, and the relationship between the emergency and permanent executive branch agencies.

Only after he defined the research agenda and assured himself of editorial control did Roosevelt agreed to sponsor the study. On Mar. 20, 1936, he formally appointed Brownlow, Merriam, and Gulick to the President's Committee on Administrative Management, better known as the Brownlow Committee.[28] It was attached as an adjunct to the National Emergency Council (NEC) and funded through relief appropriations.[29] Publicly, the Committee's mandate was to study "the relation to the existing regular organizations of the Executive Branch of the Government, of the many new agencies which have been created during the emergency."[30] In fact, however, the study's core objectives, as indicated by Brownlow's memoranda, were to strengthen FDR's staff resources, so

28 The Committee operated under a relative tight deadline; FDR wanted its Report in time to present to the 75th Congress, which took office in January 1937. However, the Committee was not to meet with FDR until after the November presidential election, in order to avoid charges that its recommendations were politically motivated.

29 Apparently, Roosevelt initially wanted the study conducted by the National Resource Committee's Advisory Committee working jointly with some but not all of the five-member NRC cabinet committee. However, by not including the entire NRC cabinet committee, some cabinet officers would undoubtedly be alienated. His solution was to exclude both the cabinet and the formal NRC advisory committee. In this way the Brownlow Committee was solely responsive to FDR, rather than to any cabinet members. See Barry Karl, *The Uneasy State: The United States from 1915 to 1945* (Chicago: University of Chicago Press, 1983), pp. 156–7.
   Others were apparently also considered for membership; Frank Lowden declined a position due to ill health, and Delano felt he could not serve while also chairing the NRC advisory committee. See Louis Brownlow, file copy, A-II-7 (Mar. 4, 1936), PCAM, FDRL, esp. p. 6. (According to Gulick, however, Lowden – a Midwest Republican – was prepared to chair the Committee if asked by FDR, but that FDR was never satisfied with the list of names given him to balance Lowden's selection. "I concluded that the White House staff buried it [list of prospective candidates] every time," Gulick recalled (see Mosher, *The President Needs Help*, pp. 29–30.)
   Funding was to prove another, and continuing, problem. Roosevelt's initial attempts to use $50,000 in emergency relief money to finance the study were ruled invalid by the Comptroller-General, thus forcing FDR to ask Congress to appropriate $100,000 to conduct the Brownlow study. But the Senate and House studies raised questions of duplication of effort and institutional prerogatives. Roosevelt's funding request was finally granted in late June 1936, with the provision that copies of the report be presented to Congress, and that the president's Committee focus on simplifying governmental activities with the goal of improving efficiency and achieving economy. However, by agreeing to give $20,000 of their appropriation to the Brookings Institution, which was working for the Senate, the Brownlow Committee exempted itself from the requirement to achieve economy. The Committee also gave $10,000 to the House committee and an additional $20,000 to the Senate Committee, leaving $50,000 for themselves. Of this total, it spent about $45,000. See "Journal," document A-II-58, PCAM, FDRL, esp. pp. 3–17; and Herbert Emmerich, *Federal Organization and Administrative Management*, (Birmingham: University of Alabama Press, 1971), p. 66.

30 This was for public consumption only; Roosevelt apparently thought it impolitic to boldly announce he wanted administrative authority commensurate with his growing

that he might acquire the necessary "information and recommendations," and strengthen his "managerial direction and control."[31]

In later years, Brownlow defended the Committee against charges it had sacrificed its intellectual independence to write a report catering to FDR's interests:

> We had been appointed to an official committee by the President and we thought we should consult him, especially about his office, inclining to the notion that he might know more about the presidency than any or all of us. And finally [the criticism] does not seem to have taken into consideration the possibility that perhaps the President persuaded us to his own view.[32]

Of course, as Peri Arnold points out,

> The committee's report was an eloquent call for presidential authority. Yet, in none of what it recommended was the committee simply a conduit for Roosevelt's views. . . .

responsibilities. Thus he and Brownlow decided "the springboard was to say that the time had come to consider the new agencies created during the emergency," were they to be made permanent, and if so, how to integrate them with existing agencies.

31 Brownlow had been appointed by FDR to chair the committee, and he had, at FDR's request, drafted a four-page project precis:

> What is needed is a careful study of the managerial and administrative relationships of the President to *all* the farflung and complicated agencies of the federal government. After all the President is responsible in fact if not always in law and cannot escape that responsibility. The recognition of this fact makes it impossible to devolve his prerogatives. . . . In its exercise [of these prerogatives] he must work with and through staff agencies for the control and direction of *fiscal, personnel, planning, legal* (?) aspects of all agencies.
>
> Over-all management requires coordination of all these relationships to make effective the President's responsible control but without depriving him of coordinate *information* and *recommendations* and without *adding to his burdens* and *by diminishing the number of agencies reporting directly to him*. (Brownlow memorandum [February 1936], PCAM, FDRL. [Underlining and question mark in parentheses in original; italics added].)

Much of this initial draft was incorporated into a later memorandum by Brownlow in which he formally stated the goals of the Brownlow Committee. See his "Management Study." The objectives were also reiterated in the Mar. 4 meeting between Brownlow and FDR:

> We discussed in considerable detail the problem of over-all management in the Government, the relation of the President to the staff agencies, the line agencies, and the regulatory bodies, and found ourselves in quite close agreement as to the nature of the problem.
>
> Essentially the problem is how to implement the President with simple but effective machinery which will enable him to exercise managerial direction and control appropriate to the burden of responsibility imposed upon him by the Constitution. (Brownlow memorandum for the record, document A-II-7, [Mar. 4, 1936], PCAM, FDRL, pp. 3–6).

32 Louis Brownlow, *The President and the Presidency* (Chicago: Public Administration Service, 1949), p. 106.

The Brownlow Committee devised recommendations that reflected Roosevelt's interests for a combination of reasons, the character of administrative theory, the political sophistication of its members, their admiration of Roosevelt, and their sense of crisis for democracy.[33] But if Roosevelt did not dictate the Report to the Committee, neither did he leave the final product to chance.[34] By sponsoring the study, Roosevelt positioned himself to block findings with which he did not agree. That included even the mildest attempts by the Committee to nudge him down the road toward a White House staff-centered presidential branch.

The study

After commissioning the Brownlow Committee and setting its research agenda, Roosevelt refrained from any further contact with its members until after his November 1936 reelection.[35] In the intervening months, the Committee conducted interviews, solicited reports, and gathered data,[36]

33 Arnold, *Making the Managerial Presidency*, pp. 106–7.
34 Indeed, he sanctioned the study only after determining the Committee's members, its mandate, its funding, the method of presidential supervision, the Committee's likely impact on his congressional relations, and the potential public relations fallout, if any.
35 However, the Committee continued to touch base with Roosevelt's White House aide Marvin McIntyre, usually to discuss administrative matters, such as funding. However, FDR ordered the Committee not to discuss the specifics of their activities with his personal White House assistants (Brownlow, *A Passion for Anonymity*, 441). As Brownlow noted in retrospect, "There was no doubt whatever that his [FDR's] secretaries, Stephen Early and Marvin H. Mcintyre had taken from the beginning a dim view of the whole procedure" (ibid., p. 394). In part, their opposition stemmed from their fear that FDR was treading in politically dangerous waters (ibid., p. 348).
36 The initial Committee meeting took place Apr. 11. Thereafter, a good deal of that month was spent creating the administrative infrastructure through which to conduct the study. Political scientist Joseph P. Harris was appointed staff director, responsible for staff management and securing financial support. A research staff, eventually numbering twenty-six, was assembled from among leading political scientists and public administration experts (six served as president of the American Political Science Association and, at the time of appointment, more than half held doctorates and about 70 percent were in academia).
    During a two-day staff conference Apr. 9–10, 1936, the three Committee members met with a group of fifteen staff members, reviewing the mandate and suggesting topics and methods of research. Brownlow pointed out that the time constraints under which they were operating prevented original data collection, and thus they were directed to "skim the cream off the top of their memories." Roosevelt wanted a report on "principles, not methodology," Brownlow told the staff (see "Minutes of the N.Y. Meeting, Apr. 9–10, 1936, PCAM, FDRL).
    During the summer months, while the staff compiled their studies, Brownlow and Merriam traveled in Europe, conducting interviews and reviewing administrative practices in several European governments. The frequency of the Committee meetings increased when the two committee members returned from Europe and the various supporting reports came trickling in. On Aug. 12, Harris complied a progress report of the various studies. Four days later he drafted a preliminary outline.

all guided by its fundamental objective: "[T]o discover and invent ways and means to give the president effective managerial direction and control commensurate with his responsibility over all departments and agencies of the executive branch of the Federal Government."37

Eventually, Committee thoughts began to crystallize around a two-part staff division, metaphorically described by staff members as the managerial "arms" and a coordinating "brain."38 The staff arms would help re-

The Committee met with most of the research staff during Aug. 17–19, and again to discuss individual reports with their respective authors on Sept. 2, 9, 23–7, and Oct. 3–4, 10–11, 16–18. Staff member James Fesler likened these to "the dissertation experience that I had experienced a year earlier." Mosher, *The President Needs Help*, p. 9. Herbert Emmerich, another participant, thought the conferences between the Committee and staff more useful than the Reports themselves, most of which were never used. "The real value of the research group was in their service as staff aides, advisers, and stimulators to Committee thinking" (Emmerich, *Federal Organization and Administrative Management*, p. 68).

37 Brownlow, "Management Study," pp. 1–2. See also the memorandum by Joseph Harris, the project's executive director, reiterating the by now familiar theme to focus on "executive management" rather than executive branch reorganization. By that he meant supplying the president with adequate staff resources for "planning, coordination, financial and personnel supervision. . . . It is important . . . that the Executive Office be developed on the side of management and administrative supervision as well as on the political side if its full possibilities are to be realized in national affairs" (Joseph Harris "A Tentative Draft of Memorandum Proposing An Inquiry into the Reorganization, Management, and Personnel of the Administrative Agencies, with Particular Reference to the New Independent Agencies," [Apr. 1936], document A-II-12, PCAM, FDRL, pp. 1, 3.

    Gulick later acknowledged: "The Committee wrote the introduction and the conclusions before the report was finalized because, truthfully, most commissions have their conclusions before they are appointed" (Gulick in Mosher, *The President Needs Help*, p. 6).

38 See, for example, Herbert Emmerich's memorandum listing four staffing alternatives, which differed only in the extent of the coordination power entrusted to the staff brain. Each of Emmerich's alternatives envision three managerial staff agencies: a "Planning Secretariat" for planning, the "Office of the Budget" for budgeting and fiscal affairs, the "Office of Legislative Counsel" for legislative and legal advice, and the "Office of the Executive Secretary to the President" to centralize staff coordination.

    The planning secretariat would handle: presidential liaison with executive branch departments, including research and statistical agencies; the provision of secretarial support for interdepartmental committees; clearance with executive departments of all programs submitted to, or initiated by, the president; serving as a secretariat to the cabinet, responsible for minutes, agendas, and circulating memoranda.

    The Office of Legislative Counsel would take charge of: clearing proposed or pending legislation; reviewing executive orders; and furnishing legal advice. The Office of the Budget, meanwhile, would continue the functions of the existing BoB, including rendering organizational advice. The Executive Secretary duties depended on the degree of coordinating authority entrusted to it. Curiously, his memo does not mention personnel management. See "Organization of President's Staff" with chart and memorandum from Herbert Emmerich to Joseph Harris (Oct. 29, 1936), document G-XX, PCAM, FDRL. Emmerich was serving in the Farm Credit Administration at this time. His views regarding the role of the president as administrative manager are summarized in Herbert Emmerich, *Essays on Federal Reorganization* (Birmingham, AL: University of Alabama Press, 1950).

duce bargaining uncertainty in the recurring budgeting, personnel, and policy planning processes. The brain would be responsible for coordinating the managerial activities on the president's behalf. Initially, both Brownlow and Merriam wanted to model the administrative brain after the British cabinet secretariat.[39] Comprised of a corps of permanent government officials headed by a career civil servant, the British cabinet secretariat provided administrative support for the Prime Minister's meetings with his ministers.[40] Although not formally charged with enforcing cabinet orders, the secretariat informally monitored compliance through routine interaction with careerists in the various ministries.[41]

The secretariat was not without critics, as Lindsay Rogers, a Brownlow Committee staff member, admitted. Some felt it unnecessarily interposed itself between the Prime Minister and the cabinet ministries.[42] Others believed that Maurice Hankey, who headed the secretariat, wielded excessive power with little accountability.[43]

39 Recall that both had conducted several interviews with European government officials, including members of the British civil service. Additional input about the British system came from political scientists Lindsay Rogers, Arthur Holcombe, Harold Laski, and Herman Finer. See in particular Lindsay Rogers, "The British and French Cabinet-Secretariats," document G-XXVII, PCAM, FDRL, and Arthur Holcombe, "The Administrative Principles Exemplified by the War Department General Staff and Their Applicability to the Civil Departments and Establishments of the Federal Government," (with Annexes prepared by Merle Fainsod), (Aug. 15, 1936), document G-V, PCAM, FDRL.

40 The British staff secretariat, which grew out of the British Committee on Imperial Defence during World War I, prepared and circulated cabinet agendas, meeting minutes, and background briefing papers, and informed ministries of the cabinet's decisions. In 1936 it was headed by Maurice Hankey, assisted by a private secretary, a deputy secretary, a principal on detail from Treasury, and a chief clerk. Typically, Hankey met with the Prime Minister to develop a cabinet agenda, then directed his staff to gather relevant information for distribution to the cabinet ministers prior to the cabinet meeting. To help with preparation, members of the secretariat attended cabinet and subcabinet meetings. There were also a number of interdepartmental committees operating on both the cabinet and the subcabinet level, and Hankey's organization often provided the secretariat for these meetings as well. "The indirect results of this phase of the cabinet secretariat's work cannot be measured. There are innumerable improvements and adjustments in intradepartmental administration," Rogers told the Committee (Rogers, "The British and French Cabinet-Secretariats," pp. 53, 56–8). See also "Minutes of Meeting of Committee" (Aug. 17, 1936), document A-II 33a, PCAM, FDRL, p. 17; Brownlow, *A Passion for Anonymity*, p. 357. On Hankey's role, see John F. Naylor, *A Man and an Institution: Sir Maurice Hankey, the Cabinet Secretariat and the Custody of Cabinet Secrecy* (New York: Cambridge University Press, 1984).

41 This informal consultation between secretariat members and those in the ministries also provided smoother coordination of departmental work as well as better preparation for cabinet meetings.

42 Critics argued that this was especially true under Prime Minister David Lloyd during the immediate post – World War I era, when the secretariat allegedly siphoned functions from the Foreign Office.

43 This was Harold Laski's concern, as reported by Brownlow. However, Herman Finer felt the "system wouldn't run without him [Hankey]" ("Minutes of the Meeting," PCAM,

But Brownlow's enthusiasm for instituting a prototype of the British cabinet secretariat was bolstered by his talk with Tom Jones, a former secretary to the British Prime Minister, who told Brownlow: "[Y]ou have just got one thing to do. You have got to look all over the United States and find the Maurice Hankey and persuade Roosevelt to put him in and the rest of your report will be written in action rather than on the typewriter."[44]

It was Jones who also provided the famous job description for Hankey's counterpart that Brownlow, to Roosevelt's amusement, incorporated into the final Brownlow Report: "[Jones] said, 'I think I can put it in one sentence: He should be a man of tremendous physical vitality with a passion for anonymity.'"[45]

But if the British secretariat concept appealed to the Committee, there remained the question of implementing it in a presidential, as opposed to a prime ministerial cabinet government.[46] Rogers proposed establishing a permanent cabinet secretariat, staffed by careerists, but headed by a presidential appointee.[47] This appointee would help bridge the gap between the permanent secretariat and the president's political staff of personal aides.[48]

> FDRL, pp. 12–15.) Rogers conceded Hankey's influence, but argued that "a person who heads an organization like Hankey's must be powerful in order to make that organization successful." If Hankey was powerful, he was also, according to Rogers, indifferent to policy. Furthermore, his power was often used to prevent the secretariat from meddling in issues, such as policy implementation, with which it had no business (ibid., pp. 64–5).
>
> Hankey later wrote about his wartime experiences in the British secretariat. See Maurice Hankey, *Government Control in War* (New York: Cambridge University Press, 1947).
>
> 44 "Minutes of Meeting of Committee," pp. 19–20. Additional support for the cabinet secretariat system came from Walter Runciman, a British cabinet minister. He told Brownlow that without the secretariat, the British governing system would have "broken down" in the face of the great increase "in the activities of government, with consequently increasing complexities."
> 45 Ibid., pp. 19–20. Brownlow records that when Roosevelt first read the phrase, he burst out laughing.
> 46 As Rogers noted: "One problem that would have to be faced is that of a secretariat's personnel holding on from one administration to another. . . . If President Roosevelt were to attempt to set up a cabinet secretariat and were to choose as its head a man who was not interested in politics; who was admirably equipped for the post and who for four years did the job especially well, it is almost inconceivable that President Roosevelt's successor, even though he were of the same political party, would not want to put in his own man" (ibid., pp. 58–9).
> 47 In effect, emulating the BoB, which was staffed by careerists but headed by a presidential political appointee. Ibid., pp. 59–60.
> 48 "It seems to me that in the United States there is not much of a problem along these lines. The cabinet secretariat could attempt what Hankey's show attempts in Great Britain. It could be attempted in the name of the cabinet, but it would really work for the President. Its functions would go no further than they go in Great Britain. At the head of the secretariat would have to be a person in whom the President felt great personal confidence. . . . [H]e should probably be on par with the director of the budget" (ibid., 62–3).

A similar plan was proposed by political scientist William Y. Elliott, who suggested using the NEC's administrative support staff as the core of an expanded presidential staff secretariat: "As I see it . . . we should have in the Secretariat, around the President, a reconditioned N.E.C. or something of that sort of administrative council, a group of assistants to the President."[49]

Efforts to incorporate a British-style staff secretariat, however, had one major drawback: They were perceived to link the president too closely to his cabinet. By 1936, of course, FDR did not hold the cabinet-based NEC in high regard, a point reiterated in several reports submitted to the Committee.[50] His dissatisfaction with the NEC, or any cabinet coordinating committee, apparently prompted the Brownlow Committee to

Rogers envisioned utilizing the NEC's support staff as the nucleus of this secretariat, perhaps by merging it with the White House Executive Clerk's office under the direction of an executive secretary appointed by the president. "The Forster side of the White House executive offices would probably become in considerable measure part of a cabinet secretariat. The President's personal secretariat would continue to do everything that it does now with the exception of routing executive business to him. It would maintain liaison with Congress, relations with the press, arrange appointments . . . interest itself in patronage, do ghost writing, etc." Others might be drawn from the Army or Navy. These careerists, by retaining rank in the armed services, would have the prestige to withstand political pressures. They would also provide the agency with the expertise needed to deal with defense-related issues ("Journal of Meetings of PCAM," PCAM, FDRL, pp. 17, 59–62.

49 "It will be seen that the organization of the President's machinery of control at the present time presents no such central agency, outside of the working of the National Emergency Council. . . . [H]e [FDR] obviously feels it necessary to increase the Cabinet somewhere to around 15 members, with the possibility that one or more of them may be members without portfolios, or may combine several agencies now existing. But it is apparent he is convinced . . . that all work of administrative coordination of management requires that it be done below the Cabinet level. He feels strongly, I judge, that he requires several administrative assistants. These assistants would be allotted functions not along the lines of the existing vertical divisions of the Cabinet. For example, I should think so far as I could gather, that he might well choose about four or five of them, one for Social Security in all its aspects, one for fiscal aspects of government, one for conservation of the general programs, which might well include physical planning, one for commercial policy and finally one to deal with the functions that center around the national defense policy in the broadest aspect" (see William Y. Elliott, "The President's Role in Administrative Management," PCAM, FDRL, p. 2).

Elliott elaborated his vision of an enhanced NEC staff in a discussion with Robert Randall, a member of the National Resources Committee: "There would, of course, have to be some sort of Cabinet Secretary who would to some degree insist on getting everyone to clear all matters through him and the Secretariat before coming to the President. . . . Also . . . this new sort of Secretariat for the President would not affect his private secretaries. They are, or should be, engaged in a different sort of activity. Relations with them should be cordial and cooperative" (notes of Elliott's talk with Robert Randall, of the National Resources Committee [cover letter dated Aug. 17, 1936], document GXX, Brownlow Files, John F. Kennedy Library [hereafter JFKL], p. 5).

50 As Frank Walker, the NEC's former executive secretary, admitted, the NEC was not a "guiding force in the direction of governmental policy." Instead, Walker thought it more effective as a liaison device providing department and agency heads regular access to the

back away from plans that even remotely appeared to lean toward "cabinet government."[51]

Instead, as revealed by Brownlow's Nov. 5 draft outline (which evidently amplified ideas in an earlier memorandum submitted by Herbert Emmerich), the Committee decided to recommend vesting significant staff oversight functions in a staff agency separate from the cabinet.[52] This staff entity would report directly to the president and would be responsible for coordinating the other managerial agencies.

president. "Mr. Walker," Harris reported, "thought the important thing was for the President to have an opportunity to talk to and with the heads of those agencies without much regard to what he talked about, and in this way to give the heads of these agencies the feeling of personal contact with the President which some of them would not get otherwise ("Confidential Memorandum on the National Emergency Council," J. P. Harris [Aug. 15, 1936], document G-II, Brownlow Files, JFKL).

Furthermore, as Harris noted, even when the NEC performed a policy-making role during its first months of existence, it focused primarily on the emergency agencies, not the regular departments. As the New Deal emergency activities were reduced and routinized the functions performed by the NEC's support staff changed from administering council meetings to supporting field service functions. Of 475 total employees, 214 were in the state offices, and another 35 worked in Washington, D.C. offices coordinating the field services. In contrast, the Executive Director's office employed 10 people, with another 64 in the Administrative Division.

Indeed, the BoB recommended curtailing the NEC entirely, reducing its staff, and integrating it into the budget bureau. "The Report recommended that the service of the National Emergency Council should be greatly curtailed and the organization should be place in the Budget Bureau" ("Notes upon a Survey of the National Emergency Council by Mr. Ahern of the Budget Bureau, made in June 1936, at the Request of Mr. Allison," document G-XII, Brownlow Papers, JFKL).

51 At a more basic level, the Brownlow Committee's negative reaction to the Elliott/Rogers plan suggests they saw a difference in principle between presidential and prime ministerial forms of government. In the presidential system, where political responsibility for presidential decision making is centered in the president alone, the staff secretariat would be totally ineffective as a coordinating device, or it would pose a threat to presidential leadership – there could be no middle ground.

52 "Memo, Nov. 5, 1939, Brownlow, dictated in New York," document A-II-33, PCAM, FDRL, pp. 1–3, and organizational chart titled "Possible Organization of President's Staff" [Nov. 5, 1936]. See also Brownlow, *A Passion for Anonymity*, p. 376; and "Organization of President's Staff," with chart and memorandum from Herbert Emmerich to Joseph Harris (Oct. 29, 1936), document G-XX; PCAM; FDRL.

Brownlow assigned his White House secretariat functions that represented a meshing of some of the roles Emmerich assigned to the Executive Office and the Planning Secretariat. Brownlow's White House staff would:

1. Maintain contact with all research and statistical agencies and advise the president as to the proper sources of information on matters of interest to him. 2. Maintain liaison between the president and interdepartmental and other committees on policy and programs; transmit the president's views to them and vice versa; also report to the president on the progress made by such committees. 3. Provide for clearance of programs submitted to the president or initiated by him, with all departments affected. 4. Recommend to the president the abolition or creation of committees on policy or programs, and suggest projects to be undertaken by them. 5. Upon request of the president, act as secretary to the cabinet,

The proposed relationship between the central executive coordinating staff and the BoB proved, however, to be a sticking point.[53] At one point, the Committee considered having the BoB, rather than another staff entity, take responsibility for staff coordination, in addition to its managerial functions.[54] Eventually, however, it backed away from this and instead adopted a middle ground: The BoB would expand beyond its traditional budgeting activities to handle most of the managerial functions, including budgeting and accounting, but also legislative research and coordination. But it would not be responsible for coordinating staff.[55] That task was to be entrusted to a separate White House "Executive Secretariat," headed by an Executive Secretary reporting directly to the president. In Brownlow's outline, the Executive Secretary was assisted by five assistants, all "government career men," supplemented by others loaned

preparing agenda, minutes, briefs memoranda, and so forth, for the expedition of its business. 6. Direct the activities of a small staff of specialists in various phases of federal service.

53 In mid-October, the Committee met with Emmerich, Daniel Bell, and William McReynolds to "discuss the problem of the location of the Bureau of the Budget, [and] the question whether it should be made a staff agency in other than budgetary matters" ("Journal of Meetings of PCAM," PCAM, FDRL, p. 17).

54 Arthur Holcombe, for one, had suggested transforming the BoB into an "Office of Fiscal Economics and Administration," in effect making it the general staff to the president, albeit with an economic orientation. Under Holcombe's plan, the BoB, numbering close to 100 members, would be divided into eight divisions, each dealing with a different policy area: budgeting, monetary policy and banking, agriculture, and so forth. A chief of staff appointed by the president would attempt, through formal power and informal consultation, to coordinate the range of departmental and agency activities falling within these policy areas. But, Holcombe hinted, this office might also develop into a more powerful coordinating device: "[T]he logic of the development envisaged in this memorandum might seem to imply transforming the Bureau of the Budget into such a super-staff agency directly attached to the office of the President, and concentrating within it all of the functions of over-all management, including financial control, personnel administration, material and procurement, planning, reporting, and proposed legislation and executive orders" (Holcombe "The Administrative Principles Exemplified by the War Department General Staff," pp. 26–8).

Meriam, however, felt less sanguine regarding plans to make the BoB a general coordinating instrument. "The difficulty in my judgement is that our modern problems do not fall into departments of knowledge. They cut across them. We need not an Economic General Staff made up of economists but a general staff that can bring to bear on the current problems expert knowledge on every aspect of that problem" (undated memorandum from Lewis Meriam to Joseph Harris regarding "The Administrative Principles Exemplified by the War Department General Staff," document G-IV, Brownlow Papers, JFKL, p. 2.) He proposed instead creating a separate staff agency, albeit one closely tied to the BoB. Meriam thought this "central agency" might consist of individuals detailed from existing departments, as well as outside experts brought in for varying periods depending on the requirements of the case at hand. This new agency would report directly to the President, but work closely with the BoB and committees in Congress. "I should hope that the whole central agency of administration would play close team ball with Congress as a whole and especially with the appropriation committees of Congress."

55 See Brownlow's Nov. 5 draft outline listing four BoB divisions for budgeting, research and coordination, accounting, and legal issues.

from existing departments and agencies. Only the Executive Secretary would be located in the White House; his assistants' offices were to be next door in the State, War and Navy Building (the Old Executive Office Building).[56]

In the three days after Brownlow submitted this proposal, the Committee and staff huddled in what Brownlow described as "perhaps the most significant and deterministic sessions."[57] From these meetings a penultimate draft, entitled "Tentative Outline on Administrative Management in the Federal Government," was produced.[58]

The most notable change in this version was a distinct muting of the coordinating powers entrusted to the "Executive Secretariat." Rather than a separate staff coordinating agency, the Committee now suggested simply expanding the existing White House office by adding several administrative assistants under the direction of an "executive secretary" who clearly would not be mistaken for an "Assistant President"[59]:

> His effectiveness in assisting the President will, we think, be directly proportional to his ability to discharge his functions with restraint. He will remain in the background, issue no orders, make no deci-

56 Ibid.
57 Brownlow, *A Passion for Anonymity*, p. 378.
58 "Tentative Outline on Administrative Management in the Federal Government," document A-II-39 (no date), PCAM, FDRL. In addition to clarifying the functions of the proposed "executive secretariat" this draft more clearly delineated the roles of the institutional staff agencies serving the president in the areas of finance, personnel, planning, research, and the clearance of executive orders and rules. In this regard five proposals were made:

> 1. Transfer the power to settle accounts and supervise accounting systems from the General Accounting Office to the Treasury. 2. Strengthen the Bureau of the Budget and charge it with continually researching administrative problems. 3. Reorganize personnel administration in the government under a single Civil Service Commissioner, advised by a citizen board (to serve without salary), and extend the merit system to all positions except those that are policy determining. 4. Provide a permanent agency to facilitate long-term planning and to guide and coordinate research on current programs affecting several departments or agencies. 5. Improve the machinery for the preparation and clearance of executive orders and administrative rules.

Each recommendation was elaborated in subsequent pages and were eventually incorporated into the final version of the Report without much change. Of particular importance were provisions to strengthen the Bureau of the Budget through increased appropriations, a larger staff, and the creation of a research division to carry out BoB's statutory duties to improve government management. This latter function had heretofore remained largely unfulfilled. In addition, the BoB was to assimilate the informational, coordinating and legislative clearance functions then assigned to the NEC.
59 To wit: "1. Equip the President with staff assistance on administrative problems. Enlarge the White House secretariat by the addition of an Executive Secretary and a small corps of assistants specifically to aid the President in his administrative duties." The Executive Secretary would be assisted by "highly qualified associates in the office of the White House," to assist the president "in maintaining contact (a) with operating departments and establishments which do the work of government; (b) with the staff and

sions, emit no public statements. He will facilitate rather than impede appropriate, direct access to the President. He will punctiliously refrain from assuming any authority that could possibly lead to his role being construed as that of 'Assistant President.'[60]

In his autobiography, Brownlow says conversations with Roosevelt and Frank Lowden (then the chair of the Public Administration Clearing House), as well as internal Committee deliberations, prompted the decision to minimize the coordinating functions originally envisioned for the "executive secretariat."[61] As he recalled, "[I]n our conversations with the President, the members of the Committee . . . found Mr. Roosevelt reluctant to set up any sort of secretariat under one person. After hearing him at length we agreed with him, and came to recommend a corps of administrative assistants instead of an administrative secretariat under a single head."[62]

But even this went too far for FDR. On Nov. 14, 1936, the Committee (minus Merriam) met the newly reelected president at the White House to discuss the latest draft.[63] Although FDR reacted quite favorably to the preliminary outline, saying it was in the right direction, he balked at the idea of a fifth assistant serving as a de facto staff director, citing his experiences with Richberg and others.[64] Brownlow backtracked, suggesting formally assigning this fifth executive assistant responsibility for planning and personnel, while tacitly allowing him to function as primus inter pares. Roosevelt accepted the compromise: "Yes, that's the person who never goes out." He reserved the right to specify who that would be, and the extent of coordinating duties the person might assume. Such privileges would not be institutionalized through formal designation. Subsequently,

---

60 control agencies which keep the machinery going; and (c) with the planning activities and committees" (ibid., 1–2).

60 Ibid., p. 4. This draft also incorporated Jones' famous description of qualities needed by the executive assistant. "It is essential . . . that the Executive Secretary shall be a man of 'high competence, great physical vigor, and a passion for anonymity.'"

Assisted by "five or six" assistants (some of them detailed from other parts of the government) he would "insure that all matters coming to his [the president's] attention have been examined from the overall managerial or housekeeping point of view, as well as from all standpoints that would bear on policy and operation." The assistants would also transmit presidential decisions to ensure "coordinated cooperation" from affected agencies. Roosevelt's political secretaries would continue "in their work of aiding the president in his relations with the public, with the Congress, and with press; the Executive Secretary and his assistants would aid the president in his relations with the administrative departments and agencies" (ibid., p. 4).

61 Brownlow, *A Passion for Anonymity*, pp. 376–7.

62 Louis Brownlow, *The President and the Presidency*, pp. 105–6.

63 Brownlow, *A Passion for Anonymity*, pp. 381–2.

64 Gulick reports that Roosevelt said, "You can't have just one Executive secretary. The damn columnists would never let him alone. They are always looking for the 'white haired boy.' Just now they are writing up Corcoran. Way back it was Raymond Moley, and there was no truth in that either" (ibid., p. 381).

however, FDR never even implicitly followed Brownlow's advice; no aide was ever designated responsibility for managing other staff on FDR's behalf. That function he reserved for himself.[65]

By rejecting plans to institute an executive secretariat, FDR reaffirmed the fundamental principle governing his use of staff. As Karl put it, Roosevelt realized that "the problem of information was the central problem of the presidency, given the essential isolation and singularity of its constitutional responsibility."[66] Roosevelt himself explained to the Committee that he wanted the "Executive Assistant[s] to the President" to operate largely as extensions of himself, acting as his eyes, ears, and voice in gathering and transmitting information and expertise vis à vis the executive branch.[67] One assistant would report on foreign affairs, FDR said. He would start out the day "talking to [Secretary of State Cordell] Hull, then go to Treasury, Agriculture, etc. . . . touching foreign relations wherever it was." Another assistant would cover business relations, a third financial affairs, the fourth welfare and conservation.[68] Because FDR alone bore the impact of his bargaining choices, however, he refused to delegate staff "coordination" to any single subordinate. That remained a presidential prerogative.

Summary: Roosevelt's plan for organizing the presidency

Roosevelt's administrative philosophy, as expressed in the Brownlow Committee Report, is clearly antithetical to subsequent staff developments during the last half century.[69] The critical difference is in the realm of White House staffing. Despite Brownlow's efforts to create even a diluted version of the British staff secretariat, Roosevelt would accept in the final Report only the exceedingly vague recommendation to augment his White House staff by a handful of executive assistants to serve as liaison with a rapidly expanding executive branch.[70] Brownlow himself, after conferring with FDR, wrote this section dealing with the White House

65 Karl, *Executive Reorganization and Reform in the New Deal*, p. 245.
66 Ibid., p. 246.
67 In effect, they would continue the functions already performed by men like Cohen and Corcoran who served on detail from other departments.
68 Note the similarity here to what Roosevelt discussed with Elliott that summer, during the Committee's deliberations. This suggests FDR had a firm and relatively consistent notion of what he wanted from these additional staff members.
69 "None of these concepts [in the Brownlow Report] survive," James Fesler commented fifty years after it was published. See his remarks in Mosher, *The President Needs Help*, pp. 15–18.
70 Roosevelt told the Committee, "I thought the White House office was all set for 25 years, but already it is too small."

Office.[71] The passage is noteworthy for the care Brownlow took in specifying what these assistants would *not* do as much as what they might accomplish.

The White House Office, he wrote, was to be increased "by not more than six administrative assistants." As Gulick recalled, the number of assistants envisioned was not chosen at random. The Committee did *not* expect that as the demands increased on the president the number could be revised upward. "You will remember that your committee reached the conclusion that the staff in the White House should be distinctly limited. What we suggested was not in excess of six technical experts as additional assistants," Gulick recalled.[72] James Fesler, a research assistant for the Brownlow Committee, amplifies this point: "[T]he number of aides, both secretaries and assistants, was about ten, a number permitting the President to give personal direction to his staff and to have regular meetings of the whole group. No question was likely to arise as to 'what did the President know and when did he know it.'"[73]

In short, by keeping the White House staff small, FDR could more easily supervise its activities, thereby reducing his management costs.[74] Moreover, their activities were severely circumscribed. Gone were Brownlow's expansive and detailed listings of staff functions. Instead, as Fesler recalls: "[T]he aides were to engage purely in staff assistance activities that facilitated the president's own decision-making and communicated his decisions to affected agencies. They were not to involve themselves in line (operational) activities."[75]

Finally, these individuals would remain in the background, issue no orders, make no decisions, emit no public statements – in short they would have few opportunities to escape anonymity. Rather than assistant presidents, they were to be little more than presidential "gofers," working alongside FDR's political secretaries who continued to assist the president in his dealings with the public, the Congress, and the press. To be sure, Roosevelt expected that each assistant would build up an area of expertise within his locus of activities; thus, one would emphasize foreign policy, another legal matters, and so on. But they were not to formulate policy in these areas; their duties were primarily liaison and information transmission.[76]

71 Ibid., p. 14.
72 Gulick, in Mosher, *The President Needs Help*, p. 7.
73 Fesler, in Mosher, *The President Needs Help*, p. 15.
74 Note that the Committee also recommended the president be provided a discretionary fund through which to hire detailees and other experts as needed. *Brownlow Committee Report*, pp. 5–6.
75 Ibid.
76 Moreover, FDR was unwilling to have those functions codified in statute.

But if Roosevelt resisted every effort to bureaucratize a specialized corps of White House – based advisers, he accepted the Committee's proposals to strengthen the non-White House managerial staff. These institutional staff agencies were responsible for the "great managerial functions of the Government which affect all the administrative departments," including "personnel management, fiscal and organizational management, and planning management."[77]

In effect, then, the Committee established a two-part distinction in staff: "managerial" and personal.[78] Indeed, the most controversial portions of the Report were those advocating stronger staff arms to assist the president in budgeting, planning and personnel.[79] Specifically, these recommendations include:

1. *Budgeting:* Strengthen the BoB's fiscal and budgeting policy role; increase the Director's staff; have him attend Cabinet meetings and report directly to the President. Also, enhance the BoB's administrative research functions; emphasize its watchdog role overseeing the expenditure of federal funds; and expand its legislative clearance of both enrolled bills and executive orders.[80]

2. *Planning:* Institutionalize the National Resources Board [at the time operating under the provisions of executive order] through legislation. The NRB would function as a clearinghouse for planning-related information; collect and analyze data regarding the nation's natural resources;

77 See the *Brownlow Committee Report*, p. 6; and sections II. Personnel Management, III. Fiscal Management, and IV. Planning Management, pp. 7–30.

78 Karl calls this distinction the most important contribution the Brownlow Committee made: "What the Committee had done, in effect, was to distinguish two forms of information relevant to administration, only one form of which could be directly and specifically defined as administrative information – that relating immediately to the three managerial functions. The other form of information came specifically from concerns in the world itself and were scientific or diplomatic or economic or sociological – anything which circumstances would, from time to time, define them as being," (Karl, *Executive Reorganization and Reform in the New Deal*, p. 243).

79 *Brownlow Committee Report*, p. 6.

80 Roosevelt began immediately upgrading the BoB, despite the two-year delay in implementing the Committee's plan, by doubling its appropriations and manpower. Congress, in its second Deficiency Appropriation Act (June 25, 1938) authorized a supplementary BoB appropriation for fiscal year 1939 of $132,710, almost equal to the original appropriation of $187,000. Acting director Bell argued that the money was necessary to hire fifty-five additional employees in light of the increased demands for BoB services. Roosevelt followed up by appointing Harold Smith as a full-time, permanent BoB director on Mar. 8, 1939. See A. J. Wann, *The President as Chief Administrator: A Study of Franklin D. Roosevelt*, (Washington, D.C.: Public Affairs Press, 1968), p. 163.

cooperate with state and local agencies to facilitate resource planning; and generally substitute "careful scientific study" for political expediency in making national resource policy. In short, operate as a general long-range policy planning staff – preparing reports, conducting research, gathering data – but not as a decisionmaking body.[81]

3. *Personnel*: Replace the three-person Civil Service Commission with a single personnel director appointed by the President, subject to Senatorial confirmation. This director would advise the President on personnel issues, subject to oversight by a seven-person (non-salaried) personnel board, also appointed by the President with Senatorial consent, whose members served overlapping terms. The board would act in effect as a watchdog, meeting periodically to review presidential personnel policy.[82]

Two related subjects – fiscal and accounting procedures,[83] and executive branch administration, including reorganization – were also ad-

---

81 The Committee suggested a five-member board, appointed by the president, serving with no salary and for indefinite terms. The board would be supported by a staff of careerists, specialists detailed for short periods from departments, and other experts brought in during emergencies. The director would be appointed by the board, and the board itself would be funded through annual appropriations. The *Brownlow Committee Report*, pp. 27–30.

 At this time the NRC had expanded to a staff of about 200. See Roth, *The Executive Office of the President*, pp. 168–9.

82 The Committee also proposed a system of pay raises for cabinet heads, their assistants, and members of the higher civil service. The *Brownlow Committee Report*, pp. 12–14. Reform of the civil service board would be accompanied by an extension of the merit system to cover all nonpolicy-making positions (in effect, leaving only the following civilian positions to be filled by presidential appointment: departmental secretaries, as well as assistant and undersecretary positions; the regulatory commissions; the diplomatic posts; and the heads of several bureaus and agencies with policy functions).

83 Specifically, the Committee argued that fiscal procedures in the United States were hampered by four defects: the understaffed BoB; an overly powerful Comptroller-General's Office; the absence of a truly independent agency to conduct post-audits of government transactions, and the lack of an efficient system of accounts and records. The Committee was particularly critical of the Comptroller-General's ability to both rule on the legality of government financial transactions prior to their occurrence, and then to conduct post-audits of those transactions. The Committee believed that spending appropriated funds was an executive prerogative, while the ability to audit those transactions was strictly legislative. The Comptroller-General's Office, as an independent agency, surely could not legitimately do both.

 To counter this, the Committee recommended vesting control of much of the accounting system in the Secretary of the Treasury under the president's direction, while limiting the Comptroller-General to auditing expenditures after they occur. This would entail changing the title of the Comptroller-General to the Auditor-General, and that of the General Accounting Office to the General Auditing Office. The *Brownlow Committee Report*, pp. 21–5.

dressed.[84] Although important components of the entire Report, these sections are less germane to the argument here and thus will not be discussed. The cabinet, the Committee thought, should function "more or less as a council of state upon which the president may rely for advice and whose jurisdictional differences of opinion he will have the power and authority to umpire."[85] Aided by assistant and under secretaries chosen by the president, the cabinet secretaries would formulate departmental policy.[86]

84 Executive branch reorganization, the Committee argued, was "inherently executive in character." Its purpose was to reduce the president's administrative span of control but without bringing unrelated activities within one department. To accomplish this, the Committee suggested two broad strategies: centralizing policy making at the top, while decentralizing administration of departmental activities toward state and local agencies. This would encompass four tactics: creating two cabinet-level departments to deal with social welfare and public works; requiring the president to determine on a continuing basis the appropriate functions of each department; equipping the president with the management tools necessary to undertake that responsibility; and developing an independent audit function to ensure executive accountability. Other than the specific recommendations for two new cabinet departments, then, the Report stayed clear of specifying where existing bureaus and agencies should be moved. *Brownlow Committee Report*, pp. 33–6.
    The Committee also proposed a number of additional changes to facilitate presidential control of the executive branch. First, it advocated replacing boards and commissions with single directors, in order to improve accountability.
    Second, it proposed giving the president continuing reorganization authority. Congress would retain administrative influence through its appropriation authority, postaudit functions, and investigatory powers. Ibid., p. 37.
    Third, the Committee recommended that government corporations be brought under existing departments, to act as semiautonomous divisions. The Committee acknowledged that these corporations served useful functions, but argued that accountability was a problem. Most had been authorized during periods of financial depression. There generally were two types:
        1. business corporations that had federal charters but privately held stock; among the approximately 14,000 corporations in this category were farm loan associations, credit unions, and saving and loans institutions. 2. "Government corporations," which were federally owned and controlled; these included the RFC, the FDIC, the TVA, the Federal Surplus Commodity Corporation – altogether about 90 such corporations were active. Ibid., pp. 43–6.
    Fourth, it advocated placing the administrative functions of all independent regulatory commissions within existing departments, headed by a career civil servant responsible to the department secretary. The commissions' judicial functions, on the other hand, would remain wholly independent of the departments and the president. The Committee believed that by exercising both judicial and executive authority, regulatory commissions violated the constitutionally mandated separation of powers and raised questions of accountability.
    Under its recommendations, officials performing judicial activities would be appointed by the president, with senatorial consent, serving staggered terms. Ibid., pp. 39–42.
    Fifth, the BoB would act as a presidential staff agency investigating organizational questions and helping adjudicate jurisdictional disputes between two or more departments.
85 Ibid., 46–7.
86 Departmental organizational issues, however, would fall under the supervision of careerists serving in each institution. Ibid., pp. 36–8.

Although the Committee's recommendations proved controversial, they are in one sense distinctly limited in scope. Presidential functions, Committee members believed, encompass three general tasks: political leadership, ceremonial duties, and administrative functions. In writing the Report, however, the Committee focused solely on the latter function; in their words, the inquiry was limited to the "realm of administrative management."[87]

Critics have charged that in so doing the Committee placed unrealistic faith in an administrative–political dichotomy. In fact, however, Committee members themselves adopted no such scheme. Instead, the decision to couch the Report in terms of general administrative principles, refraining from specific policy recommendations, was largely politically motivated. True, they hoped to make FDR view his administrative needs not just in light of his immediate political situation, but from the long-term interests of the presidency as well.[88] But they wrote the Report in "neutral" language in order to reduce the political opposition it engendered.[89]

Despite their best efforts to minimize the political aspects of the recommendations, however, the Brownlow Committee Report was viewed by Congress, and others, as a thoroughly presidential document. Its operating assumption was clearly spelled out in FDR's introductory statement (which was in fact written by Gulick): The Committee's recommendations provided "tools of management and authority to distribute the work so that the President can effectively discharge these powers which the Constitution now places on him."[90] The Committee, defending their quest to strengthen the presidency, argued that augmenting the president's management tools in fact *increased* presidential accountability by improving the president's actual control of the government. Accountability, in turn, was the cornerstone of effective democratic government.[91]

---

87 Nor, wrote the Committee, was the immediate objective to save money, although that would be an incidental outcome should the recommendations be implemented. Ibid., p. 51.

88 Roosevelt, according to Gulick, "was personally inclined to drive for great ideas with great enthusiasm and so was less inclined to the routines of good budgeting, good personnel administration, and the organization of planning staff. 'Sure, that's right, but what are we going to do about our enemies over there who are getting us into all kinds of trouble.' Brownlow and Merriam would bring him back to the details" (Mosher *The President Needs Help*, pp. 3–7).

89 "We were trying very hard to keep government reorganization out of politics," Gulick recalled fifty years later. "We had to be very careful not to let the legislative branch get the feeling that they were being downgraded." A committee staff member, John Millet, concurs: "It has been my conception that the effort to draw a distinction between politics and administrative management in 1936 was a political decision."

In retrospect, James Fesler, another staff member, acknowledges that the attempt to emphasize administration and not politics might be regarded as "naive." See Gulick's, Millet's and Fesler's retrospective evaluations of the Brownlow Committee in Mosher, *The President Needs Help*, pp. 3–7, 18, 23, 29, 59.

90 *Brownlow Committee Report*, p. v.   91 Ibid.

In the final analysis, however, the distinctly presidential perspective of the Report, no matter how justified, was bound to stimulate congressional opposition. Roosevelt's tactical errors in his presentation and during the ensuing legislative battle to implement the Report merely compounded the problem. The result was a two-year delay before any of the Committee's recommendations became law.[92]

Epilogue: From Report to law

On Jan. 10, 1937, the Brownlow Committee Report was publicly unveiled, together with proposed legislation embodying its recommendations, in a White House conference attended by congressional leaders and others.[93] Roosevelt, showing total mastery of the material, presented a forthright overview of the proposals, a four-hour presentation whose "suggestion of radical changes necessarily shocked Congressional habit patterns."[94] Brownlow recalled: "They could scarcely believe their ears."[95] Ominously, congressional leaders said nothing as Roosevelt discussed plans to bring all the regulatory agencies within the purview of the twelve cabinet departments.

Roosevelt's presentation at this meeting is noteworthy for its clear enunciation of the functional division between a White House personal staff and the managerial staff agencies. His choice of words suggests that

92 Bills incorporating almost all the Committee's recommendations were introduced in the first session of the 75th Congress in 1937. In the House, the proposals were spread among four different measures; in the Senate they were combined in one omnibus bill. Two of the bills quickly passed the House, including one providing for six administrative assistants. The Senate, meanwhile, held hearings, but took no action. Early in the third session of the same Congress, Senator Byrnes, working on Roosevelt's behalf, introduced a new omnibus bill that included the provisions of the two bills that had already passed the House, as well as the more controversial recommendations regarding the Civil Service Commission and the Comptroller-General Office. This bill then passed the Senate, but in the House a motion to send the bill back to committee passed by eight votes, essentially killing the legislation for the time being. See Emmerich, *Federal Organization and Administrative Management*, pp. 78–81; Roth, *The Executive Office of the President*, pp. 150–8.

93 Those in attendance included Vice-President Garner, Speaker Bankhead, Representatives Rayburn, Doughton, and Buchanan; Senators Robinson and Harrison; the Brownlow Committee; and Harris, Emmerich, McReynolds, Hester, and James Roosevelt. Emmerich's notes on this presentation, reproduced in Emmerich, *Federal Organization and Administrative Management*, Appendix I, provide a glimpse of the opposition the recommendations would stir. This was followed the next day by a formal press conference at which FDR publicly unveiled the Committee's recommendations.

94 Brownlow, *A Passion for Anonymity*, p. 387. Brownlow notes that congressional leaders were particularly offended by FDR's decision to draft legislation to implement the Report before consulting with them.

95 Ibid., p. 390.

this staff division genuinely reflected his views. Regarding the White House assistants, he noted:

> The problem of better administrative management is one that has troubled me for some time. In 1933 we were too busy with the problems of the emergency program to give it the consideration it deserved, but . . . an attempt was made by the establishment of the National Emergency Council to improve the coordination of the government's program. The President's task has become impossible for me or any other man. A man in this position will not be able to survive White House service unless it is simplified. I need executive assistants with a "passion for anonymity" to be my legs.[96]

At this point a Senator interjected – in what was a remarkably prescient aside – "Try and find them." Roosevelt continued:

> I have to contact eight people alone on foreign affairs. . . . [O]ne of my assistants could save me many of these contacts. . . . One of the assistants would not go out. I have no legal help directly available. When I am called about a bill from Congress, I have no one to advise me on the legal and parliamentary aspects. . . . These are only two examples.[97]

He then turned to the managerial agencies:

> But I also need managerial agencies to help in this job on fiscal, personnel and planning. Greater aid should be given me by the Bureau of the Budget, which now reports to me directly. It should be authorized to improve its staff and to perform certain services on coordination of informational activities. On the personnel side, the President needs a single administrator to operate the civil service system. He should be part of my establishment.[98]

This was followed by FDR's brief in support of a planning board to evaluate the numerous public works projects submitted to him. He then turned to the other provisions designed to augment his bargaining capacity within the executive branch. These included strengthening presidential control of the regulatory agencies, revamping the civil service system, increasing the salaries of civil servants, and adding two cabinet departments. These suggestions prompted the first serious objections raised during the presentation. "After the legislative leaders left, the President predicted a hard fight."[99] In this he was quite correct. Roosevelt's subsequent struggle to persuade

---

96 Emmerich, *Federal Organization and Administrative Management*, p. 207.
97 Ibid. Those in the room from Congress indicated at this point that Roosevelt would have no problem getting additional assistance through an appropriation bill.
98 Ibid., p. 208.
99 See the "Journal," PCAM, FDRL, p. 19; and Emmerich, *Federal Organization and Administrative Management*, pp. 208–2. Emmerich, in the immediate aftermath of the meeting, wrote, "The President told them – he did not ask them, except on ways and means of getting it through. They knew it and they knew who was the boss." This euphoria was not to last.

Congress to implement the Brownlow Report has been well documented by Richard Polenberg, among others.[100] It culminated in passage of the 1939 Reorganization Act that, together with subsequent legislation, strengthened the Executive Office of the President in a way that largely comported with FDR's views as expressed in the Brownlow Report, although some specific details differed.[101] Roosevelt was able, despite congressional intransigence, to broaden his institutional staff resources and thus gain greater control over the activities of the federal government. He did so by using his two-year reorganization authority to formalize the existence of the Executive Office of the President and to transfer a strengthened BoB and a National Resources Planning Board (in effect the National Resources Committee with additional functions) into it.[102] And, although not able to gain control of the Civil Service Commission, he did

100 See also Roth, *The Executive Office of the President*; and Karl, *Executive Reorganization and Reform in the New Deal*, pp. 247–65.
101 The 1939 Reorganization Act became law on Apr. 3, 1939. Strictly speaking, it – together with subsequent Executive Orders – incorporates only two of the Brownlow Committee's original suggestions: FDR gained reorganization authority, subject to congressional veto, and he was authorized to hire up to six administrative assistants, to be paid not more than $10,000 annually. However, FDR was prohibited from reorganizing the Civil Service Commission, from making any change in the name or number of the ten existing cabinet departments, and from reorganizing twenty-one agencies specifically listed by Congress. See Wann, *The President as Chief Administrator*, p. 99.
     Nevertheless, as Emmerich points out, the changes Roosevelt made under the Reorganization Act "conformed to the principle enunciated by the President's Committee two years earlier." Emmerich, *Federal Organization and Administrative Management*, p. 84. The subsequent reorganization plans and the Executive Order organizing the EOP were drafted by members of the Brownlow Committee, working in conjunction with FDR's new BoB director Harold Smith. Brownlow himself wrote the final draft of E.O. 8248, which more clearly delineated the functions of the different entities within the EOP. He was assisted by Smith, Donald Stone, head of the administrative division of the BoB, and Judge Townsend of the Department of Justice. Brownlow, *A Passion for Anonymity*, p. 428.
102 Reorganization Plan I actually transferred the functions and personnel of the National Resources Committee, except for the Committee itself, to the EOP. In addition, it transferred some of the functions carried out by the Federal Employment Stabilization Office, then located in the Department of Commerce. These were combined and reported to a National Resources Planning Board (NRPB), composed of five members appointed by the president, serving on a part-time basis. Technically speaking, only those functions performed by the stabilization office had a statutory basis; the NRC operated under authority of an emergency appropriation and thus its functions could not legally be transferred to the NRPB. The upshot was that, despite Plan I, FDR continued to seek congressional legislation for a NRPB. Due to a variety of factors, however, including congressional reluctance to spend money for "planning," Roosevelt's disinclination to fight for that money during World War II, and the competition from other agencies, especially the Bureau of the Budget and the Office of War Mobilization, the NRPB expired in 1943, never to be resurrected. See Roth, *The Executive Office of the President*, pp. 175–6.

designate one of his administrative assistants as his Liaison for Personnel Management, charged with advising him on personnel matters.[103]

The Brownlow Report, as implemented, represents the clearest articulation of FDR's views regarding the proper utilization of presidential staff. But it raises two critical question: Were the reforms effective? And are they applicable today? To find answers, the next four chapters assess Roosevelt's staff effectiveness prior to and during World War II – a period in which he confronted bargaining demands in many respects similar to those faced by his successors in the postwar era. As these chapters will demonstrate, the existence of a war emergency did little to reduce Roosevelt's costs to bargain in what soon became many separate institutions sharing powers. And yet, despite the emergence of "big government" FDR's administrative response remained largely true to the principles enunciated by the Brownlow Report: a small White House Office supported by a vastly expanded institutional staff. More importantly, the staff system appears to have worked; for the most part Roosevelt's bargaining choices during the war years produced the outcomes he desired, without sacrificing his sources of bargaining power. To see why, we turn next to examine the most significant domestic issue FDR confronted during the war: mobilizing for military production.

103 Furthermore, the extension of civil service status gradually came about during the next few years, aided by the Hatch Act of 1939 and the Ramspeck Act of 1940. The former prohibited executive employees from engaging in political campaigning. The latter allowed Roosevelt to extend the merit system from 61 percent coverage in 1936 to 73 percent in 1943. See Fesler, in Mosher, *The President Needs Help*, pp. 11–13. He also brought all but two government corporations into existing departments.

PART III

Testing Roosevelt's staff system: The war years, 1939–45

4

Economic mobilization and World War II

To test whether Roosevelt's institutional response is relevant today, its effectiveness must be evaluated under circumstances in which bargaining costs rival those faced by his successors. Economic mobilization during World War II is one such case. The need to mobilize the nation's economy for war confronted FDR with bargaining demands of unprecedented magnitude and complexity.[1]

Roosevelt's objective on the home front was simple: to convert the nation's economy to munitions production as quickly as political constraints would allow. The execution, however, was politically and administratively complex. It encompassed two phases. The first, lasting roughly from 1938–41, laid the foundation for defense production within the constraints imposed by isolationists who actively campaigned against any American military involvement overseas.[2] Phase two, covered in Chapter 5, began with the Japanese attack at Pearl Harbor in December 1941 and extended through the end of his presidency in 1945. In this period, FDR successfully sought to prosecute the war by integrating military strategy with war production while protecting his sources of bargaining support.

To accomplish these ends, FDR took three administrative steps: progressively imposing production and price controls to maximize munitions output while limiting civilian economic disruption; establishing institutional means to implement those controls; and, most important, devising coordinating agencies to ensure that these institutions worked in FDR's bargaining interest.[3]

---

1 R. Elberton Smith, *The Army and Economic Mobilization* (Washington, D.C.: Office of the Chief of Military History, Department of the Army, 1959), pp. 4–31, provides a succinct overview of the administrative complexity mobilization entailed.

2 As Herbert Emmerich recalls, "The spirit of non-involvement and minding our own business was rampant. There was resistance to preparedness moves and to aid to the allies. . . . In this atmosphere, a good deal of our early steps for preparedness had to be sugar coated and coaxed through a reluctant Congress" (Herbert Emmerich, *Federal Organization and Administrative Management*, [Birmingham, Ala.: The University of Alabama Press, 1971], pp. 67–8; Smith, *The Army and Economic Mobilization*, p. 83).

3 These controls included mandatory wage and price guidelines; preference ratings specifying the products to be moved to the head of production lines; allocation controls

The various war mobilization and production agencies, most of which reported directly to FDR outside existing executive branch jurisdictions, eventually oversaw almost every sector of the nation's economy, including manufacturing, agriculture, manpower, wages and prices, import/ export trade, shipping, science research, and information and propaganda.[4] To retain some semblance of administrative control within the presidency, FDR typically invested these agencies with weak statutory authority, ill-defined jurisdictions, and divided leadership. As a consequence, lacking clear mandates or the authority to carry them out, the war agencies invariably clashed with one another in pursuit of organizational objectives. Such conflicts pushed controversial production decisions up the administrative ladder to FDR for resolution, precisely as he had intended.

But if this strategy preserved FDR's sources of bargaining power, it also imposed an extraordinary management load on his shoulders. By 1943, he was no longer able to carry that weight. With munitions output faltering and Congress threatening to usurp FDR's responsibility for war production, he delegated extensive oversight of the "home front" to James Byrnes and the Office of War Mobilization.

The details of Roosevelt's delegation of authority to Byrnes are highly instructive. Byrnes, limited by a small staff that never numbered more than ten aides (most of them performing clerical functions), eschewed both policy-making and operational functions. Instead, he functioned essentially as a judge, adjudicating production disputes on FDR's behalf – a role that fit Byrnes' experience and temperament.[5] And because his authority

governing the distribution of scarce materials; conservation orders restricting the use of those scarce materials to certain end products; limitation orders curbing the production of nonessential civilian products; and inventory controls limiting materials stockpiling. Through these devices almost the entire American economy came to be regulated during World War II.

    It was necessary to substitute controls for pricing strategies, profit calculations, and other free-market mechanisms that normally regulate supply and demand, because the latter were inadequate in wartime to ensure that munitions were produced in the time, quantity, and quality necessary for national survival.

4 Altogether some 160 war-related agencies, departments, boards, commissions, and other institutions operated during 1940–5. For a list and description of their functions, see Bureau of the Budget, *The United States at War: Development and Administration of the War Program by the Federal Government* (Washington, D.C.: Government Printing Office, 1946), Appendix I.

    In 1943, at the peak of the war, a handbook of emergency war agencies lists forty-four agencies, commissions, boards, offices and departments with responsibility for some war-related functions, and which reported directly to FDR. This probably understates the extent of organizational growth; many of these wartime agencies contained administrative subdivisions that essentially operated as autonomous units within particular policy areas (see Office of War Information, *Handbook of Emergency War Agencies* [Washington, D.C.: Government Printing Office, 1943]).

5 He was a former Senator and then a Supreme Court Justice before resigning that post to head the OWM

derived not from congressional statute, but from presidential executive order, Byrnes remained answerable only to Roosevelt, who was thus positioned to revoke Byrnes' authority when the war emergency ended.

Economic mobilization provides strong evidence that FDR's administrative principles, as articulated in the Brownlow Report and operationalized during the war years, remain relevant today. Despite the extraordinary demands of World War II, Roosevelt acquired bargaining resources needed to accurately gauge the likely impact of his administrative choices on his wartime objectives. And even at the peak of those demands, FDR managed to delegate significant authority to staff subordinates without jeopardizing his sources of bargaining power. Modern day presidents can learn much from studying this period.

Creating the foundation for economic mobilization

After a long interwar period of relative isolationism, U.S. military production began rising during 1938-9, initially driven by overseas orders from France and Great Britain reacting to Germany's military resurgence.[6] But because there was no effective system of administrative controls through which FDR could tell manufacturers what to produce, these early efforts were largely voluntary and uncoordinated. Facing a potential third-term reelection campaign, FDR found himself caught politically between the isolationists and the "all-outers," who pushed for an aggressive response to German and Japanese militarism. Alarmed by the developing European and Far East military conflicts, but constrained by the neutrality acts and general congressional resistance to overseas aid, Roosevelt spent these prewar years from 1937 to 1941 quietly building the organizational base necessary to put the American economy on a war footing.[7]

Roosevelt's administrative preparations quickened, however, after the German invasion of Western Europe in May 1940, which prompted him

---

6 The most visible component was an expansion in aircraft production for overseas use. The American military, however, resisted these efforts, forcing Roosevelt to use Treasury Secretary Henry Morgenthau as his point of contact with foreign governments seeking U.S. planes. (For details on FDR's efforts to stimulate plane production, see Chapter 7. For an overview of the defense buildup in this period, see BoB *The U.S. at War*, p. 21.)

7 The Neutrality Act, initially passed in Aug. 31, 1935, and amended several times afterward, made it "unlawful to export arms, ammunition, or implements of war" from the U.S. to any country at war. Nor could munitions be carried on U.S. ships to those countries. Roosevelt was forced to expend tremendous political capital to revise the neutrality laws in 1939 to permit foreign nations to buy American munitions, albeit on a for-cash-only basis, and only if transported in non-U.S. ships. All other military transactions were still prohibited.

to declare a national emergency.[8] The declaration allowed FDR to invoke a little noted provision in E.O. 8248 empowering the president, in times of national emergency, to activate an "office of emergency management" [OEM]."[9] This was an important step, for the OEM served as the ad-

8 The May 25, 1940, declaration followed Roosevelt's earlier (September 1939) declaration of a limited emergency in the aftermath of the German invasion of Poland.

9 Section I of E.O. 8248 states: "There shall be within the Executive Office of the President the following principal divisions, namely: (1) The White House Office, (2) the Bureau of the Budget, (3) the National Resources Planning Board, (4) the Liaison Office for Personnel Management, (5) the Office of Government Reports, and (6) *in the event of a national emergency, or threat of a national emergency, such office for emergency management as the President shall determine* [italics added]."

Simultaneous with declaring the national emergency, FDR issued an administrative order clarifying the OEM's functions and structure:

Section 1. There is established in the Executive Office of the President an Office to be known as the Office for Emergency Management, which shall be under the direction of one of the Administrative Assistants to the President, to be designated by the President.

Section 2. The Office for Emergency Management shall: (a) Assist the President in the clearance of information with respect to measures necessitated by the threatened emergency;

(b) Maintain liaison between the President and the Council of National Defense and its Advisory Commission and with such other agencies, public or private, as the President may direct, for the purpose of securing maximum utilization and coordination of agencies and facilities in meeting the threatened emergency;

(c) Perform such additional duties as the President may direct.

The OEM's functions were subsequently altered slightly by administrative order (Jan. 7, 1941) when the Office of Production Management was established. The relevant provisions are:

(a) To advise and assist the President in the discharge of extraordinary responsibilities imposed upon him by any emergency arising out of war, the threat of war, imminence of war, flood, drought, or other condition threatening the public peace or safety.

(b) To serve as a division of the Executive Office of the President, with such subdivisions as may be required, through which the President, during any emergency, may coordinate and supervise and, in appropriate cases, direct the activities of agencies, public or private, in relation thereto.

(c) To serve as a channel of communication between such agencies and the President concerning emergency activities, to keep the President currently advised of their progress, to assemble and analyze information concerning additional measures that should be taken, and to assist in the preparation of recommendations for any necessary legislation.

(d) To provide and maintain liaison during any such emergency with other divisions of the Executive Office of the President and with other agencies, public or private, for the purpose of bringing about maximum utilization and coordination of their services and facilities.

(e) To advise and assist the President upon or before termination of any such emergency with respect to any measures that may be needful to facilitate a restoration of normal administrative relations and to ameliorate the consequences of the emergency.

(f) To perform other such duties and functions with respect to any such emergency as the President may from time to time direct.

ministrative umbrella that eventually sheltered almost all of the nation's wartime agencies.[10]

Roosevelt's decision to create the OEM followed several months of careful preparatory work.[11] On Aug. 9, 1939, he had directed Louis Johnson, the Assistant Secretary of War, to appoint a civilian-based War Resources Board (WRB).[12] This advisory committee, composed primarily of prominent business leaders, was charged with reviewing the M-Day Plan, an eighteen-page military plan for mobilizing the nation's economy in the event of war.[13]

> There followed a section listing the defense-related agencies that were to be housed within the OEM.

10 A partial listing of those agencies includes: the Foreign Economic Administration, the National War Labor Board, the Office of Production Management, the Office of Alien Property Custodian, the Office of Civilian Defense, the Office of the Coordinator of Inter-American Affairs, the Supply Priorities and Allocations Board, the Office of Defense Health and Welfare Services, the Office of Defense Transportation, the Office of Economic Stabilization, the Office of Scientific Research and Development, the Office of War Information, the War Manpower Commission, the War Production Board, the War Relocation Authority, the War Shipping Administration, and the Office of War Mobilization. See A. J. Wann, *The President as Chief Administrator: A Study of Franklin D. Roosevelt* (Washington, D.C.: Public Affairs Press, 1968), p. 127.
    In theory, of course, the OEM might have developed into a presidential staff unit responsible for coordinating the activities of these agencies on FDR's behalf. This did not happen because FDR never invested the necessary authority in the people charged with supervising the OEM. These include McReynolds, FDR's administrative assistant who also served as his Liaison for Personnel Management; Wayne Coy, who replaced McReynolds in April 1941, and who was also appointed Assistant Director of the BoB in 1942, holding both positions until June 1943; and James Byrnes who briefly occupied the OEM liaison post when appointed director of the OWM until his resignation as OEM liaison on Nov. 3, 1943. Thereafter the position went unoccupied although the OEM remained on the books as an emergency agency until the end of the war. See also Herman Somers, *Presidential Agency: OWMR The Office of War Mobilization and Reconversion* (New York: Greewood Press, 1969), pp. 43.

11 Roosevelt's foresight was in part prompted by his wartime experience as Woodrow Wilson's Assistant Secretary of the Navy, which convinced him that U.S. involvement in a second European war would likely necessitate substantial executive branch growth. FDR thus instructed Brownlow to include a provision in E.O. 8248 that would ensure he had the authority to create emergency war agencies without asking for congressional authorization.

12 The appointees included Edward H. Stettinius, Jr., Chairman of the Board of U.S. Steel; Walter S. Gifford, President of AT&T; John Lee Pratt, director of General Motors; General Robert E. Wood, chairman of Sears, Roebuck and Co.; John Hancock, a Lehman Brothers partner; Karl T. Compton, President of M.I.T.; and Harold G. Moulton, President of the Brookings Institution. The prominence of business representation on the board was to prove a distinct political handicap. See Donald Nelson, *Arsenal of Democracy: The Story of American War Production* (New York: Harcourt, Brace and Company), pp. 87–9; Albert A. Blum, "Birth and Death of the M-Day Plan," in Harold Stein (ed.), *American Civil-Military Decisions: A Book of Case Studies* (Birmingham, Ala.: The University of Alabama Press, 1963) (hereafter *Civil-Military Decisions*), pp. 74–5.

13 Under the 1920 National Defense Act, primary responsibility for preparing the American economy for war was delegated by Congress to the Assistant Secretary of War, working through the Army and Navy Munitions Board (the ANMB, created on July 22, 1922,

Johnson assumed, as did the appointed board members, that the WRB would be delegated implementation of the M-Day Plan if war broke out.[14] Roosevelt, however, had no intention of delegating this authority, as he explained in a private session with the WRB two weeks after it was formed. He particularly objected to the M-Day Plan's stipulation that a defense "czar" be appointed to oversee the nation's conversion to a war economy.[15] Rather than delegate that authority to someone else, Roosevelt wanted to administer defense mobilization out of his own executive office.[16] Taking a cue from Brownlow, who shared the president's

by administrative action to coordinate Army and Navy mobilization efforts). The first M-Day Plan, ostensibly distilling the lessons of economic mobilization during World War I, was written in 1931 and subsequently revised in 1933, 1936, and 1939. See "Industrial Mobilization Plan Revision of 1939" (hereafter "M-Day Plan") (Government Printing Office: 1939) Senate document no. 134, 76th Congress, 2nd sess. A copy is contained in the Harry Hopkins Papers – Sherwood Book Manuscript Collection, Book 2: Organization of NDAC #3 Folder, FDRL. Although the main text is approximately eighteen pages, appendices add considerably to that total.

The Report itself was meant to provide only general guidelines for economic mobilization; detailed annexes held by the armed services fleshed out these plans considerably. See also Smith, *The Army and Economic Mobilization*, pp. 74–97; Blum, "The Birth and Death of the M-Day Plan," pp. 61–96; and U.S. Bureau of Demobilization *Industrial Mobilization for War: History of the War Production Board and Predecessor Agencies, 1940–45*, vol. 1, (Washington, D.C.: Government Printing Office, 1947) (hereafter *Industrial Mobilization*), pp. 3–5.

14 This is clearly spelled out in the press release Johnson, a vigorous supporter of industrial preparedness, issued announcing the board's appointment. See Smith, *The Army and Economic Mobilization*, pp. 98–99. The military shared Johnson's assumption. Indeed, the board's survey of the nation's defense posture was aided by Johnson, Acting Navy Secretary Charles Edison, Chief of Staff General George Marshall, Colonel James H. Burns, Colonel Harry K. Rutherford, and Sumner Welles at the State Department.

15 More specifically, the M-Day plan proposed creating, in the event of war, a War Resources Administration, under the direction of a civilian appointed by the president. This individual would be assisted by an advisory council consisting of individuals selected to oversee conversion in the spheres of industrial facilities, commodities, power, fuel, and transportation. Representatives from the State, War, and Navy departments and from the Army Chief of Staff and Chief of Naval operations would also report to the defense czar, as would representatives of other emergency agencies handling public relations, selective service, finance, trade, labor and prices. See "M-Day Plan," chart on p. 2; *Civil-Military Relations*, p. 73; and the discussion in Smith, *The Army and Economic Mobilization*. Smith describes the proposed War Resources Administration as "the key superagency with supervisory power over all other superagencies whose principal functions were directly related to economic mobilization" (Smith, *The Army and Economic Mobilization*, p. 80).

16 As he explained to the WRB, he wanted the advisers overseeing the various mobilization processes to report directly to him, not to a mobilization czar. (There is a diagram – probably sketched by Roosevelt himself – in Hopkins' papers summarizing FDR's ideas. See Harry Hopkins Papers, General Correspondence, 1933–40 File, Franklin D. Roosevelt Folder, FDRL; and Smith, *The Army and Economic Mobilization*, pp. 100–2.)

Roosevelt's plan for a group of aides who would act as liaison to departments and agencies carrying out related functions foreshadowed with remarkable clarity his use of his White House administrative assistants (six of which were authorized by E.O.

aversion to the M-Day document, FDR planned to revive a six-member "war cabinet" and its civilian advisory committee, by invoking a 1916 war statute still on the books.[17] Thereafter, the cabinet committee would be mothballed, and the civilian advisory commission transferred as an independent entity to what would become the OEM. The purpose, FDR explained, was to "tell the Cabinet officers to get lost, and run the thing [economic mobilization] through the advisory committee as part of my own office."[18]

> If we are really headed for trouble, I will at least be my own boss and will not be compelled to turn over the presidency of the United States to some other man, a man who, I am sure, would never be nominated by a Democratic convention and never be elected by the people.[19]

Predictably, the WRB balked at FDR's plans, but to no avail.[20] After only two months in existence, it was dissolved by FDR (effective Nov. 24, 1939) with its recommendations tabled, for the war's duration as it turned

8248 in 1939) during the next five years. William McReynolds served as defense liaison (after Brownlow refused the position). Lauchlin Currie performed as Roosevelt's economic liaison; Admiral William Leahy was eventually recalled from his post as Ambassador to Vichy France and installed as FDR's military chief of staff, although Harry Hopkins, as FDR's special assistant, more nearly filled this foreign policy liaison post; and Lowell Mellett took charge of the Office of Government Reports, fulfilling an information role.

17 Brownlow had examined the M-Day document at FDR's request and told the president, "Well, it seems to me that any President who accepts the recommendations of these mobilization plans would do little better to resign" (Louis Brownlow *A Passion for Anonymity* [Chicago: University of Chicago Press, 1955], pp. 424–7). Subsequently, after Roosevelt asked whether there were any World War I statutes still on the books which might legally allow him to create his own economic mobilization agency, Brownlow unearthed the 1916 provision for a cabinet-level Council of National Defense. See *Civil-Military Relations*, p. 79.

Brownlow's aversion to the M-Day Plan was echoed by others. After the German invasion of the Low Countries in May 1940, there were renewed calls to implement the original M-Day Plan. Roosevelt asked Lauchlin Currie, one of his administrative assistants, to scrutinize the document one more time. Currie did so and concluded it was "deficient in a number of respects" in part because it ignored changes in military tactics and strategy that had taken place since 1918. See "Comments on our Industrial War Plans" Memorandum by Lauchlin Currie (read by FDR on May 20, 1940), President's Secretary's File (hereafter *PSF*), Lauchlin Currie Folder, FDRL.

18 Brownlow, *A Passion for Anonymity*, pp. 424–7.

19 Ibid.

20 In November 1939, the WRB issued two alternatives to FDR's plan. Neither met FDR's approval. The first proposed creating a superagency under the direction of a czar with almost total control of the nation's wartime economy. The second option, favored by the WRB and somewhat closer to Roosevelt's proposal, would establish seven different agencies, each exercising a war power and each reporting directly to the president. This alternative was similar to the existing M-Day Plan, except that the proposed War Resource Administration would have limited power to direct the other war agencies. See *Industrial Mobilization*, pp. 8–11; *Civil-Military Relations*, pp. 86–7; Smith, *The Army and Economic Mobilization*, pp. 101–2

out.[21] Six months later, having declared a state of emergency, FDR then revived the cabinet-level Council of National Defense, and appointed the civilian National Defense Advisory Commission (NDAC).[22] As planned, the NDAC was then transferred to the OEM under FDR's direct control, and the war cabinet, after one session, ceased to function.[23]

Roosevelt's machinations served several purposes. First, by dissolving the WRB and tabling its recommendations, FDR countered widespread perceptions that the board was dominated by big business.[24] With an elec-

21 Actual board deliberations extended from Aug. 17 to Oct. 12, 1939. See Nelson, *Arsenal of Democracy*, p. 87. Roosevelt's decision to dismiss it without commenting on its recommendations did not sit well with all board members; Stettinius told Currie that, "while he was satisfied that [FDR's] action in dismissing the Board was no reflection in any way on the members of the Board, nevertheless there was much misunderstanding and he, personally, would be very gratified if you received his Report graciously" (Currie to Roosevelt, [Oct. 12, 1939]; *PSF* Personal Files, Currie Folder, FDRL. Despite the request, the board's recommendations were not publicly released until 1946.

22 As stipulated by the 1916 statute, the National Defense Advisory Commission (NDAC) was to consist of not more than seven individuals, "each of whom should have some special knowledge of some industry, public utility, or the development of some natural resource, or are otherwise specially qualified." Those chosen by FDR (with area of specialty) included: Stettinius (industrial materials); William Knudsen, president of General Motors, (industrial production); Sidney Hillman, president of Amalgamated Clothing Worker of America (employment policies); Chester Davis, member of the Federal Reserve Board (farm production), Leon Henderson, member of the Security and Exchange Commission (prices); Ralph Budd, chairman of the board, Chicago, Burlington & Quincy Railroad (transportation); and Harriet Elliot, dean of women, University of North Carolina (consumer interests).
    On June 27, 1940, Donald Nelson, formerly the executive vice-president of Sears, Roebuck & Co. and later in charge of defense procurement in the Treasury Department, was appointed to coordinate defense purchases. He operated as a de facto member of the Advisory Commission, although by statute the board was restricted to seven members.
    The initial rules and regulations governing the NDAC's activities are summarized in the undated document titled "Rules and Regulations Council of National Defense," Harry Hopkins Papers, Sherwood Book Manuscript Collection; Book 2: Organization of NDAC Folder, FDRL.

23 See, regarding the first meeting of the Cabinet Council, Harold L. Ickes, *The Secret Diary of Harold L. Ickes: The First Thousand Days*, vol. 3 (New York: Simon & Schuster), p. 194; see also Frances Perkins, *The Roosevelt I Knew*, paperback ed. (New York: Harper & Row, 1964), pp. 355–7. Perkins records that there was "a mild protest from cabinet officers" when Roosevelt announced the members of the NDAC.

24 This impression was reinforced by a phrase in the M-Day document stating that the War Resources Administration would be filled by "patriotic business leaders of the nation." Ickes, in his diary, tells of a meeting in his office attended by Cohen, Corcoran, Currie, Jerome Frank, Robert Jackson, Isador Lublin, and Frank Murphy in which they discussed how to prevent Johnson and Morgenthau from appointing a cadre of business-oriented advisers. Ickes, *Secret Diaries*, vol. 3, pp. 4–5. See also, A. Blum, "The Birth and Death of the M-Day Plan," pp. 76–7.
    Roosevelt was fully aware of the perception that business interests dominated mobilization planning, and he hoped to include labor representatives as a countervailing force in his industrial mobilization agency. However, the split between the C.I.O. and the A.F. of L. constrained his ability to do so; he could not ask one in without the other. See Roo-

tion pending and isolationism running strong, FDR would not risk publicly endorsing defense mobilization plans proposed by a business-dominated board.

Second, the OEM gave FDR the means to create emergency war agencies that reported directly to him, without having to seek congressional authorization to do so.[25] He thus avoided provoking extended debate on his war aims.[26] This was particularly important during the eleven-month period between the expiration of reorganization authority granted him by the 1939 Reorganization Act and the passage of the First War Powers Act on Dec. 18, 1941.[27]

sevelt's letter to Lindsay Rogers (Sept. 11, 1939). "The dovetailing of labor into the new plans has not yet been thought out. . . . In this regard also we have to look very carefully at the political effects of any plan and the whole subject is complicated by the personality of [John] Lewis and the deeper troubles between the C.I.O. and the A.F. of L." (reprinted in Elliot Roosevelt (ed.), *F.D.R. His Personal Letters, 1928–1945*, (New York: Duell, Sloan & Pearce, 1950), p. 920 [hereafter *FDR's Personal Letters*]).

25 The M-Day Plan gave Congress, not the president, authority to create the War Resources Administration and related mobilization agencies. But it was not until the fall of France, in July 1940, that Congress voted to embargo shipments of munitions and critical materials to hostile nations and to authorize the building of a two-ocean Navy, a land force of 1,200,000 soldiers, and an additional 18,000 airplanes. It was another two months before it passed legislation for selective service. By this point, of course, most of Europe was under German control, and Great Britain, almost totally denuded of armaments, was preparing for the anticipated German invasion. See Nelson, *Arsenal of Democracy*, p. 72. Incredibly, on Aug. 12, 1941, at the peak of German domination of the European continent, legislation to extend selective service registration passed the House by one vote.

26 Although, as Emmerich recalls, the Senate subcommittee on appropriations, in hearings during 1941, questioned the legality of FDR's method for creating wartime agencies. Knudsen, a member of NDAC and widely respected as the ex-chairman of General Motors, was forced to testify to gain the subcommittee's support. See Emmerich, *Federal Organization and Administrative Management*, pp. 72.

27 The 1939 Reorganization Act I expired on Jan. 21, 1941. During the eleven-month period afterward, several critical defense agencies, including the Office of Production Management, the Office of Price Administration and Civilian Supply, the Office of the Coordinator of Inter-American Affairs, the Office of Scientific Research and Development, the Office of Lend-Lease Administration, and the Office of Facts and Figures, were established by executive order as elements within the OEM.

Roosevelt tried to get his reorganization authority extended, but was told by Representative John Cochrane, chairman of the House Committee on Government Organization, that the House leadership wanted to delay the matter. See the exchange of memos between Smith, FDR, Cochrane, and Ickes accompanying Roosevelt's memo to Smith (May 14, 1941), *PSF* – Subject Files, Reorganization Folder, FDRL.

The First War Powers Act, passed Dec. 17, 1941, (55 *stat.*) (Title I) remained in effect until June 30, 1947, six months after the official termination of the war. The Act authorized the president to make transfers and consolidations of government agencies by executive order, without being subject to congressional approval or legislative veto. See the memorandum from Oscar Cox to Harry Hopkins (Dec. 18, 1941) listing some presidential powers under this act (Hopkins Papers, Special Assistant to the President, 1941–5, Organizing Government for War [Presidential Emergency Powers] Folder, FDRL).

Third, by invoking the 1916 statute to create a "war cabinet" and advisory commission, Roosevelt successfully wrested defense production from the War Department, again without directly confronting Congress.[28] Finally, the advisory commission helped Roosevelt broaden his political support by serving as a repository for individuals who otherwise might have opposed his war leadership, while simultaneously functioning as an administrative proving ground.[29]

But, as Labor Secretary Frances Perkins complained, FDR's desire to personally manipulate the administrative strings of defense production had drawbacks:

> A more systematic administrator . . . would have made fuller use first of the great resources of the Government's permanent staff. He would have made the Advisory Commission members policy consultants. Instead, as administrative officers, they invented their own jobs as they went along and had, at least in the first year, only the vaguest conception of the resources of the Government agencies which might have been made available to them if they had asked.[30]

This lack of experience among NDAC's members and their failure to learn from the events of the World War I proved costly. Eliot Janeway, in his study of economic mobilization, argues: "To hindsight the story of things left undone during the lost year of 1939–40 is unbelievable."[31] Janeway's observation rings particularly true in reference to the develop-

---

However, this authority was to be exercised only "in matters relating to the conduct of the present war." Furthermore, proposals to abolish statutory functions of agencies had to be submitted to Congress to be enacted as legislation. Under this authority FDR issued 135 executive orders pertaining to wartime organizations during the almost forty-five months the United States was at war.

28 A particularly important consideration in a period when Roosevelt's political influence with Congress was quite low. Remember that Roosevelt was trying to rebound from both the unsuccessful Court-packing fight and the failed party purge of 1938, neither of which had helped his influence in Congress. (The "purge" was Roosevelt's attempt to intervene in a number of Congressional races in 1938 in order to elect Democrats who shared his New Deal philosophy. See Robert Sherwood *Roosevelt and Hopkins* rev. paperback ed. [New York: The Universal Library, 1950], p. 162.)

29 That same logic governed FDR's decision, three weeks after reestablishing NDAC, to bring two long-standing Republicans, Henry L. Stimson and Frank Knox, into his cabinet as Secretary of War and Secretary of the Navy, respectively. Again, Roosevelt drew on his experiences in World War I; Brownlow recalled that Roosevelt believed Woodrow Wilson's major mistake as president was not appointing to his wartime administration individuals representing as many different political interests as possible.

30 Perkins, *The Roosevelt I Knew*, p. 357.

31 Eliot Janeway, *The Struggle for Survival: A Chronicle of Economic Mobilization in World War II* (New Haven, Conn.: Yale University Press, 1951), p. 80. Janeway argues that the M-Day Plan, as modified by Bernard Baruch and others, in fact would have addressed FDR's concerns to control mobilization and thus should have been implemented.

ment of administrative controls affecting defense procurement and contracting in this period.[32]

During the eighteen months after Roosevelt's declaration of a national emergency, the military began issuing preference certificates, or priority orders, giving precedence to the production of military munitions in the nation's factories.[33] This prioritization of end products was soon supplemented by additional controls focusing on the use of critical raw materials, such as aluminum and steel, deemed essential to the war effort.[34] However, these production controls were typically applied on a spot basis; as shortages were anticipated, the military limited consumption to ensure that the required materials were available to the factory producing the requested end products. Because they were largely uncoordinated efforts, the initial produc-

---

32 Military procurement refers to the purchasing, inspection, and delivery of munitions. As Smith notes, "Military procurement in time of war represents the very heart of the entire economic mobilization process. Without a solid foundation in procurement planning, emergency production for war could not get started" (Smith, *The Army and Economic Mobilization*, p. 72).

  Probably the most critical aspect of procurement is the power to award military contracts: "[T]he placement of contracts is the force which sets the economic machine in motion" (David Novick, Melvin Anshen, and W. C. Truppner, *Wartime Production Controls* [New York: Columbia University Press, 1949], p. 386). Other procurement controls, such as priority orders, preference ratings, and allocation authority, come into play after military orders have already been placed.

  Before the U.S. entrance into the war, civilian procurement was handled by the Treasury Department's Procurement Division, whereas military procurement was administered by the War and Navy departments, operating through their own procurement offices. See the memorandum by Bruce Berkman regarding National Defense Procurement (July 1940), in Harry Hopkins Papers, Special Assistant to the President, 1941–5; Procurement Folder, FDRL, and Somers, *Presidential Agency*, p. 110.

33 Under Public Law 671 (June 28, 1940) the Army and Navy were directed at the president's discretion to issue priority lists specifying items that were critical for fulfilling military contracts and which therefore took precedence over all private manufacturing contracts. The assistant secretaries of War and Navy had, on June 17, 1940, already established a priorities committee within the Army – Navy Munitions Board, responsible for determining production priorities related to military contracts. The first formal priority order was issued by the ANMB on Aug. 12,1940, and thereafter they were produced on an expanding scale.

  However, debate regarding the scope of manufacturing that should be subject to priority orders, as well as who should issue them, was extensive during this period. Nelson stated flatly, "If any single issue constantly loomed larger than any of the rest, it was that of priorities" (Nelson, *Arsenal of Democracy*, p. 110).

  Moreover, below the level of the primary production contract, compliance with priority orders remained essentially voluntary until September 1941.

34 This was the first step toward mandatory allocation of certain critical raw materials. Eventually, there developed a system of "M" orders limiting the use of raw materials in nonmilitary manufacturing as well. Individual advisory material committees, consisting of industry representatives, were established to oversee the use of raw materials in each manufacturing sector.

tion controls created materials shortages and manufacturing bottlenecks.[35]

That NDAC was unable to impose some administrative order on the early attempts to mobilize the economy for defense production was due to several reasons. The most important was the military procurement agencies' failure to acknowledge NDAC's procurement authority, despite congressional legislation in June 1940, giving NDAC the authority to review all War Department and Navy Department military contracts.[36]

Indeed, this period marks the start of a bitter administrative struggle between a succession of civilian defense agencies and the military's procurement agencies, each of which asserted their supremacy in defense contracting.[37] The military services, operating through the joint Army – Navy Munitions Board (ANMB) and their own individual procurement arms, consistently argued that by controlling military procurement, they could ensure their forces were properly equipped to carry out specific military strategy.[38] It followed logically that they should be granted sole authority to award and prioritize military production contracts.[39] But the heads of the civilian agencies responded that allowing the military to place

35 As Novick, Ashen, and Truppner write, "From mid-1940 to the end of the year the organization of American industry for national defense was planless" (Novick, Ashen, and Truppner *Wartime Production Controls*, p. 76).

36 Congress passed legislation on June 26, 1940, stipulating that the secretaries of War and Navy could only enter into contracts with the approval of the "Council of National Defense, and the Advisory Commission thereof, and with the approval of the President" (Public No. 671, 76th Congress). This was reaffirmed in appropriation acts passed in September and October, and by the ruling of the Attorney General in February 1941 (see Novick, Ashen, and Truppner, *Wartime Production Controls*, p. 384). Despite this, "[t]he Army and Navy . . . went ahead with specific programs without waiting for the formal approval which NDAC often felt should have been obtained in advance of action" (Smith, *The Army and Economic Mobilization*, p. 110).

37 On the relation between NDAC, especially Nelson, and the ANMB regarding priorities control in this period, see Smith, *The Army and Economic Mobilization*, pp. 530–1.

38 Note that the ANMB's importance as a procurement agency was frequently overstated by civilians during the war years; in fact the more important procurement agencies were those within each military branch. These included some forty-six field procurement offices in the War Department, and twenty-seven in the Navy. See John Millet, *The Organization and Role of the Army Service Forces* (Washington, D.C.: Office of the Chief of Military History, Department of the Army, 1954), pp. 281–94. Millet was an adviser to General Somervell who headed the Army Service Forces (the chief military procurement department after 1942) during World War II.

39 The War Department defended the military's control over procurement in a document published in 1942, in response to congressional attempts to transfer that power to civilian agencies. See "The Necessity for Continued Military Responsibility for Equipping the Armed Services," contained in Hopkins Papers, Special Assistant to the President, 1941–5, Organization of Military Forces File, FDRL. See also Smith, *The Army and Economic Mobilization*, p. 235; and Millet, *The Organization and Role of the Army Service Forces*, pp. 281–4.

production contracts without regard for the nation's productive capacity would inevitable grind the economy to a halt.[40]

American business interests were no less divided on the issue. At the risk of simplification, the cleavage among the business community tended to run between large and small firms. The former were awarded the brunt of the defense contracts and thus sought as little government interference as possible in their dealings with the armed services. Smaller firms, however, wanted the government to ensure a more equitable spread of military contracts, and they eventually enlisted a congressional investigating committee in their cause.[41] Those not directly involved in military production, such as farmers, sought government protection in order to survive in an economy increasingly dependent on munitions production.[42]

Rather than resolve these administrative divisions, however, FDR tried to turn them to his advantage.[43] By refusing to vest procurement authority in a single agency, he was able to use the administrative competition between civilian and military agencies to control the pace of defense

40 Recall that Nelson, who formerly headed the Treasury's Procurement Department beginning November 1938, joined NDAC in 1940 as coordinator of defense purchases. From this position he shared civilian oversight of military procurement with William Knudsen, who cleared ordnance and other "hard goods" contracts, whereas Nelson was responsible for quartermaster and "soft goods" contracts (see Novick, Ashen and Truppner, *Wartime Production Controls*, p. 384; Somers, *Presidential Agency*, p. 110; and Smith, *The Army and Economic Mobilization*, pp. 109–11).

41 Congress held a series of committee hearings and produced several reports examining the impact of the defense program on small businesses. See the records of the Senate, Hearings of the Special Committee to Study and Survey Problems of American Small Business Enterprises (77th Congress., 2nd sess., 1942) and the Select House Committee to Investigate the National Defense Program in Relation to Small Business (77th Congress., 2nd sess., Hearing on House Resolution 294).

42 As an added political complication, neither the military nor the business community in general commanded much public support, especially after well-publicized congressional investigations suggested that these "merchants of death" had driven the United States to intervene in World War I. But the civilian war agencies, especially after the impact of administrative controls were extended to all parts of the civilian economy, also incurred growing resentment.

43 He did agree to establish a Priorities Board ostensibly with the authority to formally establish production priorities on behalf of NDAC in conjunction with the ANMB. E.O. 8572 (Oct. 21, 1940) states that the Priorities Board could require that "persons with whom naval and Army contracts and orders have been or are placed, to grant priority for deliveries pursuant thereto over all deliveries for private account or for export." (The Board consisted of Knudsen, Stettinius, and Henderson, with Nelson serving as administrator.) See also *Industrial Mobilization*, pp. 24–5; Nelson, *Arsenal of Democracy*, pp. 84–6; and Smith, *The Army and Economic Mobilization*, pp. 513–16, for a discussion.

Roosevelt subsequently issued E.O. 8612 (Dec. 15, 1940), containing additional rules governing the administration of priority orders. Essentially, however, by stipulating that major policy changes were to come through consultation among Nelson, the AMNB, and the procurement agencies Roosevelt did nothing to resolve the bureaucratic squabbling.

mobilization. His strategy is evident in the organizational and statutory makeup of NDAC.⁴⁴ As an advisory commission, NDAC possessed limited legal authority.⁴⁵ Its weak statutory base was compounded by organizational defects, the most glaring of which was the lack of a chairman.⁴⁶ This made it difficult for NDAC members to coordinate activities across different production areas.⁴⁷ Nor could commission members speak with one voice to the military services.

As 1940 came to an end, the expanding defense program threatened to outstrip the nation's productive capacity. Individual military orders continued to be issued without regard for the cumulative impact on the nation's manufacturing capacity.⁴⁸ Subsequent shortages in materials, tools, and component parts exacerbated the manufacturing bottlenecks.⁴⁹

Although NDAC had helped initiate defense conversion, a more effective administrative system was clearly needed to match the nation's in-

---

44 An overview of its internal organization and spheres of activity is provided in the NDAC's "Weekly Progress Report," first submitted to FDR on July 24, 1940. See *PSF* – Subject Files; Council of National Defense Folder, FDRL, pp. 1–7.

45 On paper, of course, its most significant power was contract clearance, vested in Knudsen and Nelson. In addition, NDAC possessed limited authority to review applications for accelerated tax amortization on defense plants, to establish production priorities, to stockpile critical materials, and to establish production estimates.

46 Nelson considered this NDAC's greatest weakness. See Nelson, *The Arsenal of Democracy*, pp. 82–3. McReynolds, who headed the OEM, was officially designated to chair Commission meetings in FDR's absence, but he was not empowered to make decisions. See also the memo from Sidney [?] to Roosevelt, asking him to strengthen McReynolds's role in "clearance, procedure and administrative control." "A word from you to McReynolds, to take a stronger hand, would do the trick" (Nov. 26, 1940, [?] to FDR, *PSF* – Subject Files, Council of National Defense Folder, FDRL, pp. 1–2).

47 As Nelson recalled, "Someone had to have the authority to say what should be produced, in order that a balanced war program might be carried out" (Nelson, *Arsenal of Democracy*, p. 112). Leon Henderson agreed, writing Roosevelt that, "[t]he Commission still needs a Co-ordinator and Don Nelson is still the best bet. He [Nelson] would be elected, almost unanimously, if you wanted to handle it this way" (Henderson to Roosevelt [Nov. 20, 1940], *PSF* – Subject Files, Council of National Defense Folder, FDRL, p. 2). Hopkins made a similar proposal.

48 "As military requirements grew, the operational impact of this type of [spot] control procedure were all in the direction of disorganization, waste, and planlessness" (Novick, Anshen and Truppner, *Wartime Production Controls*, p. 66).

49 The primary problem was the lack of administrative means for balancing total production requirements with total manufacturing capacity. Without any mechanism for aggregating the sum of individual priority production orders, uncoordinated production efforts led to material shortfalls, thus producing manufacturing bottlenecks. This problem became more acute as the size of the defense effort expanded. "The larger the program, the greater was the impact on production capacity and the more difficult the task of administration" (Ibid., p. 49). Moreover, inadequate stockpiling, and later the hoarding, of raw materials exacerbated the problem.

dustrial capacity with its strategic needs.⁵⁰ (This was particularly true after Lend-Lease went into effect in the spring of 1941.⁵¹)

Congress began urging FDR to appoint a single administrator to oversee defense preparation.⁵² Labor leaders, meanwhile, continued to complain about lack of representation on NDAC. The press, egged on by Republican candidate Wendell Willkie's charges, gave substantial play to these criticisms during the 1940 presidential campaign.⁵³

50 See the memo from Henderson to FDR, summarizing the NDAC's accomplishments through November 1940. ([Nov. 20, 1940], *PSF* – Subject Files, Council on National Defense Folder, FDRL, pp. 1–2.) Henderson acknowledged NDAC's progress in placing production contracts, but he pointed out the need to integrate production planning with strategic considerations, especially in the critical areas of production scheduling, procurement planning, and labor supply.
   The failure to adequately organize defense production in part reflected a simple lack of knowledge regarding the minimum level of materials needed to maintain the civilian economy, as well as the fact that there was as yet no agreed upon military strategy. For example, at what point did the military's desire for rubber threaten the construction of farm tractors necessary to harvest crops? Nobody knew. The lack of reliable statistical data eventually prompted NDAC to bring in Stacy May to head a Bureau of Research and Statistics. Subsequently, the May organization was transferred to NDAC's successor, the Office of Production Management. It was May who was responsible in 1941 for compiling the crucial report that for the first time listed British and American war needs and capacities. See Nelson, *Arsenal of Democracy*, pp. 129–38.

51 Lend-Lease was established Mar. 11, 1941, to provide American assistance to the Allied nations. It followed Churchill's urgent request to FDR for assistance in late 1940, at a time when Great Britain had exhausted both military hardware and her cash reserves. (On the background to Churchill's request, see Blum, "Birth and Death of the M-Day Plan," pp. 340–6; James McGregor Burns, *Soldier of Freedom* (New York: Harcourt, Brace Jovanovich, 1970), pp. 23–6. Roosevelt's response was a plan to lend or loan military equipment to Great Britain, with repayment "in kind." (He remained vague as to what constituted "in kind" repayment and no one thought to pin him down.) A formal request for the legislation was made in FDR's annual message to Congress in January of the following year, and the legislation was passed two months later, with an initial appropriation of $7 billion dollars. (On its legislative history, see Samuel I. Rosenman, *Working with Roosevelt* (New York: Harper & Row, 1952), pp. 257–74; Sherwood, *Roosevelt and Hopkins*, pp. 228–9; and Blum, "Birth and Death of the M-Day Plan," pp. 349–58.)
   Although FDR initially considered administering Lend-Lease through a State-Treasury-Army-Navy cabinet committee, he instead created a "Division of Defense Aid Reports" within the OEM, ostensibly under the direction of General James Burns. In fact, Lend-Lease officials reported directly to Roosevelt, with Hopkins appointed "to advise and assist" him in this area. (The title Division of Defense Aid Reports was not changed to Lend-Lease Administration until seven months later.) See Blum, "Birth and Death of the M-Day Plan," p. 357; Sherwood, *Roosevelt and Hopkins*, p. 278.
   Throughout the summer of 1941 the principal recipient of Lend-Lease aid was Great Britain, with China receiving some material as well.

52 On Nov. 21, 1940, Senator Robert Taft was reported to have announced that he would introduce a bill to create a War Resources Board under a single administrator. Somers, *Presidential Agency*, p. 14. This would be the clarion call of several congressional committees investigating defense production during the next two years. See Somers, *Presidential Agency*, pp. 110–11.

53 For instance, see the memo from Early to FDR (May 23, 1940), in which Early complains, "A careful reading and analysis of the editorials and contributions of columnists in the Scripps-Howard papers during the past two weeks justifies the charge that these

Roosevelt, however, resisted entreaties to place a single person at the head of an NDAC with statutory teeth.[54] Instead, after winning reelection to a third term in November 1940, he removed the four most critical mobilization-related activities from NDAC: production, materials procurement, employment, and purchasing, and placed them within a newly created Office of Production Management (OPM).[55] Subsequently, in the spring of 1941, all of NDAC's appropriations were allocated to the OEM, and the commission, while never formally terminated, decreased in importance, holding its last meeting on Oct. 23, 1941.

The Office of Production Management

Like NDAC, the Office of Production Management was placed within the OEM where it reported directly to FDR. Rather than the relatively vague legal guidelines given NDAC, however, the OPM was issued explicit statutory authority to administer industrial mobilization.[56] Nevertheless, OPM authority was split between William Knudsen as Director General

papers are distorting the facts in dealing with the question of national defense." Early subsequently met with Roy Howard, one of the directors of this newspaper chain, in an attempt to muffle the criticism. Howard asked Early if FDR "was going to put one man in charge of national defense" (Early to FDR [May 28, 1940]; both memoranda contained in *PSF* – Subject Files, Executive Office – Early Folder, FDRL).

54 There was no shortage of advice to FDR on how to improve NDAC; Leon Henderson wrote Roosevelt that, "I understand many persons have charts or plans for reorganizing the Commission, including Knudsen, Harold Smith and Stettinius" (Henderson to FDR, [Nov. 20, 1940], *PSF* – Subject Files, Council on National Defense Folder, FDRL, p. 3). Knudsen's advice was to place him in sole charge of defense production. Roosevelt refused, however, because he feared labor's reaction should he appoint a businessman like Knudsen to the post. Wann, *The President as Chief Administrator*, p. 141.

55 See E.O. 8629 (Jan. 7, 1941). Consumer protection, agriculture, and transportation were left for the time being under the jurisdiction of NDAC. However, various other divisions within NDAC were either reassigned to the OPM or established as separate entities within the OEM. The Bureau of Research and Statistics went into the OPM, whereas the Division of Information and the Office of Coordinator of National Defense Housing (E.O. 8632, Jan. 11, 1941) were established as separate divisions. The divisions of Price Stabilization and Consumer Protection were eventually merged into an independent Office of Price Administration and Civilian Supply on Apr. 11, 1941 (E.O. 8734).

56 E.O. 8629 (Jan. 7, 1941) stated that the OPM was to: "Formulate and execute in the public interest all measures needful and appropriate in order (1) to increase, accelerate, and regulate the production and supply of materials, articles, and equipment and for provision of emergency plant facilities and services required for the national defense, and (2) to insure effective coordination of those activities of the several departments, corporations, and other agencies of the government which are directly concerned therewith."
   In addition, Roosevelt delegated to the OPM the power to place compulsory orders and requisition materials, drawing on authority granted him by Congress through the Selective Service and Training Act of 1940, as well as powers granted FDR by Congress on June 28, 1940. See also Nelson, *Arsenal of Democracy*, pp. 117–18 for an overview of the OPM powers.

and Sidney Hillman, the Associate Director General. These two were expected to operate, as Roosevelt explained to a skeptical group of reporters, much as controlling partners in a law firm.[57] Moreover, the secretaries of the Navy and of War were appointed with Knudsen and Hillman to a policy council designed to integrate military and civilian needs and to develop the underlying principles to guide the day-to-day operational activities of the OPM.

In a Dec. 20, 1940, press conference, Roosevelt tried to explain the administrative philosophy governing his choice of a new defense production setup:

> There were two or three cardinal principles; and one of them is the fact that you cannot, under the Constitution, set up a second President of the United States.
>
> In other words, the Constitution states one man is responsible. Now that man can delegate, surely, but in the delegation he does not delegate away any part of the responsibility from the ultimate responsibility that rests on him.[58]

Roosevelt argued that industrial production necessitated balancing three very different interests: the buyer and user, management, and labor.[59] "[I]t is impossible to find any one 'Czar' of 'Poobah' or 'Akhoond of Swats,' who combines all three of those elements in his own person," he asserted. In truth, the practical effect of this arrangement was to leave ultimate control in FDR's hand, precisely where he felt it belonged. Donald Nelson acknowledged as much.

---

57 Quizzed during his Dec. 20, 1940 press conference as to who would hold final authority in the proposed OPM, Roosevelt replied, "I have a single, responsible head; his name is Knudsen and Hillman." See Samuel I. Rosenman (ed.) *The Public Papers and Addresses of Franklin D. Roosevelt*, (New York: Random House, 1940) (hereafter *FDR's Public Papers*), p. 684.

58 Cited in Wann, *The President as Chief Administrator*, pp. 142–3. See also Rosenman, *Working with Roosevelt*, p. 258.

59 Knudsen and Hillman represented management and labor, respectively, and the secretaries of War and the Navy represented the "buyers and users." Internally, the OPM was divided into three independent administrative sectors: a Division of Production, a Division of Purchases, and a Division of Priorities. These were headed by John D. Biggers, Donald Nelson, and Edward Stettinius, respectively. To a great extent these divisions operated independently of one another. They were soon supplemented on Mar. 17, 1941, by the inclusion of the NDAC's Division of Labor, headed by Sidney Hillman, and the Bureau of Research and Statistics under May.

In addition, FDR again established a Priorities Board, to serve as an advisory policy-making body regarding defense production priorities and materials allocation. The board was chaired by Stettinius, and included Biggers, Major General R. C. Moore, Captain A. B. Anderson, and Nelson, along with Knudsen and Hillman as ex officio members. Ickes notes that FDR asked Morgenthau and Harold Smith, director of the BoB, to participate on the Priorities Board as ex officio members, but that Morgenthau wanted no part of an organization that he felt was sure to explode through internal bickering.

The President's announcement . . . had informed us that he was going to run the new show just as he had run the headless NDAC. He
was not going to cede or delegate any powers to any "economic" czar.
The new machine was to operate with co-pilots, a Director General
and an Associate Director General – which apparently meant that the
Boss would be the Super-director General, just as he had been with
NDAC.[60]

Thus, despite somewhat more impressive statutory language and some
structural improvements, the OPM was in fact not much more powerful
than NDAC.[61] Although the OPM could advise, summarize, survey, analyze, and prioritize (in consultation with the military) the placement of defense orders, it could not determine military requirements, nor did it
actually control the provision of defense production contracts.[62] That authority remained essentially with the Army and Navy departments, operating through their procurement arms.[63]

Moreover, as the OPM subdivided internally into more administrative divisions in addition to the ones absorbed from NDAC, its
administrative cohesion broke down.[64] At the top, co-directors Knudsen and Hillman frequently found themselves working at cross-
purposes.[65] To make matters worse, Roosevelt – perhaps reflecting
his ambivalence toward creating a superagency – appointed "czars"
in several defense-related production fields, most of whom reported
directly to him rather than to the OPM.[66] The Office of Price Administration and Civilian Supply (OPACS), headed by Leon Henderson,

60 Nelson, *Arsenal of Democracy*, p. 117.
61 "Structurally, OPM suffered from the same deficiencies which had caused NDAC to
    sicken," Nelson recalled, adding that "Boiling down its provisions, it may be seen that
    it was largely a planning and advisory body, and all of the rhetoric celebrating its cre-
    ation could not make it more than that" (ibid., p. 118).
62 *Industrial Mobilization*, pp. 93–4, 115–19; Smith, *The Army and Economic Mobili-
    zation*, pp. 513–17; Harold G. Vatter, *The U.S. Economy in World War II* (New York:
    Columbia University Press, 1985), pp. 36–7, and Wann, *The President as Chief Ad-
    ministrator*, pp. 146–9.
63 Somers notes that some consideration was given to eliminating the ANMB and center-
    ing all procurement authority within the OPM's Priorities Board. Navy Secretary Frank
    Knox suggested entirely abolishing the ANMB priority functions, but the Army, led by
    Under Secretary of War Robert Patterson, disagreed. See Somers, *Presidential Agency*,
    pp. 15, 115.
64 Beginning with about 1,000 employees inherited from NDAC, the OPM grew by the
    end of 1941 to approximately 7,600 employees. Moreover, it became increasingly diffi-
    cult to keep up with the paperwork generated by its growing production control system.
    An overview of the internal workings of the OPM is provided in *Industrial Mobiliza-
    tion*, pp. 96–102.
65 See Perkins, *The Roosevelt I Knew*, pp. 363–5, regarding conflict between the two.
66 Ickes, appointed by FDR as Petroleum Coordinator for National Defense in May 1941,
    was the first. Later czars were created for labor and rubber.

proved to be the most troublesome, but each helped undercut the OPM's authority.[67]

In the spring of 1941, more comprehensive production controls focusing on entire production lines, including all parts necessary to manufacture the priority end products, were instituted.[68] This was an improvement over the system of spot controls and preference ratings, but it still did not balance aggregate military needs with the nation's overall economic capacity.[69] Instead, in the face of the geometrically expanding defense program, a domino effect was created by the competition among manufacturers for scarce materials. Shortages rippled downward from the factory producing the end product to those responsible for providing the necessary components, such as tools and raw materials that went into building the military item. Manufacturers responded by requesting

67 The Office of Price Administration and Civilian Supply (OPACS) was created by FDR Apr. 11, 1941 (E.O. 8734), as a price control agency. Directed by Leon Henderson, it in effect merged the NDAC's price stabilization division, which had used voluntary controls to try and stem the rise in prices of materials and commodities, with NDAC's consumer protection division (under Harriet Elliot). In addition to price control, OPACS took charge of civilian rationing.
    The OPM and OPACS presented distinct and opposing perspectives on the objectives of industrial mobilization. As Nelson recalls (Nelson, *Arsenal of Democracy*, pp. 125–6) OPACS' policy makers (the "all-outers") sought a rapid movement to a wartime economy through expedited conversion of industrial plants to war production and the stockpiling of raw materials. In contrast, the OPM directors advocated a much slower transition to a wartime economy. In this they were supported by Jesse Jones and members of the Reconstruction Finance Corporation (RFC), which provided much of the financing necessary for purchasing raw materials and for industrial conversion. Moreover, many viewed OPACS as a "New Deal" agency, whereas OPM was perceived as more responsive to industry. (BoB, *The U.S. at War*, pp. 73–9).
    The different perspectives were exacerbated by the clash engendered by the agency's peculiar division of jurisdictions that administratively separated product and materials pricing and rationing from manufacturing control. In actual practice, however, the two could not be separated so easily. For instance, manufacturers who feared price inflation would frequently stockpile more raw materials than they needed to fill current orders. This, of course, produced more shortages and higher prices. Although OPACS was responsible for rationing and price control, it could in fact only recommend production programs to meet its targets; actual power to implement those recommendations was vested in the OPM through its priorities orders. As Somers notes, "This splitting of the priority power and OPACS' lack of authority to enforce any of its recommendations made the system administratively unworkable" (Somers, *Presidential Agency*, p. 18). See also *Industrial Mobilization*, pp. 102–5, 174–7.
68 These "general" preference orders, first issued Mar. 12, 1941, essentially shifted the focus of administrative controls from the end product itself to the raw materials and other items from which the end product was made. For additional details, see Smith, *The Army and Economic Mobilization*, pp. 516–49.
69 The OPM did compile for the first time an estimate of the overall production needs of the United States, given Lend-Lease, military and civilian requirements. That demonstrated clearly that the nation would need to convert to a wartime economy. See *Industrial Mobilization*, pp. 134–40.

priority ratings for their particular product. But as the number of priority items multiplied, the ratings themselves became meaningless.[70]

In addition, the impact of military production demands spilled over into the civilian sector, drawing away materials and manufacturing capacity once reserved for civilian needs. In the spring of 1941, the first controls were thus slapped on nonmilitary production, again on a spot basis, in an attempt to reduce consumption.[71] These were followed in August 1941 with broader restrictions, intended to limit the aggregate use of materials, facilities, and labor across a class of products.[72]

The institution of across-the-board production priorities and controls created a new problem. As production shifted to prioritized items and as other items were cut back, unanticipated shortages appeared in areas previously considered nonessential to the war effort.

By the summer of 1941, it was increasingly obvious there needed to be a more comprehensive production control system regulating almost the entire economy.[73] But the OPM lacked the authority or organizational means to implement such a system. Despite an administrative reorganization that June, it was still plagued by internal coordination problems.[74] These deficiencies became particularly acute after the German invasion of the Soviet Union that month caused a significant expansion in the Lend-Lease program and further fueled inflationary pressures.[75]

---

70 As all items were rated top priority, determining which were truly critical to the war effort became difficult.

71 These were conservation orders, issued in the "M" series beginning in March 1941 with aluminum.

72 Usually by forbidding the production of the product entirely or reducing it to some percentage of a prewar base. Although these limitations, or "L" orders were tailored to fit the requirements of different manufacturing spheres, they tended to be inflexible and time-consuming to establish. See Novick, Anshen, and Truppner, *Wartime Production Controls*, pp. 67–75.

73 The breakdown in the priorities system prompted Bernard Baruch to write FDR, complaining, "Unless production is greatly increased, tragic results lie in front of us. The principal difficulty in production lies in the final priority authority which should be immediately centralized in O.P.M." (Baruch to FDR [May 7, 1941], *PSF* – Subject Files, OPM Folder, FDRL. Baruch had developed his thoughts regarding the need to centralize priority control in the OPM more fully in previous memoranda; See Baruch to FDR (Apr. 16, 1941), *PSF* – Subject Files, OPM Folder, FDRL. He also warned Roosevelt regarding the need to institute price controls: "I see no way of getting away from a ceiling over all prices." See also Nelson, *Arsenal of Democracy*, pp. 139–44.

74 Under this reorganization, commodity sections were established to serve as liaison with major industries in different fields. In addition, industry advisory committees, consisting of representatives of particular industries, were established. Both innovations were carried over to the OPM's successors. Nelson, *Arsenal of Democracy*, pp. 144–5. Interestingly, provisions for both commodity sections and industry advisory committees were contained in the M-Day Plans never implemented.

75 For the particulars of Lend-Lease to the Soviet Union, see *Industrial Mobilization*, pp. 122–33. On the inflationary pressures, see Somers, *Presidential Agency*, p. 19.

To complicate matters, congressional oversight of defense production intensified.[76] Alarmed, Roosevelt's subordinates warned him of the possible political consequences, given the disorganized state of the defense preparedness program.[77] Prominent outsiders, like Bernard Baruch who had served as a prototype of a mobilization czar during World War I, were also highly critical:

> The production of these things is not moving well. . . . I think it is because of the organization.
>
> I am sorry to find myself in disagreement with what has been done. . . . But I can assure you that I still think as I did in the beginning. We are improperly organized. It has cost us 20% more in money (which is comparatively unimportant) but also 33⅓% in time which cannot be measured except by success or failure.[78]

In May 1941 Roosevelt had beat back proposed legislation that would have established a Director of Priorities, appointed by the president but subject to senatorial confirmation.[79] Soon after, however, a bill was introduced to replace the OPM with a War Resources Administration. By the summer of 1941, it was evident that the OPM was, in Nelson's words, "ready for the oxygen tank."[80]

76 On Mar. 1, 1941, the Senate Committee to Investigate the National Defense Program (the Truman Committee) was established to provide continual oversight of the war agencies. For an overview, see Donald H. Riddle, *The Truman Committee: A Study in Congressional Responsibility* (New Brunswick, N.J.: Rutgers University Press, 1964). In addition, a Senate Committee to Study and Survey Problems of Small Business Enterprises (the Murray Committee), and a House Committee Investigating National Defense Migration (the Tolan Committee) were appointed. In 1941 alone fifty-one OPM officials appeared before nineteen Congressional committees on over 130 separate occasions. *Industrial Mobilization*, pp. 114–15; Nelson, *Arsenal of Democracy*, p. 128.

77 A week after the Truman Committee was established, James Rowe, one of Roosevelt's White House assistants, wrote Roosevelt: "But if something isn't done, OPM, the Army and the Navy will be a shambles. Congress is 'gunning' for them . . . and, under the present set-up a child could do the job" (Rowe to Roosevelt, [Mar. 8, 1941], *PSF* – Personal File, Rowe Folder, FDRL).

   Roosevelt had already suggested to the OPM Policy Council that they organize a division to prepare for any possible congressional investigation of the national defense program. See FDR to the Secretary of War, et. al. [Mar. 6, 1941]; *PSF* – Subject Files, OPM Folder, FDRL.

78 Baruch to Hopkins [May 7, 1941], Hopkins Papers, Sherwood Book Manuscript Collection, Book 3: Developing Crisis of May 1941 #3 Folder, FDRL. Baruch's frustration with Roosevelt's defense organization is illustrated in an undated memo he sent to "Pa" Watson, one of FDR's political secretaries: "How in hell can he [FDR] make a decision worth a D__ with all this hooey being handed him" (Baruch to Watson, *PSF* – Subject File, Office of Production Management Folder, FDRL).

79 The proposed legislative amendment would have prohibited FDR from delegating priority power to anyone but the Director of Priorities, who would then only exercise powers with the approval of the Army – Navy Munitions Board. See the memo from Wayne Coy to FDR (May 9, 1941), *PSF* – Subject File, OPM folder, FDRL.

80 Nelson, *Arsenal of Democracy*, p. 139.

The Supply Priorities and Allocations Board

In response, Roosevelt decided on Aug. 28, 1941, to create a seven-member Supply Priorities and Allocations Board (SPAB).[81] This was still another administrative compromise, based in part on plans worked up by Samuel Rosenman.[82] The board was comprised of the four OPM policy council members (Knudsen, Hillman, Stimson, and Knox), most of whom advocated incremental wartime conversion, and three people (Hopkins, Leon Henderson, and Vice-President Henry Wallace) known to favor rapid mobilization. Moreover, SPAB's production authority was considerably increased over that of the OPM.[83] It was essentially given the power to determine the total materials and commodities needed for defense and civilian purposes, including Lend-Lease, and the power to recommend policies to obtain those requirements.[84] The OPM, meanwhile, continued to handle the operational side of defense mobilization, subject to SPAB's policy directives.[85]

But SPAB too suffered from administrative flaws.[86] Officially it was chaired by Vice-President Henry Wallace, who also headed the Economic Defense Board.[87] Because Wallace could not devote full time to SPAB, ac-

81 See E.O. 8875, (Aug. 28, 1941).
82 Asked at this time by FDR to investigate defense production, Rosenman concluded that there needed to be a central production agency with the power to decide all matters of supply and priority.
83 Donald Nelson was made SPAB's executive director. Jesse Jones, the Secretary of Commerce, was added later to supervise financing from the Reconstruction Finance Corporation.
84 As stated in E.O. 8875, SPAB would:
(a) Determine the total requirements of materials and commodities needed, respectively, for defense, civilian, and all other purposes; establish policies for the fulfillment of such accomplishments, and, where necessary, make recommendations to the president relative thereto.
(b) Determine policies and make regulations governing allocations and priorities with respect to the procurement, production, transmission, or transportation of materials, articles, power, fuel, and other commodities among military, economic defense, defense aid, civilian, and other major demands of the total defense program.
85 The OPM added two new divisions: Materials and Civilian Supply (which had formerly been part of OPACS). Leon Henderson was appointed head of civilian supply, although he continued as well to head the Office of Price Administration (OPA – OPACS' administrative remnant). In this capacity, Henderson was responsible for determining civilian needs, submitting his requests to SPAB through the OPM. The OPA survived until the end of the war as the agency responsible for price control and rationing.
86 Roosevelt had stopped short of ceding total authority over industrial production to the SPAB; its jurisdiction extended only to the allocation of the materials necessary to manufacture war materials. It was the president, in consultation with the military services, who continued to make the final decisions regarding the disbursement of finished products, such as guns, planes, and ships. See the press release announcing SPAB's creation (Aug. 28, 1941).
87 Established July 30, 1941, the Economic Defense Board was responsible for overseeing the import and export of military items.

tual administrative responsibility devolved to Nelson, as executive director. But Nelson lacked the statutory authority to enforce decisions, and the lines of authority connecting him to Knudsen, who still headed the OPM, and to Henderson, who headed OPACS as well as the OPM's newly created Division of Civilian Supply, were hopelessly tangled.[88] In effect, SPAB merely transformed an interagency dispute between the OPM and the OPACS into an intraagency dispute within SPAB. Moreover, without full power to award war contracts, SPAB's attempts to administer price control and civilian production could never be fully effective.

Nevertheless, SPAB served an important planning purpose during its brief four-month history.[89] In particular, SPAB's compilation of overall figures on the supplies required to prosecute the war, including the Lend-Lease program, conclusively demonstrated that the United States would need to convert to a full war economy. That compilation was also a prerequisite for determining production priorities and for developing a policy governing civilian production.[90] And, by eschewing operational duties, SPAB was better able to coordinate the activities of its subordinate agencies, especially the OPM and the OPACS – a lesson its administrative successor, the War Production Board, did not learn.

Despite these accomplishments, Roosevelt's handling of defense production as 1941 drew to a close remained a politically vulnerable spot. This was partly because the general public was increasingly feeling the impact of defense mobilization as administrative controls expanded to non-military products and rationing went into effect.[91] Moreover, the continuing dispute between civilian and military agencies threatened the Democratic margin of control in Congress.[92]

---

88 Nelson points out that, as executive director of SPAB, he gave orders to OPM, but as director of OPM's Priorities Division, he received orders from OPM. See Nelson, *Arsenal of Democracy*, pp. 159–60; *Industrial Mobilization*, pp. 112–13.

89 Its first meeting took place Sept. 2, 1941, the last on Jan. 13, 1942. On its accomplishments, see Nelson, *Arsenal of Democracy*, pp. 159–68.

90 As Nelson summarizes: "By the end of summer . . . the Supply, Priorities and Allocations Board had made three basic decisions without which war production of the size we later attained would never have been possible. It had committed us to an all-out program; it had established the policy of providing the necessary productive equipment for such basic civilian industries as agriculture; and it had agreed that the civilian economy would be protected in its ability to do the job required of it" (Nelson, *Arsenal of Democracy*, p. 170). See also Somers, *Presidential Agency*, pp. 22–3.

91 Moreover, the shortage of raw materials and the tendency of the armed services to award contracts to large firms created great animosity among small businesses.

92 As the midterm congressional elections drew near, Eugene Casey, one of FDR's administrative assistants, warned: "The 1942 elections will be lost by the Democratic Party if the straight lines of action of the ultimate aims of the all-out Defense Program are not defined at once. . . . Procurement of all supplies must be placed under civilian control and taken away from the Army and Navy to the end of better and complete coordination of planning, priorities, and allocations" (Casey to FDR [Nov. 26, 1941], *PSF* – Personal Files, Casey Folder, FDRL).

Most ominous, however, was the leveling of war-related production during the second half of 1941: Aircraft totals were lower than projected; military and cargo shipbuilding actually declined; so did the production of key raw materials.[93] This fueled the perception that economic mobilization was in disarray. Again, Roosevelt was urged, this time by the Truman Committee, to delegate oversight of defense production to a single czar.[94] On Dec. 6, 1941, a member of a special congressional committee investigating defense preparedness submitted legislation to centralize administration of war production within a proposed Department of Defense Coordination and Control, to be headed by a new cabinet officer.

Within a day, however, the surprise Japanese attack on Pearl Harbor entirely changed the nature of FDR's administrative problems. No longer need he concern himself lest he push too quickly to convert the nation to defense production. Instead, the fear now was that of not moving quickly enough.

93 See Burns, *Soldier of Freedom*, pp. 192–3.
94 See *The New York Times*, (Dec. 7, 1941) and Report No. 480, pt. 5 (Jan. 15, 1942), 77th Congress, 2nd sess., Senate, Special Committee Investigating the National Defense Program (cited in Wann, *The President as Chief Administrator*, p. 23).

5

Managing war production

The Japanese attack and America's formal entry into World War II all but ended Roosevelt's concern regarding the isolationists' opposition against United States' military intervention overseas. Now his primary objective became maximizing the nation's military output as quickly as possible. That, however, necessitated overhauling the administration of war production.[1] Accordingly, on Jan. 16, 1942, he replaced both SPAB and the OPM with the War Production Board (WPB), and charged it with insuring the production of finished capital goods and materials, military items, and consumer products (except for food, housing, and transportation).[2] To accomplish these goals, the WPB was authorized to

[1] Shortly after the Japanese attack on Pearl Harbor, FDR met with Churchill and Lord Beaverbrook, the British Minister of Supply, to discuss Allied strategy and production needs. Subsequently, in his State of the Union address to Congress on Jan. 6, 1942, Roosevelt laid out America's war production goals for the coming year: 60,000 planes in 1942 and 125,000 the following year; 45,000 tanks, followed the next year by 75,000; 20,000 antiaircraft guns in 1942 and 35,000 the following year; and 8 million deadweight tons of shipping in 1942. (For a more detailed breakdown, see the memorandum from FDR to Stimson [Jan. 3, 1942] listing projections for 1942 and 1943 [copies were sent to Knox, Knudsen, and Hillman], Harry Hopkins Papers, Special Assistant to the President, 1941–5, Production File, FDRL.)
Roosevelt's production targets were met with disbelief, even among his own production advisers who were most familiar with the administrative disarray characterizing the mobilization efforts to date. The evidence suggests FDR largely cut the targets from whole cloth by adding to existing baseline projections. For details, see "The Feasibility Dispute: The Determination of War Production Objectives for 1942 and 1943" (Washington, D.C.: Committee on Public Administration Cases, 1950).
[2] E.O. 9024 (Jan. 16, 1942). See also Harold G. Vatter, *The U.S. Economy in World War II* (New York: Columbia University Press, 1985), p. 69. The OPM's and SPAB's powers were transferred to the WPB. Nelson recalls that Roosevelt delegated the drafting of the executive order creating the WPB to him. See Donald Nelson, *Arsenal of Democracy: The Story of American War Production* (New York: Harcourt, Brace and Company, 1946), pp. 195–7. But James Byrnes says that he drafted it in consultation with Smith and Hopkins. James Byrnes, *Speaking Frankly* (New York: Harper & Brothers, 1947), pp. 16–9.
The WPB's powers were later amended by E.O. 9040 (Jan. 24, 1942) and E.O. 9125 (Apr. 7, 1942).

force manufacturers to accept military contracts, to requisition private property, and to stop the production of specified goods and services.

In effect, however, it was Donald Nelson who assumed these powers; the WPB served in a purely advisory capacity to him.[3] Except for price control, Nelson essentially wielded authority over every aspect of the domestic defense effort.[4] A Roosevelt memorandum to Nelson summarized the president's expectations regarding the division of labor between Nelson and the military:

> [T]he Army and Navy should advise me what they want to fight with, how many of each munition is required and when they should be delivered. That is clearly a strategic military function.
>
> . . . I do not expect the Army and Navy to then determine . . . how these items are to be rated as priorities or allocations. . . . The weapons are all important and they all must be built on schedule.
>
> If there is any rating to be done for allocation purposes of machine tools, equipment, materials or labor, I think you should do it. . . . [Y]ou should start from scratch with all these various priorities which have been assigned by the munitions board and review them in relation to my directive.[5]

There are a number of reasons why Roosevelt decided to finally appoint a single war mobilization czar, after resisting for so long.[6] First, of course, America's entrance into the war removed any remaining political obstacles to converting to a full war economy. Second, military strategy had been elevated to the forefront of FDR's concerns, necessitating a corresponding decline in his attention to production issues. Third, by establishing the WPB through executive order, Roosevelt preempted congressional efforts to create a war production agency less amenable to presidential influence. Fourth, ultimate responsibility for war production

---

3 With membership consisting of Stimson, Knox, Jones, Wallace, Henderson, and Hopkins, the WPB in fact was not much more than a reconstituted SPAB.

4 "The Chairman may exercise the powers, authority, and discretion conferred upon him . . . through such officials or agencies and in such a manner as he may determine; and his decision shall be final." Furthermore, the Army – Navy Munitions Board was directed to report to the president through Nelson. On Apr. 7, Nelson assumed the allocation power initially granted to the president under title III of the Second War Powers Act. Wann writes, "The authority delegated to Nelson constituted Roosevelt's greatest delegation [sic] of authority since he became president in 1933" (A. J. Wann *The President as Chief Administrator: A Study of Franklin D. Roosevelt* [Washington, D.C.: Public Affairs Press, 1968], p. 157).

5 Roosevelt to Nelson (Feb. 11, 1942), Hopkins Papers, Special Assistant to the President, 1941–5, Production File, FDRL.

6 According to Byrnes, Roosevelt initially considered creating still another multimember production board, but decided against it after Byrnes and Hopkins warned that only a single individual with strong presidential backing would be able to arbitrate the inevitable production disputes. See James Byrnes, *All in One Lifetime* (New York: Harper & Brothers, 1958), pp. 150–1.

still rested with Roosevelt, who retained – and frequently exercised – his authority to intervene in the production decisions as he saw fit.[7] Fifth, it was clear the OPM simply was not organizationally suited to ensure the level of production necessary to win the war.

The most fundamental reason, however, may be that Roosevelt in fact did not see Nelson as the all-powerful defense mobilization czar Baruch and others had long pushed for. In fact, having appointed Nelson, Roosevelt then took steps that in retrospect appear to have undercut Nelson's authority.[8] This partly reflected FDR's suspicion, not unfounded, that WPB members did not believe FDR's production targets were realistic.[9] Moreover, Nelson's own conception of his job reinforced FDR's reluctance:

> As interpreted and executed by me, it was not the one man job conceived by the President when the Board was created. The economic power vested in me at that time was potentially greater than that ever held by any other civilian, except a wartime president. The records will show that of my own initiative I shed controls and authorities not directly germane to my principal function (which was war production) as rapidly as I could be sure that they had been placed in competent hands. This was done not to escape responsibility, but to allocate responsibility in such a way that the administrative capacity of no one person – including myself – would be spread so thin that it would lose its tensile strength.[10]

7 For example, just prior to the invasion of North Africa, Roosevelt directed Nelson to accelerate the production of landing craft, heretofore not a priority item. See Nelson, *Arsenal for Democracy*, pp. 252–9.

8 Perhaps this is not so surprising, given FDR's first-term dealings with Donald Richberg, the so-called Assistant President whose authority he effectively undermined.

9 Indeed, a study by the WPB planning office concluded that the supplementary production targets the military services deemed necessary to achieve FDR's primary production objectives could not be obtained in the specified time period. See "The Feasibility Dispute."

Hopkins, after receiving reports regarding pessimism within the WPB, sent them along to FDR with a cover memo stating: "I hope you will have time to read this, because it indicates the kind of thing that you are going to have to watch out for. There are still a good many defeatists about in your production program" (Hopkins to FDR [Feb. 23, 1942]; see also Lubin to Hopkins [Feb. 21, 1942]; both in Hopkins Papers, Special Assistant to the President, Production File, FDRL).

10 Nelson, *Arsenal of Democracy*, pp. xi–xii. See also his testimony before the Truman Committee, cited in the Bureau of the Budget, *The United States at War: Development and Administration of the War Program by the Federal Government* (Washington, D.C.: Government Printing Office, 1946), p. 107: "I have gone even to the point of being overzealous in seeing that the contracting power is kept within the Army and Navy," he told the Committee. Nelson argued that the American political tradition emphasizing self-rule and freedom from government coercion meant the WPB had to effectuate industrial mobilization without resorting to outright coercion; in effect, he viewed the war as a test case determining whether democracy could outproduce totalitarian regimes without adopting totalitarian tactics. Nelson, *Arsenal of Democracy*, pp. 198–210;

However, by delegating production tasks to other agencies, Nelson diluted his own authority; the WPB came to be seen as one of several agencies vying for the president's ear, rather than as the administrative court of last resort. This perception was reinforced as the WPB developed into a full-fledged operating agency, rather than retaining its original function as the coordinating body at the top of the production hierarchy.[11] By taking on operational duties, the WPB's clashes with other war agencies and departments, particularly the military, increased.

But FDR's repeated creation, with Nelson's concurrence, of "claimant" agencies under the direction of "czars" greatly diluted the WPB's authority.[12] Almost immediately after taking charge in 1942, Nelson had delegated partial oversight of rationing to the Office of Price Administration.[13] Within the next year at least a dozen more "claimant" agencies, responsible for manpower,[14] petroleum, solid

207–11. See also U.S. Bureau of Demobilization *Industrial Mobilization for War: History of the War Production Board and Predecessor Agencies, 1940–5*, vol. 1, (Washington, D.C.: Government Printing Office, 1947), pp. 208–12 for a balanced discussion of Nelson's administrative qualities.

11 The WPB gradually expanded from about 6,600 employees to a peak of some 23,000 people in February 1943, two thirds of whom worked in Washington, D.C., with the remaining third in field offices. The growth coincided with the changing objective from industrial mobilization and conversion to the integration of military and production strategy.
    Nelson initially grouped the WPB into the following divisions: Production, under William Harrison; Industry Operations, under James Knowlson; Materials, under William Batt; Civilian Supply, under Henderson; Labor, under Hillman; Statistics, under May; Purchases, under Douglas MacKeachie; Legal, under John O'Brian; and Planning, under Robert Nathan. For staff support he had a Planning Committee (for details see "The Feasibility Dispute") and an Office of Progress Reports. These are described in *Industrial Mobilization*, pp. 236–48; and Nelson, *Arsenal of Democracy*, pp. 203–5. The WPB was reorganized in July 1942.

12 As Smith noted in his monthly report to Roosevelt, "The alienation or withdrawal of powers from the War Production Board and the vesting of additional powers in the Food Administrator, the Petroleum Administrator, the War Manpower Commission, the Rubber Director, the Office of Defense Transportation, etc., has given rise to a considerable number of program disputes among these agencies" (Smith, BoB Report, [September – December 1942], p. 29, FDRL). Other claimants included the National Housing Agency, the Maritime Commission (responsible for shipbuilding), the War Shipping Administration (overseeing ocean shipping), the Foreign Economic Administration (created in 1943 to supervise all agencies, including Lend-Lease and the Board of Economic Warfare, with functions related to foreign aid), and, of course, the Army and Navy procurement agencies.

13 Recall the struggle between OPM and OPACS to integrate production and price controls. This dispute continued when the WPB was formed; although Nelson retained control over commodities and the amount to be rationed, the OPA under Henderson competed with the WPB's Division of Civilian Supply for operational control of rationing. See Nelson, *Arsenal of Democracy*, pp. 190–1.

14 Three months after creating the WPB, FDR offered Nelson oversight of a new manpower control agency, but Nelson refused. Consequently, the War Manpower Commission (WMC) under Paul McNutt was established as a separate organization, despite the critical importance of the labor supply for industrial production.

fuels, transportation, housing, food, and, in practice, rubber[15] were operating.[16]

The WPB's biggest struggles, however, were with the military, and they continued to center on procurement control.[17] When drafting the executive order specifying his authority, Nelson – in what looks retrospectively like a monumental blunder – decided not to formally lodge procurement power in his own hands.[18] He reasoned that to strip the military of this power at so critical a stage in the war might cause production delays that would be fatal to the nation. He also thought the armed services understood their production needs more completely than did a civilian board, and he believed the two could work out an informal procurement agreement.

> Labor strikes were a continuing problem almost from the beginning of the mobilization effort, although they did not become severe until 1942. Roosevelt initially created (Mar. 11, 1941) an eleven-member Board of Mediation for defense industries within the OPM, but it was rendered ineffectual by the resignation of labor representatives during the steel worker dispute in the fall of 1941. Subsequently Roosevelt appointed a War Labor Board that was relatively successful for a time in holding down labor unrest. On Roosevelt and Labor, see Frances Perkins, *The Roosevelt I Knew*, paperback ed. (New York: Harper & Row, 1964), pp. 362–76.
>
> The WMC under McNutt, who also headed the Federal Security Agency, took over the responsibilities formerly assumed by the OPM's Labor Division under Hillman. Although McNutt was instructed to coordinate with the WPB's Labor Requirements Committee, in practice this administrative dividing line was hard to maintain. The WMC's activities were further complicated by the need to integrate labor requirements with the demands of the selective service system. See Vatter, *The U.S. Economy in World War II*, pp. 69–71.

15 The scarcity of natural rubber due to Japanese domination of the Southeast Asia archipelago had forced the United States to embark on a crash program to produce synthetic rubber. Farm interests were pushing to use alcohol rather than petroleum as the raw material for the synthetic rubber, and they were well represented by congressional agricultural committees. Eventually Roosevelt vetoed legislation intended to establish a separate agency outside the WPB to control rubber production and, instead, in 1942 he established the Office of the Rubber Director, headed by William M. Jeffers, within the WPB. But Nelson then delegated all his authority as WPB chairman in the realm of rubber production to Jeffers, essentially establishing the latter as rubber "czar." See Nelson, *Arsenal of Democracy*, pp. 290–306; *Industrial Mobilization*, pp. 255–7.

16 The situation was exacerbated by the WPB's tendency to form internal divisions, including ones for shipbuilding, labor production, manpower requirements, and international supply, as well as internal units responsible for worker housing and civilian goods. These duplicated the responsibilities delegated to the claimant agencies under the czars. See Vatter, *The U.S. Economy in World War II*, p. 74.

17 Nelson pinpointed the root cause of these continuing disputes: "[T]he Army wished to assume greater control over war production and the civilian economy than the War Production Board deemed it prudent to have" (Nelson, *Arsenal of Democracy*, pp. xvii, 368–90). See also Herman Somers *Presidential Agency: OWMR The Office of War Mobilization and Reconversion* (New York: Greenwood Press, 1969), pp. 28–30; *Industrial Mobilization*.

18 This despite explicit recognition by FDR that Nelson's authority extended to the ANMB; E.O. 9024 (Jan. 16, 1942) stipulated that the ANMB report to the president through Nelson.

In fact, however, rather than negotiate a division of labor, Nelson ended up practically abdicating procurement control to the military.[19] Eventually, rather than reporting through Nelson, the military procurement agencies pushed disputes beyond him to FDR for adjudication.[20] The conflict between the two came to a head with Nelson's attempt to institute the Controlled Materials Plan (CMP), a production control procedure that allocated resources to the various claimant agencies on a schedule determined by the WPB.[21] On Sept. 18, 1942, Nelson appointed Charles

19 See WPB General Administrative Orders nos. 2–23, and 2–33 (March and April 1942) and General Order 2–71 (Dec. 9, 1942) essentially giving procurement control back to the military. Also, see Somers, *Presidential Agency*, 115–17; Vatter, *The U.S. Economy in World War II*, pp. 71–2, and *Industrial Mobilization*, pp. 212–22.

20 In fact, Roosevelt eventually formally acquiesced to the ANMB's efforts to evade Nelson's control by signing a document that, among other provisions, stated that the ANMB "will report, when necessary, to the President through the Joint Chiefs of Staff" (see memorandum to the president regarding the Reconstituting of the Army-Navy Munitions Board [July 27, 1943], Section 3, *PSF* – Subject Files, Army – Navy Munitions Board Folder, FDRL.

In fact, however, the ANMB had become less important due to the War Department reorganization effected in February 1942. As part of that reorganization, an Army Services of Supply (later renamed the Army Service Forces) was established, encompassing all the Army procurement functions except those of the Army Air Force. The ANMB, although still ostensibly representing the Army and Navy, in fact was absorbed within the newly established Army Supply division.

Although the Navy too was reorganized at this time, its procurement bureaus remained relatively autonomous from centralized control. See *The U.S. at War*, pp. 107–8.

21 Under the CMP, announced on Nov. 2, 1942, claimant agencies, with WPB approval, allocated materials to prime contractors, who in turn allocated their allotment to their suppliers. The CMP scheduling process could thus be used to match strategic requirements with resources, and not incidentally strengthened the WPB's ability to control production through material allocations. But it also engendered strong military opposition. See Smith BoB Monthly Report #26 (September – December 1942), p. 26, FDRL.

The CMP was the outgrowth of a fourth phase in the evolution of production controls. Beginning on a voluntary basis in 1942, a Defense Supplies Ratings Plan had been introduced, under which defense-related shipments, orders, and requirements were grouped in broad classifications and previewed on a quarterly, rather than on a spot basis. This system was soon made mandatory and expanded to cover entire production programs. The first integrated control plan was issued June 10, 1942, under Priorities Regulation no. 11. See David Novick, Melvin Anshen, and W. C. Truppner, *Wartime Production Controls* (New York: Columbia University Press, 1949), p. 105. Manufacturers were required to report anticipated production requirements for the coming months as well as consumption in the previous quarter. By aggregating these reports, the WPB was able to gauge total supply and demand within programs and thus establish realistic end- product and materials priorities.

However, the Defense Supplies plan was flawed in two respects. First, allocation took place "horizontally" – between the production agency and the individual manufacturers. Thus, the WPB had no mechanism for controlling production within a production line, from raw materials to finished product. More importantly, this system did nothing to control the armed services' ability to place military orders. Contracts continued to be awarded without regard for the nation's manufacturing capacity; the WPB was limited to reacting to these contracts by adjusting controls accordingly.

This prompted the CMP, announced in November 1942, but not implemented until the following year. It remained in effect until the end of the war.

Wilson, chairman of General Electric, to implement the CMP.[22] Two days later, however, he also appointed Ferdinand Eberstadt, who had formerly served on the ANMB, as WPB Vice-Chairman on Program Determination in charge of materials allocation. Eberstadt, backed by the military, was soon feuding with Wilson. Those responsible for military procurement opposed the CMP, complaining that although the WPB could allocate materials, it should not schedule the placement of war contracts.

When, in February 1943, Nelson tried to augment Wilson's authority by transferring several industry divisions to his control, the Army retaliated by seeking Nelson's removal. Harold Smith, FDR's budget director, summed up the predicament to Roosevelt: "[T]hese transfers of certain divisions do not resolve the fundamental issues: should production programs be determined by scheduling decisions of Mr. Wilson or by the materials allocations decisions of Mr. Eberstadt? Nor do they resolve the lack of unity, vigor, and definite policy by WPB as a whole."[23] Nelson reacted to the Army's efforts to have his job by firing Eberstadt. Rather than back Nelson publicly, however, FDR opted to fire him as well. Only the timely intervention of Smith and Hopkins temporarily saved Nelson's job.[24]

As Smith noted dryly in his monthly report, "[T]he conversion of these differences of opinion [between the armed services and the WPB] into a public 'knock-down and drag-out' fight can hardly promote the winning of the war."[25] Roosevelt was only too well aware of this; Nelson recalls, "President Roosevelt was not pleased at newspaper stories that hinted at slugging within the War Production Board and upon occasion bawled me out in his quizzically reproving manner."[26]

22 Wilson chaired the newly established WPB Production Executive Committee (PEC). Nelson hoped Wilson's appointment would help the WPB regain some of the procurement powers lost in the struggle with the military branches earlier that year. See Somers, *Presidential Agency*, pp. 114–15.
23 Smith to FDR (Feb. 8, 1943), *PSF* – Subject Files, Budget Folder, FDRL.
24 Roosevelt, perhaps at Byrnes' prompting, had evidently decided to replace Nelson with Baruch, even going so far as to send a letter asking Baruch to take over the WPB. But, at Hopkins' and Smith's urging, Roosevelt changed his mind. "Washington is full of stories that Baruch is to succeed Nelson. It seems to me that at this particular time any further changes in WPB would be unwise. Nelson's removal in favor of anyone other than Wilson would indicate that he had been removed because of his dismissal of Eberstadt" (Smith to Roosevelt [Feb. 19, 1943], *PSF* – Subject Files, Budget Folder, FDRL).
25 Smith, BoB Monthly Report #29 (February 1943), p. 26, FDRL.
26 Nelson, *Arsenal of Democracy*, p. xvi. In fact, FDR issued a public letter admonishing the heads of his war production agencies that he would not tolerate continued dissent. *FDR Public Papers*, vol. 1942, p. 333. In addition to Nelson's feuds with the ANMB, Henry Wallace, head of the Board of Economic Warfare (BEW), was engaged in a virulent dispute with Jesse Jones, Secretary of Commerce and director of the Reconstruction Finance Corporation. The BEW controlled all exports from the United States (other than Lend Lease) and purchased essential materials in foreign countries for the U.S. needs or to keep material from the enemy. The problem was that the Board's activities were

The Office of Economic Stabilization

While these jurisdictional disputes were airing, the nation's economy appeared to reach maximum production capacity. Hundreds of production lines were shut down, and the specter of rampant inflation – a recurring concern since at least the United States' entrance into the war – was again raised.[27] Roosevelt, worried by the OPA's failure to rein in prices, created an Office of Economic Stabilization (OES), headed by Supreme Court Justice James Byrnes, in October 1942.[28] Byrnes was authorized to control prices, wages, and rationing.[29] As he recalled, however, Roosevelt expected Byrnes to do more than fight inflation:

funded by the RFC under Jones' direction. The separation of policy from financing led to acrimonious fighting between Wallace and Jones. Eventually, when the dispute went public, an exasperated FDR relieved both men of their duties, and he consolidated their functions under a new Office of Economic Warfare, supervised by Byrnes. See also Somers, *Presidential Agency*, pp. 33–5. Similarly, when in 1944 reports of a feud between Wilson and Nelson received much media play, Nelson was sent by FDR on a diplomatic mission to China, and Wilson resigned. See Robert Sherwood, *Roosevelt and Hopkins*, rev. paperback ed. (New York: The Universal LIbrary, 1950), pp. 699–700, 820; and Nelson, *Arsenal of Democracy*, pp. 410–16. Julius Krug replaced Nelson as head of the WPB.

27   The need for price control became apparent quite early in the mobilization process, as the impact of overseas orders, resistance by the farm bloc to price control, and a general rise in wages and costs fueled by the economic expansion produced inflationary pressures. After the U.S. entered the war these pressures intensified; from December 1941 to March 1942 (when the OPA first issued price guidelines) food prices rose 4.9 percent, and clothing went up 7.7 percent (*The U.S. At War*, p. 253). They were partly caused by economic havoc created when the armed services contracted for finished products to an extent far beyond the nation's existing industrial capacity (see Vatter, *The U.S. Economy in World War II*, pp. 72–3).

28   The OPA had, under authority granted it by the Emergency Price Control Act (passed Jan. 30, 1942), issued the General Maximum Price Regulation (General Max) guidelines in April 1942, governing price increases in nonmilitary, nonfarm producer and consumer goods. Despite these guidelines, price control under the OPA remained ineffectual through most of 1942. (This contrasts with the OPA's rather successful efforts at instituting rationing, beginning with tires in January 1942. See Vatter, *The U.S. Economy in World War II*, pp. 89–91.) The OPA's failure partly reflects weak administrative controls and limited authority, as well as political resistance to price control efforts. Specifically, the OPA had no authority to limit wage increases; that was the purview of the OEM's War Labor Board, which in turn was restricted to resolving disputes referred to it through the U.S. Labor Department's Conciliation Service. That left for a time a sizeable sector of labor wage agreements outside any administrative control. (See Vatter, *The U.S. Economy in World War II*, pp. 92–101; *The U.S. at War*, pp. 253–71).

29   Roosevelt initially threatened to institute price controls through executive order, using a plan developed by Rosenman. But Byrnes recommended going through Congress first. Consequently, legislation was introduced and Congress responded with a stabilization bill signed by Roosevelt on Oct. 2. Byrnes, *Speaking Frankly*, pp. 16–19; *The U.S. at War*, p. 271.

The next day Roosevelt appointed Byrnes to head the Office of Economic Stabilization (OES), whose functions as outlined in E.O. 9250 (Oct. 3, 1942), were:

Jimmy, most of my time is devoted to the consideration of problems . . . connected with the conduct of war. It just isn't possible for me to devote sufficient time to the domestic problems. All these new agencies we have had to create mean an increasing number of jurisdictional conflicts which come to me for decision. I want you to settle those conflicts for me; I'll issue an executive order giving you power to settle them, and I'll let it be known that your decision is my decision.[30]

Indeed, Byrnes was soon functioning as the de facto "assistant president on the homefront."[31] His political clout was enhanced by FDR's decision to give him an office in the East Wing of the White House, providing symbolism as well as proximity to Roosevelt.[32] Armed with a formidable political reputation and with Roosevelt's backing, Byrnes' duties inevitably encroached on Nelson's functions.[33]

> To formulate and develop a comprehensive national economic policy relating to the control of civilian purchasing power, prices, rents, wages, salaries, profits, rationing subsidies, and all related matters – all for the purpose of preventing avoidable increase in the cost of living, cooperating in minimizing the unnecessary migration from one business, industry, region to another, and facilitating the prosecution of the war. To give effect to this comprehensive national economic policy the Director shall have power to issue directives on policy to the Federal departments and agencies concerned.

From Oct. 15, 1942 through April 1943, the cost of living increased 4.3 percent, whereupon Roosevelt issued his famous "Hold the Line" executive order on Apr. 8, directing the Price Administrator and Food Administrator to place ceilings on all commodities affecting the cost of living. In addition, the order extended the OES director's authority to control prices and wages. From then until April 1945, the cost-of-living index rose only 3.2 percent. See Byrnes, *Speaking Frankly*, pp. 18–19; Smith, BoB Monthly Report #31 (April 1943), pp. 30–2, FDRL.

30 Byrnes, *Speaking Frankly*, p. 18; see also his account in Byrnes, *All in One Lifetime*, pp. 155–7.

31 The characterization is from Sherwood, *Roosevelt and Hopkins*, pp. 632–4. But note that Byrnes quotes FDR as telling him when he was first appointed to head the OES: "For all practical purposes you will be Assistant President" (Byrnes, *All in One Lifetime*, p. 155).

32 Byrnes was supported by a permanent staff of five. See Byrnes, *All in One Lifetime*, pp. 160–5.

33 As Smith noted in his monthly report to FDR in regard to disputes among the war agencies: "Most of these [disputes] have been referred to the Director of Office of Economic Stabilization to be resolved. This has led many to infer that we are in the process of replacing the War Production Board as the over-all coordinator of economic activity by the Office of Economic Stabilization developed into an "Office of War Mobilization" on the order of the Tolan Committee proposal" (Smith, BoB Monthly Report #28, [February 1943], p. 29, FDRL). Byrnes' specific functions are listed in Byrnes, *All in One Lifetime*, pp. 164–6.

Nelson and Byrnes were a study in contrasts; the former had spent a lifetime in the private sector, the latter was a professional politician, having served many years in Congress before FDR appointed him to the Supreme Court. In a revealing comment, Nelson recalls Roosevelt telling him: "It is my experience with businessmen in government that they always get into these battles, not alone with one another but with the heads of other

Congress, meanwhile, was considering legislation to create an Office of War Mobilization (OWM), which would take responsibility for overseeing war production.³⁴ Others were pushing their own solutions to the production problems, including the full transfer of mobilization authority to the military, appointing more czars in particular production areas, and revamping the production control system administered by the WPB.³⁵

It appeared that no one short of the president could adjudicate the recurring production-related policy disputes and personality clashes.³⁶ But it was equally clear that Roosevelt was increasingly preoccupied with military strategy.³⁷

Byrnes, meanwhile, seemed to have effectively adjudicated a number of problems that fell outside his official domain as inflation fighter. He was also well known to Roosevelt.³⁸ The upshot was FDR's decision, on May

government agencies. They don't know how to administer the things they must administer as well as the politicians know how." These remarks provide a clue to Roosevelt's decision to appoint Byrnes, a long-time politician (see Nelson, *Arsenal of Democracy*, pp. 382–90).

34 The congressional plan, submitted as H.R. 7742 on Oct. 22, 1942, proposed creating a super mobilization office, encompassing many of the existing war agencies, but under the direction of a single "Director of War Mobilization." A copy of the proposed legislation is contained in Hopkins Papers, Sherwood Collection, Book 5, Organizing for War, War Cabinet File, FDRL, attached to a memorandum from Oscar Cox to Hopkins (Oct. 26, 1942); see also Somers, *Presidential Agency*, pp. 49–51.

35 *The U.S. at War*, p. 279–81.

36 As Somers notes, "[S]hort of the President, who could not possible attend to all these disputes personally, there was no place to go for any effective resolution or to determine what the controlling policy would be" (Somers, *Presidential Agency*, p. 40).

37 This led some to advocate the creation of a "War Cabinet" with specific focus on production issues. Lubin sent a memorandum to Hopkins at this time suggesting exactly that: "If we are ever really going to do our job, it will be absolutely essential to coordinate production possibilities with strategy plans. Only through a War Cabinet or something similar to it will it be possible to get some semblance of order into the present picture. It is becoming increasingly evident that at the moment there is not a relationship between what is being asked for by the Armed Services and what can be produced within a given period of time" (Lubin to Hopkins [Oct. 13, 1942]). A month later Oscar Cox wrote Hopkins: "The public's impression of the fight between WPB and the Army and Navy is an additional indicative reason for setting up the kind of President's War Policy Committee that I wrote you about on Wednesday" (Cox to Hopkins [Nov. 27, 1942]; both in Hopkins Papers, Sherwood Collection, Book 5: Organizing for War, War Cabinet File, FDRL.

38 Recall that Byrnes led the Senate floor fight to ratify the Brownlow Committee report in 1937–9. He later sought the 1940 Democratic presidential nomination, but dropped out when FDR decided to run for a third term. Byrnes then worked on FDR's behalf, helping secure Henry Wallace's selection as FDR's running mate at the Chicago Democratic convention, and was rewarded for his support when FDR nominated him to the Supreme Court. See Byrnes, *All in One Lifetime*, pp. 60–7; Samuel Rosenman, *Working with Roosevelt* (New York: Harper & Row, 1952), p. 202.

27, 1943, to establish the OWM through executive order, responsible for overseeing all aspects of war production, to be headed by Byrnes.[39]

The Office of War Mobilization

Byrnes' appointment represents a clear break by FDR with past administrative practices. He evidently expected Byrnes to act as his troubleshooter on the home front, adjudicating disputes and smoothing production bottlenecks that otherwise would have absorbed too much of Roosevelt's time.[40] The OWM was placed at the top of the administrative hierarchy, at the same level as the OEM and above the WPB.[41] Except for Byrnes' expanded jurisdiction, organizationally and statutorily the OWM was based to a considerable extent upon the OES.[42] It was expected to:

> develop unified programs and to establish policies for the maximum use of the nation's natural and industrial resources for military and civilian needs, for the effective use of the national manpower not in the Armed Forces, for the maintenance and stabilization of the civilian economy, and for the adjustment of such economy to war needs and conditions.[43]

To achieve these objectives, Byrnes concentrated on adjudicating disputes as they emerged from below, rather than allowing the OWM to assume operational and lower-level coordinating duties itself, as Nelson had with the WPB.[44] Nor did the OWM engage in long- term planning.[45] Although

39 Byrnes was to remain in this post until resigning ten days before FDR's death in April 1945. Sanders notes that Byrnes wanted to resign after FDR failed to nominate him for vice-president in 1944, but was persuaded to stay on.

40 Coy told Somers after the war that Roosevelt's clear intent in appointing Byrnes was "to create 'a chief of staff' for the entire domestic front" (Somers, *Presidential Agency*, p. 48).

41 According to Somers, Byrnes' White House location reflects Roosevelt's belief that "real integration would have to come out of his own office" rather than through a separate agency. Somers, *Presidential Agency*, p. 48. Byrnes was replaced as OES director by Fred Vinson, although the two maintained a close working relationship for the war's duration. Vinson eventually replaced Byrnes as head of the OWM's successor agency, the Office of War Mobilization and Reconversion.

42 The executive order establishing the OWM was drafted by Byrnes' assistant, Donald Russell, Ben Cohen, and Wayne Coy. Rosenman, who reviewed the plan, wrote Roosevelt on May 24, 1943: "I have talked with Jimmy Byrnes and have gone over the proposed order which he has drawn up. I think, in the present form, it is fine and that Jimmy is the perfect man for the job. The set-up will work, in my opinion, and will leave you free really to spend most of your time fighting the war and arranging for 'post-war'" (*PSF* – Subject Files, Rosenman Folder, FDRL). See also Byrnes, *All in One Lifetime*, pp. 183–5.

43 E.O. 9347 (May 27, 1943).

44 Edward H. Hobbs, *Behind the President: A Study of Executive Office Agencies*, (Washington, D.C.: Public Affairs Press, 1954), pp. 188–9; Vatter, *The U.S. Economy in World War II*, p. 87.

45 The exception is his decision to appoint Baruch to draw up a plan for postwar reconversion.

Byrnes was ostensibly assisted by a War Mobilization Committee, in practice it served more as a sounding board than as a policy-making body; Byrnes essentially answered only to Roosevelt.[46]

As with the OES, Byrnes's OWM staff was quite small, numbering only four professionals.[47] For additional expertise, Byrnes relied on existing agencies, especially the BoB. He also employed outside help, especially Baruch, who continued to provide advice on war production during this entire period.[48]

As Somers' detailed study makes clear, the OWM under Byrnes was relatively successful at coordinating policy and adjudicating disputes involving war production agencies, both civilian and military, on FDR's behalf.[49] Byrnes' effectiveness, however, was not based on any significant revision of the basic wartime administrative machinery governing procurement, resource allocation, and production controls.[50] Instead, his success was due to the combination of his own political experience, his close ties to FDR, and his decision, aided by his small staff, to avoid operations and concentrate instead on adjudicating disputes.

Although a complete accounting of the OWM's activities is impossible here, a review of archives and secondary sources indicates that the

46 The War Mobilization Committee was comprised of Byrnes, the secretaries of War and Navy, the chairman of the Munitions Assignment Board, the chairman of the WPB, and the director of Economic Stabilization.

47 Somers writes, "After a year of operation, the OWM had a regular staff of only ten paid persons of all ranks." This included four permanent professionals: Cohen; Walter Brown, assistant for press relations; Donald Russell, an administrative assistant; and Fred Searls, Jr. Byrnes lists six assistants, including a secretary, but notes that others were borrowed as needed. These were described as expediters, not buffers. See Byrnes, *All in One Lifetime*, pp. 185–7; Alfred Dick Sander, *A Staff for the President: The Executive Office, 1921–52*, (New York: Greenwood Press, 1989), p. 57, and Somers, *Presidential Agency*, pp. 54–5.

48 Baruch, of course, was highly critical of FDR's wartime economic management. But he was coopted by Byrnes who hired him as a consultant to the OWM responsible for drafting a report on postwar planning. Eventually Baruch joined the OWM, heading a special unit studying the postwar economy. See Jordan A. Schwarz, "Bernard Baruch and the Vocation of Presidential Adviser," in Wilbur J. Cohen (ed.), *The Roosevelt New Deal: A Program Assessment Fifty Years After* (Richmond, Va: Lyndon B. Johnson School of Public Affairs, Virginia Commonwealth University, 1986), pp. 277–9; Vatter, *The U.S. Economy in World War II*, p. 82.

49 Somers, *Presidential Agency*, pp. 130–7.

50 As Somers notes, integration of civilian and military production strategy was easier to accomplish in any case by 1943, when military strategy was more clearly established and the prospects for victory exceedingly brighter. But Byrnes helped his cause by getting FDR to establish a Joint Production Survey Committee within the Joint Chiefs of Staff. Although the production committee was dominated by members of the JCS, Byrnes' subordinate Fred Sears attended meetings as a nonvoting member. In addition, Byrnes himself was able to effect some coordination between production and military strategy by meeting separately with Admiral Leahy, FDR's representative on the Joint Chiefs. Somers, *Presidential Agency*.

OWM's purview was extensive, ranging over food rationing, military procurement,[51] wartime shipping allocation,[52] analysis of foreign petroleum preserves,[53] the administrative consolidation of foreign economic programs, reconversion and postwar planning,[54] and ad hoc troubleshooting, often at FDR's direction.[55]

Perhaps Byrnes' most important accomplishment was gaining some control over military procurement. He did so by establishing procurement review boards, with OWM representatives on each, within the military procurement agencies.[56] This ensured OWM's input to military procurement decisions and eventually was instrumental in persuading the military services to revise their production targets downward as the end of the war drew near.

In addition, Byrnes helped create a policy blueprint for manpower allocation. By 1943, at the peak of war production, labor shortages were proving to be the most critical bottleneck.[57] That fall Byrnes hammered through a working agreement, using a report drafted by Baruch and his assistant John Hancock, that governed manpower allocation among war agencies and remained in effect for the war's duration.[58]

The BoB

Inevitably, of course, Byrnes' extensive purview led to clashes with other staff agencies, including the Bureau of the Budget. In the fall of 1942, prior to Byrnes' appointment to head the OWM, Wayne Coy, the assistant director of the BoB, had suggested making BoB Director Smith the "chief of staff" for the EOP, with the BoB acting as Smith's staff support.[59]

---

51 See the two reports from Byrnes to Roosevelt (Sept. 15, 1943, and Sept. 16, 1943) regarding Army and Navy procurement procedures, *PSF* – Subject File, Byrnes Folder, FDRL.

52 See Byrnes to FDR (Mar. 3, 1945), and attached, *PSF* – Subject File, Byrnes Folder, FDRL.

53 Roosevelt to Byrnes (June 23, 1943); Byrnes to FDR (June 26, 1943); Byrnes to FDR (Nov. 11, 1943), (and attached all in *PSF* – Subject File, Byrnes Folder, FDRL).

54 This task was mandated by Congress when it transformed the OWM into the Office of War Mobilization and Reconversion (OWMR).

55 Byrnes did not, however, play an extensive role in military strategy and international political relations. Somers, *Presidential Agency*, p. 48.

56 Byrnes, *All in One Lifetime*, pp. 187–92; Somers, *Presidential Agency*, pp. 62–4; 117–22.

57 Recall that although ostensibly under the control of the War Manpower Commission, manpower allocation was in fact dispersed among several agencies.

58 Somers, *Presidential Agency*, pp. 143–53.

59 Coy's three-page memo observed that: "With ever-increasing problems of broad strategy, war policy and over-all leadership crowding upon your time and attention, it is easy to see how such an 'administrative secretary' could be of immeasurable help to you.

Roosevelt, of course, opted instead to appoint Byrnes, first as head of the OES, and then the more powerful OWM. Thereafter Smith complained that the OWM duplicated many of the BoB's functions, but without the expertise or personnel to effectively carry them out.⁶⁰ And as the war drew to a close, he urged FDR to conduct "a thorough reexamination of the Executive Office of the President."⁶¹

Roosevelt, of course, had begun expanding the BoB's functions in the Brownlow Report's aftermath, and Smith's appointment to head the agency in March 1939, confirmed that trend.⁶² Reorganization Plan I

Briefly, he could (1) assist in reconciling divergent views of civilian war agencies, (2) help in the integration of their efforts to conform with your general plans, and (3) work toward a better balance in the individual portions of broad programs" (Wayne Coy to Roosevelt [Oct. 13, 1942]; *PSF* – Subject File, EOP – Coy Folder, p. 1, FDRL).

Coy argued that by relieving Smith of responsibility for budget estimates and procedures, the BoB director would be free to serve as Roosevelt's point man on administrative issues related to war production. In this capacity he would be part of the president's four-man staff secretariat, joining Admiral William Leahy, Roosevelt's liaison to the Joint Chiefs of Staff; Hopkins, FDR's roving minister on foreign affairs; and Byrnes, whom Coy likened to the President's "economic chief-of-staff" (ibid., pp. 2–3).

60 Smith argued that policy oversight ought not to be separate from budgetary control and administrative management. From his perspective the OWM was simply one among many wartime agencies. But Byrnes saw himself as *the* assistant president in charge of the entire domestic front. From this vantage point, then, the BoB provided staff assistance to the OWM. Sander, *A Staff for the President*, pp. 40–1, 44–6. On OWM – BoB relations more generally, see Somers, *Presidential Agency*, pp. 67–70; and Richard E. Neustadt, "Presidential Clearance of Legislation: Legislative Development, Review and Coordination in the Executive Office of the President," Ph.D. dissertation, Harvard University, Cambridge, 1950, pp. 100–17. (Note that Neustadt tends to downplay the agencies' differences. See Neustadt, "Presidential Clearance of Legislation," p. 100, footnote 40.)

61 The budget director wrote FDR in late 1944: "For several years you have not been able to give this matter careful consideration because of the many other pressing problems before you. Now . . . the conflicting delegations and assumptions of authority are compounding trouble for you. The prestige of both the White House and the Executive Office, in their relations with the operating agencies, is involved . . . Central executive direction is not only important during the war but will be more important than ever before in the postwar period when the Government will be called upon to solve pressing domestic problems.

"The greatest contribution which can be made during the next four years is to organize that Office in such a way that it will be an effective instrument of management" (Smith to Roosevelt [Nov. 9, 1944], *PSF* – Subject Files, Bureau of the Budget Folder, FDRL).

FDR responded, "I will have a little more time after January first and I do want to talk with you some more about the organization of the Executive Office" (Roosevelt to Smith [Dec. 9, 1944], *PSF* – Subject Files, Bureau of the Budget Folder, FDRL). But there is no evidence FDR did so.

62 Smith had been highly recommended to FDR by Brownlow and Morgenthau, who both had been asked by FDR to find the best state budget director, regardless of political affiliation. Simultaneous with Smith's appointment, the BoB was authorized in fiscal year 1939 to create fifty-five more positions. See Donald Stone, "Administrative Management: Reflections on Origins and Accomplishments," *Public Administration Review* 50, no. 1 (Jan. – Feb. 1990), pp. 3–20. See also Sander, *A Staff for the President*, pp. 45–6.

and E.O. 8248 subsequently established the BoB's organizational structure for the next decade.[63] Smith had soon developed strong ties to the

63 By 1937, of course, the BoB had largely absorbed the National Emergency Council's legislative clearance functions. (See Neustadt, "Presidential Clearance for Legislature," pp. 68–70.) In the fall of 1938, acting director Daniel Bell reorganized the bureau, establishing a Division of Coordination responsible for clearing and coordinating all legislation. The intent was to increase the BoB's ability to provide a governmentwide perspective on the clearance of proposed legislation. Simultaneously, the Division of Organizational Activities was renamed the Division of Estimates, and its staff also enlarged.

E.O 8248, issued in 1939, formally recognized the BoB's growing influence. Recall the pertinent provisions:

1. Assist the President in the preparation of the Budget and the formulation of the fiscal program of the government.
2. Supervise and Control the administration of the Budget.
3. Conduct research in the development of improved plans of administrative management, and to advise the executive departments and agencies of the Government with respect to improved administrative organization and practice.
4. Aid the President to bring about more efficient and economical conduct of government Service.
5. Assist the President by clearing and coordinating departmental advice on proposed legislation and by making recommendations as to Presidential action on legislative enactments, in accordance with past practice.
6. Assist in the consideration and clearance and, where necessary, in the preparation of proposed Executive orders and proclamations, in accordance with the provisions of Executive Order 7289 of February 18, 1936.
7. Plan and promote the improvement, development, and coordination of Federal and other statistical services.
8. Keep the President informed of the progress of activities by agencies of the Government with respect to work proposed, work actually initiated, and work completed, together with the relative timing of work between the several agencies of the Government; all to the end that the work programs of the several agencies of the Executive Branch of the Government may be coordinated and that the monies appropriated by the Congress may be expended in the most economical manner possible with the least possible overall pain and duplication of effort.

E.O. 8248 also created three other divisions within the BoB – Fiscal, Statistical Standards, and Administrative Management – in addition to the divisions of Estimates and Legislative Reference. The Fiscal division focused on budget and analysis and later conducted analyses of government programs. The Division of Administrative Management was an outgrowth of the old Division of Research and Investigation. The Division of Coordination was renamed the Division of Legislative Reference, the result of Smith's fears that "coordination" sounded too imposing. The Central Statistical Board was incorporated into the BoB through the 1939 Reorganization Plan I, and became Statistical Standards. (See Stone, "Administrative Management," pp. 5–7. Neustadt gives a slightly different chronology; see his "Legislative Reference," pp. 70–2; Sander, *A Staff for the President*, pp. 41–4.)

According to Stone, this internal reorganization of the BoB was deliberately designed to prevent excessive accumulation of power in any one division. Instead, major issues were now subject to analysis from several perspectives, with none predominating. However, Neustadt notes that in practice the Division of Administrative Management and, to a lesser extent, the Fiscal division became the spearheads of this new BoB. He also observes that the influx of new staff to fill positions in these expanded divisions helped

president and began actively recruiting personnel who shared their activist outlook.[64]

The BoB's physical transfer in August 1939 from the Treasury Building to new offices in the Executive Office Building alongside the White House signaled its preeminence as a *presidential* staff agency.[65] By 1940 then, the BoB was positioned to play the dominant role in domestic and economic policy formulation, due to its expanded legislative clearance and coordination functions, coupled with the agency's strengthened capabilities in administrative organization and fiscal analysis.

But several factors prevented it from taking on these duties, despite Coy's efforts to the contrary. First, the BoB operated from an *institutional* perspective; even during its heyday overseeing legislative clearance, Roosevelt was careful to use his White House assistants to double-check BoB recommendations, so that he received a personal political perspective.[66] Furthermore, the BoB was limited to correlating and reacting to input from other departments; budget review and administrative management served essentially as checks on policy formulation and as means of program evaluation, not as instruments for policy development.[67] Third, as Neustadt notes, the BoB was already burdened carrying out its assigned tasks:

> Smith was spread very thin. Even if he had wanted to play the top coordinating role on domestic operations and requirements, it is hard to see how his organization could have absorbed it. Even if it could physically have done so, the task called for a different orientation, different personnel, and an entirely different set of relationships to the President and the agencies than the Budget Bureau could

broaden the BoB's perspective beyond its traditional focus on budgeting and cost containment. Neustadt "Presidential Clearance of Legislation," pp. 94–9.

64 Until Smith's heart attack in 1943, he met with FDR approximately three-to-four times daily; thereafter they met about once a month. (Sander, *A Staff for the President*, pp. 40–1.) On BoB personnel, see Sander, *A Staff for the President*; Stone, "Administrative Management," pp. 5–12; Neustadt, "Presidential Clearance of Legislation," pp. 94–6.

65 Stone recalls, "The organizational and physical transfer from the Treasury was electrifying in changing attitudes within the government. No longer were BoB staff looked upon as agents of a peer department, poking their noses into other departments' affairs. They were representatives of the President." (Stone, "Administrative Management," p. 6).

66 James Rowe, who began as an assistant to FDR's son Jimmy Roosevelt in the White House and who was appointed as one of the newly authorized administrative assistants in 1939, performed this political function under FDR for a couple of years. Every enrolled bill went to him for review, and he often worked directly with the BoB before formulating a recommendation. These functions were taken over by Rosenman when he joined the White House staff in the newly created position of White House Special Counsel in 1943.

67 Smith himself acknowledged the limits of the BoB's policy role in testimony before Congress regarding postwar planning. See U.S. Congress, House, Special Committee on Postwar Economic Policy and Planning, Hearings, 78th Congress., 2nd sess., Mar. 15 – May 3, 1944, pp. 410–11. See also Wayne Coy, "Basic Problems," *The American Political Science Review* (December 1946), p. 1124.

have produced without profoundly altering its character and basic purposes.[68]
Consequently, although the BoB continued to be the dominant staff work-horse during the war years, its activities were submerged and diffused within the broader military effort.[69] It was the OWM, rather than the BoB, that took on the task of coordinating war production.[70]

The Office of War Mobilization and Reconversion

By 1944, as it became apparent the Allies were going to win the war, policy makers began grappling with the problems associated with conversion to a peacetime economy.[71] Members of Congress who thought their role had been eroded by wartime deference to FDR became particularly concerned to reassert their institutional prerogatives. This is clearly indicated by congressional passage of legislation, in October 1944, that

68 Neustadt, "Presidential Clearance of Legislation," p. 99. Berman provides an succinct description of the BoB's strengths and weaknesses in this period (Larry Berman, *The Office of Management Budget and the Presidency 1929–79*) [Princeton, N.J.: Princeton University Press, 1979], pp. 16–31.

69 The BoB essentially fulfilled three primary war-related functions (in addition to its traditional budgeting, legislative clearance, and fiscal advising duties): organizing wartime agencies, analyzing wartime management needs, and assisting federal agencies in their internal administrative problems. (Berman, *Office of Management Budget and the Presidency*, pp. 28–9). The BoB's organizational expertise proved particularly useful in this period, as indicated by the doubling, from thirty-seven in 1940 to seventy-seven by June 1942, of personnel in the BoB's Division of Administrative Management. The BoB's staff studies were instrumental in setting up the War Manpower Commission, the OWM, the OEM, the OPA, the Foreign Economic Administration, the Office of Strategic Studies, the OES, and a Defense Projects Unit, established to collect information regarding defense expenditures. See also Stone, "Administrative Management," pp. 16–20; Neustadt, "Presidential Clearance," pp. 96–100.

70 Sander, *A Staff for the President*, pp. 44–5; Somers, *Presidential Agency*, pp. 67–70. Note, however, that the BoB continued to dominate budgetary matters. In fact, in late 1944 FDR essentially delegated to Smith the responsibility for producing the president's fiscal 1946 budget, thus freeing FDR to focus on the war. In addition, Roosevelt evidently planned for the BoB to play a major role in planning for the liquidation of the war agencies and the establishment of a peacetime administrative structure.

71 In fact, the WPB initiated postwar planning in 1943, but FDR's request that Congress consider the role of the National Resources Planning Board prompted both Houses to establish their own committees on Postwar Economic Policy, chaired by Senator George and Representative Colmer, respectively.
Meanwhile, on Nov. 4, 1943, Byrnes announced Baruch's appointment to head a post-war planning unit within the OWM. The Baruch – Hancock Report was subsequently made public on Feb. 15, 1944, and served as a blueprint for a series of administrative reconversion activities implemented during the next several months regarding the chief reconversion issues: settlement of war contracts, disposition of surplus property, relaxation of wartime controls, and curtailment of war production. These are described in Somers, *Presidential Agency*, pp. 176–200.

converted the OWM into the Office of War Mobilization and Reconversion (OWMR).[72]

The OWMR was largely patterned after the OWM, and Byrnes was retained as director. Nevertheless, there were significant differences between the two agencies that reflected the congressional assertiveness. First, the OWMR was organizationally placed outside the president's Office of Emergency Management (OEM). Second, Byrnes was now subject to Senate confirmation. Third, by creating an agency with specific responsibility for postwar planning, Congress consciously limited FDR's bargaining options in this area, in part by creating incentives for the agency to pursue its own agenda.

After Byrnes' departure and FDR's death in April 1945, the OWMR soon expanded in size and internal specialization, thus losing the OWM's characteristic traits.[73] This internal expansion prompted OWMR employees to extend the range of issues with which they dealt, leading to frequent clashes with other agencies.[74] And it meant that the OWMR's interests increasingly diverged from the president's.[75] Accordingly, by December 1946, it was essentially terminated, although legally it hung on until June 30, 1947.[76]

Some concluding thoughts on economic mobilization and the wartime staff

Secretary of War Henry Stimson complained in March 1943, "[T]he President is the poorest administrator I have ever worked under in respect to orderly procedure and routine of his performance. He is not a good chooser of men and he does not know how to use them in co-ordination."[77] Stimson's views were shared by others who served under FDR at this time.

72 Through the War Mobilization Act (58 *Stat.* 785). See also ibid., pp. 76–7.
73 One month after its creation, the OWMR staff totaled 16 persons. In June 1945, there were 80 staff employees. By May, 1946, at its peak strength, the OWMR numbered 146 employees. For details regarding the OWMR's functional expansion, see Hobbs, *Behind the President*, pp. 190–1; Somers, *Presidential Agency*, pp. 80–1.
74 In fact, the OWMR actually took on some clearance functions pertaining to war-related legislation. Under Truman, the jockeying between the OWMR and the BoB regarding postwar planning became particularly intense. See, generally, Sander, *A Staff for the President*, pp. 57–9; Somers, *Presidential Agency*, pp. 90–108.
75 Hobbs, *Behind the President*, pp. 191–2.
76 Byrnes was replaced by Fred Vinson on Apr. 2, 1945. Vinson served until August 1945, to be replaced by John Snyder, a long-time associate of Truman. Snyder served almost a year, succeeded in June 1946, by John Steelman, one of Truman's White House assistants. It was Steelman who oversaw the agency's termination soon after.
77 Henry Stimson (with McGeorge Bundy), *On Active Service in Peace and War* (New York: Octagon Books, 1971 [originally published in 1948]), p. 495.

Indeed, the prodigious U.S. economic output during the war should not obscure the equally important fact that the United States experienced significant delays in converting to a war economy – delays that are partly attributable to FDR's administrative strategy.[78] Despite the advice of almost everyone, he refused until 1943 to vest mobilization authority within a single individual of sufficient stature to mandate effective production controls and coordinate the activities of related defense production agencies.

To be sure, the mobilization of the nation's productive capacity for the war effort during 1939–45 was a monumental task whose complexity and scope rivals any government program implemented since. Thus it arguably demanded more bargaining resources than any series of bargaining transactions taken on by FDR's successors. To discharge his presidential responsibilities in this period, Roosevelt essentially had to devise the means for administering almost the entire American economy, from production priorities to commodity rationing, from plant expansion to farm policy, from job training to manpower allocation.[79] A failure to achieve bargaining objectives in almost any of these spheres threatened not just economic prosperity, but the nation's very survival.

And yet *success* in war production bred additional problems. The massive expansion in industrial output sparked inflation, particularly in food products, while simultaneously creating shortages on the home front. Roosevelt's resort to government- mandated wage and price controls provoked a storm of controversy. At the peak of industrial production in 1944, when the nation reached full employment, labor shortages threatened to grind the economy to a halt.

78 Scholars typically cite a slew of impressive production figures as evidence that the United States was the "arsenal of democracy." Thus, the total output of American goods and services, measured in 1939 dollars, rose 52 percent from 1939 to 1944; in the five years and two months from July 1940 to August 1945, the U.S. produced munitions having a total value of \$183.1 billion; during the critical war years of 1943–4 the United States produced about 40 percent of the world's munitions, and so forth. (All statistics are from *Industrial Mobilization for War*.) What is lacking, however, is a means to estimate what production might have been under an alternative administrative strategy, such as that contained in the M-Day Plan.

79 Wartime labor policy is further evidence regarding the complexity of the mobilization task. Attempts by civilian manpower agencies to mobilize skilled workers for critical production activities were hampered by the military's competing need for skilled labor. The result was a running battle between relatively autonomous selective service boards, in charge of military recruitment, and industrial manpower agencies, charged with mobilizing the work force for war production. The situation was further exacerbated by farmers' complaints that the dwindling labor supply hampered the harvesting of food, thereby jeopardizing the war effort – complaints that received a thorough airing in public congressional committee hearings. Indeed, it was the allocation of manpower that most threatened to prevent the United States from achieving production objectives during the war. And it was Roosevelt who was held responsible for ensuring that the optimal labor allocation policy was produced.

Production success also brought the postwar reconversion problem home to roost. There was tremendous fear that the wartime economic boom, fueled by military contracts and the expansion of the nation's industrial capacity, would collapse just as millions of returning service men flooded the workforce, looking for jobs. Many anticipated massive economic dislocation on the scale of the Great Depression – a calamity that Roosevelt's New Deal had never completely licked.[80]

Note, too, that FDR's administrative decisions had international repercussions. Indeed, the integral relationship between military strategy and war production was perhaps the primary reason FDR refused to delegate administrative control to anyone else.[81] To abdicate responsibility for war production was to jeopardize his ability to fulfill his responsibility as commander in chief. The need to integrate military with production strategy meant devising an administrative structure flexible enough to adjust to changing priorities in either field.

In addition to military strategic considerations, other factors complicated FDR's ability to achieve mobilization objectives. Economic production, even in war, continued to a great extent to be driven by nongovernmental processes relatively immune to Roosevelt's influence.[82] And there was the complexity of the production task itself. Simply understanding what and how many munitions were needed, and how to create the appropriate controls for insuring the desired output, proved to be a prodigious administrative task of unprecedented complexity.

A single-minded focus on economic output, however, overlooks the fact that war production was not simply a technical administrative exercise – it was primarily a political problem. Although the exigencies of war infused the actions of government officials with an added sense of urgency, they did *not* diminish the political clashes inherent in a system of what was now many separate institutions sharing rather extensive powers. Indeed, the proliferation of government agencies with overlapping powers meant bargaining became more central to presidential influence than ever before. But the costs to do so increased dramatically as well, driven by bargainers' quite plausible claims that the nation's survival

---

80 Indeed the nation had undergone another severe economic slump in 1937, rivaling that experienced in the three to five years after the 1929 crash.

81 As Nelson recalled: "[T]he styles in arms had everything to do with the way which our defense and war production were organized, everything to do with the methods and extent of industrial conversion, everything to do with all preparations. . . ." (Nelson, *Arsenal of Democracy*, p. 50).

82 One must remember that, even at the height of federal control of wartime industrial mobilization, much of the nation's economic activity continued to take place through free-market mechanisms, albeit fueled by extensive military orders and funded by federal monies.

depended on their success in obtaining their particular bargaining objectives.

From Roosevelt's vantage point as president, then, speed of conversion alone was not the relevant criteria for measuring administrative effectiveness – mobilizing for defense while maintaining the political support necessary to prosecute the war on all fronts was. He knew that to convert to full economic mobilization without adequate political support risked permanently damaging his sources of bargaining influence. That would jeopardize not only his control of economic mobilization, but also his ability to influence the war effort across a range of issues.[83]

To truly judge FDR's administrative effectiveness in this period, then, one needs to look at his choices from his perspective as president, juggling several bargaining objectives simultaneously. Subordinates like Stimson, who saw only one slice of the problem, were highly critical of his methods. But taken as a whole, the evidence suggests Roosevelt's administrative methods fulfilled his bargaining needs. In the final analysis, the United States fulfilled its role as the "arsenal of democracy" because FDR did not squander his political reserves on a fruitless effort to mobilize the nation before it was ready.

Lessons and precedents

The details of economic mobilization are important in judging FDR's administrative effectiveness. But the implication of this phase of history for the postwar presidency is equally noteworthy.[84] To the extent that his bargaining objectives were driven by the exigencies of total war, of course, Roosevelt's task was not identical to that faced by peacetime presidents. Nevertheless, this period portends the growth in expectations regarding the responsibility of the federal government to maintain economic growth. Moreover, the brunt of those expectations are centered in the American presidency. Consciously or not, then, Roosevelt through his actions in World War II ushered in the era of modern American government, and with it the expectation that the president function as the "manager of prosperity."[85] In this respect, Roosevelt's wartime administrative actions *are*

---

83 Of what use would a rapid conversion to industrial production in the prewar years have been if it cost Roosevelt the influence necessary to loosen congressional restrictions on U.S. military aid imposed by the Neutrality acts, for instance?

84 Indeed, at the end of the war most of the production controls and war agencies were dismantled with astonishing speed.

85 The phrase is Clinton Rossiter's; for details see Clinton Rossiter, *The American Presidency*, paperback ed. (New York: Time Incorporated, 1960), pp. 26–9.

quite relevant today. As Somers noted in 1950, "The situation which faced the President during the war and which graphically called for such an instrument as OWM is essentially perennial, regardless of general government organization."[86]

The ensuing four decades have done nothing to invalidate Somers' assertion; many of the problems the OWM was designed to meet persist today. Although most of the wartime emergency agencies were terminated with the war's end, the federal government's fiscal and regulatory role had permanently expanded. The Employment Act of 1946 irrevocably committed the president to active intervention in the nation's economy. And the international preeminence of America's postwar economy made the president's economic decisions even more important.

Although FDR acceded to these demands for a more activist presidential economic policy role, he steadfastly rejected pressure to form a White House–centered domestic or economic policy staff.[87] During the entire war, the core of Roosevelt's personal senior staff, including his White House political secretaries, Hopkins, Leahy, Byrnes, Smith, and the various administrative assistants scarcely totaled a dozen people (support staff not included.)[88] Moreover, Roosevelt continued to personally supervise their activities, handing out assignments, correlating their reports, and generally acting as his own executive assistant.

But what of FDR's delegation of authority to Byrnes? Is the OWM a precursor of postwar staff developments? Might it have become a domestic or economic policy staff, had FDR lived? The evidence regarding FDR's postwar intentions in this regard is inconclusive. As his re-

---

86 Somers, *Presidential Agency*, p. 205.

87 Samuel Rosenman, appointed Special Counsel in 1943, was the closest FDR came to a domestic policy adviser during the war. He took on James Rowe's duties when the latter left in 1942, handling legislative review, speech writing, fact-finding, (including overseas trips later in the war), ad hoc troubleshooting, background checks on potential judicial appointments, public opinion analysis, presidential pardons, and rendering political advice.

88 As the Brownlow Report recommended and E.O. 8248 spelled out, Roosevelt's White House staff expanded during the war through the addition of several administrative assistants who functioned essentially as general-purpose aides, troubleshooters, facilitators, and intelligence gatherers. In addition to Rowe, these included William McReynolds; Lauchlin Currie; Daniel J. Tobin; Lowell Mellett; Sherman Minton; David K. Niles; and James M. Barnes. Eugene Casey served as a special executive assistant beginning in 1942. Donald Nelson was named personal representative to the president in 1945. A review of archives indicates that their duties varied across a range of issues, although some specialization occurred. For instance, Rowe handled civil aviation matters; general political advice; judicial appointments; and some patronage questions. But neither he nor anyone else in FDR's White House was responsible for policy development. See generally the memos contained in *PSF* – Subject files, EOP – [subject's name], FDRL. See also Hobbs, *Behind the President*, pp. 86–7, Wann, *The President as Chief Administrator*, p. 38.

sponse to Harold Smith's memo suggests, FDR evidently anticipated further reorganization of the EOP.

For reasons that will become more obvious below, it is unlikely FDR would have sanctioned the creation of a White House–based policy staff. Recall that Byrnes' office was never responsible for developing legislation; he was a judge, who adjudicated policy disputes as they came to him. For the most part, FDR's most important White House aides like Hopkins and Rosenman continued to act as facilitators and expediters, not as policy specialists.

Moreover, as Chapter 6 will make clear, Roosevelt conspicuously avoided dividing his personal staff into domestic and foreign policy experts; indeed, he evidently never saw a distinction between the two issue spheres. To better understand why, the final piece to FDR's staff puzzle must be examined. Accordingly, the next two chapters will recount his handling of foreign and military policy, particularly during the war years. They will show that the demarcation between domestic economic and foreign policy, so distinct in White House staffs today, was anathema to FDR. And for good reason.

6

FDR and the national
security bureaucracy

The most intense criticisms of the presidential branch in the post-Roosevelt era are directed toward the national security staff.[1] When institutionalizing a national security bureaucracy, critics charge, presidents are tempted to obtain foreign policy objectives by circumventing domestic political constraints, thus laying the groundwork for an "imperial Presidency."[2] The long-term impact, they claim, is an erosion not just of the presidents' national security bargaining influence, but of the constitutional system of checks and balances more generally.[3]

Charges of presidential "imperialism" are not new, of course; recall that FDR's 1937 reorganization plan was characterized by some as a "dictator bill.[4]" However, neither the Brownlow Report nor the legislation it spawned mentions a national security council or staff. Indeed, as this chapter tries to demonstrate, FDR's administrative instincts, as embodied by the Brownlow Report, precluded the development of both. In the words of former Brownlow Committee research assistant James Fesler: "The charge that the Brownlow Committee set in train the development

---

1 By "national security" I mean both military policy making and diplomatic activities. Note that this differs from usage common to FDR's time; then, "national security" emphasized military decision making, whereas foreign policy referred to diplomacy conducted by the Department of State. See Anna Kasten Nelson, "National Security I: Inventing a Process," in Hugh Heclo and Lester Salamon (eds.), *The Illusion of Presidential Government*, (Boulder, Colo.: Westview Press, 1981), pp. 257–8.

2 The charge of presidential imperialism, most vociferously aired during the Johnson, Nixon, and Reagan presidencies, reflects concern regarding presidents' more prolific use of executive orders and other discretionary powers to obtain foreign policy objectives; their alleged abuses of intelligence-gathering methods both domestically and abroad; and their generally sweeping claims as to the extent of their war powers. Perhaps the most cogent review of these charges is Arthur Schlesinger, Jr., *The Imperial Presidency* (Boston: Houghton-Mifflin, 1973).

3 On this general point, see Harold Hongju Koh, *The National Security Constitution: Sharing Power After the Iran-contra Affair* (New Haven, Conn.: Yale University Press, 1990), pp. 54–7.

4 Richard Polenberg, *Reorganizing Roosevelt's Government 1936–1939 (The Controversy over Executive Reorganization)* (Cambridge: Harvard University Press, 1966).

of 'the imperial presidency' can only be advanced by those who have not read the Committee's report."[5]

In fact, the National Security Council's (NSC) origins are traced to Congress' postwar rejection of FDR's wartime administrative strategy.[6] As Mark Lowenthal points out, Roosevelt's seemingly ad hoc management approach was judged too personalized and thus dangerously antiquated in a nuclear weapons–dominated Cold War era:

> The World War II system had largely reflected the preferred working methods of President Roosevelt, who maintained central control by establishing numerous satrapies.
>
> However, the complex demands of the war and post-war world rendered this system inadequate, and it was generally recognized that a return to the simple and limited prewar system would not be possible if the United States was to face up to the responsibilities thrust upon it by the war and its aftermath.[7]

Reflecting this judgment, Congress in 1947 passed the National Security Act, creating the National Security Council, with administrative support to be provided by an executive secretary heading a staff secretariat.[8] The intent was to ensure closer consultation between presidents and their foreign policy experts, particularly the secretaries of State and Defense and the military branches, the military service chiefs, and the intelligence community.[9]

5 Fesler, in Frederick C. Mosher, *The President Needs Help*, (Lanham, Md.: University Press of American, 1988), p. 13.

6 See the diary of James Forrestal, the Secretary of the Navy who was a strong advocate of a national security council (James Forrestal, *The Forrestal Diaries* [New York: Viking Press, 1951] p. 19). See also Alfred D. Sander, "Truman and the National Security Council, 1945–47," *Journal of American History* 59 (September 1972).

7 See Mark M. Lowenthal, *The National Security Council: Organizational History*, Congressional Research Service (June 27, 1978), p. 8; Charles Neu, "The Rise of the National Security Bureaucracy," in Louis Galambos (ed.), *The New American State: Bureaucracies and Policies Since World War II* (Baltimore: Johns Hopkins University Press, 1987), p. 87.

8 See The National Security Act (P.L. 80–253) (July 26, 1947). In addition to the NSC, the legislation also established the Central Intelligence Agency and unified the Army, Navy, and Army Air Corps within a single Department of Defense. It was amended in 1949 to strengthen the Defense Secretary's authority over the military services.

9 Section 2 of the National Security Act declares: "In enacting this legislation, it is the intent of Congress to provide a comprehensive program for the future security of the United States; to provide for the establishment of integrated policies and procedures for the departments, agencies, and functions of the Government relating to the national security."

   Under Title I, section 101, regarding the establishment of the National Security Council, the act states: "The function of the Council shall be to advise the President with respect to the integration of domestic, foreign, and military policies relating to the national security so as to enable the military services and other departments and agencies of the Government to cooperate more effectively in matters involving the national security."

   The NSC members included: the President; the secretaries of State, the newly established Department of Defense, Army, Navy, and Air Force; and the Chairman of

That did not happen. For the most part, presidents, beginning with Truman who opposed Congress' efforts, have largely ignored the full National Security Council, and have instead utilized the NSC's staff for national security advice.[10] Beginning as a small clerical unit, that staff had by the Nixon administration become a large, functionally specialized *bureaucracy*, headed by a White House–based assistant to the president for national security affairs.[11]

It is the NSC staff that is most frequently targeted by those seeking to reform the presidential branch.[12] And yet, even the NSC's most fervent critics do not advocate a return to FDR's national security advising system. But why not? He successfully headed the United States–led Allied coalition during World War II. And he deserves some acknowledgment for constructing the institutional foundation for a lasting postwar order – one generally credited with "winning" the Cold War.[13] Why, then, when searching for remedies to the current NSC system, are FDR's administrative methods almost universally ignored?

the National Security Resources Board. Secretaries of other departments and the chairmen of the Munitions Board and the Research and Development Board could be designated as members from time to time. Any other appointee required Senate confirmation.

10 For histories of the NSC, see John Prados, *Keepers of the Keys: A History of the National Security Council from Truman to Bush* (New York: William Morrow & Company, Inc., 1991); Nelson, "National Security I," and I. M. Destler, "National Security II: The Rise of the Assistant (1961–1981)," in Hugh Heclo and Lester Salamon (eds.), *The Illusion of Presidential Government* (Boulder, Colo.: Westview Press, 1981), pp. 263–85; I. M. Destler "A Lost Legacy? The Presidency and the National Security Organization, 1945–1960" paper delivered at the U.S. Military Academy, April 1982; and I. M. Destler, "National Security Advice to U.S. Presidents: Some Lessons from Thirty Years," *World Politics* 29, no. 2 (January 1977); Stanley Falk, "The Role of the National Security Council Under Truman, Eisenhower and Kennedy," in Demetrios Caraley (ed.), *The President's War Powers from Federalists to Reagan* (New York: Academy of Political Science, 1984), pp. 131–62; Neu, "The Rise of the National Security Bureaucracy," pp. 85–108; and (for the period before the Kennedy presidency) the Jackson subcommittee hearings and report, formally entitled the Senate Government Operations, Subcommittee on National Policy Machinery, Hearings (and Report): Organizing for National Security (Washington, D.C.: Government Printing Office, 1960). Excerpts were published in Henry Jackson (ed.), *The National Security Council: Jackson Subcommittee Papers on Policymaking at the Presidential Level* (New York: Frederick Praeger, 1965).

11 Officially the NSC staff, except for the assistant to the president for national security affairs, is not part of the White House Office. In practice, however, the distinction is less clearcut.

12 There are four general critiques regarding NSC staff activities: it operates with little congressional oversight; it undercuts the State Department's foreign affairs role; its objectives tend to be too militaristic; and it has become overbureaucratized. See Lowenthal, *The National Security Council*, pp. 35–6; *The Tower Commission Report: The Full Text of the President's Special Review Board*, paperback ed. (New York: Bantam Books, Inc., and Time Books, 1987); and Prados, *Keepers of the Keys*.

13 See, generally, Robert Dallek, *Franklin D. Roosevelt and American Foreign Policy, 1932–1945* (New York: New York University Press, 1979).

One obvious response is that his administrative strategy unfolded during a shooting – as opposed to a cold – war, when support for his foreign policy objectives was practically universal. But, in fact, until the Japanese attack on Pearl Harbor in 1941, the divisions in public sentiment regarding U.S. involvement overseas were similar to those encountered by presidents during the Korean or Vietnam conflicts. Even after the United States entered World War II, FDR's strategy for its prosecution engendered bitter debates, as did his postwar plans.[14]

Roosevelt, then, operated under constraints as daunting as those his successors faced. Hence his staff principles are highly instructive today. Presidents can learn much from his ability to extract national security expertise from his advisers without becoming captive to their bargaining interests. This chapter tells how he did so.

Prelude to war: FDR, the White House and the departments of State, War, and Navy, 1938–41

National security issues began to dominate FDR's bargaining agenda midway through FDR's second presidential term, during congressional debate regarding the Brownlow bill.[15] With public opinion in the prewar period split between isolationists who wanted no U.S. involvement overseas and internationalists pushing for intervention abroad, FDR pursued a middle course: lending military support to the European democracies and to China; engaging in both bilateral and multilateral diplomatic efforts with the totalitarian governments; and strengthening American defenses as much as political constraints would allow.

Administratively, FDR sought to increase his control of diplomatic and military expertise through three means: personnel selection, organizational restructuring, and changes in the policy-making process. He began by handpicking the new Army Chief of Staff, George C. Marshall, effective Sept. 1, 1939.[16] In 1942, Admiral Ernest King replaced Admiral

---

14 For evidence, see the discussion in Chapter 5 regarding economic mobilization.

15 If there is a specific point at which FDR became convinced war was inevitable, it may well have been Hitler's Sept. 12, 1938, Nuremburg address, in the midst of the crisis instigated by Hitler's demand that Czechoslovakia cede the Sudetenland to Germany. This came on the heels of the 1938 German-Austrian Anschluss and preceded the infamous Munich conference. Roosevelt, who understood German, listened to Hitler's speech on radio. For evidence regarding FDR's reaction, see Samuel I. Rosenman, *Working with Roosevelt* (New York: Harper & Row, 1952), p. 181.

16 Roosevelt's decision to replace retiring General Malin Craig with Marshall was actually made Apr. 23, 1939. See War Department Special Order 1149. Although not, by virtue of seniority, next in line for promotion, Marshall had impressed FDR with his candor

Harold Stark as Chief of Naval Operations, and that same year Admiral William Leahy became FDR's White House military liaison to the Joint Chiefs. Together with General Henry (Hap) Arnold, Deputy Chief of Staff and head of the Army Air Corps, these four served as FDR's primary source of military advice and support during the war years.[17] Roosevelt utilized their military expertise to achieve his primary bargaining objective in this period: victory for the Allied coalition.

It was, however, a sometimes testy collaboration, reflecting different bargaining vantage points.[18] Generally speaking, the service chiefs evaluated national security decisions according to their military value and likely impact on their respective military organizations. In contrast, Roosevelt saw military strategy in terms of its potential effect on his broader bargaining objectives, both foreign and domestic.

These different vantage points are illustrated by the clash between Marshall and Roosevelt over how best to modernize the U.S. military in the period beginning during the 1938 budget deliberations. The U.S. Army at this time was in a state of neglect. Numbering only 174,000 men, well below its authorized strength of 210,000 men, it ranked nineteenth in the world in size. It had no air force to speak of and its mechanized capabil-

and independent thinking and received strong backing from Harry Hopkins, Secretary of War Harry Woodring, Assistant Secretary of War Louis Johnson, and former Army Chief of Staff General John J. Pershing. By patiently tutoring Hopkins in the fall of 1938 and spring of 1939 regarding the need to strengthen the American military, Marshall had also helped his own cause.

17 Although Marshall and King were the most influential military strategists, King was probably closer to FDR. James Roosevelt, FDR's eldest son, writes, "I knew [FDR] thought Admiral King the wisest of his staff of military men. I remember him being asked why he kept King in the White House instead of sending him up front to take command. 'The president has to have close to him the shrewdest of strategists. Most critical decisions must be made here. You don't send these men into the front lines where their lives may be endangered'" (James Roosevelt, *My Parents: A Differing View* [Chicago: Playboy Press, 1976], p. 166).

Although Marshall had great respect for Roosevelt's political skills, he complained about FDR's tendency to vacillate on policy questions, and he felt FDR's disorderly administrative habits left him vulnerable to conflicting advice. Forrest Pogue, Marshall's biographer, also suggests the two had contrasting temperaments; Marshall was determined to resist being "taken in" by FDR's congenial manner – toward this end, he made it a point never to laugh at Roosevelt's jokes.

Of course, Roosevelt was always partial to the Navy. And air power was viewed primarily in tactical, rather than strategic terms, at least at the war's outset, which partially explains Arnold's lesser influence.

18 For details, see Eric Larrabee, *Commander-in-Chief: Franklin Delano Roosevelt, His Lieutenants, and Their War* (New York: Harper & Row, 1987); Ed Cray, *General of the Army: George C. Marshall, Soldier and Statesman* (New York: W. W. Norton & Co., 1990); Forrest Pogue's multivolume work on Marshall, especially *Ordeal and Hope, 1939–1942* (New York: Viking Press, 1965); Thomas Parrish, *Roosevelt and Marshall: Partners in Politics and War* (New York: William Morrow, 1989); and Robert William Love Jr. (ed.), *The Chiefs of Naval Operations*, (Annapolis, Md.: Naval Institute Press, 1980).

ities were woeful.[19] In response, Marshall pushed to reorganize the War Department by replacing older officers with younger blood, to expand the size of the Army through a peacetime draft, and to increase the military budget.[20]

But for several reasons, Roosevelt was lukewarm to Marshall's efforts, particularly the proposal to significantly increase defense expenditures. First, he did not think an expanded army would, in the short run, deter German aggression. As Arnold put it, "Roosevelt didn't think Hitler would be too worried about building barracks in Kansas."[21] Instead, FDR initially sought to quickly upgrade the U.S. capacity to produce war planes, which he then intended to ship overseas to France and Great Britain.[22] Moreover, these overseas orders might stimulate the U.S. aviation industry.

But the primary constraint on FDR was political. An extended, across-the-board military buildup could jeopardize congressional and public support for FDR's New Deal programs during a time when isolationism was strong and the economy – and FDR's political influence – weak. The Republicans had made major gains in the 1938 midterm elections,

19 In contrast, the Navy, although also in need of modernization, nevertheless had fared slightly better during the interwar period.

20 The draft was a particularly risky issue in this period, given the strong isolationist sentiment. Roosevelt, who was pursuing reelection, remained noncommittal for more than a month while Marshall spearheaded the lobbying effort, starting July 12, 1940, with testimony on Capitol Hill in support of a draft bill. Finally, in August 1940, FDR threw his support behind the legislation. Congress approved the mobilization of the National Guard on Aug. 27, and on Sept. 16, 1940, a month after the Battle of Britain began, Roosevelt signed into law the Selective Service Act, establishing a draft. Both the draft act and the mobilization of the National Guard were good for one year. Subsequent efforts to extend the draft entailed a bitter political struggle.

21 Indeed, FDR told Morgenthau, "Had we had this summer 5,000 planes and the capacity to immediately produce 10,000 per year . . . Hitler would not have dared to take the stand he did" John Blum (ed.), *Roosevelt and Morgenthau: A Revision and Condensation of the "From the Morgenthau Diaries"* (Boston: Houghton-Mifflin Co, 1970), p. 273.

22 William Bullitt, the U.S. ambassador to France, had met with FDR on Oct. 14, 1938, to warn of French and British vulnerability to a German air attack. A week later FDR told Treasury Secretary Henry Morgenthau he wanted to sign contracts to produce 10,000 planes over a two-year period, including 3,750 combat-ready aircraft, another 3,750 reserve combat planes, and 2,500 training craft. On Nov. 12, he reiterated this goal in a conversation with Morgenthau, Hopkins and Assistant Secretary of War Johnson.

At this time, of course, the United States had no separate air force, although the Army and the Navy had their own air wings. (A separate air force staff did not begin to materialize until July 1941, when the positions of Deputy Chief of Staff for Air [the Chief of the Army Air Forces] and the Chief of the Navy's Bureau of Aeronautics were added to the Joint Army – Navy Board. See the revision to Army regulation 95–5 [June 1941]). Moreover, despite congressional endorsement in 1936 of the Baker Board recommendation to increase U.S. plane production to 2,320 planes, only 1,600 planes had actually been turned out by the fall of 1938, and few of these were bombers. The rest were on order.

whereas FDR's efforts to purge conservative Democrats had largely failed.[23] His "court-packing" and reorganization plans had been stymied, and he was widely perceived to be a lame-duck president, unlikely to challenge the third-term "taboo" by running again in 1940.[24]

Understandably, given the appalling state of American air power, FDR's military experts were not keen on denuding American defenses by selling U.S. planes to European allies. Nor did they support FDR's effort to strengthen defense on the cheap, without a significant budget increase.[25] The result, as Marshall's biographer Forrest Pogue notes, was that, "[T]hrough the months of ostensible neutrality Roosevelt called the arms assistance tune, and his service chiefs, believing further diminution of their resources unwise and dangerous, hopped to it with something less than wholehearted enthusiasm."[26]

See Mark S. Watson, *Chief of Staff* (Washington, D.C.: Office of the Chief of Military History, Department of the Army, 1951), p. 127; Blum, *Roosevelt and Morgenthau*, pp. 270–1; Parrish, *Roosevelt and Marshall*, pp. 15–17; and Larrabee, *Commander-in-Chief*, pp. 214–15.

23 The Republicans had gone from 88 to 170 seats in the House, and picked up eight senatorial seats, which, combined with the conservative Democratic coalition, gave them commanding power in the Senate.

24 A measure of his lack of influence within Congress was his inability during the period 1938–9 to get the Neutrality Act reformed or eliminated. It was not until the German invasion of Poland in September 1939, that Congress agreed to pass the less stringent cash-and-carry provision. Roosevelt signed cash-and-carry into law Nov. 4, 1939. His struggle to repeal the neutrality legislation is summarized in Dallek, *Franklin D. Roosevelt and American Foreign Policy*, pp. 180–92; 199–205.

25 A point almost all of FDR's national security advisers made to him in a Nov. 14, 1938 White House meeting. Marshall, at this time the Deputy Chief of Staff of the Army, thought FDR's proposal wholly unrealistic and told him so during this encounter. Roosevelt answered Marshall's objection by ending the meeting, whereupon Marshall was advised by his associates that his chance to be promoted to Chief of Staff of the Army had probably vanished. Fortunately, this was not the case. The story is recounted in Cray, *General of the Army*, pp. 131–3; see also Parrish, *Roosevelt and Marshall*, pp. 15–17; and Watson, *Chief of Staff*, p. 130.

Marshall's sentiments were shared by Secretary of War Woodring, an isolationist, and Assistant Secretary Johnson, an interventionist – one of the few instance in which they were on the same side of an argument. After the meeting, former Army Chief of Staff John J. Pershing wrote Roosevelt on Nov. 25, 1938 to argue Marshall's case. Roosevelt's reply (Dec. 3, 1938) is noncommittal. (Both letters reprinted in Elliot Roosevelt (ed.), *F.D.R. His Personal Letters, 1928–45*, [New York: Duell, Sloan & Pearce, 1950], pp. 837–8 [hereafter *FDR's Personal Letters*].) Arnold, head of the Army air force, also agreed with Marshall, as did Joseph Kennedy, Roosevelt's ambassador in London, who cabled FDR, "It seems to me that if we had to fight to protect our lives, we would do better fighting in our own backyard." Blum, *Roosevelt and Morgenthau*, p. 317; see also Dallek, *Franklin D. Roosevelt and American Foreign Policy*, p. 213.

To bypass this opposition, Roosevelt assigned Morgenthau responsibility for selling American planes to the French and British. See Blum, *Roosevelt and Morgenthau*, pp. 274–84.

26 Pogue, *Ordeal and Hope*, p. 52. In part the difficulty FDR faced was statutory; by law (P.L. 671 approved June 28, 1940) defense material could not be shipped overseas unless declared surplus by the Chief of Naval Operations and the Chief of Staff. This led

The initial result was budget compromise; FDR asked Congress for $1.3 billion in defense funding for fiscal year 1940 (out of a total budget request of $8.996 billion), of which about $170 million was targeted for the production of 3,000 planes. This significantly increased the military budget, but funded less than half FDR's original production goal for planes. Roosevelt was not happy with the compromise, as he told Johnson in January 1939: "I am not satisfied with the limit of $170,000,000 provided for airplanes themselves. This item should be increased and the other items reduced."[27]

During the next fifteen months Roosevelt continued to pursue short-term fixes, such as selling planes, while postponing long-term commitments for across-the-board military expenditures until political sentiments had crystallized. His strategy is captured in a note he wrote to Navy Secretary Frank Knox in December 1940: "This is a period of flux. I want no authorizations for what may happen beyond July 1, 1942. All of us may be dead when that time comes!"[28]

In fact, however, the domestic political winds had already begun to shift that spring, in response to the deteriorating European situation.[29] In April 1940, the House began debating an appropriations bill granting the War Department almost 10 percent less than the $853 million FDR had initially requested for fiscal year 1941. Then the Germans, fresh from their conquest of Denmark and Norway, invaded the Low Countries beginning May 10, 1940. Three days later, at a White House meeting, Treasury Secretary Henry Morgenthau was pleading with a reluctant Roosevelt to support Marshall's request for a supplementary military appropriation.[30]

to some intricate negotiations between FDR and his two commanders. For instance, Stark initially felt compelled to reject the destroyer-for-bases deal negotiated by FDR and Churchill because he could not in good conscience declare the destroyers not necessary for American defense. Only some delicate negotiating convinced Stark to approve the trade with the British. See Pogue, *Ordeal and Hope*, pp. 46–79; Love, *Chiefs of Naval Operations*, p. 123.

27 FDR to Johnson (Jan. 18, 1939), reprinted in *F.D.R.'s Personal Letters*, p. 854. Moreover, Roosevelt's efforts to allow the British and French to buy American planes met stiff resistance from Woodring, Arnold, and members of the Senate Military Affairs Committee. Nevertheless, this budget marks the start of the modernization of American air power from 20,000 men flying a few hundred semiobsolescent planes in 1938 into a potent military arm numbering 2.4 million men and 80,000 modern planes by 1945. See Watson, *Chief of Staff*, pp. 142–5.

28 FDR to Knox (Dec. 23, 1940) *FDR's Personal Letters*, p. 1088–9.

29 Germany moved into Denmark and Norway on Apr. 9, 1940, began its sweep through the Low Countries on May 10, and by June was in control of most of France. Even then, however, opposition to direct military intervention by the United States into the European conflict continued, as evidenced by the resistance to FDR's plan to swap American destroyers for British bases. See Dallek, *Franklin D. Roosevelt and Foreign Policy*, pp. 243–7.

30 Marshall was asking for $657 million in supplementary funds to increase the Army to 280,000 men by the end of September 1940, and to 750,000 by the end of the follow-

When British Prime Minister Winston Churchill formally requested U.S. military aid three days after that, FDR – sensing a shift in congressional sentiment – agreed to request a supplementary $1.08 billion defense appropriation from Congress, more than half of which was to go to the Army. As the German onslaught progressed, a suddenly alarmed Congress tacked on $320 million to FDR's request, and on June 13 he signed legislation appropriating $1.5 billion for the War Department for fiscal year 1941.[31] A supplementary appropriation signed into law on June 26 increased that total to nearly $3 billion. That same month, following the fall of France, Congress passed the "Two Navy Act," laying the foundation for the construction of the American fleet that fought World War II.

By the summer of 1940, then, American rearmament was finally underway.[32] Pogue notes that, "Marshall always spoke of this action afterward as the breaking of the logjam. In April, he recalled in later years, he had struggled to get 18 million dollars restored to the budget; in May the president asked for a billion for defense."[33]

The increase in military expenditures was accompanied by organizational changes designed to make the military more responsive to FDR's leadership. On July 5, 1939, four days after Marshall began serving as acting Army Chief of Staff, FDR overhauled the Joint Army–Navy Board, an interdepartmental administrative body created in 1903 to smooth over Army–Navy differences.[34] Roosevelt's military order effectively removed the secretaries of War and the Navy from the military

ing year. He had prepped Morgenthau on the request during a meeting on May 11, 1940. Two days later Morgenthau, Marshall, Woodring, Johnson, and Budget Director Harold Smith met with FDR at the White House. Morgenthau noted, "At first the President was entirely opposed to Marshall's program and when I put up a strong argument for it, he said, 'I am not asking you. I am telling you'" (Blum, *Roosevelt and Morgenthau*, p. 315).

31 Watson, *Chief of Staff*, p. 169. A breakdown of the War Department supplementary request is contained in a memo from Stimson to FDR (May 29, 1940), Harry Hopkins Papers, Sherwood manuscript, Conceptions of Strategy – Pre-Pearl Harbor Folder, FDRL.

32 Army personnel was expanded from 280,000 to 375,000. A Joint Resolution passed on Aug. 27, 1940 granted FDR the power to mobilize the national guard. He signed the Selective Service Act on Sept. 16, 1940, which together with the national guard resolution gave FDR legislative authorization for an army of 1.4 million men.

33 Pogue, *Ordeal and Hope*, p. 32.

34 Created in the aftermath of the Spanish-American War, the Joint Board was the brainchild of Secretary of War Elihu Root and Secretary of the Navy John D. Long, who sought administrative means to improve interservice cooperation. It was comprised of four Army and four Navy officers, who met monthly. However, because board members each had full-time duties within their respective military branches, they could not devote full attention to Joint Board issues. Consequently, in 1919 the board was reconstituted, its members designated by position rather than by name, and it was given a staff support system – the Joint Planning Committee, consisting of three or more officers from the General Staff's War Plans Division and from the Office of Naval Operations Plans Division.

chain of command; henceforth, the Board reported directly to the president in regard to matters of tactics, strategy, and military operations.[35]

Roosevelt's action was prompted by two Joint Board deficiencies. First, the German blitzkrieg had demonstrated the effectiveness of synchronized military action by the separate service branches, especially the army and air force. But until FDR's reorganization order, the Joint Board was primarily an instrument of consultation, not coordinated execution.[36]

Second, Joint Board decisions could not be implemented without the approval of the War and Navy secretaries. Roosevelt, of course, was always uneasy at having cabinet heads interposed between him and his staff. His unease was exacerbated in this case due to Secretary of War Woodring's increasingly isolationist views and continuing feud with Assistant Secretary of War Louis Johnson.[37] By cutting the departmental secretaries out of the Board's decision-making process, then, Roosevelt could personally coordinate military operations across a global expanse.[38]

Roosevelt followed the same administrative logic in 1942 when he shuffled the War Department chain of command in the aftermath of Pearl Harbor.[39] As he explained to Henry Stimson, who had succeeded Woodring as Secretary of War:

> After 1923, membership on the Joint Board included the Army Chief of Staff, the Deputy Chief of Staff, and the Chief of the General Staff's War Plans Division, together with the Navy Chief of Naval Operations, the Assistant Chief of Naval Operations, and the Director of the Office of Naval Operations' Plans Division. Remember that at this juncture, both the Army and the Navy contained their own aviation branches; there was no separate air force service.
>
> See Demetrios Caraley, *The Politics of Military Unification: A Study of Conflict and the Policy Process* (New York: Columbia University Press, 1966), pp. 14–15; Watson, *Chief of Staff*, pp. 79–81.

35 The military order, effective July 1, 1939, transferred control of the Joint Army – Navy Board, the Joint Economy Board, the Aeronautical Board, and the Joint Army and Navy Munitions Board from the secretaries of the Navy and War to Roosevelt. The Joint Economy Board functioned to eliminate overlaps or duplications in operations of the two services; the Aeronautical Board focused on securing greater coordination in the use of Army and Navy air power; and the Joint Army and Navy Munitions Board worked to harmonize procurement policies affecting the two services.

36 Roosevelt, a former Assistant Secretary of the Navy, was particularly interested in naval organizational matters; his papers are full of memoranda to Navy officials regarding promotions, shipbuilding techniques, funding, and other related items. Marshall, aware of FDR's partiality toward the Navy, knew it could cut both ways; he might have more latitude to restructure the Army to his liking, but he also had less leeway for mistakes.

37 In addition to hampering the effectiveness of the War Department, the continuing dispute put Marshall in a rather delicate position, because he reported to both individuals. See Pogue, *Ordeal and Hope*, pp. 19–23.

38 Weekly, rather than monthly, Joint Board meetings were instituted July 2, 1941, reflecting the increased tempo of events as well as FDR's desire for greater inter-service coordination. See Watson, *Chief of Staff*, p. 80.

39 The Mar. 9, 1942, reorganization established a central command post (the War Plans Division, renamed the Operations Division on Mar. 23) within the War Department. Its

I am quite willing to approve this order which you and General Marshall have worked over so carefully, in so far as it concerns the reorganization of the Army. . . . I wish, however, that the wording . . . be
rephrased to make it very clear that the Commander-in-Chief exercises his command function in relation to strategy, tactics and operations directly through the Chief of Staff. You, as Secretary of War,
apart from your administrative responsibilities, would, of course, advise on military matters.[40]

Roosevelt was no less jealous of his command prerogative toward
the Navy, actively monitoring reorganization efforts there to protect his
interests.[41]

Roosevelt's actions converted the Joint Board into "the keystone in the
structure of authority that made the president commander-in-chief in fact
as well as name."[42] During the prewar period, the newly reconstituted
Joint Board served as FDR's primary administrative means for developing a strategy that addressed both his military and political objectives. But
even before Pearl Harbor, that strategy was increasingly devised in consultation with the American Allies.[43]

intent was to provide Marshall with more effective strategic command of the Army without burdening him with peripheral administrative details. It also established three Army
command divisions. For details, see Ray Cline, *Washington Command Post: The Operations Division* (Washington, D.C.: Office of the Chief of Military History, Department
of the Army, 1951), pp. 90–106.

40 Roosevelt to Stimson (Feb. 26, 1942) in the Harry Hopkins Papers, Special Assistant to
the President, 1941–5, Organization of Military Forces File, FDRL. See also E.O. 9082
(Feb. 28, 1942) regarding reorganization of the Army of the United States; and Larrabee,
Commander-in-Chief, pp. 141–2.

41 On Mar. 12, 1942, FDR issued E.O. 9096 combining two Navy posts – the Commander in Chief United States Fleet, and Chief of Naval Operations – into one position. King
was given this title and thereafter served as FDR's primary naval aide. But when King
tried to strengthen his control over Navy bureau chiefs through a series of orders in May
of that year, FDR vetoed the move. See "Ernest Joseph King" in Love, *The Chiefs of
Naval Operations*, pp. ix, 162.

42 Larrabee, *Commander-in-Chief*, p. 167. It also laid the groundwork for the subsequent
creation by FDR of the Joint Chiefs of Staff, which beginning in 1941 became his primary
instrument for exercising his commander-in-chief functions for the duration of the war.

43 Military strategy was detailed in the Joint Board's Basic War Plans. Each plan was color-
coded in reference to the nation anticipated to be the principal enemy. For instance, War Plan
Orange, revised by the Joint Board and approved by the secretaries of War and the Navy in
February 1938, presented the American response to Japanese military aggression. It provided
the strategic rationale for the increase in naval strength passed by Congress in May 1938.
    Until November 1938, these war plans generally focused on engaging one enemy at a
time. Thereafter, however, the Board began seriously studying the military implications
of an alliance between Japan, Germany, and Italy. Eventually, the Board devised five
"rainbow" war plans, each contemplating a different scenario in which the United States
battled multiple enemies across a broad geographic expanse. Four of the five plans were
rendered obsolete by events. Rainbow Five, which made provisions for sending U.S.
forces to Africa or Europe to defeat Germany or Italy, or both, served as the basic document for subsequent strategic talks with the British, described below. See Watson, *Chief
of Staff*, pp. 92–3, 103–4; and Cline, *Washington Command Post*, pp. 34–7.

The first serious military talks with the British began in January 1941. These were preceded by strategy sessions among FDR and his own generals. At Admiral Stark's suggestion, the Americans decided to adopt an Atlantic-first strategy designed to defeat Germany and Italy, while maintaining a defensive posture in the Pacific.[44] This battle plan became the basis for the high-level "ABC" (American-British Conversations) beginning later that month.[45]

Conducted in the utmost secrecy, the ABC talks produced a set of military agreements regarding joint U.S.-British strategic objectives, and plans for obtaining them, that would eventually guide the Allies through the entire war.[46] But the meetings also revealed fundamental divisions between the two countries regarding military strategy and tactics, providing

---

44 "Plan Dog" (or "D") was in fact chosen from among four options. The others were Plan A (limiting U.S. action to the Western Hemisphere), B (primary attention to Japan), and C (equivalent pressure in both the Atlantic and Pacific theaters). Plan D reversed the interwar period American military strategy that had been predicated on the assumption that the French and British navies would protect U.S. interests in the Atlantic. France's defeat and the near demise of Great Britain in 1940 forced Roosevelt to revise the planners' assumptions; Britain's survival now seemed the key to any successful American war plan. See Robert Sherwood, *Roosevelt and Hopkins*, rev. paperback ed. (New York: The Universal Library, 1950), pp. 271–2; Watson, *Chief of Staff*, pp. 117–25; Maurice Matloff and Edwin Snell, *Strategic Planning for Coalition Warfare* (Washington, D.C.: Office of Chief of Military History, Department of the Army, 1953), pp. 25–8; and Love, *Chiefs of Naval Operations*, p. 125.

45 These lasted from Jan. 29 through Mar. 29, 1941. Due to their potentially explosive political implications, no high-ranking political officials from either nation dared attend; only military officers did. Recall that during the 1940 presidential campaign Wendell Willkie charged FDR with leading the nation toward war. In response, Roosevelt repeatedly promised "your boys are not going to be sent into any foreign wars." For most of the campaign he qualified this promise by ending it with the clause "unless attacked," but in an uncharacteristic moment of ill-timed pique, he dropped the qualifying clause during a speech on Oct. 30, 1940, at Boston. Given this public statement, he was understandably reluctant to acknowledge military talks with the British. (See Watson, *Chief of Staff*, pp. 369–70, and Matloff and Snell, *Strategic Planning for Coalition Warfare*, pp. 33–42, for a list of participants and details of the meetings.)

46 The ABC-1 and ABC-2 (focusing on air strategy) reports, basically reaffirmed the Germany-first strategy and provided the basis for American military planners to adopt the Rainbow Five war plan. A summary of the major points is contained in Watson, *Chief of Staff*, pp. 375–82. Roosevelt read the reports but did not at this time formally approve them.

Agreement on military strategy, of course, was essential to determine production guidelines. Subsequently, the so-called Victory program was laid out in the "Joint Board Estimate of the United States Over-all Production Requirements," dated Sept. 11, 1941, and given to FDR on Sept. 25. A copy of this twenty-three page document, signed by Marshall and Stark, is contained in Hopkins Papers, Sherwood Manuscript, Conception of Strategy – Pre-Pearl Harbor Folder, FDRL. Sherwood called it "one of the most important documents of the pre-Pearl Harbor period," (Sherwood, *Roosevelt and Hopkins*, pp. 410–8). See also Watson, *Chief of Staff*, pp. 331–66; and Chapter 4.

See FDR's directive (July 9, 1941) to the secretaries of War and Navy asking that such a study be undertaken. *PSF* – Subject, Safe File, FDRL.

the first indication of the difficulty FDR would face in conducting a wartime alliance.[47]

This also marked the beginning of fears among Roosevelt's military advisers that he would succumb to British pressure and support strategic objectives that served primarily British interests. The first alarms in this regard were raised by British efforts to enlist the U.S. Pacific fleet in the defense of British-held Singapore. They were renewed when the British began arguing that Germany could be defeated through naval and air power alone, without a large ground commitment. Hence, the British argued, American forces could be used elsewhere, presumably (the Americans feared) to protect British colonial interests.

The generals' suspicions were furthered aroused by the establishment of the Lend-Lease program in March 1941. Rather than entrust Lend-Lease to his military officials, Roosevelt chose to administer it through a Defense Aid Division created within the Office of Emergency Management, under the direction of Harry Hopkins.[48] In this way, he circumvented opposition from his service chiefs to the further dissipation of American military materials.

The move recognized Hopkins' growing influence as FDR's chief foreign policy confidant.[49] In May 1940, he had set up shop full-time in the White House, working out of what used to be Lincoln's study in the main residence.[50] That location, combined with a lack of competing institu-

47 The details are in Watson, *Chief of Staff*, pp. 367–82, 393–400; and Matloff and Snell, *Strategic Planning for Coalition Warfare*, pp. 34–8.
48 Although nominally administered by General James Burns, Lend-Lease in fact operated under Hopkins' direction. On Mar. 27, 1941, FDR designated Hopkins "to advise and assist me in carrying out the responsibilities placed upon me by the act of March 11, 1941 [the Lend-Lease Act]" (see the copy of the memo [Mar. 27, 1942], from FDR to Hopkins, *PSF* – Subject Files, Hopkins' Folder, FDRL). Officially Hopkins left Lend-Lease in late 1941, although he continued to make policy decisions affecting that program. Subsequently the Defense Aid Division was eventually officially transformed into the Office of Lend-Lease Administration when Edward R. Stettinius assumed charge. See Edward Stettinius, *Lend-Lease: Weapons for Victory* (New York: MacMillan, 1944), pp. 95–6.
49 On Hopkins' wartime duties, see especially Sherwood, *Roosevelt and Hopkins*. See also George McJimsey, *Harry Hopkins* (Cambridge: Harvard University Press, 1987). Hopkins was first brought into foreign policy discussions because FDR wanted to build aircraft in WPA-constructed factories. Hopkins, of course, headed the WPA. Subsequently, in 1938, he was appointed Secretary of Commerce to improve his relations with the business community and thus his presidential prospects. But ill health ended those ambitions, and Hopkins resigned the Commerce post. Thereafter, he did not hold an official position until 1942, when FDR made him a special assistant in charge of Lend-Lease, followed by his appointment as Chairman of the Munitions Supply Board. From here he was paid not from the regular White House appropriations, but from a special emergency fund available to FDR.
50 On May 10, 1940, after dinner at the White House, Hopkins felt so poorly that FDR asked him to stay overnight. He remained in the White House for three and one-half years. Hopkins' room was situated on the second floor in the southeast section of the

tional loyalties, allowed Hopkins to view foreign policy from a perspective most closely matching Roosevelt's. The military staff, realizing this, cultivated Hopkins' support.[51] Through these ties Roosevelt increasingly found Hopkins extraordinarily useful. Soon he was relying on him to carry out sensitive diplomatic missions, beginning with a trip in January 1941 to confer with Churchill.[52]

Hopkins' influence was cemented at the Arcadia conference in January 1942, when the Allies agreed to establish a series of combined boards to oversee all joint war activities: munitions assignments, shipping, materials, food production, and resources.[53] Roosevelt appointed Hopkins to head the Munitions Assignment Board responsible for allocating military supplies to all of the Allies in every theater for the duration of the war. It was "by all the odds the most important and controlled to a large extent the determination of the others."[54] From this post Hopkins became the "supreme office boy of them all," intervening across the range of wartime activities, much as he did on the domestic front by virtue of his position as de facto head of the Lend-Lease program.[55] This extensive purview led

main White House residence. In addition to the main bedroom, there was an adjoining room that Hopkins used for his secretary. See the general description in Sherwood, *Roosevelt and Hopkins*, pp. 202-6.

   Samuel Rosenman, who continued to work on FDR's speeches during this period, also had a bedroom in the main residence in which he stayed during his frequent visits to Washington.

51 So as not to wear out his welcome with FDR, Marshall frequently relied on Hopkins to intervene with FDR on his behalf. They had first met when Hopkins used the Army to train Works Progress Administration workers. On the relationship between the two, see Pogue, *Ordeal and Hope*, pp. 24–6; Larrabee, *Commander-in-Chief*, pp. 106–9.

52 This six-week visit beginning in January 1941 was the first of two Hopkins made to Churchill. He reported back to FDR through secret cable, bypassing the State Department (Sherwood, *Roosevelt and Hopkins*, pp. 253–63). Subsequently, after a return visit to Churchill in July 1941, Hopkins flew directly to Moscow to confer with Stalin regarding the status of the Soviet resistance to the German invasion. Hopkins' sole authority was a note from FDR saying, "I ask you to treat Mr. Hopkins with the identical confidence you would feel if you were talking directly to me." Sherwood, *Roosevelt and Hopkins*, pp. 319–22. He then returned to England and sailed with Churchill in August to meet FDR in the Bay of Newfoundland.

53 "Notes on Informal Conferences Held During the Visit of the British Chiefs of Staff in Washington" (Jan. 14, 1942, Arcadia Conference), Harry Hopkins Papers, Special Assistant to the President, 1941–45, Organization of Military Forces File, FDRL.

   An attempt to coordinate production among the two countries by creating a Combined Production and Resources board on June 9, 1942, with Oliver Lyttelton and Donald Nelson never really was effective. Sherwood, *Roosevelt and Hopkins*, pp. 578–9.

54 Sherwood, *Roosevelt and Hopkins*, p. 470. Marshall opposed Hopkins' appointment, hoping instead to place the munitions board under the joint authority of the combined military chiefs representing both nations. However, the British wanted each country to retain control of supplies within their respective spheres of influence. Thus Marshall was overruled. (Minutes, Jan. 14, 1942 meeting, p. 3.)

55 Sherwood, *Roosevelt and Hopkins*, pp. 202–3, 173. Foreign leaders frequently used Hopkins to communicate information which they felt that for political or personal

Roosevelt to make sure all the cables from Churchill and other heads of state were "coordinated through Harry because so much of them refer to civil things."[56]

As Hopkins' biographer Robert Sherwood summarizes: "The extraordinary fact was that the second most important individual in the United States government during the most critical period of the world's greatest war had no legitimate official position nor even any desk of his own except the card table in his bedroom. However, the bedroom was in the White House."[57]

Hopkins met FDR daily, attended all the key wartime conferences and most of the White House military strategy conferences. Moreover, he functioned with a minimal staff, numbering no more than two to three individuals.[58] It was not until 1944 that Hopkins' influence began waning, a victim of his worsening health.[59]

While he was ascendant, however, Hopkins unquestionably weakened Cordell Hull's position as Secretary of State.[60] Indeed, Hopkins, with

reasons they could not say directly to their opposite number; "Because of the utter informality of his position as well as of his character he could act in an extra-official capacity and thus bring about ready settlement of disputes which might have been greatly prolonged or completely stalled if left to traditional . . . machinery of international negotiation" (ibid., p. 457). Leahy, noting Hopkins' role in almost all aspects of presidential decision making at this time, called him "Harry the Hop." He "was usually the first man to put a finger on the essential element of the problem," Leahy recalled (Admiral William Leahy, *I Was There: The Personal Story of the Chief of Staff to Presidents Roosevelt and Truman Based on His Notes and Diaries Made at the Time*, (New York: Whittlesey House – McGraw-Hill Books, 1950), p. 138. Sherwood also characterizes Hopkins as FDR's "one man Foreign Office." In addition to overseeing Lend-Lease and chairing the Munitions Board, Hopkins served as Roosevelt's channel of communication with all the defense-oriented agencies, especially the War Department. Some indication of the scope of Hopkins' duties can be gleaned by reading his memos from FDR. Frequently, they took the form of "H. H. Will you check on this and speak to me about it?" See generally the Harry Hopkins Papers, Special Assistant to the President, 1941–5; and *PSF* – Subject Files, Hopkins' Folder, FDRL.

56 See the general description of Hopkins as Roosevelt's "foreign secretary" in Sherwood, *Roosevelt and Hopkins*, pp. 636–40.

57 Ibid., p. 212.

58 His primary assistant during much of this time was Isador Lubin, although he made use of a range of individuals working on the payroll of other departments and agencies.

59 At this point it was apparent, as Leahy said, that Hopkins was "living on borrowed time" (Leahy, *I Was There*, p. 220). See also Sherwood, *Roosevelt and Hopkins*, p. 814. Forced to the sidelines by ill health for seven months, he lost his place as FDR's key confidant. Thereafter Roosevelt never invested such trust in another aide. Leahy notes, "There was no one close to Roosevelt who could take his place." Sherwood argues that during Hopkins' illness, Roosevelt made a couple of errors – endorsing the Morgenthau Plan for the reduction of Germany to an agrarian economy, and almost sanctioning a separate meeting between Churchill and Stalin – which Hopkins would have stopped. Sherwood, *Roosevelt and Hopkins*, p. 833.

60 Although in his memoir, Hull professes not to be bothered by Hopkins' activities: "Although Hopkins' work was now on an international scale, I never had any friction, much

FDR's acquiescence, frequently bypassed the State Department altogether in his dealings with foreign leaders. On more than one occasion, Hull had to ask Hopkins for copies of critical foreign policy cables that were routed through other channels. Not surprisingly, Hull resented this treatment, especially his exclusion from the major war conferences.[61]

But Roosevelt evidently believed the State Department, on the whole, had become too conservative during the long interwar period of American isolationism.[62] (He was also infuriated by the department's tendency to leak confidential matters.[63]) As a result, FDR cultivated secondary channels, include Hopkins, to bypass the State Department whenever possible.[64]

The Lend-Lease program offered one means for doing so, since communications from Lend-Lease officials went through military channels. Averell Harriman, officially in London to oversee the Lend-Lease mission, in fact served as a conduit between Churchill and Roosevelt, bypassing Ambassador John Winant of the State Department.[65] Moreover, Roosevelt used second-level State Department aides as informal liaisons to the White House. Assistant Secretary of State Sumner Welles served this function for several years until Hull, in 1943, revolted against the

less clashes, with him. To the best of my knowledge, he did not undertake to interfere with important policies of the State Department. . . .

While I and many others differed with Hopkins' views on numerous domestic questions prior to 1941, my later estimates of him were that he possessed splendid ability and rendered valuable service during the war" (Cordell Hull, *The Memoirs of Cordell Hull* [New York: MacMillan Co., 1948], vol. 2 p. 923).

61 "After Pearl Harbor I did not sit in on meetings concerned with military matters. This was because the President did not invite me to such meetings. . . .

I feel it is a serious mistake for a Secretary of State not to be present at important military meetings . . . The President did not take me with him to the Casablanca, Cairo or Teheran conferences . . . nor did I take part in his military discussions with Prime Minister Churchill in Washington, some of which had widespread diplomatic repercussions" (ibid. pp. 1,109–11).

62 See FDR's letter to Hull (Aug. 28, 1939) complaining about State Department promotion policies, reprinted in *FDR's Personal Letters*, pp. 913–14; Sherwood, *Roosevelt and Hopkins*, pp. 756–7.

63 Regarding leaks, see Roosevelt's complaint to Sumner Welles (FDR to Welles, Jan. 7, 1938), reprinted in *FDR's Personal Letters*, pp. 741–2.

64 For instance, Leahy, while serving as U.S. Ambassador to Vichy France in 1940, communicated directly with Roosevelt or with Sumner Welles, the Undersecretary of State, bypassing Hull completely. Leahy, *I Was There*, p. 94.

65 Harriman began in 1940 as a Lend-Lease official stationed in Great Britain, reporting directly to Hopkins through naval communications. Churchill, knowing of the arrangement, dealt directly with Harriman. See Sherwood, *Roosevelt and Hopkins*, pp. 268–70; 755–6. Subsequently Harriman was appointed U.S. Ambassador to the Soviet Union in September 1943. See Rudy Abramson, *Spanning the Century: The Life of W. Averell Harriman* (New York: William Morrow, 1992).

Later, a Lend-Lease mission was established in Moscow with a similar communications process. And Roosevelt sent Administrative Assistant Lauchlin Currie on several trips to China after Lend-Lease aid was extended to that nation. Currie thus served as FDR's direct liaison to Chiang Kai-shek.

affront:[66] "From our earliest association I had sought to give him [Welles] reasonable latitude in carrying on his work. . . . I found, however, that Welles abused this privilege by going to the President at times without my knowledge, and even attempting to secure a decision, again without my knowledge."[67]

Hull pressured FDR into accepting Welles' resignation in 1943.[68] Subsequently, when Hull quit the next year due to poor health, FDR replaced him with Assistant Secretary of State Edward Stettinius.[69] Stettinius then officially designated long-time State Department employee Chip Bohlen, FDR's interpreter at the 1943 Teheran conference with Stalin, as his White House liaison. In fact, this merely formalized an existing arrangement; Bohlen had been performing unofficially as FDR's link to the State Department since early 1944.[70]

What purpose, then, did Hull serve? Despite Roosevelt's Machiavellian treatment of him, Roosevelt found Hull to be an extremely useful Secretary of State. Because of Hull's strong public standing as a former Congressman, Roosevelt used him on Capitol Hill and in public appearances to muster domestic support for FDR's foreign policies.[71] Moreover, Roo-

---

66 Roosevelt's correspondence is filled with memos to Welles directing him to intervene in various situations, in addition to undertaking direct diplomatic activities. Welles also conducted overseas diplomacy for FDR; in 1940, FDR sent him on a European fact-finding tour during which Welles met the leaders of Germany and Italy. See Sumner Welles, *The Time for Decision* (New York: Harper & Brothers, 1944), pp. 73–147.

67 Hull, *Memoir*, p. 1,227. Hull acknowledged that "[t]here was perhaps some explanation for this tendency in the fact that Mr. Roosevelt and Welles were old family friends with the same social and school background." For Hull's views on the issue, see, generally, ibid., pp. 1,227–31.

68 Welles quit on Sept. 25, 1943. To minimize the backlash created by Welles' forced resignation, FDR, with Hull's concurrence, tried to get Welles to take an ambassador post or to head a special mission to Russia. "Hull has been telephoning me almost daily about the Welles matter," James Byrnes wrote Roosevelt at this time, adding that Hull wanted Welles "kicked upstairs." But Welles refused to take another governmental post (Byrnes to FDR [Sept. 3, 1943]), *PSF – Subject Files: Executive Office, Byrnes Folder, FDRL.*

69 In fact, Stettinius was a compromise candidate; FDR's first choice was probably Welles, but to appoint him would likely have incurred the wrath of Congress. The other possible candidate for the post, James Byrnes, was opposed by Hopkins, who felt Byrnes would not be content to serve as FDR's mouthpiece. (Sherwood, *Roosevelt and Hopkins*, pp. 834–5.)

70 Bohlen's appointment came on Hopkins' recommendation. He was a career State Department official who was fluent in Russian and served under Harriman while the latter was ambassador to the Soviet Union. Beginning with the Teheran conference in 1943, he became FDR's personal interpreter in meetings with the Soviets. See Sherwood, *Roosevelt and Hopkins*, pp. 774–5; Leahy, *I Was There*, pp. 280–1; T. Michael Ruddy, *The Cautious Diplomat: Charles E. Bohlen and the Soviet Union, 1929–1969* (Kent, Ohio: Kent State University Press, 1986), p. 21–3; and Walter Isaacson and Evan Thomas, *The Wise Men: Six Friends and the World They Made* (New York: Simon & Schuster, 1986), pp. 225–6.

71 One indication of Hull's prestige both on the Hill and among the public is Wendell Willkie's promise to reappoint Hull as Secretary of State should Willkie win the presi-

sevelt expected the State Department to handle the formal diplomatic intercourse among nations: meetings with foreign ministers, treaty negotiations, economic trade talks, the lodging of diplomatic protests, exchanges of ambassadors – all but the highest diplomatic negotiations.[72] For instance, it was Hull who met almost continually with the Japanese ambassador in the years leading to Pearl Harbor.[73] And it was Hull who organized the Havana conference in 1940 designed to gain hemispheric solidarity against Nazi influence.[74] Hull was also a primary force in working with the foreign ministers of other nations to lay the groundwork for the postwar United Nations.[75]

Although Roosevelt had no formal staff mechanism in this period for integrating advice from his major foreign policy departments, he did meet about once a week with his "War Council": the secretaries of State, War, and the Navy; the Chief of Staff; and the Chief of Naval Operations. But this served primarily as an information exchange rather than a decision-making purpose, much as FDR's full cabinet meetings did[76]; as Hull recalled, the meetings were "a sort of clearinghouse for all the information and views we had under discussion with our respective contacts and in our respective circles."[77]

Rather than sanction a cabinet-level council, Roosevelt preferred that interdepartmental coordination in foreign affairs take place informally, at the subcabinet level. These meetings were instigated by Hull, who grew alarmed in 1938 when Germany and Italy began establishing military liaison posts in Latin and South American nations.[78] At Hull's suggestion,

dency in 1940. Willkie's deference to Hull is in marked contrast to his devastating attacks on other members of FDR's staff. Sherwood, *Roosevelt and Hopkins*, p. 185. Hull also harbored presidential ambitions, which FDR frequently seemed to encourage, but without taking concrete steps to make it happen.

72 For example, see FDR to Hull [Jan. 28, 1938] regarding the proper U.S. response to looting of American-owned property in China by Japanese soldiers, reprinted in *FDR's Personal Letters*, p. 753.

73 These are described in Hull, *Memoirs*, pp. 982–1,105; for a more critical view, see Frederick W. Marks III, "Facade Failure: The Hull-Nomura Talks of 1941" from Gordon Hoxie, (ed.), *The Presidency and National Security Policy* (New York: Center for the Study of the Presidency, 1984). pp. 115–30.

74 See Dallek, *Franklin D. Roosevelt and American Foreign Policy*, p. 235; Hull, *Memoirs*, pp. 822–9.

75 See Hull, *Memoirs*, pp. 1,277–1,307 regarding the 1943 Moscow conference and plans for a postwar organization.

76 "Our meetings were mostly exchanges of views on the information that was coming to us" (ibid.).

77 Ibid., p. 1,079.

78 "The Committee would be charged with the study of coordination and liaison both at home and abroad of the three departments concerned, and of the Foreign Service and the two combatant services. Matters of national policy affecting the three departments would also be taken up and discussed by the Committee" (Hull memo to the President, reprinted in Watson, *Chief of Staff*, pp. 89–90).

Roosevelt sanctioned the establishment in April that year of the Standing Liaison Committee, consisting of the Under Secretary of State, the Chief of Staff of the Army, and the Chief of Naval Operations. But he warned Hull that the liaison committee should remain low-key. "I call special attention to the absolute necessity of secrecy regarding discussions or recommendations of such a liaison committee."[79]

Subsequently, during military talks preceding the secret ABC talks with the British in 1940, Hull agreed to meet with the two military service secretaries "each Tuesday re National Defense matters." This was the start of high-level meetings between State, War, and the Navy, superseding the Standing Liaison Committee meetings.[80]

As Harold Smith noted, Roosevelt's aversion to standing cabinet committees reflected his belief that departmental secretaries did not share his bargaining vantage point: "Roosevelt saw the cabinet members as theatre commanders, each with his own special area, interests, problems and demands. You couldn't expect any of them to see the picture whole, as the President had to do."[81]

As it turned out, this logic governed FDR's interaction with his generals, even during war, as well. Despite pressure from Marshall to the contrary, FDR resisted formally creating a Joint Chiefs of Staff under the control of a single, dominant chairman. Instead, as Chapter 7 makes clear, Roosevelt exploited the divisions among his military commanders to broaden his sources of bargaining information and expertise. This enabled him to effectively fulfill his commander-in-chief functions in conditions far more demanding than any his successors have confronted. And his successful prosecution of the war, combined with his reluctance to institutionalize a cabinet-level military or diplomatic advising council, calls into question the post–World War II creation of the National Security Council and staff.

79 FDR to Hull (Apr. 4, 1938) reprinted in *FDR's Personal Letters*, p. 770.
80 See Watson, *Chief of Staff*, pp. 122–3; and Matloff and Snell, *Strategic Planning for Coalition Warfare*, pp. 27–8, footnote 44.
81 As Smith noted, this was why "Hopkins became so valuable after he left the Department of Commerce. Hopkins' sole job was to see everything from the President's point of view. He was bound by no preconceived notions, no legal inhibitions and he certainly had absolutely no respect for tradition" (quoted in Sherwood, *Roosevelt and Hopkins*, p. 159).

7

The commander in chief

America's entrance into the war relieved the isolationist pressure which FDR had found so constraining. But it also greatly multiplied his administrative burden. First, he had to construct a staff structure by which to exercise his military duties as commander in chief. Moreover, as part of a multination military coalition, he also had to devise means for integrating command of the American and British military forces, as well as those of other Allies, without violating norms of national sovereignty. How he did so, and what lessons are offered for contemporary presidents, is this chapter's subject.

Creating the Joint Chiefs of Staff (JCS)

The December 1941 conference with Churchill regarding U.S.–British military collaboration first demonstrated to FDR his need for a military command structure.[1] The British Prime Minister arrived in Washington, D.C., with his Chiefs of Staff Committee in tow, comprised of the heads of the three British military services: the Army's Chief of the Imperial General Staff, the Navy's First Sea Lord, and the Chief of the Air Staff. Roosevelt, in contrast, had no comparable military staff; the Joint Army–Navy Board was primarily a planning tool, not an instrument of military command.

1 This was the conference code-named "Arcadia." A summary of the major issues is found in the document titled "Notes on Informal Conferences Held During the Visit of the British Chiefs of Staff in Washington" Harry Hopkins Papers, Special Assistant to the President, 1941–5, Organization of Military Forces File, FDRL. See also Maurice Matloff and Edwin Snell *Strategic Planning for Coalition Warfare* (Washington, D.C.: Office of the Chief of Military History, Department of the Army), pp. 97–119.

   Although the staffs met separately as well, it was at the plenary sessions that FDR and Churchill reviewed the work of their military advisers and reached general agreement on strategy. During these plenary sessions FDR was joined by Hopkins, his military advisers (King, Arnold, Stark, and Marshall), his military aide Edwin Watson, and usually Stimson and Knox.

This lack of an American military staff proved problematic when the Allies tried to fashion an integrated command structure in order to respond to Japanese aggression in the south Pacific "ABDA" area (the area of strategic interest to Americans, British, Dutch, and the Australians). After some debate the British and Americans agreed generally on the principle of unity of command in each military theater;² all joint military forces would be commanded by the nation whose interests were predominantly at stake in the affected region.³ But to whom would these theater commanders report?

Roosevelt initially sought to create a new military staff and superimpose it on the existing command structures of both nations. But the American and British service chiefs, not wanting to give up their autonomy, objected. As a compromise, it was decided instead to join them together into a Combined Chiefs of Staff.⁴

This, however, created concerns among the American military commanders that Roosevelt, lacking adequate staff support, would succumb to British military proposals that did not serve the U.S interests.⁵ Although the British shared the Americans' preference for a Germany-first military strategy, the two staffs differed on the tactics to achieve this goal. The British sought to "close the ring" by landing relatively small forces at sev-

2 Marshall, with backing from FDR and Secretary of War Stimson, pushed for a unified command. But, in a preview of the debate regarding the postwar plan for a unified defense establishment, Admiral King opposed the plan except in limited instances. Churchill also was at first opposed, because Marshall wanted General Wavell, a British general, to take charge of the ABDA area. It was clear, however, that no matter who commanded the Allies in the ABDA area, they were likely to suffer heavy losses at the hands of the Japanese. Churchill did not want the onus of defeat placed on a British commander. (See the minutes of the Dec. 28, 1941 and Jan. 2, 1942 meetings, in "Notes on Informal Conferences Held During the Visit of the British Chiefs of Staff in Washington" Harry Hopkins Papers, Special Assistant to the President, 1941–5, Organization of Military Forces File, FDRL. See also Matloff and Snell, *Strategic Planning for Coalition Warfare*, pp. 123–5; and "Ernest J. King," in Robert William Love, Jr. (ed.), *The Chiefs of Naval Operations* [Annapolis, Md.: Naval Institute Press, 1980], p. 145.)

3 Churchill and FDR essentially divided the world into American and British zones of military influence. The United States was chiefly responsible for military decision making in the Pacific, including the American continents, and shared control of the Atlantic and Europe with the British. The latter was paramount in the Indian Ocean and the Middle East.

4 See FDR to Hopkins (Dec. 31, 1941) with attached memo from Marshall, King, Stark, and Arnold to FDR (Dec. 30, 1941), describing the Allied command structure in the ABDA area (*PSF* – Safe File, Combined Chiefs of Staff Folder, FDRL). See also Eric Larrabee, *Commander-in-Chief Franklin Delano Roosevelt, His Lieutenants, and Their War* (New York: Harper & Row, 1987), pp. 16–20. The memorandum for this decision had in fact been developed in staff talks held in Washington the previous year. See Robert Sherwood *Roosevelt and Hopkins* rev. paperback ed. (New York: The Universal Library, 1950), pp. 466–70.

5 Marshall particularly worried about Roosevelt's tendency to make seemingly off-the-cuff decisions, which he characterized as FDR's "cigarette holder decisions." On the Joint Chiefs of Staff as a counterbalance to Churchill's influence on FDR's strategic thinking, see Sherwood, *Roosevelt and Hopkins*, p. 446.

eral places on the perimeter of German-held territory, while softening German resistance through bombing and naval blockade. The centerpiece was Churchill's "soft underbelly" strategy: military operations in the Mediterranean with a view to knocking Italy out of the war. Accordingly, at Arcadia Churchill attempted to enlist FDR's support to invade North Africa (Operation Torch) with American troops, as a first step in clearing the German and Italian forces out of the Mediterranean.

The Americans, in contrast, wanted to land a major Allied force in northwest Europe to directly engage the main part of the German forces, preferably in concert with Soviet attacks from the east. To provide the organizational means for shoring up FDR's resistance to British entreaties, the U.S. military chiefs gained FDR's approval to informally establish a Joint Chiefs of Staff (JCS), comprised of Marshall, Stark, King, and Arnold.[6] The JCS (with two personnel changes) would serve as Roosevelt's primary military strategic command instrument for the war's duration. (Stark was replaced by King in March 1942, and, as discussed below, Admiral William Leahy was appointed FDR's personal representative to the JCS in July 1942.[7])

Roosevelt, however, refused to vest the JCS with statutory authority. Instead, for the duration of his presidency it served entirely at FDR's pleasure.[8] As he told Leahy, formalizing the JCS would "provide no benefits and might in some way impair flexibility of operations."[9] Above all else, the JCS was to remain a *presidential* staff resource.

Leahy's 1942 appointment as Roosevelt's military liaison to the JCS clearly underscores this point. Critics were blaming the disaster at Pearl Harbor on the division between the Army and Navy command structures. In response, Congress began hearings on legislation to unify the military branches within a single Department of National Defense under a civilian

6 The Army Chief of Staff, Chief of Naval Operations, Commander in Chief of the United States Fleet, and head of the Army Air Corps, respectively.

7 After the fiasco at Pearl Harbor, Navy Secretary Knox urged FDR to remove Stark from control of all Navy operations. This was done through E.O. 8984, which placed operational command of naval forces under King, who was assigned the newly created position of Commander in Chief of the Navy. Stark was limited to long-range planning and oversight of shipbuilding. King, although officially reporting to the Navy Secretary, in fact answered directly to FDR. However, under this new arrangement, the division of responsibility between Stark as Chief of Naval Operations, and King as Commander in Chief, was never very clear. The result was what some called an "an administrative nightmare" although it was typically Rooseveltian. In view of these difficulties, Stark eventually resigned his position on Mar. 7, 1942. Five days later FDR signed E.O. 9096, essentially giving King both jobs. The practical effect of FDR's order was to give King control of the entire Navy, although he continually quarreled with both Knox and his successor James Forrestal regarding the extent of his authority. See "Ernest J. King," in Love, *The Chiefs of Naval Operations*, p. 143.

8 The only legal basis for the JCS during the war was a memorandum describing the organization and its members. It has FDR's "OK" scrawled across it.

9 Quoted in Larrabee, *Commander-in-Chief*, p. 21.

secretary.[10] Marshall supported military unification, and after the war was one of the prime movers for a single Department of Defense. But Navy leaders, including King, vehemently opposed the plan, and in 1942 they had Roosevelt's support.

Marshall thus took another tact, proposing to make Leahy the chief of staff to the JCS. He reasoned that by giving Leahy the authority necessary to force the service chiefs to cooperate, the JCS would prove a more powerful counterweight to the British staff. Leahy's appointment also offered a way to redress the imbalance in service representation created by Stark's departure in March 1942.[11] Moreover, Leahy was well known to FDR.[12]

Roosevelt accepted the plan, but Leahy never functioned as the powerful chief of staff Marshall envisioned. Rather than helping to integrate the disparate views of the military services, Leahy instead served largely as the means by which FDR exploited the interservice rivalries for his own purposes. This was by Roosevelt's design. On June 6, 1942, in a half-hour meeting, Roosevelt had outlined his expectations to Leahy. It was clear, Leahy recalled, that FDR wanted him to represent the president's interests, not the Joint Chiefs'. The following day, Roosevelt spelled out how Leahy would serve FDR's interests. They would meet daily, and Leahy would be given an office in the soon-to-be-completed East Wing of the White House, rather than residing in the Joint Chiefs' headquarters.[13] Leahy would meet regularly with the military chiefs as well, reading and

10 Of course, efforts to unify the services for reasons of economy predated Pearl Harbor by many years. See, for instance, the letter from John McSwain, chairman of the House Military Affairs Committee, to FDR (Mar. 18, 1933) proposing the two military services be combined. (Official Files, Reorganization Folder 285c, FDRL.)

11 Arnold, as head of the Army Air Corps, gave the Army two votes to the Navy's one.

12 Leahy had known FDR for almost thirty years, beginning in 1913 when FDR was appointed Assistant Secretary of the Navy. From 1915 to 1916, Leahy commanded the Navy Secretary's dispatch boat, and Roosevelt was a frequent traveler. Leahy visited FDR at Hyde Park and recalls that they became "good friends." But the two had little formal contact until 1937, when Roosevelt appointed Leahy Chief of Naval Operations. He subsequently served as U.S. Ambassador to Vichy France from January 1941 to May 1942.

13 Consisting of two floors containing eight to ten offices occupied by presidential assistants, the East Wing faced East Executive Avenue, across from the Treasury Department. It also contained a bomb shelter able to accommodate over one hundred people. The JCS, in contrast, initially occupied the Public Health Building at the corner of 19th St. and Constitution Avenue. Subsequently they were moved to the new War Department Building on 21st Street and Virginia Avenue, and then to the Pentagon when it was completed. Although Leahy began serving FDR from the Public Health Building, he moved to the White House on Labor Day in 1942, occupying two large, well-furnished rooms in the East Wing. The outer office was used by Leahy's aide and stenographer, and also served as a reception room. (See Admiral William Leahy, *I Was There: The Personal Story of the Chief of Staff to Presidents Roosevelt and Truman Based on His Notes and Diaries Made at the Time* (New York: Whittlesey House – McGraw Hill Books, 1950), pp. 98, 113, 129–30.

digesting their reports, so that FDR was kept abreast of JCS decisions and underlying sentiments.[14] Although some journalists speculated that Leahy in fact would be given command of all U.S. military forces, Roosevelt squelched that rumor at the July 21 press conference announcing Leahy's appointment. Leahy was to be the president's "leg man."[15]

For the next three years, the two met almost every morning.[16] Leahy's proximity to FDR meant that he dealt with an astounding range of issues cutting across the entire war effort.[17] Moreover, the number of visitors to his office grew as others realized he provided indirect access to the president. This made Leahy, like Hopkins, a valuable intelligence source to Roosevelt.[18]

In addition to screening military cables, Leahy served other functions. As the senior officer, he chaired JCS meetings. When the United States hosted the British military staff, he also chaired the Combined Chiefs of Staffs meetings.[19] In short, Leahy's naval background and long relationship with FDR meant he generally understood FDR's bargaining preferences, which lessened FDR's need to closely monitor the JCS and the Combined Chiefs.[20]

Equally important is what Leahy did not do. Although he traveled on FDR's election junkets, Leahy professed almost complete ignorance of partisan issues and shied away from issuing advice in this area.[21] Unlike modern-day national security advisers, Leahy made no pretense of integrating military advice with FDR's political needs. Moreover, Leahy made few public appearances, always clearing them with FDR first.[22] And he had a skeletal staff: not more than two aides and two or three civilian secretaries, a far cry from the national security bureaucracies characteristic of later presidencies.

14 Leahy noted that these duties were similar to those exercised by the Navy's chief of staff. In contrast, the Army chief of staff exercised more command functions. (See ibid., pp. 96–7.)
15 Ibid., pp. 97–8.
16 These morning meetings generally took place in Roosevelt's Oval Study, and frequently the discussion of topics ranged outside purely military matters. Note that Leahy served in this post until Mar. 21, 1949, well into Truman's first term.
17 For instance, in 1945 alone, the following issues crossed his desk: the status of the U.S. Pacific command, unauthorized leaks in the Office of Naval Intelligence, unified command of the Defense Department, Lend-Lease requirements for France and Great Britain, political relations in the postwar Mideast, the trial of Marshal Petain, the roles of the Dutch and the French in the Pacific war, and the status of Lend-Lease after the end of hostilities. (See Leahy, *I Was There*, pp. 130–1; 133–5; 138–41; 146–53; 376–7.)
18 See ibid., pp. 2; 99–101; 183–4.   19 Ibid., pp. 2–3.
20 See ibid., p. 95.
21 This is just as well, for he was not particularly fond of Roosevelt's domestic policies, although he thought the president an eminently skilled political operator.
22 Leahy, *I Was There*, p. 126. Occasionally, he was asked to draft messages and statements for Roosevelt, but he admittedly never grasped FDR's style.

Roosevelt's informal creation of the JCS and Leahy's appointment as its chair, are two of the most significant staff decisions he made during World War II. The JCS essentially functioned as the supreme American military command staff within solely American areas of influence, and it represented the United States on the combined staff with the British. As Leahy recalls: "This organization assumed, under the constant direction and supervision of the President of the United States, the complete strategic and operational direction of all land, sea, and air forces."[23]

The first JCS meeting took place in February 1942. Thereafter the JCS met on a weekly basis – more frequently as circumstances warranted. When the chiefs jointly decided on a course of military action, implementation was delegated to the JCS member heading the military service primarily responsible for forces in the particular combat sector. Planning and operations were then carried out by that service's general staff, subject to JCS approval.

Generally, on routine matters when policy was clearly established, the JCS made decisions without directly consulting FDR. If the issue was significant, but the policy clearly understood, the JCS would take action, but refer the matter to FDR as a matter of course. Decisions within any new issue area required FDR's approval before going into effect.

Because JCS decisions were never made by majority vote, but instead required unanimity, Roosevelt acted as the court of last resort, arbitrating differences among the military branches.[24] This allowed him to protect his bargaining interests. In retrospect, there are few instances in which Roosevelt directly overruled his military commanders.[25] This has led some to argue that military decision-making during World War II was dominated by the Joint Chiefs.[26] But the absence of overt controversy is misleading; Leahy's presence on the JCS and FDR's incessant informal consultation with its members ensured that they were unlikely to propose orders FDR opposed.[27]

---

23 Ibid., p. 438.
24 Although Leahy chaired JCS meetings, he exercised no more authority than any other staff member.
25 For instance, Sherwood cites but two: FDR's decision in 1943 to cancel a military campaign in Burma, and his decision to invade North Africa in 1942 so as to get U.S. ground troops into the war as early as possible.
26 On this point, see Samuel Huntington, *The Soldier and the State: The Theory and Politics of Civil-Military Relations* (Cambridge: Harvard University Press, 1957), pp. 315–37.
27 T. B. Kittredge, of the Historical Section of the Joint Chiefs of Staffs, writes: "It may be true that the President formally overruled them on very few occasions but this was only because informal discussion of the President with Leahy, Marshall, King and Arnold usually led them to know in advance the President's views" (quoted in Sherwood, *Roosevelt and Hopkins*, p. 957, note 446). Kittredge's comments are supported by an analysis conducted by Kent Greenfield listing some twenty-two key decisions FDR made against the advice of his military advisers (cited in Larrabee, *Commander-in-Chief*, p. 15).

One can argue (and historians do) whether his decisions were correct, but the evidence is clear that Roosevelt fully exercised his prerogatives as commander in chief. Leahy, for one, confirms that perception, arguing that FDR's "lifelong devotion to making individual decision made it impossible for him to adequately distribute the [decision making] load . . . [W]hile [FDR] constantly obtained advice from those in whom he had confidence, he did not delegate to his subordinate the business of making decisions on international problems."[28] Hull agrees:

> [Roosevelt] loved the military side of events and liked to hold them in his own hands. Following Pearl Harbor, he preferred to be called Commander-in-Chief rather than president. He relished the title.[29]

Mark Watson, who authored one of the official War Department histories of World War II also concurs:

> President Franklin D. Roosevelt was the real and not merely a nominal Commander-in-Chief of the armed forces. Every president has possessed the Constitutional authority which that title indicates, but few presidents have shared Mr. Roosevelt's readiness to exercise it in fact and in detail and with such determination.[30]

The Map Room

In addition to the JCS, the 1941–2 Arcadia conference prompted still another administrative innovation by FDR. Impressed by the portable set of maps and communications equipment Churchill brought, Roosevelt resolved to implement a comparable communication center within the White House. In January 1942, he established the "Map Room" on the ground floor of the White House, in order to track military movements across the globe. His naval aides, beginning with Captain John L. McCrea, handled the daily communications flowing in and out of this command post.[31]

Roosevelt usually stopped in the Map Room twice daily, once in the morning as he went to the Oval Office from his residence, and again in the late afternoon while returning from the West Wing to the family quarters. During these visits McCrea would brief Roosevelt regarding the latest military dispatches from across the globe. Characteristically, Roosevelt structured the information flow to enhance his administrative

28 Leahy, *I Was There*, p. 346.
29 Cordell Hull, *The Memoirs of Cordell Hull*, vol. 2 (New York: MacMillan Co., 1948), p. 1,111.
30 Mark S. Watson, *Chief of Staff* (Washington, D.C.: Office of the Chief of Military History, Department of the Army, Government Printing Office, 1951), p. 4.
31 See the Finding Aid, Map Room, FDRL; and Leahy, *I Was There*, p. 99.

control; incoming messages were routed through the War Department, whereas outgoing messages were sent via the Navy Department. In this way, the only complete set of military dispatches remained in his possession.[32] No one was allowed in the room except for FDR, Hopkins, the Joint Chiefs, Roosevelt's military aides, and his personal secretaries.[33]

Together, the JCS and the Map Room gave FDR the means to communicate directly with his generals without relying on either the secretaries of War or the Navy. They also allowed him to better exploit the cleavages and divisions between the American and British military chiefs, and among the Americans themselves, to increase his bargaining effectiveness. For instance, the American generals, evidently with FDR's tacit acquiescence, occasionally threatened Churchill with the withdrawal of U.S. forces from the Atlantic to the Pacific. In this way they hoped to pressure Churchill to accept the American plan for a direct assault on Western Europe.[34] This tactic enhanced FDR's bargaining leverage with the British without necessarily embroiling him directly in the dispute.

Roosevelt took similar advantage of divisions within his own military command, particularly those between King and Marshall regarding the Pacific theater.[35] In 1942, General Douglas MacArthur sought the bulk of the Pacific military resources to recapture the Philippines and move north to Japan. In contrast, Admiral Nimitz proposed that Marines under Navy command island-hop across the central Pacific to the Japanese mainland. Although Marshall supported MacArthur and King backed Nimitz, both feared that the British would capitalize on the American division by persuading FDR to strip the Pacific theater of American forces and support British operations in the Mediterranean. Roosevelt used their fear of Pacific reductions to forge a fragile working alliance between MacArthur

---

32 The Map Room also functioned as the White House communication link to FDR while he was away.

33 Larrabee, *Commander-in-Chief*, pp. 22–4.

34 King in particular was not committed to a Germany-first strategy, and in 1942–3 he took advantage of British resistance to a cross-channel attack by moving some naval assets to the Pacific theater. ("Ernest J. King," from Love, *Chiefs of Naval Operations*, p. 178.) Marshall, too, (although partially bluffing) urged FDR to adopt a Pacific-first strategy in response to British intransigence regarding the second front. Roosevelt declined, but the incident demonstrates how rivalries within and across the British and American military staffs could play to FDR's advantage. (Sherwood, *Roosevelt and Hopkins*, p. 971, note 691.)

35 On the relations between Marshall and King, see "Ernest J. King" in Love, Jr., *Chiefs of Naval Operations*, p. 162. Though the two probably disliked each other, the necessity of war forced them to collaborate, if for no other reason than to prevent the British from exercising undue influence over Roosevelt. Because King never had a close relationship with Knox, King's authority as Chief of Naval Operations (CNO) was heavily dependent on his relationship with Roosevelt. In contrast, Marshall worked closely with Stimson. Relations between King and Arnold were also touchy, reflecting differing philosophies regarding the use of Army and Navy air power.

and Nimitz. More generally, by playing the service branches against each other, Roosevelt gained bargaining leverage in the pursuit of his own military objectives.[36]

The White House staff, 1937–45

Along with James Byrnes, Hopkins and Leahy were the two most prominent White House aides FDR added during the war years. But several other aides also played crucial roles in the White House during this period. Initially Samuel Rosenman continued to informally assist FDR while serving as a New York state judge. He drafted executive orders, did some speech writing, mediated disputes, and performed other ad hoc presidential tasks.[37] But the strain of carrying on two high-powered functions proved too much, and FDR finally asked Rosenman to come on board full-time as Special Counsel in October 1943.[38] From then on Rosenman handled presidential speeches, drafted executive orders, reviewed legislation, oversaw presidential pardons, and generally kept track of political matters.[39] Of these, speech writing was perhaps the most important of Rosenman's tasks; as he notes, it frequently served to define policy: "[N]early every major speech of a President is, in one way or another, a policy-making speech, and those who are around when it is being prepared and while it is going through its many drafts . . . are in a strategic position to help shape that policy."[40]

It was primarily Rosenman, Hopkins, and Robert Sherwood who collectively wrote most of FDR's major public addresses during the war period.[41] They recognized that FDR's public statements, by helping to shape

36 Again, however, one must remember that FDR's competitive strategy had costs. In the China theater, for instance, General Joseph W. Stillwell's constant feuding with Chiang Kai-shek does not seem to have produced positive results; the Chinese under Kai-shek never fulfilled FDR's expectations that they would be an effective military force. See FDR's memo to Marshall (Oct. 3, 1942) asking him to look into the Stillwell situation. (Reprinted in Elliot Roosevelt (ed.), *F.D.R. His Personal Letters, 1928–45* [New York: Duell, Sloan and Pearce, 1950], p. 1,350.)

37 Rosenman, of course, had first worked under FDR while the latter was governor and continued to do so after FDR appointed him to the bench as a New York state judge. Thereafter he commuted to Washington, D.C., receiving no pay while rendering a variety of services.

38 See Samuel I. Rosenman, *Working With Roosevelt*, (New York: Harper & Row, 1952), p. 379.

39 Rosenman's title, "Special Counsel," referred to his previous position as a judge, and not to any expectations, as is currently the meaning of "Counsel," that he would serve as the president's legal adviser. To get a sense of Rosenman's functions, review the documents contained in *PSF* – Subject Files – Executive Office, Rosenman Folder, FDRL.

40 Ibid., p. 8.

41 Sherwood, a noted playwright and liberal, came on board in October 1940, after the departure of Tom Corcoran. From that point the three wrote every one of FDR's major

the expectations of Washingtonians and their publics, could dramatically affect FDR's bargaining effectiveness.[42] Roosevelt, too, understood that his speeches were an important bargaining tool and also constituted part of his historical legacy. Consequently, he worked over each word of his major speeches to ensure they addressed his bargaining interests. Naturally, others with a stake in a particular bargaining exchange frequently tried to influence the drafting process.[43] By entrusting the writing to Hopkins and Rosenman, who were senior White House aides with multiple functions, rather than to second-level speech-writing specialists (as is now commonly the case), FDR more effectively protected his bargaining stakes. As senior aides, Hopkins and Rosenman had a comparatively better understanding of FDR's bargaining objectives and interests. As an additional check, however, Roosevelt edited his own speeches to ensure they said nothing that might erode his sources of power.

There were other important changes to FDR's White House staff during the post-Brownlow period. To fill the gap created by Louis Howe's death, Roosevelt appointed his son Jimmy as a Secretary to the President in 1937.[44] Jimmy Roosevelt functioned largely as FDR's liaison to a dozen and a half executive branch agencies and commissions. But he left the post in November 1938, due to stomach problems, and was replaced by his assistant Jim Rowe. Thereafter Rowe performed many of the functions that Rosenman subsequently took up.

When illness also knocked Marvin McIntyre, FDR's appointment secretary, out of commission, Roosevelt's military aide Edwin "Pa" Watson

speeches for the next five and a half years. Rosenman and Sherwood tended to write the drafts, and Hopkins served as editor, especially careful to remove passages that might harm FDR politically. (See Sherwood, *Roosevelt and Hopkins*, pp. 183–4; Rosenman, *Working with Roosevelt*, pp. 8, 228–9.)

    Rosenman's memoirs provide the best description of Roosevelt's speech-writing process. A major speech might take a week of labor, going through many drafts. Roosevelt would begin by telling Hopkins, Rosenman, and Sherwood the major points he wished to make, the audience to which those points were addressed, and a maximum word limit. He would then dictate a preliminary version, often in very rough form, at some length. When he stopped, the speech writers went to work, integrating file material, cutting and pasting, and finally giving their version back to FDR for editing. Roosevelt would dictate inserts, run the draft by the cabinet, and then the final version was put together, with FDR editing one more time. (See also Sherwood, *Roosevelt and Hopkins*, pp. 212–19.)

42 A case in point described in detail by Rosenman concerns the drafting of a presidential message to Congress in 1942 regarding the need to enact a program of anti-inflationary measures. (See Rosenman, *Working With Roosevelt*, pp. 339–40.)

43 As Rosenman wrote later, "There is something about helping in the preparation of a speech for the President . . . that tends to make people argue over every little phrase and every shade of meaning." For instance, Rosenman recalled that the Joint Chiefs frequently submitted statistics to speech writers that reflected the military's interests. (Ibid., p. 194.)

44 Actually, he was first appointed an administrative assistant to FDR on Jan. 6, 1937, and was made Secretary to the president on July 1, 1937.

took over, acting as FDR's gatekeeper and confidant.[45] By virtue of his military background, Watson also served as a point of liaison with Marshall, in addition to screening Roosevelt's visitors.[46]

William Hassett gradually assumed duties as FDR's correspondence secretary.[47] David K. Niles took responsibility for conducting outreach to minority groups and other members of Roosevelt's coalition, as well as tracking public opinion.[48] Isador Lubin, while backstopping Hopkins, performed statistical analysis, including public opinion and voting studies.[49] With Missy Lehand's stroke, Grace Tully became FDR's primary personal secretary. Later in the war FDR's daughter Anna moved back into the White House and she gradually took charge of Roosevelt's social calendar. Of course, Stephen Early continued as FDR's Press Secretary.

These White House aides worked in concert to manage FDR's daily administrative tasks: correspondence, scheduling, appointments, and media relations. The distinguishing trait of his personal staff, however, was its small size; each of these aides had a direct relationship with FDR by virtue of a specific task Roosevelt performed on a recurring schedule. Their activities were thus determined by his needs, as they unfolded (usually on a daily basis).

A war cabinet?

Although FDR's cabinet was not a decision-making apparatus, Roosevelt continued to meet with it on an almost weekly basis, and he frequently used his cabinet secretaries collectively as a political sounding board. The most important members during the war years were Stimson, Knox, Hull, and Morgenthau. Their utility to FDR was less in providing solutions than in illuminating the range of options, and associated political implications, available to him, and as a means of providing administrative follow-through once presidential decisions were made.

45 Watson began as FDR's military aide in 1933. Sherwood describes him as a "big, florid, jovial Virginian". His death from a cerebral hemorrhage during the return from the Yalta conference visibly shook Roosevelt, who confided that his sadness equalled that felt when his mother died. (Sherwood, *Roosevelt and Hopkins*, pp. 207, 874.)
46 Much to Marshall's chagrin, Watson was not averse to meddling in internal Army affairs.
47 See William Hasset, *Off the Record with F.D.R., 1942–45* (New Brunswick, N.J.: Rutgers University Press, 1958).
48 See, for instance, FDR's memo to Niles asking him to investigate unemployment in New York City (Nov. 16, 1942), reprinted in *FDR's Personal Letters*, p. 1,368; and Niles to Tully (June 7, 1944) regarding Gallup polling in New York (Dewey versus Roosevelt), *PSF* – Personal File, Niles Folder, FDRL.
49 For example, see Lubin to FDR (Aug. 6, 1943) and (Jan. 6, 1944), regarding public opinion toward various war-related issues and the impact of the poll tax on voting turnout. (Both in *PSF* – Subject Files, Lubin Folder, FDRL.)

Hull, of course, was responsible for the nation's primary diplomatic activities, carried out under FDR's supervision. But the most sensitive negotiations Roosevelt conducted himself in face-to-face meetings with Churchill and later Stalin.⁵⁰ These took place at a series of "summit" meetings, beginning with the Newfoundland conference between Churchill and FDR in August 1941, and ending with the Big Three (FDR, Churchill, and Stalin) conferring at Yalta in February 1945.⁵¹ It was at these meetings of the Allied heads of state that the key politico-military decisions during World War II were made. Typically they were preceded by months of staff work by the JCS both alone and in collaboration with the staffs of Great Britain and, later, the USSR, supplemented by input from the State Department. At the actual conferences Roosevelt was usually accompanied by the JCS, Hopkins, military aides, and several State Department officials who functioned more as FDR's personal staff than as departmental representatives.

50 In the prewar period, FDR frequently communicated directly with all the world leaders by telegram or secret letter. Moreover, he sent personal emissaries, such as Sumner Welles, who visited Rome, Berlin and London in 1940 in an effort to forestall war. See Robert Dallek, *Franklin D. Roosevelt and American Foreign Policy*, (New York: New York University Press, 1979), pp. 216–18.
51 After the Newfoundland conference, Roosevelt's major wartime meetings, and the issues discussed, include:
    The Casablanca meeting between Churchill and FDR (Jan. 14–26, 1943), the first meeting in which political leaders and military advisers were both present. It was here that FDR, to the regret of his military advisers and without their foreknowledge, issued his call for the unconditional surrender of Germany, Italy, and Japan.
    This was followed by the Trident meeting in Washington (May 11–24, 1943). At Trident, Marshall was finally successful in getting preliminary British agreement for a cross-channel attack.
    Then came the Quadrant meeting in Quebec, Aug. 11–24, 1943, noteworthy for the split between the United States and Great Britain regarding the extent to which the Allies should conduct a military campaign up the Italian peninsula. It was during this meeting that blueprints for the Normandy invasion were drawn up. Teheran, code-named "Eureka" (Nov. 27 – Dec. 2, 1943), followed, the first meeting of the Big Three. (Churchill and FDR met separately at Cairo, Egypt, immediately before and after the Teheran conference.) In addition to persuading Churchill to reaffirm his support for a cross-channel attack, FDR also spelled out his ideas for a postwar United Nations. However, no final agreement regarding German dismemberment or final status of the Polish boundaries was reached. Roosevelt also agreed that Eisenhower would command the D-Day invasion.
    The Octagon conference, from Sept. 11–16, 1944, was the second wartime conference between Churchill and Roosevelt to be held in Quebec. The discussion focused on Great Britain joining the war against the Japanese, as well as postwar planning, particularly the shape of the zonal agreements in Germany. The target date for Japanese defeat was set at eighteen months after Germany capitulated. The Allies also adopted the MacArthur plan for retaking the Philippines.
    The major issues at Yalta, FDR's final wartime summit meeting (Feb. 4–12, 1945), centered on the Soviet Union's participation in the war against Japan, control of postwar Germany, war reparations, and settlement of the Polish boundaries.

None of his cabinet secretaries regularly attended these wartime conferences,[52] nor were they on the distribution list for key JCS papers.[53] Roosevelt was frequently urged in this period to create, formally or informally, some type of "war cabinet," similar to the British wartime coalition of cabinet ministers.[54] Among other benefits, advocates thought regular meetings of the major departmental secretaries would help to more effectively integrate strategy with production. In fact, Lubin made this point in a memorandum to Hopkins in October 1942:

> I am still of the opinion that what we really need is a "War Cabinet."
> This war cabinet should be comprised of the Secretary of War, Secretary of Navy, Admiral Leahy, yourself [Hopkins], and those responsible for manpower, production and the Director of the Budget. . . .
>
> If we are ever really going to do our job, it will be absolutely essential to coordinate production possibilities with strategy plans. Only through a war cabinet or something similar will it be possible to get some semblance of order into the present picture.[55]

The next month, after the midterm elections, Lubin renewed his efforts, writing:

> This raises again the question of a war cabinet. . . . The President must make high policy decisions but he is entitled to have a clear and adequate picture of the issues before him in order to make such decisions. Moreover, he must have a reasonable assurance that when he makes policy decisions, they will be properly and quickly executed.[56]

But Roosevelt rejected the advice. Consequently, until late in the war, there were very little formal mechanisms for ensuring collaboration between the primary executive branch departments dealing with production, military strategy, and diplomacy. The interdepartmental cabinet coordinating device established by Hull in the prewar period conceivably might have been the basis of a "war cabinet," but for several reasons this did not happen. First, its agenda was primarily determined by the State Department.[57] Second, as the military's joint board became a more

---

52 As noted above, Hull, to his consternation, attended almost none of the summit meetings.

53 These papers circulated among some fifty-five individuals within the Navy and the Army during the war.

54 Indeed, both Baruch and Oscar Cox (the latter sending memos to Hopkins) investigated the organization and functions of the British war cabinet.

55 Lubin to Hopkins (Oct. 13, 1942), Hopkins Papers, Sherwood Manuscript Collection, Book 5: Organizing for War File, War Cabinet #1, FDRL.

56 Lubin to Hopkins, (Nov. 6, 1942), Hopkins Papers, Sherwood Manuscript Collection, Book 5: Organizing for War File, War Cabinet #3, FDRL.

57 The committee met infrequently, about once a month, and focused primarily on procedural matters to increase cooperation among the three institutions, rather than major policy initiatives. See Watson, *Chief of Staff*, pp. 89–94.

effective military planning tool at the presidential level, the liaison committee's activities became less important to the military. Third, the liaison
committee's functions were gradually superseded by discussions at the departmental secretaries' level, most initiated by Secretary of War Stimson.

Soon after his appointment in June 1940, Stimson set up an informal
luncheon series between his Navy counterpart, Frank Knox, and Hull.[58]
These weekly meetings eventually evolved by 1944 into the creation of
SWNCC – the State-War-Navy Coordinating Committee. The SWNCC
developed its own administrative secretariat and a number of subcommittees focusing on regional and substantive issues.[59] This system remained in existence to facilitate interdepartmental communication until
it was superseded by the National Security Council, established by the
1947 National Security Act.

The armed forces unification controversy: Toward a postwar national security staff?

Despite the successful Allied military collaboration, many of those who
worked most closely with FDR thought his administrative system poorly
suited for the postwar era. Marshall, for one, believed the United States
needed a unified command structure to better coordinate the actions of
U.S. land, sea, and air forces across a global expanse.[60]

In fact, in 1941 Marshall had discussed with King replacing the system
of separate military services with a unified military establishment.[61] In
1943 Marshall presented a more formal plan for military unification, in
which the three service branches were placed within a single department
of national defense under the direction of a civilian secretary. He also suggested appointing a single, strong chief of staff (the position to be rotated
among the service branches) to head the JCS.[62]

58 See Hull, *Memoirs*, p. 1,079.
59 Consisting of assistant secretaries in each department, SWNCC's mandate was to aid
    the cabinet secretaries "on politico- military matters and [in] coordinating the views of
    the three departments on matters in which all have common interest, particularly those
    involving foreign policy and relations with foreign nations" (Ray Cline, *Washington
    Command Post: The Operations Division*, [Washington, D.C.: Office of the Chief of
    Staff, Department of the Army, 1951], pp. 326–7).
60 This would capitalize on advances in electronic communications – radar, high-speed
    teletype, voice communication – that allowed both centralization of high command and
    greater decentralization for tactical and operational decisions. See Kenneth Allard,
    Command, Control, and the Common Defense (New Haven, Conn.: Yale University
    Press, 1990), pp. 108–11.
61 Ed Cray, *General of the Army: George C. Marshall, Soldier and Statesmen*, (New York:
    W. W. Norton & Co., 1990), p. 682.
62 This, of course, hearkens back to the role Marshall envisioned for Leahy, which FDR
    had effectively torpedoed. Notwithstanding their views on the need for a single depart-

The details of the subsequent political tug-of-war regarding Marshall's proposal have been thoroughly recounted elsewhere.[63] Essentially, Marshall's plan split the military establishment, pitting Navy against Army, and ignited a full-scale political battle that raged for the next six years. When the shooting finally stopped in 1949, Roosevelt's politico-military advising organization was gone, replaced by the foundation supporting the current national security advising system: a single Department of Defense under a civilian secretary, a National Security Council with support staff, a Central Intelligence Agency, and a statutorily based Joint Chiefs of Staff.

This advising structure was in fact of hybrid design. It combined elements of Marshall's original plan for unifying the armed services with a counter proposal, submitted by Ferdinand Eberstadt and supported by Navy Secretary James Forrestal, that envisioned a series of coordinating committees – the NSC, CIA, and JCS – to oversee national security policy making.[64] Both plans were merged through political compromise to produce the 1947 National Security Act, amended in 1949.

Forrestal's strong support of the NSC was predicated on two factors. First, with the merging of the Navy within the Defense Department, he sought a new forum from which to protect the Navy's interests. But he also admired the British cabinet system and hoped to see its best virtues incorporated into the presidency.[65] A cabinet-based security council, he believed, would ensure more systematic national security policy making. All sides of an issue would be carefully explored, and policy would be more easily enacted because the agencies responsible for implementation had helped formulate it. This seemed to Forrestal a significant improvement over FDR's ad hoc, divide-and-conquer administrative style.

ment of defense, all of FDR's military leaders evidently felt that the JCS should become a permanent body responsible only to the president, and that, among its other duties, the JCS should also retain the power to advise the president regarding the defense budget. (Leahy, *I was There*, p. 239.)

63 See, in particular, Demetrios Caraley, *The Politics of Military Unification: A Study of Conflict and the Policy Process*, (New York: Columbia University Press, 1966); Jeffrey M. Dorwat, *Eberstadt and Forrestal: A National Security Partnership, 1909–1949* (College Station: Texas A&M University Press, 1991), pp. 69–180; Alfred Dick Sander, *A Staff for the President: The Executive Office, 1921–52* (New York: Greenwood Press: New York, 1989), pp. 201–70; and Edward H. Hobbs *Behind the President: A Study of Executive Office Agencies* (Washington, D.C.: Public Affairs Press, 1954).

64 Forrestal served about six weeks as one of FDR's administrative assistants, but quickly become bored with his duties. Subsequently FDR appointed him assistant secretary of the Navy, and he replaced Knox when the latter died of a heart attack on Apr. 28, 1944. (Leahy, *I Was There*, p. 237.)

65 Forrestal objected to the idea of single chief of staff, but he sought to create a corps of civil servants, modeled after the British staff secretariat, who would staff the senior levels of the executive branch. See Clark Clifford (with Richard Holbrooke), *Counsel to the President*, (New York: Random House, 1991), p. 152.

The problem with incorporating a cabinet-based advisory system, as Harry Truman noted, was that the American Constitution vests executive responsibility in a single individual, not a collective body. To be sure, Truman shared the common perception that FDR was a poor administrator. He also strongly supported military unification, due in large part to his wartime investigations of military production that uncovered tremendous waste and duplication in procurement practices.[66] But, as he explained in his memoirs, Truman was not a proponent of a cabinet-level national security council: "Forrestal . . . had been advocating our using the British cabinet system as a model in the operation of government. There is much to this idea – in some ways a Cabinet government is more efficient – but under our system the responsibility rests on one man – the President. To change it, we would have to change the Constitution."[67]

Indeed, Truman refused to regularly meet with the NSC for almost ten months after it was established. Nor did he begin chairing NSC meetings on a consistent basis until the outbreak of the Korean War. Indeed, no president has utilized the NSC as a decision-making instrument, although some, like Eisenhower, have found it useful as a sounding board.

Truman also resisted the bureaucratization of the NSC staff – something his successors did not do. Ironically, although many questions were raised during the unification debate regarding the NSC, very little attention was focused on the Executive Secretary's position and NSC staff.[68] This oversight proved costly. However unintended, the National Security Act and its amendments primed the soil for the emergence of the national security staff bureaucracy. Clark Clifford was the Truman White House aide responsible for brokering the unification struggle. In 1991, he looked back on the evolution of the NSC advising system:

> Over the next forty years, I watched the Executive Secretary of the National Security Council evolve into the National Security "Adviser," and become a rival for power to the Secretary of State. This was clearly not our original intention, but it was an inevitable consequence of the growth of government, the desire of some Presidents to run the national security structure personally from the White House, and the personal ambitions of several men.[69]

There is evidence to suggest that had FDR lived, he would likely have opposed attempts to unify the defense departments or to create a national

66 Clifford, who spearheaded Truman's unification fight, recalls Truman telling him on more than one occasion: "We must never fight another war the way we fought the last two. I have the feeling that if the Army and the Navy had fought our enemies as hard as they fought each other, the war would have ended much earlier" (ibid., p. 146.)

67 Harry S. Truman, *Memoirs*, (Garden City, N.Y.: Doubleday, 1955–6), pp. 59–60.

68 Instead, the focus was on the NSC's proposed organizational structure, membership, level of civilian dominance, and its relation to the unified Defense Department.

69 Clifford and Holbrooke, *Counsel to the President*, p. 164.

security council. To be sure, in this area, as in most, FDR left few tangible clues regarding his intentions.[70] But those that exist suggest Roosevelt would have rejected both.

Leahy, for one, wrote after the war that Roosevelt was not "in favor of either unification of the armed forces, or of an independent air force separate from the Army and Navy."[71] And Stimson, in his diary, records that Marshall told him it appeared "the President was siding against us on this consolidation of departments."[72]

Of course, Roosevelt characteristically refused to stake out positions on controversial issues if he did not have to. But one can also try to extrapolate Roosevelt's likely response based on his use of national security staff during World War II. First, given his partiality toward the Navy, he likely would have resisted any proposal that compromised the Navy's autonomy. As a matter of political necessity, he might have supported proposals, such as that advanced in the Eberstadt plan, to unify the services within a single department of defense, but only if the unification was largely symbolic and service autonomy in fact maintained. From FDR's vantage point as president, divisions between the military branches broadened his flow of information and range of options, maximized his bargaining leverage, reduced his management costs, and thus increased his influence.

It is equally improbable FDR would have supported formalizing the JCS structure in statute, under the command of a powerful chief of staff. When Marshall tried in 1942 to unify the JCS command structure through Leahy's appointment, Roosevelt turned the innovation to his own purposes. Leahy became FDR's personal representative, not the JCS chief of staff. And FDR refused to institutionalize the JCS system through formal means.

This same reasoning suggests he would have opposed creating a single secretary of defense. Roosevelt preferred to pit cabinet secretaries and their equivalent against one another, and he disliked limiting himself to a single channel of communication. Indeed, he removed the secretaries of War and of the Navy from the military chain of command in 1939 precisely so that he could deal directly with his military chiefs.

And, because he never believed in using his cabinet as a collective decision-making body, he likely would have opposed formalizing a cabinet-level NSC. Although the SWNCC was a means to facilitate interdepartmental interaction, Roosevelt did not meet with it, nor was it a

70 Indeed, newspapers covering congressional hearings on unification spent considerable time trying to divine FDR's likely stance. Not surprisingly, different newspapers came to completely opposing conclusions. See Caraley, *The Politics of Military Unification*, p. 31.
71 Quoted in ibid.　　　　72 Ibid., p. 31–2.

decision-making forum. He reserved the right to solicit the advice of cabinet members as he saw fit, either singly or collectively. Roosevelt's first-term experiences with the Executive Council and the National Emergency Committee had permanently soured him on the virtues of cabinet government. Moreover, SWNCC was never a statutory body.

Finally, neither Leahy nor Hopkins fit the mold of a "national security adviser" as has subsequently evolved under Roosevelt's successors. Leahy functioned as liaison to the JCS, less a policy maker than a conduit for military information and expertise. Hopkins had a more substantial policy impact, but his influence ranged beyond what are now defined as "national security" issues. Indeed, his utility to FDR derived precisely from his ability to look beyond the foreign policy implications of presidential decisions toward the domestic political ramifications. Moreover, he was never entrusted with devising national security policy per se.

Because they were not officially "policy makers," neither Hopkins nor Leahy developed the extensive national security bureaucracies characteristic of later national security advisers. Thus any temptation to perform operational tasks was lessened. Their primary value was in providing advice and support that helped FDR assess the likely impact of his day-to-day decisions on his bargaining objectives. And it was FDR who personally integrated the politically oriented advice from Hopkins with the military information Leahy provided.

In short, none of FDR's advisers served as a prototype for a McGeorge Bundy, Henry Kissinger, Zbigniew Brzezinski or Brent Scowcroft.[73] And the evidence of World War II strongly suggests FDR would have rejected efforts to institutionalize cabinet coordinating devices in the national security realm. Moreover, it is likely that he would have resisted congressional attempts to create a unified defense department unless the unification was for symbolic purposes alone. From his perspective as president, interservice rivalry broadened his options, increased his information flow, and strengthened his bargaining advantages.

Conclusion

This chapter has concentrated on FDR's efforts from 1938–45 to acquire resources to illuminate his bargaining interests in the military and diplomatic spheres. His bargaining objectives in this period were, first, to defeat the Axis powers and, second, to construct a postwar administrative structure in which American interests were protected and international

73 The national security advisers for presidents Kennedy, Nixon, Carter, and Ford and Bush, respectively.

stability achieved.[74] Until December 1941, however, Roosevelt lacked the means to commit the United States to actively opposing German, Italian, and Japanese aggression. Thus he took tactical detours in the pursuit of long-term objectives. That dictated a staffing strategy that emphasized personal control and administrative flexibility. By modifying the military command structure, moving trusted personnel into positions of influence, and strengthening American defense capabilities as far as politically possible, Roosevelt positioned himself to obtain his objectives when the political barriers against U.S. military intervention fell by the wayside.

Once committed to war, Roosevelt fulfilled his duties as commander in chief with remarkable skill. He was the supreme architect of the Allied strategy, often rejecting the advice of his own military experts. More than once Roosevelt looked beyond immediate military considerations to weigh the long-term implications of foreign policy choices on his bargaining effectiveness.

In this he was helped by his administrative approach. Others served as his bargaining foils, helping to clarify risks and options on his behalf. By allowing the JCS to argue against British war aims, and pitting the American service chiefs against one another, FDR's decisiveness was masked; each of the combatants thought the president unduly responsive to someone else. Marshall, for one, deplored FDR's tendency to vacillate, but in fact Roosevelt's behavior served his bargaining purposes.

Huntington is correct in holding that military planners enjoyed tremendous access and authority in their relations with FDR during World War II. But their influence was primarily in operational matters. The president controlled strategy, modifying military recommendations to fit both his domestic interests and the political needs of the Allied coalition. Indeed, Roosevelt occasionally did not bother to inform the JCS of decisions he made after consulting with Churchill and other allies. For instance, his unconditional surrender ultimatum issued after the Teheran conference ran contrary to military recommendations. Moreover, he seemed insensitive to military needs on issues such as resource allocations and command disputes.[75] And yet his military staff gave him high marks as a military strategist. Leahy remarked that FDR had "an almost professional understanding of naval and military operations."[76]

---

74 On this point, see Warren F. Kimball, "On Diplomatic History and FDR" in Warren F. Kimball, *The Juggler: Franklin Roosevelt as Wartime Stateman* (Princeton, N.J.: Princeton University Press, 1991), pp. 3–5.

75 See Allan Millett, *The American Political System and Civilian Control of the Military: A Historical Perspective* (Columbus: Ohio State University Press, 1979), p. 29–31.

76 Leahy, *I was There*, p. 95. Indeed, he made a point of contrasting FDR's generally positive relationship with his generals to Churchill's more strained interactions with his military commanders; Leahy believes the latter often agreed with Churchill more out of loyalty than the belief that Churchill's strategic decisions made sense.

Roosevelt employed the same strategy, with equally impressive results, in diplomacy. Not fully trusting his cabinet departments, especially State, FDR devised means of pitting diplomatic advisers and institutions against one another: Welles versus Hull, Stimson against Morgenthau, Hopkins versus Byrnes, State versus Lend-Lease. In this manner decisions were forced to him, options kept open, official channels of communications supplemented, and his bargaining choices and advantages expanded.

It is true that by flaunting official communication channels and subverting hierarchical reporting relationships, FDR irritated his staff subordinates. Indeed, most of those who worked for FDR, including Hull, Truman, Stimson, and Marshall, thought FDR's administrative methods quite horrendous. But they judged Roosevelt's actions from their perspective, not his. Sitting in the Oval Office, looking out from a president's vantage point, the disorder and bruised feelings his methods inflicted were more than compensated for by the increased flow of information and expertise – and bargaining advantages – they produced.[77]

In part, of course, FDR relied on informal channels because formal means of communication were often woefully inadequate. Sherwood argues that in crucial periods of the war, Roosevelt knew not much more about world events than what he could glean from the papers and reports from embassies around the world.[78]

Moreover, FDR's reluctance to specify policy objectives sometimes produced negative repercussions. For example, his failure to clearly articulate an early commitment to a second front left his generals to argue the point with the British without adequate presidential backing. This gave the British an opening to voice their strong opposition to the American

77 One more example regarding the range of Roosevelt's sources is when Hopkins gave a private speech with Lord Beaverbrook during a tour of London in 1940, and an FBI man happened to be there who subsequently filed a report with J. Edgar Hoover. Hoover promptly passed the report on to Roosevelt, thus giving FDR an opportunity to verify Hopkins' account. The story is in Sherwood, *Roosevelt and Hopkins*, p. 249–50.

78 See *ibid.*, footnote, pp. 947–8. This chapter has largely ignored FDR's creation of the Office of Strategic Services, the intelligence-gathering organization that preceded the CIA. See Donovan to FDR (June 10, 1941), providing a structural overview for a "Service of Strategic Information" headed by a "Coordinator of Information"; and Donovan to FDR (Oct. 1. 10, 1941), regarding the consolidation of the military undercover intelligence operations under Donovan (the Coordinator of Information) (both in *PSF* – Coordinator of Information File, Donovan Folder, FDRL); FDR to the Budget Director, with attached (Mar. 31, 1942) and subsequent memos from Donovan to FDR (Apr. 14, 1942, and May 16, 1942), regarding Donovan's attempt to get the Office of Coordinator of Information attached to the Joint Chiefs of Staff (all in *PSF* – Coordinator of Information File, Donovan Folder, FDRL; and the memorandum from Leahy to FDR (Mar. 6, 1945), recommending deferring the decision to establish a central intelligence service. *PSF* - Subject Files, Joint Chiefs of Staff Folder, FDRL.

strategy.[79] Here again, however, by closely holding his cards to his vest, FDR accrued advantages that more than compensated for the discomfiture caused his subordinates. Others made his arguments for him, leaving him free to change policy positions as he saw fit. He thus gained a broader range of options.

For Roosevelt, then, national security meant achieving politico-military objectives under the constraints imposed by governing within a democratic political system. That necessitated subjecting the advice of his experts, both diplomatic and military, to the scrutiny of his political staff, and vice versa. Effective presidential influence depended on information and options that enhanced, not subverted, a president's bargaining advantages. The evidence marshaled here suggests that FDR's national security advisory system – perhaps to a greater extent than any of his successor's – did just that. He largely accomplished his bargaining objectives during World War II without centralizing administrative control within a large, functionally specialized White House staff, despite facing bargaining costs arguably as high as any his successors confronted.

We have come full circle. This book began by noting FDR's historical reputation as a great president, a reputation partly based on his administrative prowess. In subsequent chapters we probed more deeply, seeking to discover what his methods were and why they were effective. It is now time to consider these issues more directly, using the terms and concepts introduced earlier to make sense of FDR's staff choices, and to discern whether they are feasible today. The next chapter takes on this task.

79 See, for example, "Ernest J. King," from Love, *Chiefs of Naval Operations*, pp. 151–2.

PART IV

Lessons and considerations

8

"Competitive adhocracy": The principles and implications of FDR's use of staff

Roosevelt's advisory organization evolved according to his bargaining needs. Escalating demands for presidential leadership climaxed during World War II by thrusting FDR to the head of a wartime alliance and by placing responsibility for administering war production in his hands. His organizational response in both cases was largely governed by the blueprint articulated by the Brownlow Report and incorporated through the creation of the EOP and White House Office.

That blueprint, however, was predicated on a relatively fixed set of administrative tenets that, although never consciously articulated by FDR, nevertheless were consistently used by him to organize his staff support. I extract these from the preceding chapters for consideration here. Scholars have cited several of these tenets in previous studies.[1] But typically they are explained in terms of Roosevelt's unique temperament and operating style. Personality-based explanations, however, do not tell why his administrative approach was successful.

In this chapter I try to explain the source of Roosevelt's administrative effectiveness. I begin with a review of the major tenets undergirding his staff system, which I call "competitive adhocracy."[2] I then place those

1 See, for example, Alexander George, *Presidential Decision Making in Foreign Policy: The Effective Use of Information and Advice* (Boulder, Colo.: Westview Press, 1980); Richard Tanner Johnson, *Managing the White House: An Intimate Study of the Presidency* (New York: Harper & Row, 1974); Roger Porter, *Presidential Decision Making: The Economic Policy Board* (New York: Cambridge University Press, 1980), Appendix, pp. 231–5; Arthur Schlesinger, Jr., *The Coming of the New Deal* (Vol. 2 of his The Age of Roosevelt (Boston: Houghton-Mifflin, 1959), pp. 511–73; Stephen Hess, *Organizing the Presidency*, 2nd ed. (Washington, D.C.: The Brookings Institution, 1988), pp. 23–39; Richard E. Neustadt, *Presidential Power and the Modern Presidents: The Politics of Leadership from Roosevelt to Reagan* (New York: The Free Press, 1990), pp. 128–35; Richard E. Neustadt, "Approaches to Staffing the Presidency: Notes on FDR and JFK," *American Political Science Review* Vol. 59, no. 4 (December 1963), pp. 855–63, and A. J. Wann, *The President as Chief Administrator: A Study of Franklin Roosevelt* (Washington, D.C.: Public Affairs Press, 1968).
2 The term is derived from George, *Presidential Decision Making in Foreign Policy*, and Porter, *Presidential Decision Making*, pp. 229–35.

tenets in the larger framework, presented in the introductory chapter, linking presidential staff to presidential power. Roosevelt's staff tenets, I argue, are best understood as interconnected parts in a systematic search for bargaining effectiveness. He institutionalized staff support to gain access to information and expertise relevant to recurring bargaining exchanges.[3] But he did so in a manner that proved particularly efficient at reducing his management costs, as measured in time and energy spent supervising his aides.

What were those staffing tenets? The ten most important are reviewed below.

Resist delegating inherently presidential powers

First and foremost, Roosevelt almost never delegated presidential authority to staff subordinates. The president, by virtue of the Constitution and subsequent statute and tradition, is held solely accountable for any inherently presidential act. Accordingly, Roosevelt would not allow aides to act in his name unless administrative safeguards were built in to protect him from possible repercussions. As he explained to Jim Rowe, an administrative assistant: "I do not have to do it your way and I will tell you the reason why. The reason is that, although they may have made a mistake, the people of the United States elected me President, not you."[4]

The historical record demonstrates Roosevelt's stubborn commitment to this principle. In 1939, for instance, he rejected carefully laid plans to delegate oversight of war production to a "mobilization czar." Instead, FDR created agencies – NDAC, OPM, SPAB – with multiple chairmen and weak or overlapping statutory authority, thus forcing any controversial mobilization decisions to him for resolution. Even when Donald Nelson was ostensibly granted full mobilization authority as WPB director in 1942, FDR allowed – even encouraged – Nelson's authority to be challenged.

Only at the war's full height in late 1943, when the economy was completely mobilized and FDR increasingly preoccupied with foreign affairs and postwar planning did he finally delegate partial administrative control on the home front to James Byrnes and the OWM. Even here,

---

3 Recall from the Introduction that the amount of bargaining resources (as distinguished from capital) a president seeks is a function of how important the bargain is to the president, and his uncertainty regarding the likely impact of his bargaining choices on his preferred outcomes.

4 Quoted in Schlesinger, Jr., *The Coming of the New Deal*, p. 531.

however, FDR was careful to do so on his own terms. Byrnes' authority, while broad, was tempered by his understanding of what FDR expected Byrnes to do – an understanding made possible by Byrnes' long acquaintance with the president and his own vast reservoir of political experience and by the fact that Byrnes' power was conferred by executive order rather than congressional statute.

The story is the same in the international bargaining arena. It was Roosevelt who personally integrated the military and diplomatic decision streams to produce national security policy. Almost all his major foreign policies during World War II were consummated in personal meetings with the opposing heads of state, rather than by negotiations entrusted to his military and diplomatic professionals. Indeed, Secretary of State Cordell Hull attended almost none of the major wartime conferences. Roosevelt's generals did participate, but to provide military, not diplomatic, expertise. There was no "national security" staff per se.

Employ multiple communication channels to extend the range of information received

Roosevelt devised administrative means to glean information beyond what his official channels provided. One method was to parallel official communication channels with informal sources. For instance, Sumner Welles, Chip Bohlen, and others reported directly to FDR from the State Department, supplementing Hull's official reports. Similarly, Lend-Lease officials, including Hopkins and Harriman, were used to cross-check State Department communiques from overseas embassies and military estimates regarding the defense capabilities of Britain and the Soviet Union.

Moreover, FDR jealously guarded his information sources. The Map Room, his military command post at the White House, was organized so that incoming messages came through one military channel whereas outgoing communications were handled by another. In this way the only complete set of military-related messages remained in FDR's hands.

And, as indicated by his private correspondence and the testimony of others, FDR nurtured a wide assortment of individuals, situated across all levels of government and within the private sector, as intelligence sources. His wife, Eleanor, is perhaps the most famous example, but the names of many others – Frankfurter, Baruch, O'Connor – come up repeatedly.[5] Indeed, archives suggest Roosevelt's reservoir of intelligence sources was practically endless.

---

5 Eleanor, of course, served effectively as FDR's eyes and ears during her national and global trips.

Overlap staff functions to two or
more agencies or individuals

Roosevelt invariably assigned government tasks to two or more individuals or agencies. He did so to exert effective influence on bargaining outcomes through more than one pressure point. Overlapping assignments also induced competition among staff vying to win FDR's confidence. As he noted, "There is something to be said . . . for having a little conflict between agencies. A little rivalry is stimulating. . . . It keeps everyone going to prove that he is a better fellow than the next man. It keeps them honest too."[6]

Note, in this regard, his reluctance to assign procurement responsibility to either the military or the civilian production agencies alone. By splitting procurement powers among several agencies, Roosevelt was alerted to production controversies in time to formulate solutions and protect his political interests. For the same reason FDR's work-relief policies during his first presidential term were entrusted to both Ickes at the Public Works Administration and Hopkins, heading the Civil Works Administration (later the Works Progress Administration.)[7] And Johnson and Ickes split management of the National Industrial Recovery Act.

During World War II, American military progress against Japan was accelerated by the competition between Admiral Nimitz, commanding the naval fleet, and General MacArthur, who led the Army ground forces. Nimitz pushed for a central Pacific strategy, using the Navy to island hop to Japan. MacArthur, in contrast, advocated retaking the Philippines and using it as a staging area for the invasion of Japan. Rather than choose among the competing plans, and commanders, Roosevelt capitalized on the rivalry between the two. He did the same with the British and American military staffs, using each one's fear of the other's objectives to broaden his policy options and clarify associated risks.

Of course, administrative competition had drawbacks. It sometimes demoralized staff, and festering disputes often erupted publicly, as was the case with Hull and Welles, and Nelson and the ANMB. Nor was it always the most efficient way to expend scarce resources. But, on balance, FDR judged the benefits to outweigh the costs.

6 Quoted in Schlesinger, Jr., *The Coming of the New Deal*, p. 535.
7 See Harold Wilensky, *Organizational Intelligence: Knowledge and Policy in Government and Industry* (New York: Basic Books, 1967), pp. 50–3.

"Experts" do not protect presidential bargaining interests

Roosevelt made extensive use of professionals with particular expertise in bargaining areas, be it policy, politics, or administration. But he did not let their interest determine his bargaining calculations. For example, he refused to accept predictions by his military service chiefs, concerned in 1940–41 with conserving U.S. armaments, that both Great Britain and the Soviet Union were likely to wilt before the German military onslaught. Similarly, FDR in 1942 proposed production targets most businessmen thought quite unfeasible, but which were nonetheless largely obtained.

Roosevelt felt confident discounting experts' advice because he subjected it to the scrutiny of his personal assistants whose views were less wedded to a particular bargaining outcome. Hopkins analyzed military and diplomatic issues. Currie double-checked economic forecasts. Rowe, and later Rosenman, reviewed domestic legislative proposals. Byrnes adjudicated production disputes. Each did so from a perspective more nearly matching Roosevelt's.

Apparently FDR reasoned that because experts are trained in one particular area – diplomacy, economics, military strategy, and so forth – they were less likely to render advice that addressed Roosevelt's broader bargaining perspective. Defense preparation in the two years prior to Pearl Harbor is a case in point. Roosevelt continually prodded his service chiefs to expand aviation production for overseas shipment, despite the insistence of Marshall and others that planes were not a defense priority at that time and would do the United States little good if shipped elsewhere. In a purely military sense, of course, his generals' judgments were justified. But their objections did not address FDR's interests. He therefore used Morgenthau, and later Currie and Hopkins, to spur plane production, rather than entrust the task to the War Department.

Do not institutionalize White House staff roles

Roosevelt retained administrative flexibility by refusing to institutionalize White House staff roles through statutory grants of power.[8] As Neustadt notes, Roosevelt's White House aides were organized around recurring decision-making processes, rather than by functional or pro-

---

8 Recall from the Introduction of this book that by "institutionalization of staff roles" I mean formally grounding those roles in statute, executive order, or some other official grant of power.

grammatic specialty.[9] Beginning in 1942, Hopkins used munitions ship-ments as his vehicle for intervening across the spectrum of war produc-tion and military strategic issues. Rosenman utilized the flow of executive orders, bill signings, presidential speeches, and other recurring action processes to help FDR shape a domestic program. Smith organized his job around budget deadlines. Byrnes responded to production disputes that flowed upward to him. And Leahy's duties were structured by the mili-tary decisions forced on FDR by the war.

This precluded White House staff differentiation and specialization be-cause these decision-making processes did not fall within neat substantive or functional areas. For instance, Hopkins' role as munitions allocation chair required some knowledge of budgeting, military strategy, diplo-macy, and production and price control processes – all under the purview of other presidential aides. Similarly, Roosevelt brought Byrnes with him to Yalta in 1945, although Byrnes' primary domain was domestic politics rather than international affairs. Evidently FDR wanted Byrnes' domes-tic experience to balance input from his foreign policy staff. And Smith was a key adviser regarding industrial production, nominally under Byrnes' jurisdiction.

Moreover, a formal staff assignment is difficult to revoke.[10] That explains FDR's unwillingness to statutorily convert the JCS into a permanent ad-vising body. Similarly, he resisted giving Byrnes or the OWM statutory footing.[11] Roosevelt evidently thought aides interpreted formal staff des-ignations as hunting licenses, authorizing them to exercise full control of particular administrative processes or policy spheres. To prevent this, FDR eliminated Brownlow's attempt in an early draft of the Brownlow Report to specify White House staff functions. Instead, by diluting Brownlow's description of advising roles, FDR served notice that he reserved the right to assign staff tasks according to his needs at the moment.

This aversion to staff institutionalization pertained as well to public de-scriptions of staff duties, including formal titles. Except for Rosenman,

9 Neustadt, "Approaches to Staffing the Presidency."
10 This is the prime reason why presidents should be reluctant to formally place the vice-president in charge of critical staff areas – once in place, it is very difficult to fire him or her. President Gerald Ford's difficulty with Vice-President Nelson Rockefeller, who was formally appointed to head Ford's Domestic Council, is instructive in this regard. See Samuel Kernell and Samuel L. Popkin (eds.), *Chief of Staff: Twenty-Five Years of the Managerial Presidency* (Berkeley and Los Angeles: University of California Press, 1986), pp. 173–6.
11 Indeed, when Congress transformed the OWM into the OWMR, it made Byrnes the statutory head of the new agency. Byrnes, realizing that FDR preferred that the OWMR operate under presidential, as opposed to congressional, authorization, offered to resign. Roosevelt persuaded Byrnes to stay only because he wanted him to attend the Yalta con-ference. (Conversation with Richard Neustadt, based on his discussion with those who worked with Roosevelt.)

whose title, Special Counsel, was in deference to his background as a state judge, and Hopkins, who technically was not a member of the White House staff, all of Roosevelt's White House aides were listed as either secretaries or administrative assistants. Thus none could claim, by virtue of title or job description, an exclusive mandate to manage certain policies or processes.

Moreover, these titles were granted only to those who worked directly for FDR in the White House. Roosevelt did not give White House privileges to anyone who did have not regular access to him. It was too risky to designate someone a member of the White House staff, only to allow them to operate without presidential supervision.[12]

This aversion to staff institutionalization forced Roosevelt's White House assistants to encroach on their colleagues' "turf" in order to do their own job well. Thus staff parochialism, close-mindedness, and complacency were less likely to take root.[13] To be sure, some role specialization was helpful, but not to the point that aides began attributing unwarranted preeminence to their particular functions. From the president's perspective, staff tasks are important only to the extent that they address a president's bargaining interests.[14]

Moreover, FDR's aides were primarily recruited based on a demonstrated loyalty to his interests and with a track record of government service, not on the basis of particular "expertise." Indeed, except for Howe, Early, McIntyre, and Rosenman – each of whom worked for FDR prior to his becoming president – promotion to the White House staff for all of FDR's political assistants came only after extended apprenticeship.[15] Most went through a baptism of fire serving FDR in other government capacities before being brought on board.[16] He wanted his presidential

12 As Ted Sorensen warns: "More important than who gets a White House parking permit or who eats in the White House Mess is who is able to invoke the president's name, who is using the president's telephone, and who is using the president's stationary. That's serious. If you have hundreds of people doing that, there is no way you can keep them out of mischief" (Popkin and Kernell, *Chief of Staff*, p. 106).

13 Recall Smith's evident resentment when FDR began using Currie to double-check economic forecasts. It was precisely because Smith felt this was "his territory" that Roosevelt made sure another aide was giving him advice on these issues as well.

14 This aversion to staff specialization explains Hopkins' value to FDR during World War II. Hopkins' very lack of military and diplomatic expertise combined with his broad mandate encouraged him to question the assumptions of experts in both fields with impunity. It also helps explain why FDR frequently shifted staff to new, unfamiliar assignments, as when Currie was moved from domestic economic advice to liaison with the Chinese during World War II, and why Rosenman, primarily a domestic adviser, was sent overseas to investigate Allied relief policy in 1945. These aides' lack of familiarity with the issues may have allowed them to bring a fresh perspective.

15 FDR's son Jimmy Roosevelt was a conspicuous exception to this rule.

16 Again, Hopkins is a prime example. He started as a New Deal bureaucrat specializing in work relief, but after several years achieved preeminence as FDR's primary foreign policy consultant.

assistants fully capable of operating across a broad range of activities, and thus it helped to have extensive government experience.

Keep the White House staff small

This principle follows directly from the previous two. For all the reasons mentioned above – distrust of specialization, wariness of institutionalization, and his desire to personally manage staff – FDR did not allow his White House staff to grow so large that he could not adequately supervise each member's activities. As a result, even at the height of the war, his senior White House staff, not counting clerical aides, numbered no more than a dozen. And they had few assistants of their own; there was little of the staff layering so common today.

These senior aides served three primary functions, each related to a daily activity that FDR could not escape. The White House staff secretaries – Early, Watson (actually a military aide), and Hassett – oversaw FDR's daily appointments, media relations, and correspondence.[17] Roosevelt's administrative assistants – who never numbered more than a handful – served as FDR's eyes, ears, and legs, gathering intelligence, running errands, performing liaison to departments and agencies, and generally serving as in-house office boys.

Finally, FDR had a quintet of senior advisers – Byrnes, Hopkins, Leahy, Rosenman, and Smith – organized around recurring bargaining streams. Although their functional areas were somewhat bounded, none of them were policy or program specialists. Nor did they – with the exception of Smith who headed the BoB – build extensive staffs. Instead, as noted above, each assisted FDR in handling the bargaining events and processes – budgeting, program development, war production and allocation – that flowed to the president on a somewhat regular basis. Roosevelt gave these senior aides extensive leeway to handle second-level issues within their areas of responsibility, but with the proviso that he could intervene at any moment and that their license to operate on his behalf was subject to revision or revocation as he saw fit.

Production and price control, handled by Byrnes, and munitions allocations, which Hopkins oversaw, were directly related to actions predicated on American participation in World War II. It is therefore difficult to predict with certainty what would have become of these positions after 1945. Near the end of the war, some talked of turning the OWMR into a presidential program- or policy-development staff. But there is no evidence FDR supported such proposals.

17 Recall that McIntyre, who handled appointments prior to Watson, died early in the war.

Instead, policy development remained the special province of the executive branch departments and agencies; they proposed legislation, and FDR was free to accept or reject it as his interests dictated. To be sure, he used aides, like Cohen and Corcoran, to extract, synthesize, and refine ideas that were working their way through the bureaucracies' policy mill. And he expected his White House aides to work with the permanent government to hatch legislative proposals. But the closest he came to sanctioning a permanent White House–centered policy staff was his effort to institutionalize the National Resources Planning Board, responsible for long-range policy planning. However, even this effort wavered in the face of congressional opposition.

Because he accepted "happy thoughts" from any source, then, Roosevelt showed no inclination to create White House domestic or foreign policy staffs.[18] Free from White House domination, his cabinet secretaries played a more integral policy formulation and implementation role.

At the same time, however, FDR stopped short of sanctioning "cabinet government." After his unhappy first-term experience with the National Emergency Council, he never again sanctioned the development of a cabinet-level coordinating council similar to today's National Security Council or National Economic Council.

Keep institutional and political staff functions separate

Roosevelt actively nurtured two types of staff: personal and institutional. He thought both were necessary to bargain effectively.[19] Institutional staff protected the presidency as an institution. Personal staff, in contrast, were more sensitive to the interests of the sitting president.

Because institutional staff were largely career-based, they were more responsive to congressional and executive branch entreaties than was FDR's White House staff. Thus institutional staff gave FDR a more accurate picture of how his bargaining choices would be received by these critical audiences. This explains why FDR made sure the Brownlow Committee recommendations primarily augmented his institutional staff-based resources pertinent to budgeting, personnel, policy planning, and administrative management. Indeed, after a shaky start, the BoB grew more than

18 In fact, Roosevelt evidently did not see a distinction between the two areas; his most important advisers – Hopkins, Rosenman, Byrnes, Smith – were as likely to deal with domestic issues as they were foreign policy issues.

19 On this point more generally, see Colin Campbell, *Managing the Presidency: Carter, Reagan and the Search for Executive Harmony* (Pittsburgh: University of Pittsburgh Press, 1986), pp. 3–24.

tenfold during FDR's presidency, and Smith, as director, became one of FDR's most important aides.[20] In contrast, the White House staff grew much more slowly during this same period.

Be your own staff coordinator

Roosevelt immersed himself in the actual day-to-day work of his assistants. This meant actively managing staff activities: assigning tasks, hearing reports firsthand, and personally correlating the inflow of information and expertise. At the same time, he sabotaged almost every cabinet or White House–level coordinating body he ostensibly sanctioned. Recall Richberg's brief tenure as the "Assistant President," responsible for coordinating the NEC. Richberg's authority was undercut by FDR's tendency to deal directly with those nominally under Richberg's supervision.

Similarly, FDR thwarted General Marshall's attempt to make Leahy a Chief of Staff to the JCS in order to coordinate military advice to Roosevelt. Instead, Leahy became FDR's personal military aide, keeping the president abreast of divisions among the military services that Roosevelt then was free to exploit for his own purposes.

In short, there was no room in Roosevelt's system for an "executive assistant" charged with managing the staff on the president's behalf. Today, of course, scholars argue that presidents cannot hope to function effectively without a chief of staff to supervise and coordinate staff activities.[21] But that claim is premised on the existence of a large White House staff bureaucracy, functionally specialized and hierarchically arranged. If, in contrast, White House staffs are kept small and composed primarily of generalists – precisely the impact of FDR's administrative principles – the rationale for an executive assistant becomes suspect.

Moreover, Roosevelt felt that active presidential oversight improves staff work; aides tend to understand presidential bargaining objectives in proportion to the amount of time they interact with the president. It also gives staff a greater sense of involvement in presidential bargaining.

20 True, Roosevelt was less successful at institutionalizing either a planning or personnel staff; neither the National Resource Planning Board nor his White House liaison for personnel management fulfilled his expectations in these regards. But their failures reflect the opposition he encountered more than his own staff preferences.
21 See generally the viewpoints expressed by several former White House staff members in Kernell and Popkin, *Chief of Staff*, and Richard E. Neustadt, "Does the President Need a Strong Chief of Staff?" in James P. Pfiffner (ed.), *The Managerial Presidency* (Pacific Grove, CA: Brooks/Cole Publishing Co., 1991).

By directly managing both personal and institutional staff, FDR served their needs and his. Aides gained personal access to the Oval Office, and thus professional fulfillment. And Roosevelt was generally better positioned to gauge the importance of their work for his interests. This, in turn, allowed him to shift staff arrangements as dictated by his bargaining needs.

When politically possible, create new government organizations for new governmental functions

By placing new governmental functions within new government organizations that reported to him, Roosevelt increased his bargaining implementation and management capacities. This was the purpose behind FDR's creation of the alphabet-soup, Depression-era emergency agencies, almost all of which were established outside the existing governmental framework and reported directly to him. Similarly, during World War II, the industrial production and price control agencies were placed within the Office of Emergency Management, an administrative "holding company" whose de facto head was FDR. In this way new tasks were entrusted to new agencies that were directly under Roosevelt's control, rather than to existing bureaucratic departments that might have their own agendas. Moreover, FDR was able to attract new blood into government by promising recruits freedom to work within departments or agencies dedicated solely to tasks that interested them. Finally, by placing these functions within governmental entities that reported directly to him, Roosevelt was better positioned to see that they operated in his interest. He also was free, at least initially, to circumvent civil service regulations by making unabashedly partisan appointments. Once the emergency agencies were brought within the fold of permanent government, this influx of Democratic personnel was locked in by the extension of civil service.

Set internal staff deadlines, but remain publicly flexible

The effective use of time was FDR's final staff maxim. Repeatedly, as when developing the U.S. military strategy in World War II, Roosevelt imposed internal deadlines on presidential staff work to force consideration of issues that he sensed were important to him. Recall that, in the eighteen months before Pearl Harbor, FDR's military staff actively formulated military strategic plans based on Roosevelt's assumptions regarding who would be in the war. Likewise, as early as 1936, prior to the outbreak of the European conflict, FDR directed Brownlow (and later Currie) to examine his war mobilization plans. In each case, Roosevelt set internal staff deadlines so as to be more fully prepared when actual bargaining deadlines appeared.

At the same time, however, Roosevelt was careful not to commit himself publicly to specific strategies or plans unless he sensed political support had crystallized behind them. By refusing to formally endorse long-range plans, he retained bargaining flexibility in the face of changing circumstances. Thus, he reviewed, but did not formally approve any of, the military strategic plans presented to him by his commanders in the months preceding U.S. entrance into the war. He ordered the Brownlow Committee Report withheld until immediately after the November 1936 presidential election, so that he could implement a new staff system without jeopardizing his reelection chances. In 1940 he let Marshall lobby Congress for a military draft, without formally supporting him for several months. Nor did he actively commit to the defense buildup his generals so desperately wanted in this period.

His basic philosophy was to set internal deadlines to move staff work ahead while publicly refusing to tie himself to any plan of action until circumstances made such a commitment favorable to him.

Competitive adhocracy – How effective?

In summary, then, the following basic principles guided Roosevelt's use of staff: resist delegation of inherently presidential authority; personally manage staff; recognize the different incentives driving institutional and personal assistants and organize to insure input from both; limit White House staff specialization in title, form, and actual responsibilities (which in practice meant governing with a small staff of generalists and specialists to handle daily chores he could not escape); employ overlapping staff tasks; and use internal deadlines to govern staff work while eschewing public commitments until timing is advantageous for presidential bargaining effectiveness.

Were Roosevelt's principles effective? There is room for debate, of course, but much evidence suggests they were. Consider the measures scholars typically utilize to gauge the failings of the post-FDR presidential branch: a president's electability, bargaining effectiveness, and patterns of administrative choices. Roosevelt's administrative system compares favorably with his successors' on all three measures.

He was, of course, elected to an unprecedented four terms in office, and, as noted in the Introduction, his historical reputation is higher than that of any other modern president. Moreover, a close examination of two particularly demanding bargaining arenas, economic mobilization and military strategy and command, provides evidence that his administrative principles stood him in good stead. His organization of war production made America "the arsenal of democracy" during World War II, but without sacrificing the bargaining power so critical to his other war objectives. At the same time, he held the Allied coalition together through the years of global military conflict and positioned the United States to be the dominant world power at the war's end.

This success came despite facing unprecedented bargaining costs that arguably have not been matched since. Indeed, if government budget outlays are one indication of administrative costs, note that Roosevelt's wartime national government outlays (adjusted for inflation) are not matched until 1980 – long after the appearance of the bureaucratized White House staff. (If federal grants to state and local governments are excluded, outlays under FDR are not topped until 1983.) As a percentage of the gross domestic product (GDP), peak government outlays under Roosevelt have never been matched. Moreover, federal personnel levels have remained relatively stable since his presidency; most of the growth in the public sector has taken place at the state and local level. It is true that in some respects – for instance, business and environmental regulation and social welfare entitlement programs – the scope of governmental activity has widened in the last fifty years. Again, however, much of that is implemented through state and local governments. The number of federal government institutions – cabinet departments, regulatory and independent agencies, and government corporations – for which FDR was held responsible has been matched or exceeded under other presidents only a handful of occasions, and then not by much.

By most objective measures, then, FDR did not govern in a simpler time. Moreover, the numbers do not capture the significance of the bargaining issues FDR confronted during his terms in office. Essentially, Roosevelt spent much of his presidency searching for solutions to economic and military crises that threatened the nation's existence. Arguably no other president, with the exception of Lincoln and Washington, confronted such pressing political issues.

The final tests of FDR's administrative effectiveness are the administrative lessons he evidently learned, as revealed by the steady evolution in his staff system. His initial attempt to implement the New Deal recovery program through cabinet government was, administratively, ineffective. Although FDR retained political support throughout his first term, he made only marginal gains in bringing the nation out of the Great Depression, and he found the cabinet a poor source of bargaining support.

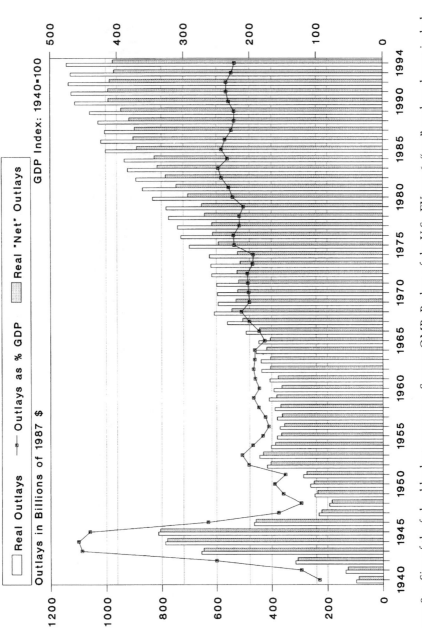

Figure 8.1. Size of the federal budget, 1940–94. *Source:* OMB, Budget of the U.S.; FY 1996; "net" outlays do not include grants to states/localities.

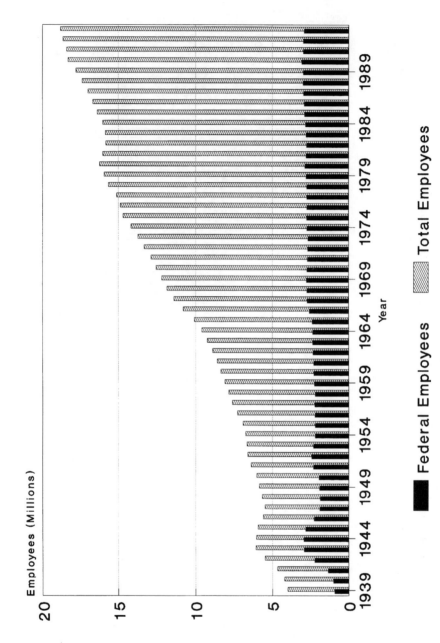

Figure 8.2. Governmental employees, 1939–93. *Source*: Bureau of Labor Statistics

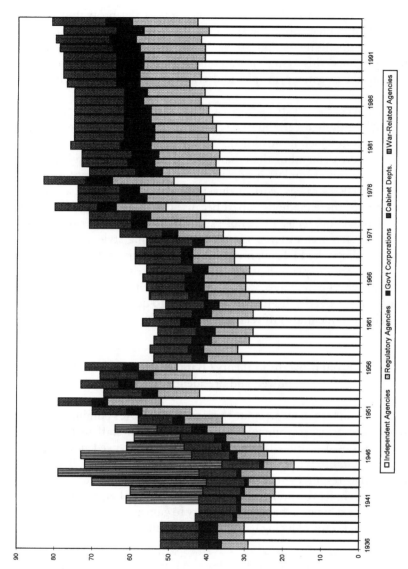

Figure 8.3. Executive branch institutional growth, 1936–95. *Source: United States Government Manual,* 1936–95

Consequently, by 1937, with the publication of the Brownlow Report, FDR began implementing the system of competitive adhocracy that was to serve him, and the nation, so well in the war years. Although he continually refined this system in response to a changing bargaining environment, the essential principles underlying it did not appreciably change after 1939.

On balance, then, a strong case can be made that FDR's administrative approach, although certainly not flawless, nevertheless was effective in the context in which he governed.[22] Moreover, that context was in many respects more demanding than that faced by his modern presidential successors. But this exemplary historical record begs a more critical question: Why did FDR's strategy work? Conventional wisdom, of course, suggests he employed these methods in part because they fulfilled a predisposition to manipulate others as a form of psychic gratification. As noted above, however, references to temperament and operating style are helpful for understanding why FDR might choose certain administrative techniques, but they cannot explain their effectiveness.[23] Instead, I argue that to understand why his methods were successful, we must move beyond administrative proverbs, useful as they may be, to develop a framework for analyzing presidential-staff relations.

From proverbs to theory? Bargaining, presidential power, and presidential staff

In this section I try to incorporate the elements of FDR's administrative approach into a larger argument linking presidential staff to presidential power. Presidents, I argued in the introductory chapter, need more than bargaining capital to wield influence; they also seek political, policy and administrative resources to help predict the likely consequences of their bargaining choices on preferred outcomes. For a given bargaining exchange or series of exchanges, then, presidents try to gain access to the advising resources helpful for reducing bargaining uncertainty to a desired level.

22 For a discussion of those flaws from the perspective of those who worked for FDR, see Frances Perkins, *The Roosevelt I Knew* (New York: Harper & Row, 1964); Henry Stimson (with McGeorge Bundy), *On Active Service in Peace and War* (New York: Octagon Books, 1971; originally published 1948); and Harold L. Ickes, *The Secret Diary of Harold L. Ickes: The First Thousand Days* (New York: Simon & Schuster, 1953), vol. 1, p. 308, and vol. 3, p. 433.

23 Indeed, similar assessments are made of Lyndon Johnson's temperament; LBJ, too, loved to hold the strings of power in his own hands, but he is generally judged less politically effective than Roosevelt. See, for example, Doris Kearns, *Lyndon Johnson and the American Dream* (Norwalk, Conn.: Easton Press, 1987 [originally published 1976).

Acquiring the requisite resources is easier for presidents when the volume of bargaining demands is small. This explains FDR's preference for limiting his bargaining agenda, as indicated by his remarks during a first-term cabinet meeting:

> If I make every bill that the Government is interested in must legislation, it is going to complicate things. . . . Where I clear legislation with a notation that says "no objection," that means you are at perfect liberty to try and get the thing through, but I am not going to send a special message. It is all your trouble, not mine.[24]

Roosevelt's cabinet officers and other lieutenants were free to pursue their own bargaining goals, of course, but they could not necessarily count on FDR to expend his scarce resources on their behalf.[25]

But limiting the presidential bargaining agenda was not always possible, nor desirable. Events, particularly the Great Depression and World War II, placed demands on FDR that he could not ignore. In these instances his response, at least until the 1939 establishment of the EOP, was to temporarily "purchase" bargaining resources through the political marketplace, utilizing detailees, acquaintances, and others on an ad hoc basis.

Note that for most of the nation's history, such "spot contracting" by presidents was presumably the rule, not the exception. That is, presidents traditionally acquired much of their information and expertise from non-institutionalized sources: party officials, state and local leaders, members of Congress, and others with the requisite bargaining resources.

The traditional system of resource acquisition proved adequate when presidential bargaining demands were limited. But, in the 1930s, the increase in the frequency and costs of particular types of bargaining transactions evidently convinced FDR that he could no longer rely on this ad hoc method for acquiring bargaining support. Faced with recurring demands for specific presidential services – program planning and development, fiscal and budgetary management, personnel recruitment – Roosevelt evidently thought it necessary to institutionalize sources of bargaining support within his presidential staff. This would reduce his cost to negotiate, hire, and monitor the work of those whose bargaining expertise he sought.[26]

By institutionalizing staff, however, Roosevelt incurred greater management costs. This is because the Constitution, statutes, and political tradition centered accountability for bargaining outcomes in Roosevelt as president, and not his assistants. Advisers thus had to be supervised. As

---

24 Schlesinger, Jr., *The Coming of the New Deal*, p. 548.
25 On this point, see Stephen Hess's proposal for a "minimalist" presidency (Hess, *Organizing the Presidency*, pp. 222–30).
26 Economists call these "transaction costs."

John Kennedy later explained, "No matter how many advisers you have, the President must finally choose. . . . [He] bears the burden . . . the advisers may move on to new advice."[27] The result, as Neustadt warns, is that: "On the one hand, [a president] can never assume that anyone or any system will supply the bits and pieces he needs most; on the other hand, he must assume that much of what he needs will not be volunteered by his official advisers."[28]

Because presidential assistants did not fully share responsibility for FDR's bargaining choices, then, he had to actively manage them.[29] This was a resource-intensive task; to supervise his advisers required an expenditure of time and energy on FDR's part.[30] Roosevelt's management costs, I argue, were determined by three factors: the size of the gap between his actual control of staff incentives and his perceived control by others; the divergence between his and his aides' preferred bargaining outcomes; and the skill with which the aide performed his assigned task.

To illustrate, consider Donald Nelson's appointment by FDR in 1942 to head the War Production Board. Nelson's appointment was forced on FDR at this juncture due to the growing size of the production program coupled with FDR's rapid immersion in military and diplomatic strategy. Burdened with conflicting advice and escalating responsibilities, FDR sought to move some of the administrative burden for war production on Nelson's shoulders.[31] But Nelson proved to be temperamentally ill-suited for the task. By shedding control of various war-related tasks and openly feuding with other staff agencies, Nelson's actual control of war produc-

---

27 Quoted in Theodore Sorensen, *Decision Making in the White House* (New York: Columbia University Press, 1963), p. 82. Under "spot contracting," presidents incurred management costs as well, but only for the duration of the bargaining support provided. Once institutionalized within the president's advisory system, however, aides had to be constantly monitored.

28 Neustadt, *Presidential Power*, p. 129.

29 The need to manage staff is a specific example of the more general issue addressed in the principal – agent literature developed mainly by economists. For an introduction to the issues, see John W. Pratt and Richard Zeckhauser, "Principles and Agents: An Overview," in Pratt and Zeckhauser (eds.), *Principles and Agents: The Structure of Business* (Boston: Harvard Business School Press, 1985), pp. 1–36.
    Political economists typically assume that agents pursue their own interest, quite consciously subverting the terms of the contract with their principal. This, I argue, is rarely the case with presidential advisers. Instead it is more common for overzealous aides to pursue what they believe to be the president's interest, when in fact it is not.

30 My assumption, of course, is that FDR's management resources were limited; for any given bargain in any specified period, he had a finite amount of time and energy to devote to staff supervision. This placed an upper limit on the size of the staff he could personally manage.

31 As FDR confided to an associate at the height of the war, "I get so many conflicting recommendations my head is splitting" (James MacGregor Burns, *Roosevelt: The Soldier of Freedom*, Norwalk, Conn.: The Easton Press, 1985 [originally published 1970]), p. 343).

tion did not match his formal responsibility. His administrative failings, however, were laid at FDR's feet. By 1943 Congress was threatening to create its own war production agency, prompting FDR's decision to establish the OWM and appoint Byrnes as its head. Thereafter Byrnes' prior political experiences, close relationship to FDR, and administrative skill eased FDR's management burden.

Generalizing from FDR's experience, then, I argue that a president who has little influence over staff actions, but is perceived by others to have more; who seeks bargaining objectives his aides oppose (or vice versa); and whose aides lack the bargaining resources the president requires will incur relatively greater management costs (as measured in time and energy). Conversely, if president and staff desire the same bargaining objectives; if actual presidential control over staff incentives meets expectations; and if aides' capabilities prove adequate to the task at hand, then the president's management costs are lessened.

The existence of management costs has important implications for presidents' efforts to reduce bargaining uncertainty through staff institutionalization. Presidents cannot simply acquire staff as needed to meet bargaining demands. The bargaining resources presidents gain must be balanced against the management costs staffs impose. This suggests, then, that for a given bargain, or series of bargains, staff institutionalization will proceed until an equilibrium between resources and costs is achieved.

The search for this bargaining equilibrium is dynamic, not static. Presidents are constantly adjusting staff arrangements in response to changing bargaining demands. Chapter 3 demonstrates that Roosevelt spent most of his first term juggling advising arrangements, trying unsuccessfully to balance bargaining resources with management costs. His difficulty is understandable, of course, for in practice he could not know with certainty beforehand if his staff resources would be adequate to ensure bargaining success; that was a retrospective judgment. Nor could he accurately predict the management costs associated with staff institutionalization until after the fact. Recall that it took several months before FDR decided his cabinet-based coordinating council, the National Emergency Council, was simply too unwieldy to administer. In short, it was only by evaluating staff information and predictions, and comparing them to outcomes over a period of time, that Roosevelt began to reliably gauge staff expertise and preferences, as well as to determine management costs.

Beneath this dynamic process, however, there is a discernable pattern to Roosevelt's staff choices. For infrequently occurring, low-cost bargains, he tended to utilize outside experts for advice and information. But as particular bargaining exchanges recurred more frequently, and became more costly, he was driven to institutionalize staff as a way of acquiring advising resources more efficiently. This suggests a simple way to categorize FDR's staff support based on bargaining frequency and cost. Depending on whether cost and frequency is "high" or "low," four categories can be identified, labeled here *spot contract, ad hoc, career,* and *personal-partisan.*[32]

Bargaining Costs

		Low	High
Frequency of Bargaining Exchange	Infrequent	Spot Contract	Ad Hoc
	Frequent	Career	Personal-partisan

Spot contracting, the mode of choice in the premodern presidential era, remains the most efficient means of acquiring expertise for presidents engaged in infrequent, low-cost bargains. Although Roosevelt relied on spot contracting throughout his presidency, he found it most useful during his first term, when transaction costs were not yet exorbitant. In this period, rather than expanding his official staff, FDR preferred instead to rely on private citizens, such as Sam Rosenman or Bernard Baruch, or government employees on the payrolls of other departments or agencies, such as Tom Corcoran and Ben Cohen, for advice and expertise.

As bargains increased in frequency and cost, however, FDR began to institutionalize staff support. Indeed, the Brownlow Committee itself perfectly illustrates an ad hoc staff structure formed in response to a one-time, but nonetheless costly bargaining transaction. In this instance, FDR sought expertise pertaining to executive branch reorganization.[33] During its lifespan, FDR controlled committee members' primary incentives: their formal standing within government (they were legally attached to one of FDR's cabinet committees); the rules governing their operation (they reported directly to – and only to – FDR, and he retained sole control over

---

32 In truth, the frequency and cost of bargaining exchanges exist on a continuum, rather than as dichotomous variables. Thus these classifications should be used with caution; they are better understood as "ideal types"; in practice, Roosevelt's staff entities frequently bridged the categories, incorporating elements from more than one classification.

As noted in the Introduction, we can further differentiate bargaining structures by *types* of information and expertise provided: policy, political or administrative.

33 Although committee members continued to assist FDR informally while the reorganization bill moved through Congress.

their recommendations); and even their pay (it came out of funds appropriated by Congress at FDR's behest for New Deal emergency agencies).

For recurring bargaining exchanges, however, Roosevelt sought permanent sources of expertise, composed of either career or personal-partisan aides. His primary source of career support was the Bureau of the Budget after its transfer to the EOP in 1939. This transfer made the BoB a "presidential" agency, with members' incentives more responsive to FDR's influence. He thus gained a ready source of expertise related to two recurring, increasingly important bargaining exercises: the annual budgeting process, and legislative clearance.[34] But in performing these chores the BoB did not become a personal-partisan advising structure. In fact, FDR took pains to protect its reputation for "neutral competence." He did so, I argue, because both budgeting and legislative clearance were administratively stable, and hence highly predictable processes. Budgeting took place in largely incremental fashion, with yearly requests based primarily on the previous year's apportionment.[35] Similarly, legislative clearance meant devising procedures to insure that enrolled bills, executive orders and legislative proposals were in accord with the president's preferences.[36] Both tasks required the expertise of government officials possessing some semblance of institutional memory, although FDR made sure his personal political advisers doublechecked careerists' recommendations.[37]

For recurring, high-cost bargains, however, FDR relied primarily on personal-partisan advising networks dominated by White House staff and key members of his cabinet. A prime example is the distribution of American military supplies to the Allies during World War II. This was largely Hopkins' province. His office in a White House bedroom and his constant proximity to FDR allowed him to view war-related bargains from a vantage point more nearly matching the president's. But, Roosevelt paid a price as Hopkins' high visibility made him a lightning rod for criticism. This, combined with Hopkins' declining health, gradually reduced his utility to FDR, so that by war's end his influence had greatly receded.

---

34 As the number of government agencies proliferated, recall that FDR responded by upgrading the BoB's administrative management section, the better to understand organizational matters [Donald Stone, "Administrative Management: Reflections on Origins and Accomplishments," *Public Administration Review* 50, no. 1 (Jan. – Feb. 1990), pp. 3–20.]

35 On this point, see Aaron Wildavsky, *Politics of the Budgetary Process* (4th ed.), (Boston: Little, Brown, 1984). As norms of budgeting broke down during the late 1970s, and the budgeting process became highly unpredictable, the Office of Management Budget moved increasingly into the ranks of personal-partisan advising structures.

36 Richard Neustadt, "Presidency and Legislation: The Growth of Central Clearance," *American Political Science Review* 48, no. 3 (September 1954), pp. 641–71.

37 And by relying primarily on civil servants, FDR gained comparatively more political insulation because they were not as beholden to him as his political aides.

Presidential style, temperament, and other caveats

The argument to this point largely ignores FDR's work habits, temperament, and other characteristics that scholars commonly cite as important for understanding any president's administrative choices. Nor does it deal with other resources a presidential staff might provide, such as emotional support and reassurance.[38] Many scholars argue that these are important influences on a president's bargaining effectiveness. Others, however, suggest that the tremendous time scholars have spent articulating differences among presidents' administrative styles has so far produced little theoretical payoff. They therefore conclude that efforts to delineate differences in style should be abandoned.[39]

There is a middle ground in this debate. Roosevelt's experiences, as documented here, suggest a president's administrative style will prove most influential as presidential staff relations move toward bargaining equilibrium, that is, as the costs to manage staff equal the bargaining resources the staff provide. Moreover, presidential management style will also prove influential in determining whether to institutionalize staff for bargains whose costs fall along the boundary separating institutional from market-based solutions. That is, when there are no clear payoffs to institutionalizing staff and incurring management costs, versus purchasing bargaining resources as needed, presidential style will determine the choice.

However, when external events occur that suddenly disrupt the equilibrium by dramatically raising or lowering the costs of obtaining bargaining support, then the impact of presidential style will be less pronounced within a given bargaining arena. And over time, significant changes in bargaining costs will lead most presidents, regardless of management styles, to adjust administrative structures accordingly.

One additional caveat is worth repeating: Roosevelt's staff choices were not solely dictated by his bargaining needs, of course. In order to institutionalize staff he had to spend political capital as well. Thus, although the National Resources Planning Board fulfilled FDR's need for planning expertise, in 1943 he allowed it to expire rather than expend the capital to overcome congressional opposition.[40]

---

38 On this point, see George, *Presidential Decision Making and Foreign Policy.*
39 Terry Moe, "Presidents, Style and Presidential Theory" (paper prepared for the Presidency Research Conference, University of Pittsburgh, Nov. 11–14, 1990). Compare to Joseph Pika "Management Style and the White House," *Administration and Society* 20 (1988), pp. 298–323.
40 Note, then, that it is possible to conceive of a president governing with a staff organization in a state of internal disequilibrium. For example, should the cost in capital to acquire bargaining resources externally, from independent sources, prove exorbitant, presidents may be forced to rely on institutionalized staff support despite high

Conclusion: FDR, presidential staff
and presidential power

In this book, Roosevelt's administrative strategy has served as the empirical grist for the conceptualist's mill. By documenting the evolution in staff support during his presidency, we can devise a logical framework that links presidential staff to presidential power. The salient points of that framework bear repeating:

All presidents seek power, whether for reelection, to achieve policy objectives, or to assure a lasting place in the history books. Power simply measures a president's effective influence on governmental outcomes. The American system of separate institutions sharing powers, however, dictates that effective influence depends on bargaining effectiveness.

But bargaining effectiveness is derived from two sets of bargaining resources. First, is a president's political capital: formal powers, presidential popularity or public prestige, and a president's bargaining reputation among his audiences. Second are the political, policy, and administrative resources used by presidents to reduce bargaining uncertainty. Presidents use more or less of these resources depending on their uncertainty regarding the bargaining outcome and its importance to the president.

Presidential staffs exist to supplement this second set of bargaining resources. When confronting frequent, costly bargains, presidents will, all other things being equal, institutionalize sources of bargaining resources within the presidential staff. For less frequent or less costly bargains, they will purchase resources from the political marketplace.

Staff institutionalization tends to proceed until the cost to manage staffs outweighs the benefits they produce. At this equilibrium point, organizational stasis sets in; presidents do not change advising arrangements within particular bargaining arenas unless bargaining costs change dramatically.

At equilibrium, presidential style plays a significantly greater role in determining the details of staff organizations.[41] Conversely, when changes in demands significantly alter the distribution of bargaining costs and benefits, then staff adjustments tend to occur regardless of differences in presidents' characteristics.

---

internal management costs. This is a different version of what Kenneth Shepsle calls a "structure-induced" as opposed to a preference-based equilibrium. (Kenneth Shepsle, "Institutional Equilibrium and Equilibrium Institutions," in Herbert F. Weisberg (ed.), *Political Science, The Science of Politics* [New York: Agathon Press, 1986], pp. 51–81.)

41 Style reflects a combination of presidential personality, temperament, work habits, and background experiences.

Why, then, was "competitive adhocracy" so effective for FDR? Because it structured staff incentives so that presidential aides supervised each other on his behalf. Pitted against one another, FDR's aides worked harder at understanding his bargaining objectives, and providing the resources necessary to obtain them. As Schlesinger, Jr., describes it, "The competitive approach to administration gave Roosevelt great advantages. It brought him an effective flow of information; it kept the reins of decision in his own hands; it made for administrative flexibility and stimulated subordinates to effective performance."[42] Stated more formally, I argue that competitive adhocracy allowed FDR to use his staff support more efficiently; by inducing competition between advisers, he reduced his staff management costs for a given supply of bargaining resources.

In contrast, the presidential branch, by expanding staff support and centralizing it within the White House Office, places a greater management burden on presidents for a comparable amount of bargaining resources. As FDR's successors have lost the ability to distance themselves from staff actions, their management costs have gone up, but without a corresponding increase in bargaining support. Indeed, as Chapter 1 suggests, White House staff growth, specialization, and layering have made the provision of presidentially oriented bargaining resources less likely. This, in turn, erodes presidential bargaining effectiveness.

Conceptually, then, there is reason to believe FDR's staff tenets are applicable today. The contextual developments in the ensuing half century have not significantly altered the constitutional and statutory foundation of presidential power; presidents continue to operate in a system of separate institutions sharing powers, in which their effective influence on governmental outcomes remains largely dependent on their bargaining effectiveness. That effectiveness, in turn, is partly predicated on how well presidents can extract the necessary resources from their advisors.

In the final analysis, of course, the proof of the conceptual pudding is in the empirical eating. Unfortunately, recent presidents have not seriously tried to implement FDR's administrative approach; indeed, they have largely contradicted it. Without documented attempts to implement Roosevelt's methods, however, how can we be sure his approach would in fact work today? In the epilogue I engage in some speculation that, I hope, will encourage further investigation into this important issue.

42 Schlesinger, Jr., *The Coming of the New Deal*, p. 537.

9

Epilogue: Roosevelt's Redux? – A Research Agenda

Roosevelt's decision to institutionalize sources of bargaining resources transformed the American presidency, enabling it to meet the unprecedented demands of the New Deal and World War II.[1] But in subsequent years presidents have strayed from the organizational precepts embraced by FDR as outlined in the Brownlow Report: a small, generalist White House staff and vastly strengthened but depoliticized institutional staff agencies. In its stead they have nurtured the presidential branch: an advisory organization dominated by a White House staff bureaucracy, functionally specialized and hierarchically arranged.

Branch growth has had debilitating consequences. Bigness, hierarchy, and specialization change staff incentives. Hierarchy and size reduce direct contact between aides and the president. Specialization attracts individuals who by virtue of prior experience may be less motivated by the president's bargaining needs and more by the parochial dictates of role requirements. Consequently, presidents must spend progressively more resources to extract bargaining resources and ensure that they serve presidential bargaining needs.

This logic, if correct, suggests at least two lines of inquiry. First, is there evidence that FDR's administrative instincts might be profitably employed under current political conditions? And if so, why have FDR's successors largely abandoned his practices? Neither question, of course, can be fully answered in the few pages remaining here; they require an additional book-length analysis.[2] Nevertheless, some preliminary if

---

1 On this point, see Clinton Rossiter, *The American Presidency* (New York: Harcourt Brace, 1956), p. 104.
2 There are several fine descriptive studies of the post-FDR developments in presidential staffing. But they do not directly address the questions raised here. Nor do they try to conceptualize the relationship between presidential staff and presidential power more generally. See John Hart, *The Presidential Branch: From Washington to Clinton* 2nd ed. (Chatham, N.J.: Chatham House Publishers, 1995); Stephen Hess, *Organizing the Presidency* 2nd ed. (Washington, D.C.: The Brookings Institution, 1989); and Alfred Dick Sander, *A Staff for the President: The Executive Office, 1921–52* (New York: Greenwood Press, 1989).

speculative responses are in order. Let us begin with the second question: Why have modern presidents largely ignored FDR's staff methods if they proved as effective as I claim?

Several possible explanations come to mind. First, staff effectiveness is not easily measured; there is no definitive "price" associated with aides' services. Lacking a true "market" for bargaining resources, then, it may be that presidents cannot readily compare the worth of alternative sources of bargaining support. Barring a staff-related scandal or the prospect of election defeat, presidents do not make organizational adjustments; administratively speaking, they are content to "satisfice" rather than optimize.

The cyclical turnover in presidential administrations, which disrupts staffs every four to eight years (or more frequently), also makes presidential "learning" more difficult. Each president essentially starts from scratch, repeating the learning curve their predecessors underwent. History suggests it takes at least a term in office before the president understands what an effective staff can and should do. Both Roosevelt and Nixon significantly realigned their staffs after four years. Carter and Bush both said they would as well, if reelected. Not yet through his first term, Clinton's staff has already undergone three significant alterations.

Lacking both adequate measures of staff effectiveness and readily apparent alternatives, presidents fall back on their own instincts and experiences in devising, managing, and evaluating advisory organizations. But they are not similarly equipped in these areas.[3] Indeed, FDR's extensive background managing executive branch agencies likely shortened his learning curve. None of his successors have duplicated that experience.[4]

Without relevant personal experience, presidents must solicit others for clues to organizing the presidency. Democratic and Republican presidents are often given different advice, however, by virtue of circulating within different political networks. This may explain why some scholars perceive organizational tendencies differentiating the two.[5] The postwar Democratic presidents – Truman, Kennedy, Johnson, Carter (initially) and Clinton (so far) – tend to adopt more freewheeling, "spokes of the wheel"

---

3 On this point, see Richard Neustadt *Presidential Power and the Modern Presidents: The Politics of Leadership from Roosevelt to Reagan*, (New York: Free Press, 1990), chapter 7, "Men in Office."
4 George Bush served more years than FDR as a federal executive, but his roles did not require him to manage departments to the extent Roosevelt was forced to do as Woodrow Wilson's Assistant Secretary of the Navy for eight years. Eisenhower was also an experienced administrator, but almost entirely within the military.
5 See, for instance, Neustadt, *Presidential Power*, pp. 218–24 and Hess, *Organizing the Presidency*, p. 189.

approaches, in which several senior White House aides report directly to the president. At least some of these presidents may have consciously emulated Roosevelt's methods.[6] In contrast, Republicans – Nixon, Ford, Reagan, and Bush – have typically assigned staff management to a single aide or, as in Reagan's first term, a triumvirate. Their more hierarchical use of staff likely reflects Eisenhower's administrative influence. In short, the difference between Republican and Democratic staff "approaches" may reflect historical legacies as much as any contrast in party or governing philosophy.[7]

Whether Republican or Democrat, however, the organizational decisions a president makes during the initial transition into the presidency are critical. Once administrative arrangements are in place, change becomes more costly.[8] As Clinton is now discovering, to alter advising arrangements is to admit that mistakes were made – never politically easy nor desirable.[9]

Moreover, even if presidents acknowledge the debilitating impact of branch growth, they may find trimming its excesses difficult due to the weaknesses of reform proposals. Scholars, perched on the periphery of the presidential experience and driven by normative concerns, are apparently unable to construct staffing alternatives that address presidential bargaining needs.[10]

6 Indeed, Neustadt's transition memorandum to JFK made explicit references to FDR's administrative tenets. And LBJ, according to his biographers, was an unabashed admirer of FDR. Truman, of course, publicly scorned Roosevelt's methods, but Neustadt argues Truman's administrative approach produced results closer to FDR's than to Eisenhower's. It is unclear on what sources Carter and Clinton drew when constructing their staffs.

7 Eisenhower and Roosevelt, of course, are a study in administrative contrasts. As the first Republican president in twenty years, following a Democratic president whose political influence was at a low ebb, Ike took office in 1953 understandably skeptical of the Democratic administrative legacy. What he knew of FDR's administrative methods came primarily while working under General Marshall, a man quite critical of Roosevelt's approach. Moreover, Ike confronted a bureaucracy saturated with New Deal Democrats. In response, he centralized power within his White House staff. His administrative legacy included a chief of staff, a national security bureaucracy, a congressional liaison office, and a core of specialized advisers – precedents adopted by his Republican successors, and all antithetical to FDR's management approach. For details, see Fred Greenstein, *The Hidden-Hand Presidency* (New York: Basic, 1982), and Phillip G. Henderson, *Managing the Presidency: the Eisenhower Legacy: From Kennedy to Reagan* (Boulder, Colo.: Westview, 1988).

8 This is a major reason why FDR resisted embedding advisory arrangements in detailed statutes.

9 See the intensive questioning by reporters regarding Clinton's most recent staff changes. Leon Panetta, Clinton's chief of staff, was asked, "Clearly, you're not satisfied or you wouldn't be doing this." When Panetta tried to cite the Clinton administration accomplishments to date, the reporter interjected, "Then why are you doing this?" (Transcript of the Sept. 23, 1994 press conference.)

10 See Hart, *The Presidential Branch*, pp. 176–213.

Conceivably, then, the post-FDR presidents' search for an effective staff organization has been hampered by personal ignorance, statutory constraints, poor advice, and the misreading of predecessors' administrative failures. Having initially adopted a particular staff arrangement, presidents then tend to muddle along without change unless faced with a major staff-induced disaster (Nixon and Watergate, Reagan and Iran-contra) or a more general decline in presidential influence that can in part be traced to the repeated actions of presidential assistants (Ford, Carter, Bush, and – so far – Clinton).

For all these reasons, it is not surprising that presidents do not easily achieve organizational equilibrium. Roosevelt had distinct advantages in this regard. For starters, he was able to call on the advice of an exceptionally intelligent and knowledgeable group of individuals who collectively had many years' experience in public administration.[11] Also, as the first modern president, FDR operated with relatively fewer statutory constraints affecting the structural design of his office. Except for yearly appropriation language, there existed no legislation restricting how FDR could organize his White House staff. And there were no relevant precedents binding him. Even with such advantages, however, FDR did not fully implement his administrative strategy until midway through his second term, and then in a somewhat circumscribed fashion. Moreover, he continued to make organizational adjustments as circumstances dictated.

But perhaps there is another, more fundamental reason why FDR's successors do not adopt his methods: Simply put, they are outmoded. I do not believe this is the case, of course; as argued in the preceding chapters, the significant political changes since 1945 do not obviate the relevance of FDR's strategy today because the essential relationship between presidential staff and presidential power has not changed in the intervening years. In terms of bargaining costs, it is hard to imagine a more demanding time than World War II.

Nevertheless, my argument would be more persuasive if scholars could document instances in which modern presidents emulated FDR's administrative approach with equally noteworthy results. This suggests a research agenda. Recall that Terry Moe, in defending the logic of the presidential branch, argued that his thesis would be borne out by subsequent historical analysis: "There need be no pretense that this argument can be thoroughly documented here. That would require, at a minimum, a lengthy and detailed historical analysis."[12] I claim no less here. A thor-

---

11 That experience is well-documented in Barry Karl, *Executive Reorganization and Reform in the New Deal* (Chicago: University of Chicago Press, 1963).

12 Terry Moe, "The Politicized Presidency," from John E. Chubb and Paul E. Peterson eds. *The New Direction in American Politics* (Washington, D.C.: The Brookings Institution, 1985), pp. 235–71.

ough investigation, using primary documents, of the administrative choices made by presidents during the last half century should help clarify whether FDR's administrative choices have been emulated, and with what results. For example, it may be that Reagan's first-term success is partly due to the competitive interaction of his senior White House advisers: James Baker, Edwin Meese, and Michael Deaver. In effect, then, a president – Ronald Reagan – whose personal characteristics are in many respects the antithesis of FDR's, nevertheless achieved comparable bargaining effectiveness by employing a similar administrative strategy. At the very least this begs for additional research.

What this suggests is the need for detailed, systematic, and theory-driven study of presidents' staff choices in the post-FDR era. This would entail specifying the interaction of staff and president during particular bargains and across specified units of time. What were the president's bargaining objectives? To what degree were they obtained? What role did staff play in the bargaining process? Most importantly, what impact did those bargains have on the president's power prospects over time? Is it plausible to argue that alternative administrative arrangements were available that might have produced a more favorable bargaining outcome?

If the argument in this book is sound, additional research should find that effective presidents tend to gravitate toward a system resembling competitive adhocracy. That is, the most effective presidential bargains will typically be those in which presidents employ administrative strategies more nearly emulating FDR's. Conversely, presidents who rely on the White House–centered presidential branch for bargaining support will tend to be less successful at predicting bargaining outcomes.

Conclusion

Ultimately, of course, the issue as to the most effective approach for organizing the presidency transcends mere academic debate. The question is important because it addresses a problem of governance that potentially affects millions of people both here and abroad. If presidential political effectiveness depends in part on the actions of the presidential staff, then the central question in this book – what type of staff organization works best? – takes on critical dimensions.

But history suggests administrative change will not come until and unless presidents are convinced that the growth of the presidential branch has, on balance, eroded presidential bargaining capacities, not enhanced them. Moreover, they must be offered realistic alternatives. That they have so far resisted reform does not mean they are enamored with the

White House staff bureaucracy. Indeed, on several occasions in the past quarter century, presidents have quite openly searched for administrative alternatives, but substantive change, I suggest, was prevented by the lack of realistic administrative options.

The foregoing study of Roosevelt's staff choices is meant to provide presidents and others with the means for constructing such an alternative to the presidential branch. It suggests, however, that the details of that alternative cannot be spelled out without first specifying the context in which the president operates. What goals does he seek? With what audiences? What type of bargaining resources will that entail? In short, lacking an operating context, the focus here must necessarily be on staff principles, not specifics.

Nevertheless, I believe the evidence, both conceptual and empirical, indicates that FDR's administrative tenets, suitably altered to take account of today's political environment, could bolster a president's bargaining effectiveness. By publicizing Roosevelt's methods and suggesting their utility to modern-day presidents, then, I hope to stimulate more rigorous scholarly and public debate regarding how best to organize the presidency.

The past as prologue

In 1943, Louis Brownlow, at FDR's behest, wrote a lengthy memorandum looking ahead to the postwar presidential staff organization. Brownlow recommended creating a system of cabinet councils, chaired by a presidential agent and staffed by a secretariat of career civil servants. The goal was to increase the president's coordinating capacity within major policy fields.[13]

Roosevelt, however, rejected Brownlow's proposals, saying: "He has not got it yet. I don't think anyone has. I am a bumblebee. I will continue bumbling."[14] In these pages I have tried to place FDR's organizational choices within a larger framework linking presidential staff to presidential power, thus providing a more coherent understanding as to why his administrative "bumbling" proved so effective.

13 The memorandum is indicative, of course, of Brownlow's continued fascination with the British cabinet secretariat. But in many respects it anticipates elements of Reagan's first-term staff system by almost four decades. (See Chester A. Newland, "Executive Office Policy Apparatus: Enforcing the Reagan Agenda" from Lester M. Salamon and Michael S. Lund (eds.) *The Reagan Presidency and the Governing of America* (Washington, D.C.: The Urban Institute Press, 1985), and Edwin Meese, *With Reagan: The Inside Story* (Washington, D.C.: Regnery Gateway, 1992).

14 The story is recounted in Don K. Price *America's Unwritten Constitution: Science, Religion and Political Responsibility*, (Cambridge, Mass.: Harvard University Press), pp. 120–3.

Admittedly, much has changed in the half century since FDR's death. But in important respects, much also remains the same. Roosevelt's influence, like that of his successors, depended on his ability to bargain effectively within a system of separate institutions, each with its own bargaining interests, sharing powers. That, in turn, required the judicious use of staff support to clarify the likely impact of his bargaining choices on governmental outcomes. The historical record suggests that, comparatively speaking, FDR bargained well.

One can criticize the modern presidential branch for producing bitter fruit, but blame should not be placed on the self-proclaimed bumblebee. Roosevelt's successors have much to learn from his administrative strategy. So do scholars.

References

Aberbach, Joel D., and Bert Rockman. "Mandates or Mandarins? Control and Discretion in the Modern Administrative State." In James P. Pfiffner, ed. *The Managerial Presidency*, pp. 158–66. Pacific Grove, Calif.: Brooks-Cole Publishing Co., 1991.

Allard, Kenneth. *Command, Control, and the Common Defense.* New Haven, Conn.: Yale University Press, 1990.

Ambramson, Rudy. *Spanning the Century: The Life of W. Averell Harriman.* New York: William Morrow, 1992.

Arnold, Peri. *Making the Managerial Presidency: Comprehensive Reorganization Planning, 1905–1980.* Princeton, N.J.: Princeton University Press, 1986.

Bailey, Stephen. "The President and His Political Executives." *Annals of the American Academy of Political and Social Sciences* 307 (1956), pp. 24–36.

Berman, Larry. *The Office of Management and Budget and the Presidency, 1929–79.* Princeton, N.J.: Princeton University Press, 1979.

Biggart, Nicole Woolsey. "A Sociological Analysis of the Presidential Staff." *The Sociological Quarterly* 25 (Winter 1984), pp. 27–43.

Blum, Albert A. "Birth and Death of the M-Day Plan." In Harold Stein, ed. *American Civil-Military Decisions: A Book of Case Studies.* Birmingham: University of Alabama Press, 1963.

Blum, John, ed. *Roosevelt and Morgenthau: A Revision and Condensation of the "From the Morgenthau Diaries."* Boston: Houghton-Mifflin, 1970.

Bodnick, Marc. "Going Public Reconsidered: Reagan's 1981 Tax and Budget Cuts, and Revisionist Theories of Presidential Power." *Congress and the Presidency* 17 (Spring 1990), pp. 13–28.

Bonafede, Dom. "White House Reorganization: Separating Smoke from Substance." *The National Journal* 10, no. 46 (1977), pp. 1,307–11.

Bond, Jon R., and Richard Fleisher. *The President in the Legislative Arena.* Chicago: University of Chicago Press, 1990.

Brace, Paul, and Barbara Hinkley. *Follow the Leader: Opinion Polls and the Modern Presidency.* New York: Basic Books, 1992.

Broder, John M. "Gergen Reveals He Has Sweeping Power." *Los Angeles Times,* June 8, 1993, p. 16A

Brody, Richard. *Assessing the President: The Media, Elite Opinion, and Public Support.* Stanford, Calif.: Stanford University Press, 1991.

Brown, Roger G. "Party and Bureaucracy: From Kennedy to Reagan." *Political Science Quarterly* 97, no. 2 (Summer 1982), pp. 279–94.

Brownlow, Louis. *A Passion for Anonymity.* Chicago: University of Chicago Press, 1955–8.

  The President and the Presidency. Chicago: Public Administration Service, 1949.

Brownlow, Louis, Harold D. Smith, Charles E. Merriam, William H. McReynolds, Lowell Mellett, and Luther Gulick. "Symposium: The Executive Office of the President." *Public Administration Review* 1, no. 2 (Winter 1941), pp. 101–89.

Buchanan, Bruce. "Constrained Diversity: The Organizational Demands of the Presidency." In James P. Pfiffner, ed. *The Managerial Presidency*, pp. 78–104. Pacific Grove, Calif.: Brooks-Cole Publishing Co., 1991.

Bureau of the Budget. *The United States at War: Development and Administration of the War Program by the Federal Government.* Washington, D.C.: Government Printing Office, 1946.

Burford, Anne M. (with John Greenya). *Are You Tough Enough? An Insider's View of Washington Power Politics.* New York: McGraw-Hill, 1986.

Burke, John P. "Responsibilities of Presidents and Advisors: A Theory and Case Study of Vietnam Decision Making." *Journal of Politics* 46, no. 3 (August 1984), pp. 818–45.

  "The Institutional Presidency." In Michael Nelson, ed. *The President and the Political System.* 4th ed., pp. 381–407. Washington, D.C.: Congressional Quarterly Press, 1995.

  The Institutional Presidency. Baltimore, Md.: Johns Hopkins University Press, 1992.

Burns, James M. *The Lion and the Fox.* New York: Harcourt, Brace Jovanovich, 1956.

  The Soldier of Freedom. Norwalk, Conn.: The Easton Press, 1985 [originally published 1970].

Byrnes, James M. *Speaking Frankly.* New York: Harper & Brothers, 1947.

  All In One Lifetime. New York: Harper & Brothers, 1958.

Campbell, Colin. *Managing the Presidency: Carter, Reagan and the Search for Executive Harmony.* Pittsburgh, Pa.: University of Pittsburgh Press, 1986.

Caraley, Demetrios. *The Politics of Military Unification: A Study of Conflict and the Policy Process.* New York: Columbia University Press, 1966.

Carey, William D. "Presidential Staffing in the Sixties and Seventies." *Public Administration Review* 29 (September – October 1969), pp. 450–2.

Carter, Jimmy. *Keeping Faith: Memoirs of a President.* Paperback ed. New York: Bantam, 1982.

Chubb, John E., and Paul E. Peterson, eds. *The New Direction in American Politics.* Washington, D.C.: The Brookings Institution, 1985.

  Can the Government Govern? Washington, D.C.: The Brookings Institution, 1989.

Clawson, Marion. *New Deal Planning: The National Resources Planning Board.* Baltimore, Md.: Johns Hopkins University Press, 1981.

Clifford, Clark (with Richard Holbrooke). *Counsel to the President.* New York: Random House, 1991.

Cline, Ray. *Washington Command Post: The Operations Division.* Washington, D.C.: Office of the Chief of Military History, Department of the Army, 1951.

"Clinton Sees Need to Focus His Goals and Sharpen Staff." *New York Times,* May 5, 1993, pp. A1, B9.

"Clinton Trimming Lower-Level Aides." *New York Times,* Feb. 10, 1993, pp. A1, A20.

"Clinton Weighs Shuffle in Top White House Staff." *Boston Globe,* May 5, 1992, pp. 1, 24.

Cohen, William, and George Mitchell. *Men of Zeal: A Candid Inside Story of the Iran-Contra Hearing.* New York: Penguin, 1988.

Cornwell, Elmer E., Jr., and Lester G. Seligman, eds. *New Deal Mosaic: Roosevelt Confers with his National Emergency Council, 1933–36.* Eugene: University of Oregon Books, 1965.

Corwin, Edward S. *The President: Office and Powers.* 5th rev. ed. Updated by Randall W. Bland, Theodore T. Hindons, and Jack W. Peltason. New York: New York University Press, 1984.

Coy, Wayne. "Basic Problems." *The American Political Science Review* (December 1946).

Cray, Ed. *General of the Army: George C. Marshall, Soldier and Statesman.* New York: W.W. Norton, 1990.

Cronin, Thomas. *The State of the Presidency.* 2nd ed. Boston: Little, Brown, 1980.

"The Swelling of the Presidency: Can Anyone Stop the Tide?" In Peter Woll, ed. *American Government: Readings and Cases.* 8th ed. Boston: Little, Brown, 1984.

Dallek, Robert. *Franklin D. Roosevelt and American Foreign Policy, 1932–45.* New York: New York University Press, 1979.

Davis, Eric L. "Congressional Liaison: The People and the Institutions." In Anthony King, ed. *Both Ends of the Avenue: The Presidency, the Executive Branch, and Congress in the 1980s.* Washington, D.C.: American Enterprise Institute, 1978.

Destler, I. M. "National Security Advice to U.S. Presidents: Some Lessons from Thirty Years." *World Politics* 29, no. 2 (January 1977).

"National Security II: The Rise of the Assistant (1961–1981)." In Hugh Heclo and Lester Salamon, eds. *The Illusion of Presidential Government,* pp. 263–85. Boulder, Colo.: Westview Press, 1981.

"A Lost Legacy? The Presidency and the National Security Organization, 1945–1960." Paper delivered at the U.S. Military Academy, April 1982.

Dickinson, Matthew J. "Neustadt and New Institutionalism: New Insights on Presidential Power?" Paper delivered at the annual meeting of the American Political Science Association, Chicago, September 1–4, 1995.

Dickinson, Matthew J. and Katie Dunn Tenpas. "Governing, Campaigning, and Organizing the Presidency: An Electoral Connection?" Paper delivered at the annual meeting of the Midwest Political Science Association, Chicago, 1994.

Dorwat, Jeffrey M. *Eberstadt and Forrestal: A National Security Partnership, 1909–1949*. College Station: Texas A&M University Press, 1991.

Eastland, Terry. *Energy in the Executive: The Case for a Strong Presidency*. New York: Free Press, 1992.

Edwards III, George C. *Presidential Influence in Congress*. San Francisco: W.H. Freeman, 1980.

At the Margins: The Presidential Leadership of Congress. New Haven, Conn.: Yale University Press, 1989.

Ehrlichman, John. *Witness to Power: the Nixon Years*. New York: Simon & Schuster, 1982.

Eisenhower, Dwight D. *The White House Years: Mandate for Change, 1953–1956*. Garden City, N.Y.: Doubleday, 1963.

Emmerich, Herbert. *Essays on Federal Reorganization*. Birmingham: University of Alabama Press, 1950.

Federal Organization and Administrative Management. Birmingham: University of Alabama Press, 1971.

Falk, Stanley. "The Role of the National Security Council Under Truman, Eisenhower and Kennedy." In Demetrios Caraley, ed. *The President's War Powers from the Federalists to Reagan*. New York: Academy of Political Science, 1984.

Farley, James. *Jim Farley's Story: The Roosevelt Years*. New York: Whittlesey House – McGraw-Hill, 1948.

Fenno, Richard F. *The President's Cabinet: An Analysis in the Period from Wilson to Eisenhower*. Paperback ed. New York: Vintage Books, 1959.

Florestano, Patricia. "The Characteristics of White House Staff Appointees from Truman to Nixon." *Presidential Studies Quarterly* 7, no. 4 (Fall 1977), pp. 184–91.

Flynn, Edward J. *You're the Boss*. New York: Penguin, 1947.

Ford, Gerald. *A Time to Heal: The Autobiography of Gerald Ford*. Norwalk, Conn.: Easton, 1987 (originally published 1979).

Forrestal, James. *The Forrestal Diaries*. New York: Penguin, 1951.

Friedel, Frank. *FDR: Launching the New Deal*. Boston: Little, Brown, 1973.

Gallup, Jr., George. *The Gallup Poll*. Wilmington, Dela.: Scholarly Resources, Inc., issues for 1986–9.

Garment, Suzanne. "Starting Over: Is Lack of Focus the Problem?" *Los Angeles Times*, July 3, 1994, Part M, p. 1.

George, Alexander. "The Case for Multiple Advocacy in Making Foreign Policy." *American Political Science Review* 66 (September 1972), pp. 751–85.

Presidential Decision-making in Foreign Policy: The Effective use of Information and Advice. Boulder, Colo.: Westview Press, 1980.

Gilmour, Robert S. "The Institutionalized Presidency: A Conceptual Clarification." In Norman Thomas, ed. *The Presidency in the Contemporary Context*. New York: Dodd, Mead, 1976.

Graham, George. "The Presidency and the Executive Office of the President." *Journal of Politics* 12, no. 4 (1950), pp. 599–621.

Graham, Jr., Otis L. *Toward a Planned Society: From Roosevelt to Nixon*. New York: Oxford University Press, 1976.

Greenfield, Kent R. *American Strategy in World War II: A Reconsideration*. Baltimore, Md.: Johns Hopkins University Press, 1963.

Greenstein, Fred. "Changes and Continuities in the Modern Presidency." In Anthony King, ed. *The New American Political System*. Washington, D.C.: American Enterprise Institute, 1978.

The Hidden-Hand Presidency. New York: Basic Books, 1982.

Greenstein, Fred, and John Burke (with Larry Berman and Richard Immerman). *How Presidents Test Reality: Decisions on Vietnam, 1954 and 1965*. New York: Russell Sage Foundation, 1989.

Gulick, Luther, and L. Urwick. *Papers on the Science of Administration*. New York: Institute of Public Administration, Columbia University, 1937.

Hamilton, Alexander. *Federalist* #70.

Hankey, Maurice. *Government Control in War*. New York: Cambridge University Press, 1947.

Hargrove, Erwin. "Presidential Personality and Leadership Style." In George Edwards, John H. Kessel, and Bert A. Rockman (eds.), *Researching the Presidency: Vital Questions, New Approaches*, pp. 69–109. Pittsburgh: University of Pittsburgh Press, 1993.

Hart, John. "No Passion for Brownlow: Models of Staffing the Presidency." *Politics* 17, no. 2 (November 1982), pp. 89–95.

"Eisenhower and the Swelling of the Presidency." *Polity* 24, no. 4 (Summer 1992), pp. 673–91.

The Presidential Branch: From Washington to Clinton. 2nd ed. Chatham, N.J.: Chatham House Publishers, 1995.

Hart, Roderick P. *The Sound of Leadership: Presidential Communication in the Modern Age*. Chicago: University of Chicago Press, 1987.

Hartmann, Robert L. *Palace Politics: An Inside Account of the Ford Years*. New York: McGraw-Hill, 1980.

Hassett, William. *Off the Record with F.D.R., 1942–45*. New Brunswick, N.J.: Rutgers University Press, 1958.

Hawley, Ellis W. *The New Deal and the Problem of Monopoly*. Princeton, N.J.: Princeton University Press, 1966.

Heclo, Hugh. "The OMB and the Presidency – the Problem of 'Neutral Competence.'" *Public Interest*, no. 38 (Winter 1975), pp. 80–98.

"The Changing Presidential Office." In Arnold J. Meltsner, ed. *Politics and the Oval Office: Toward Presidential Governance*. San Francisco: Institute for Contemporary Studies, 1981.

"One Executive Branch or Many?" In Anthony King, ed. *Both Ends of the Avenue*. Washington, D.C.: American Enterprise Institute, 1983.

"The Executive Office of the President," Harvard University Occasional Paper no. 83-4, 1983.

Henderson, Phillip G. *Managing the Presidency: The Eisenhower Legacy – From Kennedy to Reagan.* Boulder, Colo.: Westview Press, 1988.

Hess, Stephen. *Organizing the Presidency.* 2nd ed. Washington, D.C.: The Brookings Institution, 1989.

Hobbs, Edward H. *Behind the President: A Study of Executive Office Agencies.* Washington, D.C.: Public Affairs Press, 1954.

Hodgson, Godfrey. *All Things to All Men: The False Promise of the Modern American Presidency from Franklin D. Roosevelt to Ronald Reagan.* New York: Simon & Schuster, 1980.

Holden, Matthew. "Why Entourage Politics is Volatile." In James Pfiffner, ed. *The Managerial Presidency.* Pacific Grove, Calif.: Brooks-Cole Publishing Co., 1991.

Hoover, Herbert. *The Memoirs of Herbert Hoover: 1920–33, the Cabinet and the Presidency.* New York: Macmillan, 1952.

Hull, Cordell. *The Memoirs of Cordell Hull.* 2 vols. New York: Macmillan, 1948.

Hult, Karen M., and Charles Walcott. "Management Science and the Great Engineer: Governing in the White House During the Hoover Administration." Paper delivered at the annual meeting of the Midwest Political Science Association, Chicago, Apr. 9, 1987.

Huntington, Samuel P. *The Soldier and the State: The Theory and Politics of Civil-Military Relations.* Cambridge: Harvard University Press, 1957.

Ickes, Harold L. *The Secret Diary of Harold L. Ickes: The First Thousand Days.* 1st of 3 vols. New York: Simon & Schuster, 1953.

Ingwerson, Marshall. "Deficit Hawks Rise to the Top in White House." *The Christian Science Monitor,* June 29, 1994, p. 1.

Isaacson, Walter, and Evan Thomas. *The Wise Men: Six Friends and the World They Made.* New York: Simon & Schuster, 1986.

Jackson, Henry, ed. *The National Security Council: Jackson Subcommittee Papers on Policymaking at the Presidential Level.* New York: Frederick Praeger, 1965.

Janeway, Eliot. *The Struggle for Survival: A Chronicle of Economic Mobilization in World War II.* New Haven, Conn.: Yale University Press, 1951.

Jehl, Douglas. "Clinton Shuffles His Aides, Selecting Budget Director as White House Staff Chief." *The New York Times,* June 28, 1994, p. A1.

Johnson, Richard Tanner. *Managing the White House: An Intimate Study of the Presidency.* New York: Harper & Row, 1974.

Jones, Charles O. *The Trusteeship Presidency: Jimmy Carter and the United States Congress.* Baton Rouge: Louisiana State University Press, 1988.

The Presidency in a Separated System. Washington, D.C.: The Brookings Institution, 1994.

Karl, Barry. *Executive Reorganization and Reform in the New Deal.* Chicago: University of Chicago Press, 1963.

The Uneasy State: The United States from 1915 to 1945. Chicago: University of Chicago Press, 1983.

Kearns, Doris. *Lyndon Johnson and the American Dream.* Norwalk, Conn.: Easton Press, 1987 [originally published 1976].

Kellerman, Barbara. *The Political Presidency*. New York: Oxford University Press, 1986.

Kerbel, Matthew. *Beyond Persuasion: Organizational Efficiency and Presidential Power*. Albany: State University of New York Press, 1991.

Kernell, Samuel. "Explaining Presidential Popularity." *American Political Science Review* 72 (March 1978), pp. 506–22.

"The Evolution of the White House Staff." In John E. Chubb and Paul E. Peterson, eds. *Can the Government Govern?* Washington, D.C.: The Brookings Institution, 1989.

Going Public: New Strategies of Presidential Leadership. 2nd ed. Washington, D.C.: Congressional Quarterly Press, 1993.

Kernell, Samuel and Samuel L. Popkin, eds. *Chief of Staff: Twenty-Five Years of the Managerial Presidency*. Los Angeles and Berkeley: University of California Press, 1986.

Kessel, John. "The Structures of the Carter White House." *American Journal of Political Science* 27, no. 3 (August 1983), pp. 431–63.

Kettl, Donald. *Deficit Politics: Public Budgeting in Its Institutional and Historical Context*. New York: Macmillan, 1992.

Kimball, Warren. *The Juggler: Franklin Roosevelt as Wartime Statesman*. Princeton, N.J.: Princeton University Press, 1991.

King, Anthony, ed. *The New American Political System*. Washington, D.C.: American Enterprise Institute, 1978.

Both Ends of the Avenue: The Presidency, the Executive Branch, and Congress in the 1980s. Washington, D.C.: American Enterprise Institute, 1983.

Koenig, Louis W. *The Invisible Presidency*. New York: Rhinehart & Co., 1960.

Koh, Harold Hongju. *The National Security Constitution: Sharing Power after the Iran-contra Affair*. New Haven, Conn.: Yale University Press, 1990.

Kranish, Michael. "Clinton to Reduce White House Staff." *The Boston Globe*, Feb. 10, 1993, p. 3.

"McLarty out, Panetta in as Clinton Shakes Staff." *Boston Globe*, June 28, 1994, p. 1.

Lacey, Alex B. "The White House Staff Bureaucracy." *Trans- Action* 6, no. 3 (July 1969), pp. 50–6.

Larrabee, Eric. *Commander-in-Chief: Franklin Delano Roosevelt, His Lieutenants, and Their War*. New York: Harper & Row, 1987.

Leahy, Admiral William. *I Was There: The Personal Story of the Chief of Staff to Presidents Roosevelt and Truman Based on His Notes and Diaries Made At the Time*. New York: Whittlesey House – McGraw Hill, 1950.

Ledeen, Michael A. *Perilous Statecraft: An Insider's Account of the Iran-Contra Affair*. New York: Charles Scribner & Sons, 1988.

Leubsdorf, Carl P. "It Can Be Too Much Fun." *The Dallas Morning News*, Dec. 23, 1993, p. 17A.

Leuchtenberg, William. *Franklin D. Roosevelt and the New Deal*. Paperback ed. New York: Harper Torchbooks, 1963.

In the Shadow of FDR: from Harry Truman to Ronald Reagan. Rev. ed. Ithaca, N.Y.: Cornell University Press, 1983.

Light, Paul C. *The President's Agenda: Domestic Policy Choice from Kennedy to Carter*. Paperback ed. Baltimore, Md.: Johns Hopkins University Press, 1983.

Louchheim, Katie, ed. *The Making of the New Deal: The Insiders Speak*. Cambridge: Harvard University Press, 1983.

Love, Robert William, Jr., ed. *The Chiefs of Naval Operations*. Annapolis, Md.: Naval Institute Press, 1980.

Lowenthal, Mark M. *The National Security Council: Organizational History*. Washington, D.C.: Congressional Research Service, June 27, 1978.

Lowi, Theodore. *The Personal President: Power Invested, Promise Unfulfilled*. Ithaca, N.Y.: Cornell University Press, 1985.

Lyon, Leverett, et. al. *The National Recovery Administration*. Washington, D.C.: The Brookings Institution, 1935.

Maltese, John. *Spin Control: The White House Office of Communications and the Management of Presidential News*. Chapel Hill: University of North Carolina Press, 1992.

Mansfield, Harvey C. *The Comptroller-General*. New Haven, Conn.: Yale University Press, 1939.

Mansfield, Harvey C., Jr. *Taming the Prince: The Ambivalence of Modern Executive Power*. New York: Free Press, 1989.

Marcus, Ruth. "GOP Insider to Be Clinton Counselor." *The Washington Post*, May 30, 1993, p.1A

Marks III, Frederick W. "Facade and Failure: The Hull-Nomura Talks of 1941." In R. Gordon Hoxie, ed. *The Presidency and National Security Policy*. New York: Center for the Study of the Presidency, 1984.

Matloff, Maurice, and Edwin Snell. *Strategic Planning for Coalition Warfare*. Washington, D.C.: Office of the Chief of Military History, Department of the Army, 1953.

Mayer, Jane, and Doyle McManus. *Landslide: The Unmaking of the President, 1984–1988*. Boston: Houghton-Mifflin, 1988.

McJimsey, George. *Harry Hopkins*. Cambridge: Harvard University Press, 1987.

Meese, Edwin. *With Reagan: The Inside Story*. Washington, D.C.: Regnery Gateway, 1992.

Menges, Constantine C. *Inside the National Security Council: The True Story of the Unmaking of Reagan's Foreign Policy*. New York: Simon & Schuster, 1988.

Merriam, Charles. "The National Resources Planning Board: A Chapter in American Planning Experience." *The American Political Science Review* 38, no. 6 (December 1944).

Milkis, Sidney. *The President and the Parties: The Transformation of the American Party System Since the New Deal*. New York: Oxford University Press, 1993.

Miller, Gary. *Managerial Dilemmas: The Political Economy of Hierarchy*. New York: Cambridge University Press, 1992.

"Formal Theory and the Presidency." In George C. Edwards III, John H. Kessel, and Bert A. Rockman, eds. *Researching the Presidency: Vital Questions, New Approaches*. Pittsburgh, Pa.: University of Pittsburgh Press, 1993.

Millet, John. *The Organization and Role of the Army Service Forces.* Washington, D.C.: Office of the Chief of Military History, Department of the Army, 1954.

Millett, Allan. *The American Political System and Civilian Control of the Military: A Historical Perspective.* Columbus: Ohio State University, 1979.

Moe, Terry. "The New Economics of Organization." *American Journal of Political Science* 28 (November 1984), pp. 739–77.

"The Politicized Presidency." In John E. Chubb and Paul E. Peterson, eds. *The New Direction in American Politics,* pp. 235–71. Washington, D.C.: The Brookings Institution, 1985.

"Presidents, Style and Presidential Theory." Paper presented at the Presidency Research Conference, University of Pittsburgh, Nov. 11–14, 1990.

"Presidents, Institutions and Theory." In George C. Edwards III, John H. Kessel and Bert A. Rockman, eds. *Researching the Presidency: Vital Questions, New Approaches.* Pittsburgh, Pa.: University of Pittsburgh Press, 1993.

Moe, Terry and Gary J. Miller. "The Positive Theory of Hierarchies." In Herbert F. Weisberg, ed. *Political Science: The Science of Politics,* pp. 167–98. New York: Agathon Press, 1986.

Moe, Terry and Scott A. Wilson. "Presidents and the Politics of Structure." *Law and Contemporary Problems* 57, no. 2 (Spring 1994), pp. 1–44.

Moley, Raymond. *After Seven Years.* New York: Harper & Brothers, 1939.

Moley, Raymond (with Elliot A. Rosen). *The First New Deal.* New York: Harcourt, Brace & World, 1966.

Mosher, Frederick C. *The President Needs Help.* Lanham, Md.: University Press of America, 1988.

Muellar, John. "Presidential Popularity from Truman to Johnson." *American Political Science Review* 64 (March 1970), pp. 18–34.

Nathan, Richard. *The Plot that Failed: Nixon and the Administrative Presidency.* New York: John Wiley, 1975.

The Administrative Presidency. New York: John Wiley, 1983.

National Resources Committee. *Regional Factors in National Planning and Development.* Washington, D.C.: Government Printing Office, 1935.

Naylor, John F. *A Man and an Institution: Sir Maurice Hankey, The Cabinet Secretariat and the Custody of Cabinet Secrecy.* New York: Cambridge University Press, 1984.

Nelson, Anna Kasten. "National Security I: Inventing a Process." In Hugh Heclo and Lester Salamon, eds. *The Illusion of Presidential Government.* Boulder, Colo.: Westview Press, 1981.

Nelson, Donald. *Arsenal of Democracy: The Story of American War Production.* New York: Harcourt, Brace and Company, 1946.

Neu, Charles. "The Rise of the National Security Bureaucracy." In Louis Galambos, ed. *The New American State: Bureaucracies and Policies Since World War II.* Baltimore: Johns Hopkins University Press, 1987.

Neustadt, Richard E. "Presidential Clearance of Legislation: Legislative Development, Review and Coordination in the Executive Office of the President." Ph.D. dissertation, Harvard University, Cambridge, 1950.

"Presidency and Legislation: the Growth of Central Clearance." *American Political Science Review* 48, no. 3 (September 1954), pp. 641–71.

"Approaches to Staffing the Presidency: Notes on FDR and JFK." *American Political Science Review* 57, no. 4 (December 1963), pp. 855–63.

"The Constraining of the President: The Presidency after Watergate." *British Journal of Political Science* 4, no. 4 (1974), pp. 383–97.

Presidential Power and the Modern Presidents: The Politics of Leadership from Roosevelt to Reagan. NewYork: Free Press, 1990.

"Does the President Need a Chief of Staff?" In James P. Pfiffner, ed. *The Managerial Presidency.* Pacific Grove, Calif.: Brooks-Cole Publishing Co., 1991.

Newland, Chester A. "Executive Office Policy Apparatus: Enforcing the Reagan Agenda." In Lester M. Salamon and Michael S. Lund, eds. *The Reagan Presidency and the Governing of America*, pp. 135–68. Washington, D.C.: Urban Institute Press, 1985.

Nixon, Richard. *In the Arena: A Memoir of Victory, Defeat and Renewal.* Norwalk, Conn.: Easton Press, 1990.

North, Douglass C. *Institutions, Institutional Change and Economic Performance.* New York: Cambridge University Press, 1990.

North, Oliver (with William Novak). *Under Fire: An American Story.* New York: HarperCollins, 1991.

Novick, David, Melvin Anshen, and W. C. Truppner. *Wartime Production Controls.* New York: Columbia University Press, 1949.

Office of War Information. *Handbook of Emergency War Agencies.* Washington, D.C: Government Printing Office, 1943.

Ornstein, Norman, Tom Mann, and Michael Malbin. *Vital Statistics on Congress, 1987–88.* Washington, D.C.: Congressional Quarterly Press, 1987.

Ostrom, Charles W., and Dennis M. Simon. "Promise and Performance: A Dynamic Model of Presidential Popularity." *American Political Science Review* 72 (1978), pp. 334–58.

Parrish, Thomas. *Roosevelt and Marshall: Partners in Politics and War.* New York: William Morrow, 1965.

Patterson, Bradley. *The Ring of Power: The White House Staff and Its Expanding Role in Government.* New York: Basic Books, 1988.

Perkins, Frances. *The Roosevelt I Knew.* Paperback ed. New York: Harper & Row, 1964.

Peterson, Mark A. *Legislating Together: The White House and Capitol Hill from Eisenhower to Reagan.* Cambridge: Harvard University Press, 1990.

"The Presidency and Organized Interests: White House Patterns of Interest Group Liaison." *American Political Science Review* 86, no. 3(September 1992), pp. 612–25.

Pfiffner, James P. *The Modern Presidency.* New York: St. Martin's Press, 1984.

The Strategic Presidency: Hitting the Ground Running. Chicago: Dorsey, 1988.

The Managerial Presidency. Pacific Grove, Calif.: Brooks-Cole Publishing Co., 1991.

"Political Appointees and Career Executives." In James P. Pfiffner, ed. *The Managerial Presidency*. Pacific Grove, Calif.: Brooks-Cole Publishing Co., 1991.

"Can the President Manage the Government? Should He?" In James P. Pfiffner, ed. *The Managerial Presidency*. Pacific Grove, Calif.: Brooks-Cole Publishing Co., 1991.

Pika, Joseph A. "Interest Groups and the Executive Presidential Intervention." In Allan J. Cigler and Burdett A. Loomis, eds. *Interest Group Politics*. Washington, D.C.: Congressional Quarterly Press, 1983.

"Management Style and the White House." *Administration and Society* 20 (1988), pp. 298–323.

Pious, Richard. *The American Presidency*. New York: Basic Books, 1979.

Pogue, Forrest. *Ordeal and Hope, 1939–1942*. New York: Penguin, 1965.

Polenberg, Richard. *Reorganizing Roosevelt's Government 1936–1939: The Controversy over Executive Reorganization*. Cambridge: Harvard University Press, 1966.

Polsby, Nelson W. "The Institutionalization of the U.S. House of Representatives." *American Political Science Review* 52 (1968), pp. 144–68.

"Some Landmarks in Modern Presidential – Congressional Relations." In Anthony King, ed. *Both Ends of the Avenue*. Washington, D.C.: American Enterprise Institute, 1983.

Porter, Roger. *Presidential Decision Making: The Economic Policy Board*. New York: Cambridge University Press, 1980.

"Advising the President." *PS* 19 (Fall 1986).

Prados, John. *Keepers of the Keys: A History of the National Security Council from Truman to Bush*. New York: William Morrow, 1991.

Pratt, John W., and Richard Zeckhauser. "Principles and Agents: An Overview." In Pratt and Zeckhauser, eds. *Principles and Agents: The Structure of Business*. Boston: Harvard Business School Press, 1985.

President's Committee on Administrative Management. *Report with Special Studies: Administrative Management in the Government of the United States*. Washington, D.C.: Government Printing Office, 1937.

Price, Don K. *America's Unwritten Constitution – Science, Religion and Political Responsibility*. Cambridge: Harvard University Press, 1985.

Ranney, Austin. "The Political Parties: Reform and Decline." In Anthony King, ed. *The New American Political System*, pp. 213–48. Washington, D.C.: American Enterprise Institute, 1978.

Reagan, Ronald. *An American Life*. New York: Simon & Schuster, 1990.

Reedy, George E. *The Twilight of the Presidency*. Paperback ed. New York: New American Library, 1971.

Regan, Donald T. *For the Record: From Wall Street to Washington*. New York: Harcourt, Brace, Jovanovich, 1988.

Richberg, Donald. *My Hero: The Indiscreet Memoirs of an Eventful But Unheroic Life*. New York: Putnam, 1954.

Riddle, Donald H. *The Truman Committee: A Study in Congressional Responsibility*. New Brunswick, N.J.: Rutgers University Press, 1964.

Riddlesperger, Jr., James W., and James D. King. "Presidential Appointments to the Cabinet, Executive Office, and the White House Staff." *Presidential Studies Quarterly* 16, no. 4 (Fall 1986), pp. 691–9.

Rivers, Douglas, and Nancy Rose. "Passsing a President's Program: Public Opinion and Presidential Influence in Congress." *American Journal of Political Science* 29 (1988), pp. 183–96.

Roberts, Paul Craig. *The Supply-Side Revolution: An Insider's Account of Policymaking in Washington*. Cambridge: Harvard University Press, 1984.

Rollins, Jr., Alfred. *Roosevelt and Howe*. New York: Alfred A. Knopf, 1962.

Romasco, Albert U. *The Politics of Recovery: Roosevelt's New Deal*. New York: Oxford University Press, 1983.

Roosevelt, Elliot, ed. *F.D.R.: His Personal Letters, 1928–1945*. New York: Duell, Sloan & Pearce, 1950.

Roosevelt, James. *My Parents: A Differing View*. Chicago: Playboy Press, 1976.

Roosevelt and Frankfurter: Their Correspondence 1928–1945. Annotated by Max Freedman. Boston: Little, Brown, 1967.

Rose, Richard. "Organizing Issues In and Organizing Problems Out." In James P. Pfiffner, ed. *The Manangerial Presidency*, pp. 105–19. Pacific Grove, Calif.: Brooks-Cole Publishing Co., 1991.

Rosenman, Samuel I., ed. *The Public Papers and Addresses of Franklin D. Roosevelt*, Vols. 1–13. New York: Random House, 1938–50.

Working with Roosevelt. New York: Harper & Row, 1952.

Rossiter, Clinton. "The Constitutional Significance of the Executive Office of the President." *American Political Science Review* 43 (December 1949).

The American Presidency. Paperback ed. New York: Time, Inc., 1960.

Roth, Harold H. *The Executive Office of the President: A Study of Its Development with Emphasis on the Period 1939–1953*. Ph.D. Dissertation, The American University, Washington, D.C., 1953.

Rourke, Francis. "Presidentializing the Bureaucracy: From Kennedy to Reagan." In James P. Pfiffner, ed. *The Managerial Presidency*. Pacific Grove, Calif.: Brooks-Cole Publishing Co., 1991.

Ruddy, T. Michael. *The Cautious Diplomat: Charles E. Bohlen and the Soviet Union, 1929-69*. Kent, Ohio: Kent State University Press, 1986.

Sanchez, James Joseph. *Index to the Tower Commission Report*. Jefferson, N.C.: McFarland & Co., 1987.

Sander, Alfred Dick. "Truman and the National Security Council, 1945–47." *Journal of American History* 59 (September 1972).

A Staff for the President: The Executive Office, 1921–52. New York: Greenwood Press, 1989.

Savage, James D. *Balanced Budgets and American Politics*. Ithaca, N.Y.: Cornell University Press, 1988.

Schattschneider, E. E. *The Semi-Sovereign People*. Hinsdale, Ill.: Dryden Press, 1975 [originally published 1960].

Schlesinger, Jr., Arthur. *The Coming of the New Deal*. Vol. 2 of *The Age of Roosevelt*. Boston: Houghton-Mifflin, 1959.

The Imperial Presidency. Boston: Houghton-Mifflin, 1973.

Schmeckbier, Laurence F. *New Federal Organizations: An Outline of Their Structure and Functions*. Washington, D.C.: The Brookings Institution, 1934.

Schwarz, Jordan A. "Bernard Baruch and the Vocation of Presidential Adviser." In Wilbur J. Cohen, ed. *The Roosevelt New Deal: A Program Assessment Fifty Years After*. Richmond: Lyndon B. Johnson School of Public Affairs, Virginia Commonwealth University, 1986.

Seidman, Harold, and Robert Gilmour. *Politics, Position and Power*. 4th ed. New York: Oxford University Press, 1986.

Seligman, Lester G. "Presidential Leadership: the Inner Circle and Institutionalization." *The Journal Of Politics* 18 (1956), pp. 410–26.

Seligman, Lester G., and Cary R. Covington. *The Coalitional Presidency*. Chicago: Dorsey Press, 1989.

Shepsle, Kenneth. "Institutional Equilibrium and Equilibrium Institutions." In Herbert F. Weisberg, ed. *Political Science: The Science of Politics*. New York: Agathon Press, 1986.

Sherwood, Robert. *Roosevelt and Hopkins*. Rev. paperback ed. New York: Universal Library, 1950.

Simon, Herbert. *Administrative Behavior*. New York: Free Press, 1976.

Sinclair, Barbara. "Studying Presidential Leadership." In George C. Edwards III, John H. Kessel, and Bert A. Rockman, eds. *Researching the Presidency: Vital Questions, New Approaches*, pp. 203–32. Pittsburgh, Pa.: University of Pittsburgh Press, 1993.

Skowronek, Stephen. "Review of Tulis's *The Rhetorical Presidency*." *The Review of Politics* 49, no. 3 (Summer 1987).

The Politics Presidents Make. Cambridge: Harvard University Press, 1993.

Smith, R. Elberton. *The Army and Economic Mobilization*. Washington, D.C.: Office of the Chief of Military History, Department of the Army, 1959.

Solomon, Burt. "Even Clintonites Worry About Arrogance." *National Journal* (Apr. 10, 1993).

Somers, Herman. *Presidential Agency: OWMR, The Office of War Mobilization and Reconversion*. New York: Greenwood Press, 1969.

Sorensen, Theodore C. *Decision-Making in the White House*. New York: Columbia University Press, 1963.

Kennedy. New York: Harper & Row, 1965.

Sperlich, Peter. "Bargaining and Overload: An Essay on Presidential Power." In Aaron Wildavsky, ed. *Perspectives on the Presidency*, pp. 406–30. Boston: Little, Brown, 1975.

Spragens, William C. *From Spokesmen to Press Secretary: White House Media Operations*. Lanham, Md.: University Press of America, 1980.

Stettinius, Edward R. *Lend-Lease: Weapons for Victory*. New York: Macmillan, 1944.

Stimson, Henry (with McGeorge Bundy). *On Active Service in Peace and War*. New York: Octagon Books, 1971 [originally published 1948].

Stockman David. *The Triumph of Politics: Why the Reagan Revolution Failed*. New York: Harper & Row, 1986.

Stone, Donald. "Administrative Management: Reflections on Origins and Accomplishments." *Public Administration Review* 50, no. 1 (Jan.-Feb. 1990), pp. 3–20.

Sullivan, Terry. "Bargaining with the President: A Simple Game With New Evidence." *American Political Science Review* 84, no. 4 (December 1990), pp. 1,167–95.

Tower Commission Report: The Full Text of the President's Special Review Board. Paperback ed. Jointly published in New York: Bantam Books and Times Books, 1987.

Truman Harry S. *Years of Trial and Hope.* Garden City, N.Y.: Doubleday, 1956.

Tugwell, Rexford G. *The Democratic Roosevelt.* Garden City, N.Y.: Doubleday, 1957.

Tulis, Jeffrey. *The Rhetorical Presidency.* Princeton, N.J.: Princeton University Press, 1987.

"The Two Constitutional Presidencies." In Michael Nelson, ed. *The Presidency and the Political System,* pp. 91–123. 4th ed. Washington, D.C.: Congressional Quarterly Press, 1995.

Tully, Grace. *F.D.R. My Boss.* New York: Charles Scribner & Sons, 1949.

U.S. Bureau of Demobilization. *Industrial Mobilization for War: History of the War Production Board and Predecessor Agencies, 1940–45.* Vol. 1. Washington, D.C.: Government Printing Office, 1947.

U.S. Congress. Joint Committee on Government Organization. *Hearings on Reorganization of the Executive Departments.* Washington D.C.: 75th Cong., 1st sess., 1937.

U.S. Congress. Select Joint Committee of the House and Senate. *Report of the Congressional Committees Investigating the Iran-Contra Affair.* 100th Cong., 1st sess. Senate Report 216, House Report 433. Washington, D.C.: U.S. Government Printing Office, 1987.

U.S. Congress. House. Hearings of the Select Committee on Budget. 66th Cong., 1st sess., 1919.

U.S. Congress. House. Hearings of the Select House Committee to Investigate the National Defense Program in Relation to Small Business. 77th Cong., 2nd sess., 1942.

U.S. Congress. House. Hearings of the Special Committee on Postwar Economic Policy and Planning. 78th Cong., 2nd sess. Mar. 15 – May 3, 1944.

U.S. Congress. Senate. *Preliminary Report of the Senate Select Committee to Investigate the Executive Agencies of the Government.* Washington D.C.: Government Printing Office, 1937.

U.S. Congress. Senate. Committee on Government Operations, Subcommittee on National Policy Machinery. *Organizing for National Security.* Washington, D.C.: U.S. Government Printing Office, 1960.

U.S. Congress. Senate. Hearings of the Special Committee to Study and Survey Problems of American Small Business Enterprises 77th Cong., 2nd sess., 1942.

Vatter, Harold G. *The U.S. Economy in World War II.* New York: Columbia University Press, 1985.

Walcott, Charles, and Karen M. Hult. *Governing the White House: From Hoover Through LBJ.* Lawrence: University Press of Kansas, 1995.

Wann, A. J. *The President as Chief Administrator: A Study of Franklin D. Roosevelt.* Washington, D.C.: Public Affairs Press, 1968.

Waterman, Richard. *Presidential Influence and the Administrative State.* Knoxville: University of Tennessee Press, 1989.

Watson, Frank et. al. "The Draftsmen." In Katie Louchheim, ed. *The Making of the New Deal: The Insiders Speak.* Cambridge: Harvard University Press, 1983.

Watson, Mark S. *Chief of Staff.* Washington, D.C.: Office of the Chief of Military History, Department of the Army, 1951.

Wayne, Stephen J. *The Legislative Presidency.* New York: Harper & Row, 1978.

Weko, Thomas. *The Politicizing Presidency: The White House Personnel Office, 1948–1994.* Lawrence: University Press of Kansas, 1995.

Welles, Sumner. *The Time for Decision.* New York: Harper & Brothers, 1944.

White, Graham J. *FDR and the Press.* Chicago: The University of Chicago Press, 1979.

Wildavsky, Aaron. *Politics of the Budgetary Process* 4th edition. Boston: Little, Brown, 1984.

Wilensky, Harold. *Organizational Intelligence: Knowledge and Power in Government and Industry.* New York: Basic Books, 1967.

Williams, Walter. *Mismanaging America: The Rise of the Anti-Analytic Presidency.* Lawrence: University Press of Kansas, 1991.

Williamson, Oliver. *Markets and Hierarchies: Analysis and Anti-Trust Implications.* New York: Free Press, 1975.

Witte, E. E. "The Preparation of Proposed Legislative Measures." In *The President's Committee on Administrative Management, the Report with Special Studies.* Washington, D.C.: Government Printing Office, 1937.

Wolf, Patrick. "The Bureau of the Budget, 1939–48: The Golden 'Era' Examined." Paper Delivered at the Annual Meeting of the American Political Science Convention, 1990.

"Reorganization, Competition, and Crises: Fundamental Explanations for the Bureau of the Budget's 'Golden Era.'" Occasional Paper 93-14. Cambridge: Harvard University Center for American Political Studies, 1993.

Wood, Robert C. "When Government Works." In Aaron Wildavsky, ed. *Perspectives on the Presidency,* pp. 393–404. Boston: Little, Brown, 1975.

Woodward, Bob. *Veil: The Secret Wars of the CIA (1981–1987).* Paperback ed. New York: Pocket Books, 1987.

Wyszomirski, Margaret Jane. "The De-Institutionalization of Presidental Staff Agencies." *Public Administration Review.* (September/October 1982), pp. 448–58.

Index of names

Index of subjects

Advisory Committee on Allotments, 75n108

Agricultural Adjustment Act (1933), 48, 53n38, 54, 72

Air Force, U.S., 165n9, 169n22

American Political Science Association, 95n36

Arcadia Conference (1942), 177, 183

Army and Navy Munitions Board (ANMB) (*see also* economic mobilization, and military procurement), 128, 129n43, 134n63, 137n79, 207); creation of, 121n13; functions of, 121n13, 127n33; leadership and organization of, 121n13, 127n33, 142n4, 145n18, 146n20, 147

Army Corps of Engineers, 83n141

Army Service Forces (*formerly Army Services of Supply*), 128n38, 146n20

Army, U.S. (*see also* World War II, and Army, U.S.), 165n8, 9, 199

Ash Council, 39n63

Board of Economic Warfare, 144n12, 147n26

Board of Indian Commissioners, 79n124

Board of Inquiry for the Cotton Textile Industry, 52n30

Boland Amendments, 21n8

Brookings Institution, 88n11, 92n26, 93n29

Brownlow Committee (*see also* Brownlow Committee Report), 9, 46, 55n43, 58n54, 79n126, 85, 86–113, 164–5, 224; and British cabinet secretariat, 97–100, 104; and Bureau of the Budget, 101, 102n58; early proposals of, 96–102; and Executive Clerk, 99n48; and "Executive Secretary," 101–3; meetings of, 95n36, 102; members of, 83n139, 93; objectives of, 88–91, 96; and relations with FDR, 91–5, 103–4; and relations with FDR's White House

staff, 93n29, 95n35; staff of, 95n36, 96, 97n39

Brownlow Committee Report (*see also* Brownlow Committee), 31n40, 64, 86–8, 94–5, 104–13, 154, 164–5, 204, 209, 220; administrative-political dichotomy in, 109; Congressional reaction to, 109–12, 150n38; drafts of, 100, 102, 103n60, 209; executive branch organization and reorganization in, 107–8, 110, 111; fiscal and accounting procedures in, 107; and "imperial presidency," 164–5; implementation of, 2n6, 86n1, 112–3; institutional staff in, 106–8, 111, 113, 229; presidential functions in, 109; recommendations of, 86n4, 87, 96n37, 98, 104–13, 229; role for cabinet in, 107n82, 108; role for civil service in, 107, 108n84; role for White House staff in, 104–6, 111, 113, 209, 229; timing of, 91n23, 93n28, 215

budget, federal, 59n57, 78, 82, 225; size of, 50–1, 216, 217 (figure)

Bureau of the Budget (BoB), 10, 32n42, 45, 51, 75n108, 100n50, 101, 102n58, 107n83, 111, 121n10, 158n74, 195, 211; creation of, 59, 86n2; creation of Office of Management and Budget (OMB), 39n63; functions of, 59–63, 106, 108n84, 153–7, 225; and "neutral competence," 32n41, 225; placement in EOP, 86n1, 112, 120n9, 155n63, 225

Bureau of Efficiency, 62n71

Bureau of Mines, 63n77, 68n86

Bureau of Municipal Research, 83n139

Bureau of Research and Statistics, 131n50, 132n55, 133n59

Bureau of Ships, 68n86

Bureau of Standards, 63n77

Business Organization of the Federal Government, 62n71